FREEDOM'S DELAY

FREEDOM'S DELAY

America's Struggle for Emancipation, 1776–1865

Second Edition

Allen Carden

THE UNIVERSITY OF TENNESSEE PRESS / KNOXVILLE

Library of Congress Cataloging-in-Publication Data

Carden, Allen.
Freedom's delay: America's struggle for emancipation, 1776-1865 / Allen Carden.
— First edition.
    pages cm
Includes bibliographical references and index.
ISBN 978-1-62190-050-4 (pbk.: alk. paper)

1. Slavery—United States—History.
2. Slaves—Emancipation—United States—History.
I. Title.
E441.C27 2014
326'.80973—dc23
2013046938

For Our Grandchildren,
and
Thomas J. Ebert—Librarian, Historian, Friend

Contents

Illustrations

FIGURES

TABLES

Preface

What happens to a dream deferred?

Does it dry up
like a raisin in the sun?
Or fester like a sore—
And then run?
Does it stink like rotten meat?
Or crust and sugar over—Like a syrupy sweet?

Maybe it just sags
like a heavy load.

Or does it explode?
—LANGSTON HUGHES, *HARLEM*, 1951

We shall overcome because the arc of a moral universe is long, but
it bends toward justice. . . .
—MARTIN LUTHER KING JR., MARCH 31, 1968

Therefore you are no longer a slave, but a son; and if a son, then
an heir through God.
—GALATIANS 4:7

The American past has no darker stain, no more glaring hypocrisy, no greater heart-rending challenge than the story of generations of men, women, and children trapped in a demeaning and brutal system of racially based slavery. Yet a social and economic system that today seems so obviously immoral and contradictory to this nation's most sacred values was viewed by many Americans in the past as not only necessary, but even just and righteous. For nearly 250 years, slavery was at the very heart of the American experience. Even as the founders proclaimed that "all men are created equal," slavery existed legally in all thirteen of the newly independent American states. Eventually, slavery came to be the focus of a convergence of competing perspectives and crusades that culminated in a crisis more explosive and threatening to the nation's future than anything experienced before or since. To this day, there are those in the United States who still reject the Enlightenment ideal espoused by the founders, "that all men are created equal." They choose instead to embrace the creed contained in the 1861 Texas Declaration of Secession: "We hold as undeniable truths that the governments of the various States, and of the confederacy [the United

States] itself, were established exclusively by the white race, for themselves and their posterity."[1]

Many, perhaps all, of the founders themselves held those white supremacist views in 1776. Historical experience has expanded and changed our understanding of the meaning of the words in the Declaration of Independence and other great documents in the story of human freedom.[2] The Magna Carta of 1215 was an agreement between king and nobles, but the English experience broadened both its meaning and application by 1688 to an understanding between king and people, and in 1791, with the American Bill of Rights, to an understanding between people and their government.

The United States in 1776 already included free blacks who went on to serve the revolutionary cause as equals and to vote on the ratification of the Constitution of 1787. It was President Thomas Jefferson, the author of the Declaration of Independence, who added the Louisiana Territory with its non–Anglo-Saxon, Catholic, and mixed-race populations to the American commonwealth as equals under the law. By 1861, the United States already had inhabitants from around the globe, reflecting the burgeoning diversity that is now an essential part of our heritage. Since 1776, our national understanding of the words enshrined in the Declaration of Independence has grown to embrace our diversity, thanks in good measure to Abraham Lincoln's words at Gettysburg in 1863 advocating a new birth of freedom. Like the words of the Magna Carta, the words of the Declaration are static, but not their meaning. The story of emancipation is the first great struggle on the part of our nation to comprehend the full import of what the founders gave us, even though they did not fully grasp it themselves. It is hoped that those who minimize the role of slavery and the struggle for emancipation in America's history, and those who think that our country has somehow been diminished by our diversity and true equality, will be among readers of this volume who come to a fuller understanding and appreciation of the heritage bequeathed by our founding fathers, and further expanded over time by the American people and those who have led us on the journey.

Regarding the history of emancipation, "process" is a much more accurate word than "event." The process of bringing slavery to an end took nine decades, from 1776 to 1865, and was often haphazard and unsteady but of immense importance to the development of the United States. This long process involved reactions to slavery and responses to those reactions, as the nation moved incrementally, haltingly, and sometimes with backward steps, toward the dawn of freedom and equality for all Americans. It is somewhat surprising to see how long "slavery," in the abstract, theoretical sense, was discussed and used by white Americans as a weapon in fights for other causes—American independence, for example—before real flesh-and-blood chattel slavery became in its own right the cause of the day, and the process leading to emancipation could advance more directly.

The slow and painful saga of slavery's demise from the time of the Declaration of Independence to final abolition by the Thirteenth Amendment to the Constitution is a fascinating and multifaceted story of what many courageous Americans, some free and some enslaved, did in a thousand different ways to contribute to the dawning of what Abraham Lincoln called "a new birth of freedom."[3] It is also the story of how events and personalities unfolded and interacted on the national stage.

To achieve emancipation, that wondrous transition from slavery to freedom, it was necessary for the nation to grapple with the moral, theological, economic, political, and social aspects of human bondage in ways that varied significantly throughout the country over a span of nearly ninety years. Even without a unified blueprint for achieving emancipation, over time the seemingly impossible was accomplished, but at great cost and short of the realization of full freedom and equality in a nation that continued to nurture racism, in the North and the South. The movement to abolish slavery would, in 1848, inspire an early stirring of the women's suffrage movement and, in turn, the twentieth- and twenty-first-century movements for political, social, and economic justice for peoples of color, for diverse religions, gender equity, and non-discrimination in all its forms.

This narrative of emancipation includes the epic story of African Americans who with scant, if any, political power during these years helped shape the politics of slavery in major ways through their actions and reactions against the institution and its racist underpinnings. It is also the story of what other Americans did to assure that freedom's delay might be extended indefinitely.

The history of slavery in America began generations before the American Revolution, and its impact on American culture and society yet remains, long after final emancipation. One could justifiably say we are still living with slavery's legacy. However, it is in the unique and formative period between 1776 and 1865 that we find both the greatest promise of freedom and the most disappointing delay of freedom for all Americans.

The Declaration of Independence, with its soaring language and noble Enlightenment ideals, has from the time of its writing forced Americans, including the founders themselves, to encounter severe inconsistencies between our professed values and our praxis. Early in the young nation's history, most states debated, and some took action, to free their slaves. This was an issue too weighty for the fragile national government to tackle, especially in an era of far greater state authority and autonomy. Those states deciding to end slavery did so through a variety of methods and timetables, and with a multitude of motives. Not surprisingly, Northern states with the fewest slaves and the least to lose economically from slavery's demise were the most likely to embrace emancipation. But it would be a serious mistake to equate the end of slavery in the North with a commitment to racial equality, even as it would be erroneous to assume that every Southern white opposed emancipation.

The founders of the American Republic, many of them slaveholders, faced nearly insurmountable odds and challenges as they attempted to unify thirteen diverse, independent states into one nation and defeat the world's greatest military power in order to win and keep American independence. Having been victorious, they then faced the task of creating a framework for implementation of the Enlightenment republic that they had envisioned at the outset. The issue of African slavery was both a central problem facing the new nation and an unwelcome controversy to be avoided for the perceived greater good of national unity. The failure of the founders to deal decisively to end slavery preserved the national unity of the early republic, but set the stage for a bitterly divided nation and civil war decades later.

While many of the founding generation hoped for and expected slavery to die a natural death, slavery's growth due to the runaway demand for cotton production in the self-styled Cavalier Kingdom of the Deep South burst this optimistic bubble. Progress toward emancipation on some fronts would be countered by massive expansion of slavery on other fronts. Americans yearning to implement literally the republic's stated creeds of human freedom and equality experienced a time of immense frustration, as did those who chafed under criticism of their peculiar institution and who eventually rationalized slavery as inherently good and necessary. Whether the Civil War was the predestined "irrepressible conflict" envisioned by William Seward,[4] collision-course passions were unleashed that eventually led to the cataclysm of secession and civil war.

In the struggle to end slavery, at least two foundational movements, not always easy allies, worked in tandem: Enlightenment thought and reform-minded religion—a fairly broad category including, but not limited to, Quakers and evangelical Protestant denominations. These two movements, one that trusted in reason, the other that found its guiding light in the pages of Scripture, provided much of the intellectual and moral firepower aimed at the foes of emancipation, even as major American Protestant denominations divided over the great issues at hand. Instead of presenting a unified moral front against slavery, the divisions in the American churches mirrored and unintentionally blessed the deep sectional divide over the institution. However, the greatest obstacle of all to emancipation was ultimately not the economic necessity of the institution, but racial views that, for most white Americans, North and South, prevented African Americans from being accepted as true equals. Even the most enlightened intellectual and most fervent evangelical reformer struggled with the concept of racial equality in a practical, and not merely theoretical, context. That victory has still not been entirely won.

Those who opposed slavery were anything but unified in their understanding of slavery, what to do about it, and how and when to do it. Among the vast number of individual personalities contributing to emancipation's ultimate triumph, Abraham Lincoln stands as a leader without peer, although in his day he was seen as both fearfully radical by some and painfully cautious and conservative by others. Lincoln has his detractors yet today. Lincoln personally hated slavery but, as a lawyer and politician, he was willing to live with it where it existed. Then, particularly in the last decade of his life, Lincoln made a daunting intellectual journey, in part forced upon him by the war. He brought America along on that journey when he called the country to "a new birth of freedom," an America different from the one that his generation had hitherto known. In the last speech of his life, Lincoln pointed America toward not only freedom but also equality for blacks that in time would prepare the nation for the multiracial, multiethnic, pluralistic America of today. In the final analysis, it was Lincoln's political and interpersonal skills, his ability to see the how the pieces of the puzzle fit together to make a bigger picture, his willingness to change his fundamental world view and to propose a new vision of America, along with his unswerving commitment to do the right things, as he saw them, that brings our story to an end in 1865, as freedom's delay ends and freedom's hope and continued struggle for a brighter future begin.

So much has been written about slavery, abolitionism, and emancipation that a word of explanation is in order concerning what this volume seeks to contribute and where it might be placed in the historiographical landscape of such a well-ploughed field of study. Seeds for this project were sown some years ago when I searched in vain for a comprehensive overview of the national struggle for emancipation. Many parts of the antislavery story have been told by others with great skill and detail, with a focus on slavery itself and various groups targeted for enslavement including Native Americans, or on key individuals or groups involved in the antislavery struggle, or on selected geographical areas, or on specific antislavery strategies, or on the international aspect of the crusade against human bondage. These volumes often assume an understanding of the broader history of the slavery debate which neither a general reader nor an undergraduate or even graduate student is likely to possess. Additionally, much of the existing literature focuses primarily on the three decades, beginning with the 1830s, leading up to the Civil War. Many such works say little about the earlier existence of slavery or the emancipation debates that occurred in the Northern states. Likewise, the Emancipation Proclamation and the Thirteenth Amendment are often treated apart from a prior, broader context which continued to evolve during the Civil War itself. Therefore, while this volume intends to appeal to scholars in the field, it also seeks to engage the general reader and undergraduate and graduate student who might then more fully contextualize and appreciate the in-depth studies of various aspects of the struggle for emancipation already available.

I will attempt to dispel five common myths about slavery and emancipation in America, based on my decades of teaching American history at the college and university level:

Myth #1   Slavery was of little or no consequence in the North.

Myth #2   Slavery that did exist in the North was ended quickly and easily.

Myth #3   Abolition was primarily a white man's cause; blacks were passive recipients of freedom.

Myth #4   The South seceded primarily to protect states' rights, not slavery.

Myth #5   The North fought the Civil War primarily as a crusade to end slavery.

The history of the struggle to end the national addiction to slavery, from the creation of the American nation through the passage of the Thirteenth Amendment, had international connections, but my emphasis is on the American story, North and South, rather than on an expanded coverage of the broader and important Atlantic world story which has been told well by others.[5] My focus is on the struggle to end African American slavery, with no intention to diminish the enslavement of Native Americans and others, including Europeans, earlier in the American past when servitude and slavery were often separated by blurry boundaries. The topic of emancipation is vast, and as a narrative overview, this study makes no pretense to cover all that could, even with the soundest rationale, be included concerning this complex and gripping experience. I have attempted to provide more detail for aspects of the emancipation story which are less well known and where I have found the existing literature less complete. In areas where other historians have told the story well and in great detail, I have attempted to provide a meaningful, but less detailed, synthetic overview and analysis. I alone accept responsibility for the selectivity which a volume of this nature requires.

It was Jesus who said, "You shall know the truth, and the truth shall make you free."[6] Understanding the truth about our national struggle with slavery is at once both liberating and painful. We need to put aside the myths and misunderstandings, created over the years in North and South alike, which cloud our ability to see what actually transpired regarding human freedom in this critical period of our nation's history. I hope to contribute to an understanding of this quintessentially American experience and help readers to comprehend more clearly where we have been and where we yet need to go.

Acknowledgments

This history project has a history of its own. It involves many experiences that have shaped my interests, perspectives, and motivations over the years through the unique and beneficial intersection of the lives and ideas of others with my own life journey. It is not possible to express adequately in words, or in the space available, the debt and depth of gratitude that I owe to others, but that will not stop me from making the attempt.

My parents, Bill and Ruth Weaver Carden, whose time on earth has come and gone, raised me in a joyous environment of love, affirmation, faith, and intellectual stimulation. Growing up as the firstborn son of a college professor made it impossible for me even to conceive that college, and graduate school, might be optional. Our wonderful family vacations throughout the United States (including Lincoln and Civil War sites among my earliest recollections) as I grew up made a deep and lasting impression on me, conveying among other things the importance of a sense of place and the value of understanding the past.

Those in the academy who hold a special place in my heart and memory for shaping and encouraging my intellectual development, particularly as it relates to the study of history, include my professors of long ago, C. David Peters, Ronald D. Rietveld, Joyce Appleby, Gerald F. Moran, and Michael P. Johnson.

For providing encouragement and assistance with this particular project, my heartfelt thanks go to the following individuals, without whose suggestions, challenges, corrections, encouragements, and prodding, this work could not have been accomplished: Herma Williams, Rod Janzen, Ernest Carrere, Marshall Johnston, Lawrence Reid Bechtel, Annette Dale, Cherie Tremaine, Norma Luce, and Elizabeth Carden.

Special thanks is due to my wonderful wife, intellectual partner, and lover of history Denice Luce Carden, for her worthy suggestions and unfailing support and belief in me and what I have attempted to accomplish, despite the cost in time and other resources required to make this project a reality.

A truly indispensable individual who has labored with me on this work, nearly from its inception, is Thomas J. Ebert, documents librarian emeritus at California State University, Fresno, and also a historian and friend whose encouragement, insights into sources, probing questions, attention to detail, suggestions for additional material, as well as suggestions for deletion of superfluous material, and general editorial advice have enhanced this volume far beyond my original efforts.

I wish to thank the University of Tennessee Press for affirming my historical research and writing by recognizing the importance of the topic and its treatment, and by agreeing to publish this book. From my initial contact with Kerry Webb, acquisitions editor, her timely responses, encouragement, and clear and professional guidance have been tremendously helpful. She has been, in a very literal sense, an answer to this historian's prayers. I also wish to acknowledge the courteous and professional assistance of manuscript editor Gene Adair and freelance copyeditor Stan Ivester in the refining of the manuscript. It is significantly better than originally submitted. To others at the University of Tennessee Press, unknown by me, who have also labored to make this project a reality, I thank you.

I am grateful beyond measure for the various forms of assistance I have received in the research and writing of this book. If the product is good, there is plenty of credit to share with others. For errors, omissions, historical misinterpretations, inelegant wording, obfuscation, tedium, or anything else that may annoy readers, I take full and final responsibility and readily acknowledge my human frailty.

And finally, to my students of American history who I can honestly say must number in the thousands over these past four decades of teaching, I owe my continued love for sharing the amazing saga of our American past, with all its glories and disappointments, and my ongoing interest in attempting to explain complex historical realities in understandable and engaging ways that reveal meaningful truths about the human condition.

CHAPTER 1

SLAVERY AND REVOLUTION: TRUTHS NOT SO SELF-EVIDENT

They would not be enslaved. The Continental Congress, meeting in Philadelphia on July 2, 1776, had done what would have been unthinkable a few years before. On that momentous day, delegates passed a hotly debated and long anticipated resolution in favor of independence from British authority, and a new nation (or was it to be thirteen new nations?) came into existence from the former English colonies in North America. July 2 would be a day forever remembered, Massachusetts delegate John Adams excitedly wrote home to his wife Abigail, as a great day of celebration and commemoration marking the birth of the new United States of America.[1] Two days later, in what was actually an anticlimax to the events of July 2, the final editing of Thomas Jefferson's Declaration of Independence was complete and the document, in today's terminology essentially a combination public relations piece and press release, was approved by the Congress. The political slavery the colonists believed the British intended for them was not going to happen after all—assuming they could make good on their pledge to win their independence.

Drawing from the radical and refreshing well of Enlightenment thought and borrowing from the phrasing of John Locke and George Mason, Jefferson boldly asserted in the Declaration of Independence that "we hold these truths to be self-evident, that all men are created equal; that they are endowed by their Creator with certain unalienable rights; that among these, are life, liberty, and the pursuit of happiness." With that bold and inspiring introduction, Jefferson then rationalized the break with England by stating that, "whenever any form of government becomes destructive of these ends, it is the right of the people to alter or abolish it, and to institute a new government, laying its foundation on such principles, and organizing its powers in such form, as to them shall seem most likely to effect their safety and happiness." When liberty is jeopardized, rebellion is justified. Looking back with our modern understanding of the Declaration of Independence in mind, it is easy to forget that Jefferson's main point was to demonstrate the right of revolution, not the equality of men. Yet, the implications of Jefferson's axiom of human equality were indeed dire for the future of a slaveholding society, and Jefferson may have sensed it. Five years later (1781) Jefferson penned in his only published book, *Notes on the State of Virginia,* some thoughts on the interrelationship of liberty, human bondage, and the character of God:

> There must doubtless be an unhappy influence on the manners of our people produced by the existence of slavery among us. . . . [C]an the liberties of a nation be thought secure when we have removed their only firm basis, a conviction in the minds of the people that these liberties are the gift of God? That they are not to be violated but with his wrath? Indeed I tremble for my country when I reflect that God is just: that his justice cannot sleep for ever: that considering numbers, nature and natural means only, a revolution of the wheel of fortune, an exchange of situation, is among possible events: that it may become probable by supernatural interference! The Almighty has no attribute which can take side with us in such a contest.[2]

Jefferson did not originally plan to have this treatise published, fearing that his comments on slavery, including his prediction of dangers faced when "one-half the citizens . . . trample on the rights of the others" might not be well received.[3] After an unauthorized version was printed in France, Jefferson went ahead and published an English version.[4] Ironically, when Jefferson was a presidential candidate in 1800, these remarks about slavery and about Negro inferiority became a double-edged sword used by his political enemies, with Southern Federalists portraying him as an abolitionist and Northern Federalists portraying him as an advocate of slavery.[5]

While the right of revolution would have been questioned by some colonists, it was Jefferson's "self-evident truth" of human equality that may have raised the most eyebrows in 1776, and certainly would have done so earlier in the colonial past, where white bond slaves as well as Indian and African slaves toiled on behalf of the colonists. The very fact that Jefferson had to highlight this idea of equality as a self-evident truth is probably an indication that it really was not so self-evident after all. More than two centuries later, we continue to seek an understanding of

THOMAS JEFFERSON. *Author of the Declaration of Independence, vice president, president, and Virginia slaveholder who expressed his internal conflict over slavery by saying it was like holding a "wolf by the ear" and who feared for his country because of his belief in a just God.*

exactly what the slaveholding author of the Declaration of Independence meant by those words, "all men are created equal," or if indeed he could have grasped their full implications as interpreted by later generations. On the surface, he appears to be affirming the biblical passage from *Acts* often used in the later antislavery struggle, that "God has made of one blood all nations of men."[6] Jefferson is basing the case for equality on the creation of humankind by God—a statement that would resonate more broadly than a mere appeal to the rights of Englishmen. George Mason, in his *Virginia Declaration of Rights,* a source for Jefferson's Declaration, saw mankind "by nature equally free and independent." Jefferson turns up the religious rhetoric and speaks of human equality and rights brought about by divine creation.[7] Despite this emphasis on God's direct involvement in rights and equality, many God-fearing Americans were still skeptical of Jefferson's interpretation of the divine plan.

Certainly the concept that "all men are created equal" would not have been embraced by most colonial Americans of earlier generations. Those stalwart founders of the Bible Commonwealth, the New England Puritans of the seventeenth century, would have been horrified by Jefferson's egalitarian language. Few concepts would have been further from the thinking of colonial Puritans than a claim that all men are equal and should be treated accordingly. The Puritans, and most other early colonists, saw the hand of God in human inequality, the Creator having given mankind differing abilities, characteristics, and stations in life. In fact, inequality was seen as necessary to hold society together—it was part of the divine order of things.[8] Puritan preacher William Hubbard was reaffirming the obvious to his congregation when he sermonized in 1676, a century before the Declaration, "Nothing therefore can be imagined more remote either from right reason or true religion than to think that because we were all once equal at our birth, and shall be again at our death, therefore we should be so in the whole course of our lives."[9]

In the towns of early New England, social and economic distinctions among men were expected, and as long as the gaps were not too wide, as long as the elite behaved with modesty and responsibility, and if the lower rungs of society respected the upper, hierarchy rather than equality was perceived as an actual source of social harmony.[10] This attitude was summed up by the founding governor of Massachusetts, John Winthrop, who believed that "God almightie in his most holy and wise providence hath soe disposed of the condicion of mankind, as in all times some must be rich some poore, some highe and eminent in power and dignitie; others meane and in subjeccion to hold conformity with the rest of his works, being delighted to shewe forth the glory of his wisdom in the variety and difference of the Creatures and the glory of his power, in ordering all these differences for the preservacion and good of the whole and the glory of his greatness." According to Winthrop, inequality was an essential part of God's creation as an inducement for men to need and love one another. Because they were *not* equal, men would "have need of [each] other, and from hence they might be all knit more nearly together in the Bond of brotherly affeccion."[11]

The haphazard development of racially based slavery for life was a crucially important event in seventeenth-century colonial America, an age in which indentured servitude provided opportunities for significant numbers of Europeans to come to the New World. When American Indian servitude and slavery are factored into the social and legal mix, it becomes apparent that boundaries between slavery, servitude, and even apprenticeships were often blurry. As Margaret Ellen Newell has pointed out, when it came to the status of human bondage in New England,

> "Slavery" and "servitude" were slippery terms . . . contracts, writs, and bills of sale often used them interchangeably. A "slave" might be freed after a set term, just like an indentured servant. Chattel slavery as a legal system evolved slowly, the product of piecemeal construction.
>
> Moreover, English "slaves" were men, while the vast majority of the natives enslaved by the United Colonies were non-combatant women and children. This departure from precedent disturbed a few colonists.[12]

The enslavement of Indians in early New England served a dual purpose. It helped alleviate a shortage of laborers and served to punish and control native populations who were hampering the Puritans' view of the progress of God's vineyard in this new England. Laws became more protective of Indian rights in New England, but enslavement of Native Americans continued after 1700, often taking the form of "judicial enslavement" for various infractions of New England laws or to settle debts. Judicial enslavement also become far more common for blacks in New England than for the white population. Complicating the status of Native Americans was their not infrequent amalgamation with blacks, creating confusion in a society in which racial identity had great significance.[13]

Seventeenth-century New England Puritan theologians essentially demolished the prevailing view within Western Christendom that slavery was for non-Christians only. Boston's leading theologian, Cotton Mather, assured his congregation that Christian baptism did not wash away slavery, and asserted that converted slaves were more docile and productive than their heathen counterparts.[14] Ironically, years later it would be in Boston, with its Puritan heritage, where the abolitionist movement would attract such a substantial following. By 1776, Enlightenment thought was aggressively challenging the traditional Puritan obsession with inequality, but not everyone was as yet convinced, for human slavery had spread rapidly and profitably in British North America, even as Enlightenment ideas were simultaneously taking root.

Frequently, in the years of Anglo-American conflict between 1763 and 1776 following the French and Indian War, the colonists used the terrifying imagery of a descent into slavery to denounce what they thought was happening to them at the hands of their mother country. England had earlier "enslaved" the Irish, and the signs seemed all too clear, for those who were intent on finding them, that the English government intended the same fate for America. Numerous acts of Parliament appeared to many colonial patriots to be designed to subjugate rather than to protect and benefit them. The case for conspiracy and enslavement began when the Proclamation of 1763 restricted colonial settlement to the eastern side of the Appalachian Mountains. The conspiratorial rationale was strengthened with each Parliamentary enactment that followed, especially attempts to raise revenue from the colonies. Boston lawyer James Otis's famous phrase, "taxation without representation is tyranny," spawned the slogan for the colonial resistance movement—"no taxation without representation." The British Parliament could not grasp the concept that the Americans were resisting British authority on matters of principle, not only on concerns of the purse, while the colonists could not grasp that they might need to contribute further to the cost of the British Empire of which they were a key part and from which they enjoyed significant benefits.

For many colonists, the conspiratorial belief that they were facing political enslavement evolved into virtual reality. Following Boston's famous Tea Party, the conflict between Parliament and the colonies, each side with competing conspiracy theories, continued to escalate. Growing numbers of colonists saw these repeated abuses as evidence of England's malevolence, when the mother country should instead be displaying gratitude for the colonial work ethic, economic success, and cooperation that had added significantly to the prosperity of the British Empire. Were these tyrannical acts of Parliament a reasonable recompense for the colonists' military assistance that had recently helped defeat France and thus added much of eastern North America to Britain's realm? As initial shock and disbelief gave way to widely held conspiracy theories, it appeared increasingly clear to many colonial patriots that Parliament, the king's ministers, and eventually the King himself, would not rest until the colonists became their slaves.

In the years leading up to the Revolution, no word more frequently or emotionally expressed the frustration of the American colonists resisting British encroachment on their rights than the term "slavery." In the voluminous and vitriolic colonial literature of opposition and resistance, slavery was the constant theme and the ultimate political evil to be opposed at all costs.[15] Political enslavement in the eighteenth century implied not only the loss of property rights (such as quartering acts and taxation without representation), but also the loss of more abstract rights (such as "happiness"), which was anathema to a free people. After all, the colonists prided themselves greatly in the English liberties to which they thought they were entitled as political equals and which they believed were guaranteed by the most enlightened and free government in Europe. Since it was Britain that was so advanced among European states in the commitment to political liberty, British actions toward the colonies from 1763 onward were all the more incomprehensible and despicable. Yet, King and Parliament continued to treat the colonists as political inferiors. In this context, Jefferson's construct that "all men are created equal" might have been read by some of his contemporaries as "all *Englishmen* are created equal."

Pennsylvania slave master John Dickinson's logic was inescapable when he wrote in 1768, "Those who are taxed without their own consent expressed by themselves or their representatives are slaves. We are taxed without our consent expressed by ourselves or our representatives. We are therefore—SLAVES."[16] When the Second Continental Congress defended the need for armed resistance against British oppression in their *Declaration of Taking Up Arms,* approved on July 6, 1775, the argument opens by asking if it were really God's intention for "a part of the human race to hold an absolute property in, and an unbounded power over others . . . as the objects of a legal domination never rightfully resistible, however severe and oppressive."[17] As much as this may appear to be a clear and compelling antislavery argument, it was, rather, a depiction of the plight of the colonists under tyrannical British rule without reference to their own repressive practices against those they perceived as social or racial inferiors.

Two contemporary historical accounts of the Revolution offer insightful and differing perspectives concerning the ways in which slavery, or fear thereof, bolstered the patriot cause. Mercy Otis Warren, one of Revolutionary Boston's leading intellects, focused on the political slavery being attempted by the British government. She chronicled what occurred in the colonies as part of the following pattern: "the many become the slaves of the few; preferring the wretched tranquility of inglorious ease, they patiently yield to despotic masters, until awakened by multiplied wrongs to the feelings of human nature; which when once aroused to a consciousness of the native freedom and equal rights of man, ever revolts at the idea of servitude."

Fortunately for the future of America, "the intelligent yeomanry of the country, as well as those educated in the higher walks," came to their senses in time and realized that "nothing less than a systematical plan of slavery was designed against them." These patriots were sufficiently astute that "they viewed the chains as already forged to manacle the unborn millions" and took necessary preventive action by giving birth to the Revolution.[18] Without realizing it, Warren could have been writing not only of the American Revolution, but also of the struggle for emancipation yet to come.

South Carolina physician David Ramsey, on the other hand, actually credited slavery in his region with inspiring whites to seek freedom from British oppression: "In the Southern Colonies, slavery nurtured a spirit of liberty, among the free inhabitants. All masters of slaves who enjoy personal liberty will be both proud and jealous of their freedom. It is, in their opinion, not only an enjoyment, but a kind of rank and privilege. In them, the haughtiness of domination, combines with the spirit of liberty. Nothing could more effectually animate the opposition of a planter to the claims of Great-Britain, than a conviction that those claims in their extent, degraded him to a degree of dependence on his fellow subjects, equally humiliating with that which existed between his slaves and himself."[19]

Edmund S. Morgan concurred with Dr. Ramsay's observations about the role of slavery and racism in his study of colonial Virginia. Morgan sees racially based slavery as making it "possible for white Virginians to develop a devotion to the [white] equality that English republicans had declared to be the soul of liberty. . . . Racism became an essential, if unacknowledged, ingredient of the republican ideology that enabled Virginians to lead the nation."[20] David Brion Davis has noted that "this tradition helps to explain the paradox of a revolution that seemed to challenge slavery but in fact entrenched and strengthened it."[21] Despite this seemingly perverse rationalization of slavery to bolster the patriot cause, Dr. Ramsay concluded that "unhappy is that country, where necessity compels the use of slaves, and unhappy are the people, where the original decree of heaven 'that man should eat his bread in the sweat of his face' is by any means whatever generally eluded."[22]

In British eyes, much of Europe was languishing in a condition of political servitude in the late eighteenth century, and the Africans enslaved in the American colonies were simply examples of the same kind of loss of self-determination on a more extreme level.[23] Paradoxically, the use of the slavery metaphor in the rhetoric of the Revolution may actually have trivialized the reality of human bondage while simultaneously encouraging identification with the slaves as a kindred people under oppression.[24] The British government, having in reality no grand conspiratorial design to politically enslave the colonists, either ignored the Americans' fears of enslavement or observed their protests with amazement, incredulity, and irritation. But perception often becomes reality, and in 1769 Edmund Burke prophetically argued in the House of Commons, "The Americans have made a discovery, or think they have made one, that we mean to oppress them: we have made a discovery, or think we have made one, that they intend to rise in rebellion against us. . . . [W]e know not how to advance; they know not how to retreat. . . . Some party must give way."[25]

Even before the British and their American brethren began arguing over their competing conspiracy theories, broader issues of freedom and slavery had tentatively entered the American consciousness. While relatively few Americans had championed the cause of freedom for slaves prior to declaring independence, the question had been seriously raised by Pennsylvania Quakers as early as 1688, although without any resolution. Quaker belief in human brotherhood and their intense dislike of violence and coercion did result in an early abolitionist stance by the movement's founder, George Fox, and many of his followers. But the international trading networks that soon brought prosperity to Quakers in Philadelphia, New York, and Newport often involved slavery in one way or another. For this and other reasons, not all affiliated with the Society of Friends were of one mind on the issue of human bondage. Nevertheless it should be acknowledged that, when it came to seriously opposing slavery on both sides of the Atlantic, Quaker voices were among the earliest and most important to be heard.[26]

At the time of their founding, three colonies, Rhode Island, Pennsylvania, and Georgia, desired to be free of slavery. Failing in that, these colonies undertook efforts to end slavery within their borders prior to 1776, and failed in those attempts as well. The institution of slavery, with all of its social implications, was simply too firmly established in the minds of a majority of the colonial leadership and population. A generation before the revolutionary era, the evangelical Protestant stirrings of the Great Awakening brought forth some sympathy for the slave. Yet, even George Whitefield, the young English preacher who gained celebrity status while fanning the fires of religious awakening in the colonies, made use of slave labor at his orphanage project in Georgia. Methodist founder John Wesley, whose American followers would comprise the largest Protestant denomination in the country in the mid-nineteenth century, detested slavery but in the eighteenth century limited his solution to this moral injustice by calling for an end to the slave trade and urging a lengthy process of preparing the slave population for eventual freedom.[27]

However, by 1776, the spread of Enlightenment thought as applied to the colonists' political status could not fail to call into question the incongruity of the case for political liberty and the approbation of human bondage. Decades earlier, England's apostle of the Enlightenment, John Locke, had justified slavery in cases of people who deserved death but had been spared by the graciousness of their captors.[28] But to make this application to every African slave in America required an untenable stretch of interpretive imagination. It became increasingly impossible to ignore the contrast between the slavery that colonists feared for themselves and the slavery they were imposing on a significant segment of their population. Despite the logic of the antislavery argument, this embarrassing discrepancy persisted without much comment in the Southern colonies, for to free the slaves there would "complete the ruin of many American provinces, as well as the West India islands," opined an anonymous South Carolinian in 1774.[29] Thomas Jefferson briefly attacked slavery in his *Summary View of the Rights of British America* in 1774, but it was less an attack on slavery than a volley fired against King George III's "wanton exercise of power" in disallowing any restrictions on the importation of additional slaves into America despite some colonies' wishes to the contrary. Jefferson's main focus was not the plight of enslaved Africans in America, but rather his conviction that there existed a "deliberate, systematical plan of reducing us [white American colonists] to slavery" on the part of the British government.[30]

At the time of the Revolution, about one-sixth of the national population was enslaved. Ebenezer Hazard, a Pennsylvanian journeying through Maryland in 1777, made it a point in his diary to record his astonishment that "men who feel the value and importance of liberty . . . should keep such numbers of the human species in a state of so absolute vassalage. Every argument which can be urged in favor of our own liberties will certainly operate with equal force in favor of the Negroes; nor can we with any propriety contend for the one while we withhold the other."[31] James Otis was another voice examining the conundrum of colonial liberty and African slavery as early as 1764, insisting that by nature all men, regardless of race, are born free, indicting the slave trade as "the most shocking violation of the law of nature," and concluding that those who "barter away other men's liberty will soon care little for their own."[32] Such opinions were, undoubtedly, easier to voice in the Northern colonies where slavery was less widely practiced and seen as less economically necessary. Philadelphia Quaker Anthony Benezet asked in 1767, "At a time when the general rights and liberties of mankind . . . [have] become so much the subjects of universal consideration, can it be an inquiry indifferent to any, how many of those who distinguish themselves as the Advocates of Liberty, remain insensible and inattentive to the treatment of thousands and tens of thousands of our fellow men?"[33]

Incongruities and insensitivity also existed in the North between the rhetoric denouncing political slavery and the reality of chattel slavery in the colonies, as evidenced in John Dickinson's 1768 pronouncement that taxation without representation was "a state of the most abject slavery" and that there could be nothing worse than "slavery more complete, more miserable, more disgraceful, than that of a people where justice is administered, government exercised, and a standing army maintained at the expense of the people, and yet without the least dependence upon them."[34] Undoubtedly, a typical plantation slave of that day would have seen his or her situation as no less devastating. A 1764 essay by Stephen Hopkins appearing in a Newport (Rhode Island) newspaper decried the "rich, proud, and overbearing planters of the [British] West Indies" who were attempting to "distress the trade, and thereby to cramp and impoverish the poorer northern colonies." He concluded that their selfish economic policies were due to the fact that "these people are used to an arbitrary and cruel government over slaves, and have so long tasted the sweets of oppressing their fellow creatures, they can hardly forbear esteeming two millions of free and loyal British subjects, inhabitants of the northern colonies, in the same light." In other words, Caribbean slavery was harmful primarily because it made those island slaveholders more likely to economically oppress the white North American colonists.[35] Even Richard Henry Lee, who introduced the resolution for independence to the Continental Congress in June 1776, showed little empathy or respect for the slave population as he explained the growing impetus for independence. In a letter written in the spring of that year he stated that "a person [might as well] expect to wash an Ethiopian white, as to remove the taint of despotism from the British court."[36] While the white patriot elite passionately used the language of slavery and oppression as a weapon against British tyranny, most showed little concern for their own dominion over the actual slaves in their midst; the rhetoric of antislavery during the Revolution was "often more strategic than principled in its origins."[37]

When the Continental Congress declared the colonies independent from Great Britain, its members launched the ultimate Enlightenment-inspired rebellion against political slavery. It is difficult to conceive how such a momentous action could fail to influence the delegate's views toward the 700,000 chattel slaves living among them. However, during the debate over the wording of Jefferson's draft of the Declaration of Independence, there was concern about including any references to slavery. In coaxing Jefferson to draft the document, John Adams saw the importance of a Southerner taking the lead, helping to assure that the revolution would have more than a New England flavor. It also meant that a Southerner, rather than fellow Declaration draft-committee members Adams and Franklin, no friends of slavery, would address the delicate issue of slavery for a revolution based on liberty. Ironically, the slaveholding Jefferson penned an indictment of George III for his role in the slave trade, charging that the King had "waged cruel war against human nature itself, violating its most sacred rights of life and liberty in the persons of a distant people that never offended him, captivating and carrying them into a slavery in another hemisphere, or to incur miserable death in their transportation thither." While never acknowledging the colonists' active involvement in this "cruel war" both as procurers and consumers, Jefferson went on to denounce the slave trade—"this piratical warfare . . . of the *Christian* king of Great Britain" as "execrable commerce" and an "assemblage of horrors."[38] Although this passage in Jefferson's draft met with approval by Franklin and Adams, enough delegates found the language objectionable to delete it from the final draft of the Declaration, much to Jefferson's irritation. In his personal notes of the debate over the Declaration, Jefferson focused on the objections of the delegates from South Carolina and Georgia to his passage on the slave trade, but also stated that certain "Northern brethren" concurred, having a financial interest in the continued shipping of Africans to America.[39]

There may have been another reason for the deletion of Jefferson's original section on slavery, one that Jefferson was unwilling to acknowledge. On April 6, a mere three months prior to Congress's adoption of the Declaration, Congress had passed a resolution "that no slaves be imported into any of the thirteen United Colonies."[40] While Jefferson may not have admitted it, delegates to Congress may have edited out the section blaming King George III for the slave trade not out of a desire to retain that trade but because Jefferson's accusation was simply too implausible. On the other hand, Southern delegates may also have been concerned that the harshly moralistic tone of Jefferson's denunciation of the slave trade, even if questionably laid at the feet of the king, might at some point be expanded into a moralistic condemnation of slavery itself.[41] The only allusion to slavery in the final version of the Declaration of Independence was a rather vague charge that George III had "excited domestic insurrections amongst us, *and* has endeavoured to bring on the inhabitants of our frontiers, the merciless Indian savages whose known rule of warfare, is an undistinguished destruction of all ages, sexes and conditions" (emphasis mine).

While not specific, this charge was almost surely a reference to Virginia's royal governor, Lord Dunmore, who in late 1775 offered freedom to slaves who would fight with the British against their patriot masters.[42] Jefferson may also have been influenced in this statement by Thomas Paine's bold assertion in *Common Sense* that England was stirring up the Negroes "to destroy us," but Jefferson chose not to be specific, perhaps not wanting to call attention to conditions that might provoke servile uprisings. Yet, by placing domestic insurrection in the same charge with the brutality of Indian warfare, Jefferson linked the fear and horrors of slave uprisings to Indian attacks. In the minds of many colonists, the imagery and consequences of these two events were the same.

Clearly, there was not consensus in the Continental Congress of 1776 concerning slavery. It was all rather embarrassing to address such a topic in a document whose central idea was a justification for human freedom,[43] and most delegates to Congress seemed to conclude that, the less said about the anomaly of slavery in an Enlightenment-inspired crusade for liberty, the better. While the American slave trade was all but eliminated during the Revolution, it was revived when the war ended. Peter A. Dorsey has insightfully noted that use of the slavery metaphor by those favoring independence sent conflicting signals. It was "a borrowed idiom that applied an unjust racial system to a political dispute that mainly concerned white males. . . . [T]he same discourse that presented slavery as an indisputable evil and freedom as a natural right also sharpened racial distinctions and augmented racial fears. These messages would help the new nation justify slavery's continuance once the crisis of revolution and war had ended."[44]

In what surely involved mixed motives, Thomas Jefferson, along with Edmund Pendleton and George Wythe, authored a piece of legislation for Virginia in 1776 that would have emancipated slaves born after the act passed (which it did not), educated such persons at public expense, and escorted them out of Virginia when they reached adulthood.[45] Seven years later, in 1783, Jefferson still envisioned a future for Virginia without slaves. In his draft of *A Fundamental Constitution for the Commonwealth of Virginia,* no further slaves would be allowed to enter the state, and all persons born after December 31, 1800, would be free. Later, Jefferson acknowledged that the plan was ahead of its time, and it was not introduced as he originally intended.[46] Despite Jefferson's conclusion that the time for emancipation had not yet arrived, antislavery sentiment in Virginia was noted as surprisingly strong by a French general during his tour of that region in 1782. The Marquis de Chastellux wrote that many Virginians "grieved at having slaves, and are constantly talking about abolishing slavery and seeking other means of exploiting their lands." Although motives may have differed, "this opinion . . . is almost universally accepted."[47]

It is difficult for present-day Americans to understand the choice the Founders made in not taking a stronger stand against slavery in 1776. It may be clearer if the reader considers the world of 1776 from the Founders' perspectives. By late 1776, the newly declared independent states were alone in the world; not a single nation had yet risked Britain's enmity by granting them diplomatic recognition. A majority of the American population was not yet convinced that independence was the best course of action to take; many of those in opposition were strident Loyalists, while others were indifferent or tried to remain neutral. The major port city of New York was a stronghold of Loyalist sentiment, and that city was about to be invaded by the largest British seaborne military operation to that point in British history—some three hundred warships with over thirty thousand troops. Washington's Continental Army would be no match for the professional British army and navy, and most Americans realized it. Unity among the thirteen states was in short supply, and money with which to fight a war for independence against the world's greatest military power was even scarcer. Forms of indentured servitude and slavery existed in all the states, including New York's old Dutch patroon system that tied individuals to the land in a manner reminiscent of serfdom. As much as we may wish the Founders had dealt a death blow to African slavery early on, it was not at the top of their agenda. They were trying to survive, and for them the revolution was far more about political change than social revolution.

Plagued by division at home, the Continental Congress had its hands full fighting a war with Britain while attempting to forge a sense of national unity and purpose among thirteen independent states that were under no compulsion to acquiesce to any of Congress's requests. Members of Congress, such as John Adams, noted how very different the various former colonies were from one another, yet now they were attempting to forge a unified national vision based on Enlightenment ideals of liberty and freedom. A majority of Americans had to be encouraged, if not coerced, into the patriot camp. The military situation was rarely if ever good, and usually on the verge of desperation, with constant pleas from General Washington for the most basic supplies to keep the rather grandly named Continental Army from total collapse. The need for national unity, and hence survival, took precedence over antislavery impulses. In mid-1777, James Warren wrote to fellow Massachusetts patriot John Adams, then in the service of the Continental Congress, that a bill for the abolition of slavery had been tabled by the Massachusetts legislature for fear of it having "a bad effect on the Union of the Colonies." Adams's reaction was one of approval, responding that "the Bill for freeing Negroes, I hope will sleep for a time. . . . [W]e have causes enough of Jealousy, Discord, and Division, and this Bill will certainly add to the Number."[48]

Few, if any, Americans wanted the Revolution to turn into a nightmarish social upheaval. It was within this context of political formation and desperation for survival as an independent nation that early national debates over slavery sprang up. The Congress, in reality a mere shadow of a national government, had to tread cautiously regarding this issue if sectional unity were to be maintained. The importance of the institution of slavery to their economic and social orders was one of the chief differences between the Northern and Southern sections of the new nation since African slavery comprised the South's most distinctive and fundamental social arrangement.[49]

Fears of slave uprisings and general social disorder were on the minds of some Americans, including delegates to the Continental Congress, who saw independence and the formation of a republican form of government as fraught with danger. No ancient republic had survived, and more recent European attempts at such a government (including England's own seventeenth-century experience without a monarchy under Cromwell and the Puritans) had run amuck. That a wealthy American elite was managing a revolution in 1776 was a wonder in itself, and also a testimony to the power of Enlightenment ideals. Someone as initially hesitant as Carter Braxton, a Virginia delegate to the Continental Congress who had concerns about not only slaves, but poor whites and mobs in general rising up if independence were declared too quickly, and who uttered the anti-republican sentiment, "If the people rule, who will be ruled?" was, in the end, one of the signers of the Declaration of Independence.[50]

There were those in England who found it hard to take America's cries for freedom from British oppression seriously, even before independence was declared. Samuel Johnson, famed Tory essayist, had responded to some of the grievances of the American Continental Congress in a 1775 essay entitled *Taxation No Tyranny,* in which he stated, "We are told, that the subjection of Americans may tend to the diminution of our own [English] liberties. . . . If slavery be thus fatally contagious, how is it that we hear the loudest yelps for liberty among the drivers of negroes?"[51]

British reaction to America's call for independence included the scathing criticism of blatant hypocrisy. How could those who sought liberty from perceived British tyranny be taken seriously when they themselves held slaves? The American response, not quite convincing even to many Americans, was that British greed for slave-trade profits had forced slaves on the colonies in the first place and thus created a social system which would be difficult to dismantle.[52] One such voice came from "Humanus" (actually Thomas Paine), editorializing in *The Pennsylvania Journal and the Weekly Advertiser* of October 18, 1775, that Britain had, "ever since the discovery of America . . . employed herself in the most horrid of all traffics, that of human flesh, and with a deliberate brutality, unknown to the most savage nations, hath yearly [without provocation and in cool blood] ravaged the hapless shores of Africa, robbing it of its unoffending inhabitants, to cultivate her stolen dominions in the west." Paine's conclusion was that as recompense for British abuses of both Africans and Indians, "the Almighty will finally separate America from Britain," and when that day came his fervent hope was that America's gratitude would be demonstrated "by an act of continental legislation, which shall put a stop to the importation of Negroes for sale, soften the hard fate of those already here, and in time procure their freedom."[53]

Despite the deep entrenchment of slavery, especially in the South, the continuation of slavery during the Enlightenment-inspired fight for liberty became increasingly troubling throughout the revolutionary era, with growing numbers of Americans, black and white, taking measures aimed at ending the glaring incongruity. Actions ranged from the stirring words of antislavery whites to the personal escape of enslaved blacks, who often took refuge behind British lines and were willing to fight for the Loyalist cause in exchange for the promise of emancipation, even as others escaped to fight for the American cause.

Winthrop Jordan in his study of colonial slavery maintained that by the time of the Revolution there had developed a "generalized sense of slavery as communal sin" in New England, emanating from its pulpits. The real focus, however, appears to have been more on the wickedness of the perpetrators and fear of divine judgment than on the sufferings of the victims.[54] The idea of communal sin, and the idea of communal guilt, had emerged in the collective argument and would reverberate in future generations. There is also evidence that in New England the revolutionary words of the Declaration of Independence and the spirit of the patriot cause emboldened enslaved African Americans to plead their cause for personal liberty more strenuously. In Massachusetts, a petition dated January 13, 1777, implored the Bay Commonwealth to consider the reasons for the break with England, which "pleads stronger than a thousand arguments in favor of your humble petitioners." Nineteen New Hampshire slaves urged their state in 1779 to enact legislation so that "the name of slave may not more be heard in a land gloriously contending for the sweets of freedom." This same group of petitioners demanded to know "from what authority they [their masters] assume to dispose of our lives, freedom, and property."[55]

On the military front, the pressures of war brought change as well. Washington was surprised to find both free blacks and slaves among his troops when he arrived in the Boston area to take command of the newly formed Continental Army following the battle at Bunker Hill in 1775. His initial reaction was to issue an order forbidding the future enlistment of vagabonds, British deserters, and Negroes.[56] However, after Lord Dunmore began recruiting slaves to fight for the British in exchange for their freedom, Washington changed his position against re-enlisting free blacks who had already served in the conflict in Massachusetts. Slaves, however, were not welcome in Washington's army in 1775, and Congress initially prohibited their enlistment after the fall of 1775. Two reasons for this have been set forth by Benjamin Quarles: fear that the army would become a haven for runaway slaves, and fear that armed slaves were "an open invitation to trouble."[57] As the war progressed, however, Washington came to accept slaves in the army's ranks as substitutes for their masters, and eventually as bona fide recruits when the states' enlistment quotas were running short and he was desperate for manpower.[58] Connecticut encouraged manumission of slaves if they served as substitutes for their masters. Not only could masters be exempt from military duty by sending their slaves, masters were also exempted after October 1777 from any liability for the upkeep of their former slaves. Even when Northern state legislatures officially prohibited the enlistment of black recruits, recruiting officers generally ignored the law. Maryland was the only Southern state to authorize, if not embrace, the enlistment of free blacks and ultimately slaves in the patriot cause. A proposal in the legislature to create a separate regiment of 750 slaves, however, went down to defeat.[59]

The revolutionary American government broke new ground by initiating a plan for what amounted to compensated emancipation for military reasons in March of 1779. Concern over the British invasion of the Southern states prompted a measure in Congress to encourage Georgia and South Carolina to enlist three thousand slaves, with Congress to pay up to one thousand dollars per man in compensation to the owners. General Washington did not publicly support the proposal and voiced some private misgivings about it, specifically the impact that arming some slaves might have on those remaining in slavery. Nonetheless, two prominent generals in the Southern theater of the war, Benjamin Lincoln and Nathaniel Greene, both New Englanders, were advocates for slave enlistments. South Carolina and Georgia, however, remained unconvinced, and the plan did not materialize.[60] However, the use of slaves in non-armed military support roles, while officially disallowed by South Carolina lawmakers, was frequently practiced.[61] Whenever blacks, free or slave, were enlisted in the patriot cause it was primarily motivated by the need for manpower rather than any desire to extend the blessings of liberty and equality to this segment of society. By August 1778, about 5 percent of the Continental Army were African Americans, some serving alongside whites in the same units, and at least a dozen becoming noncommissioned officers. Racially integrated American fighting forces would not reemerge until President Truman ended segregation in the armed forces in 1948.[62]

The slaves' desire for freedom was stronger than an allegiance to one side or the other in this struggle, since both the United States and Great Britain were slaveholding nations. Thus it is not surprising that the British were successful in recruiting many slaves to run away from their masters and enlist in exchange for the promise of freedom. Not only did recruitment of runaway slaves boost British troop strength, it also weakened the American economy, the ability to wage a rebellion against British authority, and patriot morale. When the British command moved military operations to the South in 1780, the presence of a large slave population in that region was one of the deciding factors. Benjamin Quarles has concluded that, after the war shifted to the South, slave losses to the British side, especially in South Carolina and Virginia, were "severe." Throughout the former colonies, "the number of Negroes who fled to the British ran into the tens of thousands." Slaves provided not only manpower, but valuable specialized services to the British, acting as guides and spies. As early as 1777, an unheeded request went out from South Carolina to Congress for seven to eight thousand troops to be stationed in that state in order to stem the tide of "numerous black domestics who would undoubtedly flock in multitudes to the Banners of the enemy whenever an opportunity arrived." In a somewhat surprising move in 1780, both Virginia and Pennsylvania opened their borders for out-of-state masters in regions occupied by British troops to harbor their slaves safely until British occupation ended.[63] Some eighty years later, the same pattern would emerge during the Civil War with the Union Army assuming the role of British forces, and far-away Texas serving as the haven where out-of-state masters sought to harbor their slaves safely from the reach of Yankee emancipation.

In a fitting tribute to African Americans who fought for the American cause, Harriet Beecher Stowe wrote an introduction to an 1855 volume by William C. Nell entitled *Colored Patriots of the American Revolution.* Stowe praised these freedom fighters as "magnanimous" for serving "a nation which did not acknowledge them as citizens and equals, and in whose interests and prosperity they had less at stake. It was not for their own land they fought, nor even for a land which had adopted them, but for a land which had enslaved them, and whose laws, even in freedom, oftener oppressed than protected. Bravery, under such circumstances, has a particular beauty and merit."[64]

The end of the war required that slaves be dealt with in practical terms. The articles of capitulation agreed to at Yorktown in 1781 contained a provision for the return of any American property held by the British, largely a reference to captured or runaway slaves. This provision was often difficult to enforce, as slaves could be cleverly deceptive in describing their identity and status. Enforcement was further complicated by some American officers at Yorktown acquiring slaves once within British lines for their own use, a practice which General Washington quickly disallowed. As they evacuated their lost colonies, British forces took many former slaves with them, despite American attempts to prevent it. Failing to reach an agreement with the evacuating British in Charleston, South Carolina, Americans watched helplessly as over five thousand former slaves left on British ships in December 1782, many of them headed to Jamaica.[65] The final British evacuation of New York included former slaves who had been promised their freedom by the British. The 1783 Treaty of Paris that ended the American Revolution does contain a section dealing very specifically with slaves as a form of property to be returned to their owners.[66] Treaty provisions to the contrary, the British argued that they could not ignore pledges of freedom that had been made to slaves who served the British cause and would likely be severely punished if returned to their former owners. After fruitless negotiations with British commander-in-chief Guy Carleton in New York, a nonplussed General Washington gloomily concluded that "the slaves which have absconded from their masters will never be restored."[67] Most of the former slaves evacuated by the British ended up in the British Caribbean, or in Canada. Of course, the British did partially honor the treaty by leaving some behind—the sick, disabled, and elderly for whom they had no use.[68]

Clearly, the full implications of Enlightenment principles of freedom and equality had failed to pervade the Founders' thinking even as the war for American liberty officially ended. But the battle was just beginning. In the same year that King George III officially recognized American independence in the Treaty of Paris, Quaker abolitionist David Cooper published a typically long-titled pamphlet of that era, "A Serious Address to the Rulers of America, On the Inconsistency of their Conduct respecting Slavery: Forming a Contrast Between the Encroachments of England on American Liberty, and American Injustice in tolerating Slavery." George Washington owned a copy of the treatise, which contained the admonition,

> Let not the world have an opportunity to charge her [America's] conduct with a contradiction to her solemn and often repeated declarations; or to say that her sons are not real friends to freedom; that they have no higher motive than selfishness . . . if you wish your country to escape the reproach and lasting infamy of denying to others what she hath so often, and in the most conclusive language, declared were the rights of *all;* if you wish to retain the name of Christians, of friends to human nature, and of looking up acceptably in prayer to the common Father of men, to deal with you in the same tenderness and mercy as you deal with others; that you would even now regard the rigorous oppressions of his other children, and your brethren, which they suffer under laws, which you only can abrogate. . . . Yes, blush Americans![69]

Though few if any of the Founders realized it at the time, the egalitarian forces unleashed by the Declaration of Independence and the Revolution would profoundly affect the debate over slavery in years to come. In their own day, the revolutionaries themselves were forced to confront the inconsistencies between the commonly accepted practices of slaveholding and slave trading, and guiding principles of Enlightenment and Christian thought that provided a foundation for the struggle against British rule and the creation of the new republic.[70] While the Declaration of Independence made no direct reference to slavery, it did contain principles that seem clearly contradictory to the institution. Even though he had declined to sign the Declaration of Independence, John Dickinson freed his slaves as a consequence of the principles on which he believed the new nation was founded. Others followed the same path and freed their slaves during their lifetimes, unlike Washington who postponed manumission until after his own death. The theological construct of slavery as communal sin, and with it a sense of communal guilt, emerged as a powerful religious theme. While Massachusetts postponed the debate on emancipation for the sake of sectional unity, Pennsylvania passed legislation gradually abolishing slavery in 1780, the first state to do so. It was in Philadelphia, four years later, that the first major antislavery society was reorganized, with Benjamin Franklin as its leader. Petitions for emancipation written by slaves also began citing the Declaration as the rationale for freedom. But these actions were random, tentative, and rare.

Future antislavery rhetoric would repeatedly reference the great ideas in Jefferson's Declaration as proof that slavery could not continue forever. Perhaps Benjamin Franklin's personal relationship with slavery serves as an exemplar for the growing antislavery consciousness of the Revolutionary period. Franklin owned five slaves during his lifetime, but none at the time of his death. His views on slavery reflected the views of many Americans—"Slavery came to an end in Franklin's life by degrees and amid feelings and interests that pulled incessantly against each other."[71] While the pressures that prevented the revolutionary generation from eradicating slavery as incongruous with their own expressed ideals can be understood to a point, the consequences of this tragic failure would ultimately prove to be overwhelming for the young republic, for which a new birth of freedom would be required before the truths so eloquently stated by Jefferson would truly become self-evident and universal.

CHAPTER 2

SLAVERY AND THE CONSTITUTION: FREEDOM COMPROMISED

Having failed to reconcile the incongruity of the ideals of the Revolution with the institution of slavery in part to pursue a united front against Great Britain, the newly independent states sought to craft a new government to secure the bounties of life, liberty, and the pursuit of happiness so loftily proclaimed in the Declaration of Independence. However, the Founders were again confronted with the clash of these ideals and the protection of slavery offered by the new government they set out to create. This time, they justified their compromises, both political and moral, as necessary to create one unified nation. In the process, they chose to accept the fundamentally flawed premise that the problem of slavery would somehow resolve itself.

The American Constitution was drafted during often sweltering Philadelphia spring and summer days in 1787 in the same chamber in which the Declaration of Independence had been debated and approved eleven years earlier. The Constitutional Convention was a masterful, desperate, and highly pragmatic attempt to keep the fruits of the Revolution from spoiling and resulting in chaos and collapse. The great Enlightenment ideals which had guided the Revolution had proven easier to articulate than to put into practice. For a group of revolutionary leaders trying to assure the survival of the new nation, Philadelphia's Constitutional Convention was "show time." The intentionally weak Articles of Confederation had served their purpose for a season, but if the American states were to maintain, or indeed establish, any credibility as a true nation at home and abroad a different constitutional framework was needed.

These were desperate times. The Confederation Congress was floundering; in late 1786 and early 1787 it went for seventy-two consecutive days without a quorum.[1] James Madison had cut to the core of the issue when he stated in 1786, "The question whether it is possible and worthwhile to preserve the Union of the States must be speedily decided one way or the other. Those who are indifferent to the preservation would do well to look forward to the consequences of its extinction."[2] Shays' Rebellion, concerns over interstate bickering (or worse), Southern fear of slave revolts, and the new nation's lack of credit and standing with European powers helped goad the states (except for contrary-minded Rhode Island) to send delegates to meet in Philadelphia to review and revamp the Articles of Confederation. The Confederation Congress gave its approval to the meeting on February 21, 1787. This Philadelphia convention was no "rump" gathering of malcontents attempting to undermine the Congress. Rather, it was full of delegates who were currently serving, or had previously served, in the Congress; of the fifty-five delegates, eight had signed the Declaration of Independence, twenty-five had served in the Continental Congresses during the Revolution, and forty had served in the Confederation Congress. These men were no novices to the perils and opportunities facing the new nation. Neither were they very representative of the American public; they were all white males, educated well beyond the average (many with legal training), and wealthier than their fellow citizens. Many of them, North and South, currently owned slaves, or like Benjamin Franklin and John Dickinson, had at one time owned slaves.

It is perhaps both ironic and expected that the compromises and pragmatism of these delegates proved much less idealistic than the soaring language of the Declaration of Independence. Without such realism in the face of regional differences, factions, and the impending collapse of national unity, the great American experiment in applied Enlightenment thought would likely have failed all too quickly. Yet, there were other Americans who would see in the new and strongly nationalistic 1787 Constitution a dangerous turn, indeed a repudiation, of the revolution for which they and their states had fought so strenuously in defense of liberty. Compromise and accommodation were the orders of the day; there was little else possible at the time. Successful political leaders are pragmatists who deal with the facts as they find them, and a key fact about the Revolution of 1776 was that it was led by conservative men of wealth who essentially transferred power from London to Philadelphia.

As a backdrop to the Constitutional Convention, it should be noted that the Revolution may have removed the authority of King and Parliament, but it did not fundamentally alter the political practices or social order of the former colonies. Nowhere were there institutions that we today would consider thoroughly democratic. The franchise was limited, excluding all women and large segments of the free male population mostly on the basis of wealth but sometimes, as in the case of Massachusetts, imposing religious tests as well. In many states, the qualifications for office were stricter than the qualifications of electors. There were no leveling slogans of "Liberty, Equality, Fraternity" as the new nation exchanged an aristocracy based on lineage for one based on wealth derived from commerce in the North and agriculture in the South.

The delegates gathered in Philadelphia to determine if a form of government could be devised that would allow a people to govern themselves effectively by balancing their concepts of power and liberty and making it all work in an unheard-of immense geographical expanse. The delegates did not have the benefit of mode. historical documents from which to glean insights—they were creating a new document, fit for their times and their situation. The history of earlier republics gave them little comfort that such a lasting structure could be created and maintained.

Their deliberations were held in secret to provide more freedom to express themselves and explore ideas and options without the pressure of public passion. If the public sensed that the convention was in disarray, or that innovative or divisive proposals were being considered, enemies of a strong national government could be counted on do their best to exploit any internal divisions, and public confidence and approval of the proceedings would likely fade quickly, despite the highly respected roster of delegates. This gag rule was imposec because of the delegates' awareness, often repeated in their deliberations, that the task before them was of the utmost importance to the new nation and the world. Yet, the public was so interested in and desirous of news from what the absent Jefferson called "an assembly of demigods"[3] that, on one occasion, George Washington's dour expression as he exited the building gave rise to speculation that things were not going well.

In this atmosphere, James Madison's careful and insightful historical scholarship on republicanism provided a suitable and compelling foundation for the scrapping of the Articles of Confederation and the creation of a completely new document, a move that unapologetically overreached the original stated purposes of the convention. Madison had concluded that the Articles of Confederation were simply too feeble to warrant resuscitation, and his scholarly and theoretical insights and his impressive philosophical discourses early in the convention got things off to a promising

JAMES MADISON. *Often called "The Father of the Constitution," the slave-holding Virginian and later president was instrumental in shaping and guiding compromises through the Constitutional Convention that enabled small and large states, and Northern and Southern states, to agree on a final document. He was deeply disappointed, however, that the Constitution allowed the slave trade to continue unrestricted until 1808.*

start. However, Madison's leadership eventually gave way to a much more pragmatic and less theoretical series of compromises over which he seemed to lose a measure of control as the convention moved forward. Those compromises had at their root the feared fragmentation of the fledgling nation into factions, commencing with large states versus small states, but then centering rapidly on the division between Southern slaveholding states and Northern states where slavery seemed very likely on the path to extinction. The diminutive Madison found his voice and influence increasingly diminished as some of his ideas were ultimately rejected in an effort, in which he himself shared, to keep the Constitutional Convention from coming apart along sectional lines. While still considered the "Father of the Constitution" by many, James Madison eventually got his strong central government with proportional representation, but not according to his specifications in several important respects.

An examination of Madison's record shows that of seventy-one convention proposals moved, seconded, or addressed favorably by Madison, forty of them failed to be adopted.[4] Madison was especially disappointed in the twenty-year grace period given for continuation of the slave trade until 1808, which he hoped would end no later than 1800. After examining debates and decisions that he claims put the Lower South's proslavery imprint all over the Constitution, Lawrence Goldstone makes a case that the document's *real* "Father" was South Carolina's John Rutledge.[5] While this may be an overstatement, it is clear that Rutledge's significant role at the Philadelphia convention has been far less acknowledged than Madison's, perhaps because of Rutledge's unapologetic defense of slavery juxtaposed with Madison's careful convention note-taking, his acknowledgment of the evils of slavery, and his later service in Congress and the presidency. Appropriately, Madison has been given the honor for being on the right side of history.

Often at the center of the debates, although by no means the only challenge to harmony at the Constitutional Convention, was the future of slavery in America. There was no other single issue of such a magnitude that could have caused the convention to fail, and no other issue which could be found at the root of so many compromises. While the final document delicately avoided any direct reference to slaves and slavery, the debates over slavery were at times very direct and heated.

The role of slavery at the convention is debated by historians to this day. Whatever the exact shapes taken by the specter of slavery, its presence was clearly evident and its force powerful. James Madison at one point stated that the real division was not between the large states and the small states, but between the states where slavery played a central economic role and the states where slavery was of much less economic importance.[6] Historian Matthew Mason sees this more as a "diversionary tactic" by Madison, whose central concern, Mason believes, was getting proportional representation in the national legislature approved as a corrective to the unfair "one state—one vote" approach under the Articles of Confederation. Mason also argues that "most participants in the ratification debates made up their minds about the Constitution independent of the issue of slavery, then used its slavery clauses to attack or defend it."[7] Other historians see the slavery issue with all its social, political, economic, and moral implications as having far more profound significance in the Philadelphia debates of 1787. As Lawrence Goldstone put it, "of all the issues that would arise in Philadelphia, the one that evoked the most passion, the one that left the least possibility of compromise, the one that would most pit morality against pragmatism, was the question of slavery. To a significant and disquieting degree, America's most sacred document was molded and shaped by the most notorious institution in its history."[8]

This position is somewhat challenged by Don E. Fehrenbacher's valid conclusion that the issue of slavery exerted "a stronger influence on the deliberations of the Convention than on the text of the Constitution." Fehrenbacher asserts that

> the Convention made no calculated effort to affect the institution of slavery, and its members never conceived of themselves of having any power or responsibility to do so. The intrusions of slavery into the work of the Convention were largely side effects of progress toward a new constitutional design. . . . The Convention was severely limited, however, by its own internal differences on the subject [of slavery] and by the very nature of its task, which required the achievement of something approaching consensus on the emerging new design of a federal republic. . . . In the circumstances, it is scarcely surprising that the framers entertained no thought of trying to abolish slavery but left the institution unmolested as a creature of state law.[9]

Despite Goldstone's assertions, compromise was reached on both proportional representation and the slave trade, and there was ample precedent for a clause on fugitive slaves to be approved without much debate or compromise.

In 1787, only five of the thirteen states were truly dependent on slavery—Maryland, Virginia, North and South Carolina, and Georgia. These states comprised a region ruled deferentially by a landed aristocracy whose manners and standard of living much more resembled the English gentry than their American kinsmen to the north. Even among these five slave states, there were serious differences in their perspectives concerning the future of slavery, with Maryland and Virginia being less enthusiastic about the growth of slavery than the Carolinas and Georgia. Yet these states from Maryland south were not the only ones to profit from slavery, as Northern shipping and commercial interests were deeply involved in the trafficking of slaves. Though few and far between, calls for actual emancipation were most likely to come from the North, although pleas for curtailing the slave trade could also be heard in the Upper South which, as pointed out by both South Carolina and Georgia, had a surplus of slaves.

As the convention opened, the Pennsylvania Society for Promoting the Abolition of Slavery prepared a petition for consideration. That antislavery society, whose president was Benjamin Franklin, requested that the delegates put an end to the slave trade.[10] This put Franklin in an awkward position, but in the interests of unity he prudently declined to introduce the petition to the convention. New York delegate Alexander Hamilton, also of antislavery persuasion, similarly declined to push forward a petition given him from an abolitionist society in New York.[11] The convention never seriously discussed the abolition of slavery, only how to address it as a political reality. As the Founders had done during the Revolution, they gave priority to the unity needed to craft a viable national government over the antislavery sentiment in the minds of the majority of delegates, and probably among the American people in general. However, in the constitutional ratification process that followed, slavery, especially the three-fifths representation provision, would be a key point of contention.

The impact of the slavery debate on the actual text of the Constitution can be summarized with a discussion of three issues, all having the potential to be highly divisive. First, there was the matter of creating a national legislature that would include proportional representation based on the population and/or wealth of the individual states. Since slaves represented both wealth as property and persons for purposes of representation for a state, the issue had significant economic and political consequences. Some Southern delegates wanted slaves fully counted, while other Northern delegates wanted them not to be counted at all. Second, there was the matter of what control, if any, the new national government might have over the importation of new slaves. Could national legislative action possibly ban the slave trade outright in the future, and/or might the new government tax imported slaves beyond their economic value? Third, there was a question about what would happen to runaway slaves escaping across state lines. In the process of dealing with these issues, would the convention have the courage and take the time to debate the moral implications of slavery, or was it all just too inconvenient, embarrassing, and not really part of the agenda?

It was the nature of representation in the proposed two-house national legislature that set in motion the convention's earliest debates over slavery. After necessary preliminaries, including the selection of slaveholder George Washington as presiding officer, the convention got down to business with the presentation of a plan of action, referred to as the Virginia Plan, bearing Madison's imprint but introduced by Virginia's Governor Edmund Randolph. It was a replacement of the Articles of Confederation with something quite new—a national government with three distinct branches, including a two-house legislature. The convention adopted a useful procedure that allowed them to function first as a committee of the whole whereby they could debate and recommend key ideas for a second, and binding, vote. There was little controversy as the committee of the whole recommended a three-part governmental structure with legislative, executive, and judicial functions.

Controversy began when the convention turned its attention to the organization of the legislative branch.[12] The larger states envisioned both legislative houses having proportional representation, whereas the smaller states understandably preferred the equal state representation afforded under the Articles of Confederation. On June 11, Roger Sherman of Connecticut proposed that one house of the legislature be apportioned according to the number of free inhabitants of each state, and that the states be given equal representation in the other house. Proslavery South Carolinian John Rutledge jumped in quickly, advocating Madison's original idea for proportional representation based on states' wealth—which to the South included their slaves. To calm the divisive atmosphere, further discussion on the issue of the nature of proportional representation was postponed, but when the issue reappeared, it was Pennsylvania delegate James Wilson who suggested that "three-fifths of all other persons," a not very covert reference to slaves, be used as part of the formula for counting a state's population and wealth.[13]

This "three-fifths" concept was nothing new—it was commonly known at the time as the "federal ratio" and had been part of an equation developed by Congress under the Articles of Confederation for determining equitable tax apportionments from the states, a formula which the states rarely followed since noncompliance with the will of Congress under the Articles carried no meaningful penalty. In the meantime, an alternative to the Virginia Plan had been developed by slaveholder William Paterson of

New Jersey which emphasized state sovereignty and a much more restricted federal government with equal representation for each state in both legislative houses. Paterson's "New Jersey Plan," however, went down to defeat, and the convention continued debating the nature of proportional representation for the states.[14]

While modern sensibilities are highly offended at the thought that a man or a woman would be legally defined as three-fifths of a person, this was neither the meaning nor the purpose of this factious fraction to the framers of the Constitution. Although there was no actual data to back it up, it was agreed by many in Congress and the convention that the wealth accrued by the labors of a slave were roughly worth 60 percent of what a free laborer would produce. While delegates may have heatedly debated the application of the "federal ratio" to representation in the national legislative branch of the proposed government, they did not bother to debate the actual number; it was an arbitrary fraction pulled from previous legal precedents to which eleven of the thirteen states had agreed. The 60 percent idea had nothing to do with how human slaves were, or how much they were considered to be persons and how much they were considered to be property.[15] The South continued to argue that slaves were property *except* for purposes of representation, when they became persons. Alexander Hamilton attempted to make the distinction that they could be both property and legal persons in *Federalist* 54. The dichotomy, however, was all too apparent.

Most of the delegates took great care to avoid use of the word "slave" or "slavery" when it came to the federal ratio debate. Elbridge Gerry of Massachusetts was an exception. Stating openly that "blacks are property" in the South and used in much the same way that oxen and horses are in the North, Gerry concluded it would make as much sense to include cattle in the representational rights of the North.[16] Lest one mistake his argument as favorable to the slaves, it was not so intended. Rather, Gerry desired to distance blacks from the exalted status of freemen. In these sentiments, Gerry was not alone. Richard Beeman has summed it up well:

> In reviewing the controversy over the three-fifths clause, one comes away with a depressing sense of the near-total absence of anything resembling a moral dimension to the debate. The three-fifths compromise was, fundamentally, about states' individual interests, not the morality of slavery. Those few Northerners . . . who voiced unhappiness with the idea of counting the slave population in apportioning representation did so either out of a fear that Northern interests were being sacrificed to those of the South or, as [Pennsylvania delegate]

James Wilson phrased it, the "disgust" that their white constituents may have felt about being considered in the same category as slaves.[17]

One delegate, John Dickinson, who had freed his slaves during the Revolution, committed to his notebook some noble thoughts that he never got around to uttering on the convention floor: "Acting before the World, What will be said of this new principle of founding a Right to govern Freemen on a power derived from Slaves . . . themselves incapable of governing yet giving to others what they have not. The omitting of the WORD ["slave"] will be regarded as an Endeavor to conceal a principle of which we are ashamed."[18]

On July 12, 1787, the decision to approve the three-fifths compromise was essentially finalized, although dissenting voices would continue to be heard. Pennsylvania's Gouvernor Morris could not make peace with the compromise; he made a motion on July 17 that the issue be reconsidered, but it died for lack of a second.[19] Morris's simmering resentment came to the surface on August 7 when he rose to speak and this time let loose with the convention's first major attack on the immorality of slavery, although his primary objection was the way the counting of slaves would give the South an unreasonable representational advantage: "the inhabitant of Georgia and South Carolina who goes to the Coast of Africa, and in defiance of the most sacred laws of humanity tears away his fellow creatures from their dearest connections and damns them to the most cruel bondages, shall have more votes in a government instituted for the protection of the rights of mankind, than the citizen of Pennsylvania or New Jersey who views with a laudable horror so nefarious a practice."

Furthermore, Morris exclaimed, if counting slaves in states with large numbers of persons in bondage granted those states more representation in the new legislature, it would simply be an encouragement to such states to continue to import "fresh supplies of wretched Africans."[20] Most likely, because they had worked too hard to reach a compromise on the three-fifths concept to allow it to wither under such criticism, Morris's outburst was ignored.[21] Also largely ignored had been a thorough discussion or even a full awareness of the impact that the Three-Fifths Compromise would have on the political clout the states with high slave populations would gain from this ratio. Not only would the states with larger numbers of slaves benefit in congressional apportionment in the House of Representatives, this advantage would also serve them well in the Electoral College when it came to selecting a president (since electoral votes are based on congressional apportionment). Whoever was president would, in turn, have control of the appointments to the Supreme Court. Thus the Three-Fifths

Compromise gave high-population slave states an upper hand not only in the legislative branch, but also in the executive and judicial branches of the national government.

While the convention met in Philadelphia, the Confederation Congress, meeting in New York, was debating what would become known to history as the Northwest Ordinance, which excluded slavery in the future territories north of the Ohio River. A connection between the Philadelphia Convention's decisions involving slavery and representation and the enactment of the Northwest Ordinance has been the topic of much historical debate.[22] Was there a deal struck between the Congress and the convention that would allow North and South to simultaneously claim some victory and thus hold the country together? Was there a greater conspiracy to guarantee a slaveholding republic? Or was it all coincidental? The timing and the overlapping personnel involved give a strong hint of cooperation between the Constitutional Convention's basic agreement on the Three-Fifths Compromise on July 12 and the Confederation Congress's passage of the Northwest Ordinance on July 13, 1787.

At the same time, a pending treaty with Spain, the Jay-Gardoqui Treaty, was highly divisive along sectional lines. Known at the time as the "Spanish Treaty," it would have opened Spanish markets to American (primarily New England) goods in exchange for the United States disavowing its right to navigate the length of the Mississippi River for thirty years.[23] Without access to the Mississippi for transport of their goods to market, southwestern settlers would be hard pressed to survive economically, and growth in this region would likely be stymied if not brought to a complete halt.

It was widely anticipated that the western territories, at least south of the Ohio River, were on the verge of even more explosive growth, at least if the Spanish Treaty were not ratified. Over 100,000 settlers had moved into the region of Kentucky and Tennessee by the time of the Constitutional Convention, and about 15 percent of those persons were slaves.[24] By 1796 both of these territories would be admitted as states. Although disproved by subsequent events, there was a general belief at the convention that the South was going to grow faster than the North and would thus at some future point have the advantage in legislative representation. Congress had for several years recognized the need for policies to provide for orderly development of the region between the original thirteen states and the Mississippi River but had been deadlocked along sectional lines on precisely what those policies should be.

Suddenly, in 1787, a breakthrough seemed possible in that region north of the Ohio River. As Madison later noted in his *Federalist* 38,[25] the Confederation Congress, in the Northwest Ordinance of 1787, introduced measures which seemed to go far beyond what that Congress was actually empowered to do under the Articles of Confederation. The Northwest Ordinance of 1787 prescribed the number of new states that could be created in this region and prohibited slavery, while providing for the retrieval of fugitive slaves. An important question facing historians is what, if any, connection existed between the adoption of the three-fifths federal ratio for apportionment in the Constitution and the banning of slavery in the Northwest Ordinance. It is likely that agreeing to the ban on slavery north of the Ohio River was a Southern strategy to deflect attention from the faster-growing backcountry south of the river in hopes that nothing would impede the extension of slavery into that region. Richard Beeman is not willing to grant too much credit to antislavery forces for the antislavery provisions of the Northwest Ordinance for two reasons. First, he asserts that it was "likely that there was an informal understanding that the slavery prohibition in the Northwest Ordinance would not be applied to western territories south of the Ohio River, which quickly began to be organized by Congress after the Constitution was adopted." Beeman's enthusiasm for the Northwest Ordinance is further tempered by his observation that "it also meant that the Constitution itself could avoid directly confronting the ongoing expansion of slavery to the West and could lay the groundwork for what would eventually become the fugitive slave clause in the United States Constitution."[26]

Ninety-one miles separated the Constitutional Convention in Philadelphia from the Confederation Congress in New York. Despite the difficulties and slowness of travel at that time, several delegates to the convention who were also members of Congress moved back and forth between the two gatherings in the summer of 1787, providing the necessary quorum to pass the Northwest Ordinance on July 13.[27] Edward Coles, Madison's personal secretary during Madison's presidency, wrote in 1856 that Madison had told him years before how

> the distracting question of slavery was agitating and retarding the labours of both [Congress and Constitutional convention], and led to conferences and inter-communications of the members, which resulted in a compromise by which the northern or anti-slavery portion of the country agreed to incorporate into the Ordinance and Constitution the provision to restore the fugitive slaves; and this mutual and concurrent action was the cause of the similarity of the provision contained in both, and had its influence in creating the great unanimity by which the Ordinance passed, and also making the Constitution more acceptable to slaveholders.[28]

George William Van Cleve examines the difficulties of getting an ordinance for the Northwest Territories passed prior to 1787, focusing on sectional disagreements both on slavery and the pending treaty with Spain that would determine American navigation rights on the Mississippi River. Van Cleve's well-founded conclusion is that, after several years of disagreement among the states concerning western territorial development, the sudden passage of the 1787 Northwest Ordinance was "a remarkable achievement, even apart from its well-known territorial slavery prohibition." The timing of the ordinance's adoption in the middle of the Constitutional Convention's heated debate over representation, the deliberate creation of a congressional quorum using convention delegates to enable its adoption, the continuing interconnections and coordination between members of the convention and those of the Congress on economic-development issues, and the fact that the Northwest Ordinance and the Constitution addressed fundamentally important issues in overlapping ways that had significantly different political and legal consequences constitute a set of circumstances that, taken together, render it reasonably certain that the adoption of the ordinance was related to the bargaining at the convention.[29]

Foremost among the consequences of the passage of the Northwest Ordinance was that Congress set a precedent for exercising authority over the issue of slavery in the territories. Innovation did not stop there. Another startling feature was that territorial (colonial) possessions could enter the nation as states on an equal footing with the original thirteen states. This was an easier sell at the Confederation Congress, where it passed unanimously as part of the ordinance, than at the Constitutional Convention, where a motion by Elbridge Gerry that would have forever guaranteed that the original thirteen states would always have more representation in Congress than all future new states combined failed by one vote.[30]

After the major step of agreeing to proportional representation, including slaves according to the federal ratio, had been achieved, a second task involving slavery and the Constitution was to reach agreement on what power the proposed national government might have to tax and/or abolish slavery. When Article VII, Section 4, came to the floor of the convention for discussion, Southern interests prevailed as export taxes were banned. Maryland delegate Luther Martin (who owned half a dozen slaves at the time of the convention) was more interested, however, in attacking the proposed wording that would prohibit Congress from imposing any tax on slaves or any limit on the slave trade. It has been said of Luther Martin that he was "in a state of inebriation . . . more shrewd than many of the delegates in states of sobriety."[31] Martin, beginning to sound like a

Northerner, quickly perceived that the Constitution as proposed would guarantee the perpetuation of slavery, and would in fact encourage the importation of more slaves due to the Three-Fifths Compromise.[32]

He drew attention to the proposed Constitution's commitment to put down domestic (read "servile") insurrections, and concluded that "slaves weakened one part of the Union which the other parts were bound to protect." His closing argument blasted the slave trade as "inconsistent with the principles of the revolution and dishonorable to the American character to have such a feature in the Constitution."[33] Martin's argument prompted a heated response from the convention's most ardent defender of slavery, John Rutledge. David Waldstreicher has assessed Rutledge's rebuttal to Martin as "the most skillful stonewalling the convention had yet witnessed." Rutledge asserted that lack of a constitutional ban on slave importation did not guarantee that any slaves would actually be imported. As for putting down insurrections, he reminded his fellow delegates that it was the North that had most recently experienced domestic violence (Shays' Rebellion), and that the South could take care of itself. Then, in a startling conclusion that unashamedly attempted to make moral considerations irrelevant, Rutledge stated that "Religion & humanity had nothing to do with this question. Interest alone is the governing principle with nations. The true question at present is whether the Southern States shall or shall not be parties to the Union. If the Northern States consult their interest, they will not oppose the increase of Slaves which will increase the commodities of which they will become the carriers."[34]

When it came to the slave trade, at least some Maryland and Virginia delegates had actually hoped that constitutional limitations would be imposed. Three leading Virginians—Madison, Mason, and Washington—had strong feelings that the slave trade had outlived its usefulness and should be ended.[35] While reasons for such sentiments varied, it was no secret that the Upper South had more than enough slaves already, and found it profitable to sell surplus slaves to the Deep South. The price of slaves would remain higher if they were in scarcer supply; continued slave importation would saturate the market. Not everyone in the Upper South agreed, however. Deep South delegates began to give ground on this issue, realizing that they did not have the full support of the Upper South to maintain the slave trade in perpetuity. They also knew that compromise was essential if the Constitution were to be ratified and that unrestricted slave importation, in the words of Virginia's Edmund Randolph, "would revolt the Quakers, Methodists, and many others in the states having no slaves."[36]

George Mason presented a passionate plea for Congress to be empowered to end slave importation, stating that it was in the South's best interests to limit slavery's expansion, and warned, "Every master is born a petty tyrant. They bring the judgment of heaven on a country. As nations cannot be rewarded or punished in the next world they must be in this. By an inevitable chain of causes and effects providence punishes national sins, by national calamities. I lament that some of our Eastern brethren had from a lust of gain embarked in this nefarious traffic. As to the states being in possession of the right to import, this was the case with many other rights, now to be properly given up. I hold it essential in every point of view that the general government should have power to prevent the increase of slavery."[37]

When the debates bogged down, the convention, as it did frequently, resorted to the creation of committees to study the issues further and recommend solutions as quickly as possible. In this case a Committee of Eleven was formed including Madison, but also containing several delegates who had indicated no strong position either way regarding restricting or taxing slave imports. On August 24 the Committee of Eleven brought its four-part compromise recommendation to the convention: Congress could end the slave trade after 1800 (liked by the North and some in the Upper South), imported slaves could be taxed (liked by the North and some in the Upper South), exports could not be taxed (liked by the South), and navigation acts could be passed by simple majority vote rather than a two-thirds vote in Congress (liked by the North). The Deep South was willing to tolerate the possibility of a ban on slave importation after 1800 in part because it assumed that the population growth in slaveholding states would soon give those states a majority of seats in the House of Representatives. Just because the Constitution gave Congress the power to ban the slave trade at some future date, it did not mean that sufficient votes would be mustered to actually legislate such a ban. In the meantime, states were free to allow or ban the importation of slaves at their own ports. As for a capitation tax on imported slaves, the committee recommended that "a tax or duty may be imposed on such migration or importation at a rate not exceeding the average of duties laid on imports."[38]

A debate took place on the committee's recommendations on August 25. Charles Cotesworth Pinckney made a motion to extend the period of time during which Congress could not interfere with the slave trade to a full twenty years, to 1808. James Madison, worried about hordes of new slaves that might be imported between 1800 (the Committee of Eleven's proposed cutoff date) and 1808, was the lone voice against this extension, which he called "dishonorable to the national character."[39] As it turned out, 200,000 slaves entered the United States between 1788 and 1808.[40] Pinckney's 1808 date won the day with little difficulty. It was a much more realistic goal to end the slave trade than to end slavery itself by 1808. There was considerable optimism on the part of many advocates for emancipation that the end of the slave trade would deal a fatal blow to slavery. Elsewhere in the Western Hemisphere, slavery's continued existence was dependent on a steady new supply of imports, but this was not the case in the American South. The magnitude of the growth of the American slave population, due to natural increase, was not anticipated.[41]

The debate next moved to the committee's recommendation that imported slaves could be taxed. Although Connecticut's delegates would often vote with the South, Roger Sherman was opposed to such a tax not because it would hit Southern pocketbooks, but because it would be "acknowledging men to be property, by taxing them as such."[42] Yet slaves were already being taxed as property. Rufus King urged his fellow delegates to consider the issue of taxing slave imports from a purely political perspective and asserted that exemption from taxation would be seen as unfair by the Northern and middle states.[43] George Mason was hoping that the tax on imported slaves might be high enough to make Virginia slaves all the more attractive to the Deep South,[44] but a fairly modest ten-dollars-per-head maximum was agreed upon, in compliance with the Committee of Eleven's recommendations.

The North's desire to have navigation acts passable by a simple majority, rather than a two-thirds majority, was honored by enough Southern delegates to pass. This was a reward for Northern support of the twenty-year ban on interference with the slave trade and a relatively mild slave import tax, a bargain that was "by now enough of an open secret that Madison included it as a note in his records."[45] Probably the least happy delegates at this point were Mason and Randolph from Virginia, for they had lost their bid to discontinue the slave trade and to require a super majority for passage of navigation acts. The possibility was raised that ratification of such a Constitution might have a tough go of it in Virginia, with that state's vocal Patrick Henry already ranting against the proposed document even before it was completed. It was becoming clear that ratification of the new Constitution could not be taken for granted.

A third major issue involving slavery with which delegates had to wrestle was how the Constitution would deal with fugitive slaves. Article IV of the Articles of Confederation contained a fugitive slave provision, but the Confederation Congress did not have the means to actually implement it. What was desired by slaveholders was a fugitive slave clause in the Constitution that would be enforceable. Once again, the word "slave" was delicately avoided as South Carolina's Pierce Butler reworded his initial proposal, which found its way into the Constitution in Article IV, Section 2: "No Person held to Service or Labour in one State, under the Laws thereof, escaping into another, shall, in Consequence of any Law or Regulation therein, be discharged from such Service or Labour, but shall be delivered up on Claim of the Party to whom such Service or Labour may be due." Northerners accepted this provision without dissent, as their region still contained slaves, bonded apprentices, and a few remaining indentured servants to whom the provision would apply. On September 10, a week before the delegates ended their work, a last-minute concession was wrung from the North by John Rutledge. Concerned over what mischief the amendment process might do, Rutledge demanded, and received, a proviso that forbade amending the clauses in the Constitution dealing with the slave trade and the capitation tax prior to the year 1808.[46]

On September 17, 1787, the ailing Benjamin Franklin requested that a speech he had prepared be read by his fellow delegate from Pennsylvania, James Wilson. While Franklin had dissented from some of the document's provisions, he stated, "It therefore astonishes me, sir, this system approaching so near to perfection as it does; and I think it will astonish our enemies. . . . [T]hus, I consent, sir, to this Constitution because I expect no better, and because I am not sure that it is not the best. The opinions I have had of its errors, I sacrifice to the public good. . . . I cannot help expressing a wish that every member of the Convention who may still have objection to [the Constitution] would with me, on this occasion, doubt a little of his own infallibility—and to make manifest our unanimity, put his name to this instrument."[47] Near the bottom of the document, Gouvernor Morris had cleverly drafted a statement above the signature section which indicated that those who signed were merely witnessing that the *states* present, rather than the *delegates,* had on September 17, 1787, unanimously consented to the Constitution. Despite this somewhat manipulative attempt at unity as well as political cover for the individual delegates, George Mason, Elbridge Gerry, and Edmund Randolph would not sign.

The sectional compromise that largely centered on slavery and its implications was now completed. There was probably not a single delegate who was completely happy with the outcome. In a letter to the president of the Confederation Congress, delegates to the Constitutional Convention talked of the "mutual deference and concession" required to bring the document to fruition.[48] In reality, both North and South made concessions at the convention based on very different assumptions about the future. The North gave way to the South on certain aspects of slavery, assuming that the institution was on the path to extinction. The South gave way to the North on certain matters of political power, assuming Southern population growth would bring eventual dominance over the North. Neither section's vision for the future proved to be accurate. Those miscalculations would create increasingly dangerous sectional rifts.

But now, in the fall of 1787, it was time to begin the ratification process. Public interest in the proposed document was high. Given the importance of the printed word as a means of influencing public opinion, the positions taken by America's newspapers were extremely important to the outcome of the states' ratification proceedings.[49] Some fifty-five newspapers had printed the text of the Constitution within three weeks of the convention's adjournment, with more to follow. Editorials in support of whatever new, strong central government would emerge from the convention had appeared in the press even before the Constitution was revealed. It should be noted that neither the press nor the public had access to information from inside the convention, other than the final product of the Constitution itself. Few, if any of the debates, disputes, threats, compromises, or bargains with which historians are familiar today were available until the 1840 publication of James Madison's notes. What the public saw in 1787 was the finished product, minus the full context and controversy in which it was crafted.

It was no surprise that in the debate over ratification of the Constitution, the issue of slavery played a significant role on at least two levels. The state ratifying conventions reflected, more or less, many of the same debates over slavery that had taken place in Philadelphia. But the rhetoric of slavery as used by the Anti-Federalists, those opposed to the new Constitution, went beyond those debates over actual slavery policy to warn that approval of the new, robust form of national government would result in a repudiation of the goals of the Revolution and political slavery for all Americans.[50]

At the Pennsylvania ratifying convention, as in most Northern states, there were those critical of the Constitution for not ending the importation of slaves immediately or at least before 1808. In Massachusetts, where the vote to ratify won by a very close margin, Thomas Dawes delivered a speech aimed to convince delegates that, between the right to ban slave imports in twenty years and the right to tax imported slaves, Congress under the Constitution would eventually bring an end to slavery; "it has received a mortal wound" was his compelling, if erroneous, conclusion.

The twenty-year restriction on legislation banning the slave trade was viewed variously as a glass half-empty and half-full; it was an outrageous delay to some, while others celebrated the fact that after twenty years Congress had the power to end the nefarious trade. William Heath, an antislavery Massachusetts delegate arguing in favor of the Constitution, raised the issue of states' rights while ignoring the Puritan notion of communal sin. Heath argued that, since non-slave states could do nothing about the institution in states where it existed, "we are not in this case partakers of other men's sins."[51]

There were those in the South who were very concerned about their future under the proposed Constitution. In South Carolina, a debate erupted in the state legislature prior to its establishing a ratifying convention that would make the actual decision about joining the new Union. Rawlins Lowndes, a former governor now serving in the legislature, was convinced that the North intended to end the slave trade after twenty years and warned that, "without negroes, this state would degenerate into one of the most contemptible in the Union." In an interesting response to a question by another South Carolina legislator about the Constitution's lack of a bill of rights, Charles Cotesworth Pinckney said that most states with a bill of rights (Virginia being a prime example) began with a declaration that all men are by nature free. It would be awkward, Pinckney maintained, for South Carolina to go along with such sentiments "when a large part of our property consists in men who are actually born slaves."[52]

In Virginia's debates over the Constitution, Patrick Henry proclaimed that the United States could not survive without Virginia (which would be fine with him), but Governor Randolph argued that the opposite was true; Virginia could not survive apart from the United States. Part of his argument rested on the large number of slaves in the state and his opinion that outside help would be needed in case of servile insurrection.[53] George Mason called the Constitution's twenty-year extension of the slave trade "a fatal section" which renounced "one of the great causes of our separation from Great-Britain." "As much as I value an [*sic*] union of all the States," he went on, "I would not admit the southern States into the Union, unless they agreed to the discontinuance of this disgraceful trade, because it would bring weakness and not strength to the Union."

James Madison gave a reasoned response that he, too, found the twenty-year reprieve of the slave trade "impolitic," but it could not be excluded "without encountering greater evils": "The Southern States would not have entered into the Union of America, without the temporary permission of that trade. And if they were excluded from the Union, the consequences might be dreadful to them and to us. We are not in a worse situation than before. That traffic is prohibited by our laws, and we may continue the prohibition. The Union in general is not in a worse situation. Under the articles of Confederation, it might be continued forever: But by this clause an end may be put to it after twenty years."[54]

Eight of the nine states required to ratify the Constitution before it could take effect had done so by May 1788. The Anti-Federalists had numerous objections to the Constitution, including some who saw favoritism to the slaveholding South, but by now the momentum had clearly shifted in favor of the Federalists. The two largest states, New York and Virginia, were still debating when New Hampshire became the ninth state to ratify the Constitution on June 21, 1788. While the Constitution was now technically in effect, without New York and Virginia the Union would ring hollow without their full consent and cooperation. Virginia narrowly ratified the Constitution after twenty proposed amendments, including a bill of rights, were promised serious consideration.

The New York debate prompted *The Federalist Papers,* eighty-five essays by James Madison, Alexander Hamilton, and John Jay published in New York newspapers beginning in October 1787. These essays brilliantly analyzed and promoted the nature of federalism under the proposed Constitution, and exposed the failures of the Articles of Confederation. Of these, the papers on insurrection, navigation, and taxation touched peripherally, if at all, on the issue of slavery. *Federalist 54,* written by Hamilton, dealt directly with the Three-Fifths Clause and the dichotomy of slaves as both property and persons. None dealt directly with the fugitive slave provision. While it is difficult to measure the influence of these essays on New York's vote in favor of ratification, the essays give much insight into the thinking of the framers and are a major source for study of the Constitution and its early interpretations. The Constitution of the United States was implemented on March 4, 1789.

Of the three great provisions related to slavery in the Constitution of 1787, the abolition of the slave trade in 1808 would prove the least divisive. The Three-Fifths Clause would be a source of irritation in the future, but the South rather than the North would pay the price for it. Subsequently embedded in a number of Southern state constitutions, this arbitrary formula became, over time, a source of political tension between the plantation owner and yeoman farmer. The least controversial provision in 1787, the fugitive slave provision, proved to be the most fatal to national unity. Being a political gathering focused on compromise, Jefferson's "demigods" largely excluded from their considerations the moral aspects of slavery. The

Constitution certainly created a "more perfect union" than experienced under the Articles of Confederation, but it was essentially a slaveholders' union. As it had been with the Revolution, there was no social upheaval being promoted here; the framers "were dedicated to the proposition that government should rest upon the dominion of property."[55] Enslaved black men and women were still to be considered property. While Northern states began to move, however haltingly, toward emancipation, the day the nation would truly come to grips with slavery had been delayed again.

CHAPTER 3

STUMBLING FORWARD: EMANCIPATION PROCEEDS IN NEW ENGLAND AND PENNSYLVANIA

The founding fathers had now twice made a collective decision to ignore the incongruities of promoting liberty for themselves while keeping slaves in subjugation, first for the sake of unity in the Revolution and then to unify the nation under a new constitution. Decisions regarding slavery were left to the discretion of the individual states. At the state level, the founding generation of Northern politicians began haphazardly to address slavery in their midst.

In the early national period, slavery still existed in all parts of the country. Both the wealth and the injustice that the institution promoted were shared by the North as well as the South. It is no secret that part of the North's economic success was due to the existence of the slave trade and slave labor in the South. While actual slavery in the North was far less integral to that region's economy than in the South, Northern manufacturing interests relied on the raw materials produced by Southern slaves. Northern shipping interests not only profited by transporting raw materials and finished products between the two regions, but also were deeply involved in the international slave trade. Northern banking houses invested heavily in these endeavors. While a slave revolt occurred in New York in 1712 and a slave "conspiracy" had been brutally crushed in that city in 1741, slavery in the North was on the whole less severe when compared to the plantation system of the South. Additionally, black slavery and indentured servitude were both declining in the North during the revolutionary period.

The 1790 Census is the first reasonably accurate picture we have of the extent of slavery and the free black population in both the North and the South. According to that census, the United States contained 698,821 slaves. Of these, only 40,370 (5.8 percent) lived in the North. Of the original Southern states, only Georgia and Delaware had fewer slaves than the entire North. Less than half (27,009 or 45.6 percent) of the 59,267 free blacks lived in the North. New Jersey had the highest percentage of blacks in its population among the Northern states at 7.7 percent. New York followed closely at 7.6 percent. Percentages for other Northern states were significantly lower. The percentage of blacks, free or slave, in the Northern state populations would decline until after the Civil War. The 1790 Census also shows an unequal distribution of slaves in the North, with all of New England claiming 3,886 slaves, nearly the equal to Pennsylvania's 3,737. New Jersey's 11,423 and New York's 21,324 slaves, while significantly larger in number, paled next to Virginia's 293,427 slaves that same year. On the other hand, the number of free blacks in New England in 1790 (13,056) was slightly higher than the number of free blacks in Virginia (12,766).[1] While the North profited handsomely from slavery as a national institution, its more distant relationship with slavery and blacks in general "allowed the North to minimize and even deny its links with the institution that fueled its prosperity."[2]

Many Northerners in the early national period were rather limited in their opposition to slavery, favoring its extirpation only within their own state or region. As long as distance existed between themselves and slavery, they were comfortable with the belief that, since the American Revolution, slavery was no longer a national issue but was now essentially limited to the South, where such a labor force may indeed have its place. Furthermore, it was believed by many in the North, and some in the South, that the inevitable end of the slave trade would eventually sound the death knell of the institution, as it had elsewhere in the world. The Northern distaste for the abstract concept of slavery, while not overly concerned with the actual practice of slavery in the South, in reality gave slavery tacit permission to expand in areas remote from the North, such as in the territories of Kentucky and Tennessee and the recently organized Southwest Territory.[3] Slavery's appeal was clearly waning in much of the North in the years following American independence. While the Founders had made allowances for the slave trade to continue without interference on the national level until at least 1808, nothing prohibited individual states from outlawing either the slave trade or the practice of slavery itself at any time. Several Northern states debated and pursued the emancipation of slaves within their borders with varying levels of intensity, urgency, and success in the late eighteenth and early nineteenth centuries. This does not mean, however, that Northerners opposed to slavery in their own states were promoting equality for African Americans, or that they were necessarily opposed to slavery in other parts of the country.

For many whites, North and South, being opposed to slavery also meant being opposed to the presence of African Americans in their midst; if slavery could be eliminated, a desired ethnic cleansing might be possible in order to avoid the dreaded prospect of race-mixing. Colonization, a euphemism for deportation, was often supported as a means of fulfilling this agenda in this era and in later years, although it was rarely success-ful. For many whites, personal freedom and political equality for blacks were two very different issues. On the other hand, there were those who did have a genuine concern for human rights and desired freedom for the slaves without hoping they could be made to disappear once freed. Then there were others somewhere in the middle; we can be both perplexed and informed by the ambivalent approach of Pennsylvania's Benjamin Franklin, simultaneously an abolitionist and one who was anxiety-ridden about the results of emancipation. Franklin noted, "Slavery is such an atro-cious debasement of human nature, that its extirpation, if not performed with solicitous care, may sometimes open a source of serious evils. . . . Under such circumstances, freedom may prove a misfortune to [the slave] and prejudicial to [white] society." He suggested that a special national police force might be needed to look after the behavior of "emancipated black people."[4]

In New England, slavery historically carried with it less stigma and greater legal rights for the slave than in other sections of the country. New England's Puritan founders had attempted to justify their approach to every aspect of life from their interpretation of the Bible. They based their views of slavery on Old Testament Mosaic Law, which did not regard slaves as inherently inferior, but merely unfortunate in their present cir-cumstances.[5] In Puritan New England, with its commitment to biblical val-ues, law, and due process, precedents were established early in the colonial experience that gave blacks, both free and slave, much greater opportunity for a degree of fairness and justice than in other parts of America. Ironi-cally, it was Puritan Massachusetts that first gave slavery legal recognition in 1641—the first English colony in North America to do so.[6] While slav-ery was still slavery, in colonial Massachusetts free and enslaved blacks had access to legal counsel and could testify in court against whites. It was not acceptable to bring charges against black defendants with less evidence than would be required to charge whites, and blacks had the right to appeal legal decisions that went against them. Furthermore, New

England's slaves usually lived in their masters' homes, often had time off to use as they pleased, and were far less restricted in their mobility than in other regions.[7] Puritanism worked in the slaves' favor, although usually falling short of manumission, by encouraging masters to Christianize their slaves and generally treat them well.[8]

One of New England's earliest antislavery voices was Puritan judge Samuel Sewall, who in 1700 published *The Selling of Joseph,* in which he stated, "Forasmuch as *Liberty* is in real value next unto *Life:* None ought to part with it themselves, or deprive others of it, but upon the most mature Consideration. . . . All things considered, it would conduce more to the Welfare of the Province, to have White Servants for a Term of Years [rather than to have black slaves]." Just as the selling of Joseph by his brothers was an act without any moral or legal basis, no one at present, according to Sewall, had a right to buy another human being without the purchaser having "forfeited a great part of his own claim to Humanity."[9] Most New England Puritans in the colonial period were less bothered by slavery than Judge Sewall, however, since the institution clearly existed in the Old Testament record and did not appear to attract the wrath of God.

By the revolutionary period, opinions had largely changed in New England regarding the moral acceptability of slavery. While Puritanism as an intact religious and social system had largely disappeared by 1776, its influence lived on, including a New England penchant for fearing divine punishment for personal and collective sins that continued unabated. One revolutionary-era deacon summed up the concern by declaring slavery to be a "God-provoking and wrath-procuring sin."[10]

It was in New England that individual states first eliminated slavery. Vermont's 1777 Constitution outlawed the institution. However, while Vermont considered itself an independent state in 1777, it was not officially recognized as the fourteenth state of the United States until 1791 due to a dispute with New York over claims to the sparsely settled region, claims which New York relinquished following negotiations and a cash settlement in 1790. Thus, the first state to enter the Union after ratification and implementation of the U.S. Constitution by the original thirteen states was a "free" state. The Vermont Constitution, however, left open the possibility of binding out children whose parents had been slaves prior to 1777 until they were "of age" so as not to become a public expense. This provision could also be applied, it appears, to poor white children. Some confusion still exists over Vermont's 1790 Census, which listed seventeen slaves living in the state.[11] Eighty years later, the chief clerk of the U.S. Census Bureau, George D. Harrington of Vermont, "corrected" their status to "free."[12]

Other Northern states were not far behind in contemplating how and when to limit, and eventually end, slavery within their borders. This Northern pathway to emancipation, however, would be full of twists and turns, with each state dealing uniquely in the context of its own political, economic, and social climate. The North was never a region of large-scale slave societies providing the prevailing labor force as found in parts of the South. Slavery in the North was only one system of labor out of several options, and never the dominant model.[13] A unifying concept was the idea of gradual emancipation, which gained considerable public favor at various times in most Northern states. Such a plan was urged on the Massachusetts legislature in 1771 by a group of slaves themselves, who petitioned that all adult slaves in the Bay Colony be immediately freed and that their children be freed upon attaining the age of twenty-one years. More interested at the time in countering British tyranny and seeking colonial unity than in mitigating the plight of their slaves, the Massachusetts legislature tabled the proposed bill.[14]

In 1783, Massachusetts, the first English colony in North America to recognize the legality of slavery, became the first state (since Vermont did not attain recognized statehood until 1791) to remove from its citizens the right to possess slaves. In this case, judicial activism proved to be a more potent weapon against slavery than the legislative process. The chief justice of the Massachusetts Supreme Judicial Court, William Cushing, articulated a strong opinion in a 1783 case, *Commonwealth* [of Massachusetts] *v. Jennison,* involving an enslaved black man named Qwok Walker.[15] This case was actually the last of three cases involving Mr. Walker's ultimately successful attempt to obtain his freedom. Citing the Declaration of Rights in the 1780 Massachusetts Constitution, Chief Justice Cushing concluded in his instructions to the jury,

> As to the doctrine of slavery and the right of Christians to hold Africans in perpetual servitude, and sell and treat them as we do our horses and cattle . . . a different idea has taken place with the people of America, more favorable to the natural rights of mankind, and to that natural, innate desire of Liberty, with which Heaven (without regard to color, complexion, or shape of noses-features) has inspired all the human race. And upon this ground our Constitution of Government, by which the people of this Commonwealth have solemnly bound themselves, sets out with declaring that all men are born free and equal—and that every subject is entitled to liberty, and to have it guarded by the laws, as well as life and property—and in short is totally repugnant to the idea of being born slaves. This being the case, I think the idea of slavery is inconsistent with our own conduct and Constitution; and there can

be no such thing as perpetual servitude of a rational creature, unless his liberty is forfeited by some criminal conduct or given up by personal consent or contract.[16]

Prior to Qwok Walker's emancipation in 1783, no fewer than thirty slaves had sued successfully for their freedom in the Bay State, with only one case being reversed in the Supreme Court of Judicature. These cases reflected both the growing sophistication of Boston's black community in making use of the law, and unique Puritan traditions regarding the rights of slaves, as beneficial agents of change. The winning arguments in these cases were not based on the natural rights of humans to be free, however, but rather on the illegal ways in which these individuals had been enslaved. But everything changed when, in the 1783 *Commonwealth v. Jennison* case, Justice Cushing made reference to the natural rights guaranteed by the Massachusetts Constitution of 1780. In his legal notebook, Cushing penned an entry that "the preceding Case was the one in which by the foregoing Charge, Slavery in Massachusetts was forever abolished."[17]

While this seemed like a momentous case at the time to Justice Cushing (and no doubt to Qwok Walker, who was given his freedom), the public impact was initially less impressive. As Emily Blanck has pointed out, "Because slavery had been abolished by judicial decree rather than legislative act, the burden was on the individual rather than the system. In other words, enslaved men and women had to face their masters and assert their freedom; if the master refused, he could be brought to court, where his rights of ownership would no longer be protected. Outside of the courtroom, moreover, Jennison's significance was not widely understood. Newspapers did not carry the story, and contemporaries, who must have heard about it, apparently quickly forgot it."[18]

While little official notice was given to Cushing's constitutional pronouncement of 1783 (the case *Commonwealth v. Jennison* was first cited in an official court report in 1867 as part of an overview of the legal history of slavery in the state), slavery did decline significantly in Massachusetts. The Jennison case, however, did not mean that all slaves in the state immediately bid their masters farewell. In fact, records indicate that slaves continued to be sold in Massachusetts.[19] According to Blanck, "in the 1790 census, not one citizen claimed to own a slave. Of course, masters would have felt pressured to hide their slaveowning, and anecdotal evidence exists indicating that a scattering of people did live as slaves in the late 1780's and 1790's. Still, deprived of legal backing, slavery had withered substantially; it held on only in isolated situations, when and where local conditions allowed."[20]

The role of William Cushing in dealing a death blow to slavery is perhaps ironic, given that he himself had been a slaveholder and was essentially forced into an activist judicial role because of the failure of the Massachusetts legislature to address slavery. In 1782 the Massachusetts House did pass a bill that would have provided for gradual emancipation in the state, but the legislation got nowhere in the Senate. Two years later, in 1784, the legislature enacted fines for anyone found guilty of kidnapping a free person of color in the state (keep in mind that non-citizens of Massachusetts could bring their slaves into the state). Perhaps the true feelings of members of the legislature are best seen in their action of 1787, in which concern was addressed that Massachusetts could become a haven for free blacks and runaway slaves from other parts of the United States. Unless they had been residents of Massachusetts before 1787, blacks were limited to a two-month stay.

In 1788 the slave trade was ended legislatively in Massachusetts, with fines levied for "importing, transporting, buying, or selling as slaves individuals of African descent."[21] Not all whites in Massachusetts were delighted to see the end of slavery in their commonwealth, or approved of the manner in which its demise was accomplished. James Winthrop, chief justice of the Court of Common Pleas, whose ancestor John Winthrop had founded the Bay Colony in 1630, said in 1795 that, "by a misconstruction of our State Constitution, which declares all men by nature free and equal, a number of citizens have been deprived of property formerly acquired under the protection of law."[22]

Neighboring Connecticut had been home to the largest number of slaves in New England at the time of the Revolution. Abolitionist activity in Connecticut received the attention of the legislative assembly in 1777, when a committee was established to review the situation of Negroes in the state and recommend possible pathways toward emancipation. Much of the work of this committee involved a plan to allow slaves to serve in the Continental Army, whereby they would obtain their unconditional freedom following the war for independence from Great Britain. Furthermore, their former masters would be absolved of providing any financial support for those freed. While this plan did not come to fruition in the legislature, an alternative piece of legislation focusing on easier manumission of slaves did pass in late 1777. This meant that blacks freed in advance, or at the time, of their enlistment could enter the army as substitutes for their former masters or the sons of their former masters.[23]

While attempts at gradual emancipation failed to pass the Connecticut legislature in 1779 and 1780, a vote in January of 1784 to consolidate all state laws regarding slavery passed, including a barely noticed added section that provided for all slave children born after March 1, 1784, to be freed when they reached the age of twenty-five. This low-key, let's-just-do-it approach to gradual emancipation, whether intentional or not, had the effect of minimizing opposition to the plan. By 1810 the census showed 310 slaves remaining in Connecticut, down 89 percent from the 2,790 slaves recorded in the 1790 Census. In 1790, there were 2,801 free blacks in the state, a number which more than doubled to 6,453 in 1810,[24] evidence of substantial progress in reducing the state's slave population.

Gradual emancipation did not necessarily result in emancipation for all of Connecticut's slaves. Gradual emancipation kept in lifelong bondage any slave unfortunate enough to have been born into slavery on or before February 29, 1784. For those born on or after March 1, 1784, their masters were free to sell their property south prior to their slave's twenty-fifth birthday, and some did exactly that. While a few Connecticut masters continued to hold slaves for life, the number of slaves declined in the state as other masters freed their slaves, made labor contracts with them for limited terms, or evaded the growing social stigma of slaveholding while retaining their economic value by selling them south. As late as the 1840 Census, Connecticut, like other Northern states that had enacted gradual emancipation laws, still had slaves within its borders. The final legal end of slavery in Connecticut came when the legislature passed "An Act to prevent slavery" in 1848 which went into effect in the 1849 *Revision of the General Laws* and stated that "no person shall hereafter be held in slavery in this State."[25]

In New Hampshire, the black population was miniscule, making up only 0.56 percent of the state's populace in 1790. Of the total black population of 688 persons in the 1790 Census, 158 were listed as slaves. In the 1840 Census, only one slave was listed in the entire state and, when added to the 537 free blacks, the percentage of blacks in New Hampshire had dropped to 0.19 percent of the population.[26] A petition by 19 slaves was brought to the state legislature in 1779, but did not receive a reading in the legislature until April of 1780. The argument used was one of natural rights; the petitioners asserted that they had been born free in Africa and brought against their will to a foreign land as slaves. The petitioners pointed out the irony of having originated in a place "where (though ignorance and unchristianity prevailed) they were born free" and now find themselves in a land "where (though knowledge, Christianity, and Freedom are their boast) they are compelled . . . to drag on their lives in miserable servitude."[27]

The final legal end to slavery in New Hampshire is frustratingly obscure. The Rev. Jeremy Belknap wrote in 1788 that "the negroes in Massachusetts and New Hampshire are all free, by the first article in the Declaration of Rights [a similar statement about human freedom and equality as natural rights appeared in the constitutions of both states]. This has been pleaded in law, and admitted." However, there is a dearth of evidence concerning the legal trail in this matter, other than the removal of slaves as taxable property in a revenue bill of 1789. In 1795, Reverend Belknap revised his 1788 assertion and concluded that the New Hampshire Constitution of 1783 gave freedom only to those persons born after its adoption.[28]

In 1846, Massachusetts-born poet and abolitionist John Greenleaf Whittier published a poem called "New Hampshire" honoring that state's antislavery stand, which began:

> God bless New Hampshire! for her granite peaks
> Once more the voice of Stark and Langdon speaks.
> The long-bound vassal of the exulting South
> For very shame her self-forged chain has broken;
> Torn the black seal of slavery from her mouth
> And in the clear tones of her old time spoken!

and finally ended with these words:

> Courage, then, Northern hearts! Be firm, be true;
> What one brave State hath done, can ye not also do?[29]

Whittier's praise appears to have been premature. While only one slave was noted in the entire state according the 1840 Census, the reliability of that figure should be called into question as it was not until 1857 that the Granite State's legislature passed an act clearly forbidding slavery and declaring that "no person, because of descent, should be disqualified from becoming a citizen of the state."[30]

Rhode Island's experience with slavery was more extensive than that of the other New England states. Colonial Rhode Island was very active in importing slaves, with Newport becoming the region's leading slave port. Between the end of the Revolution and 1808, Rhode Island shipping interests controlled a majority of the American trade in African slaves. While the number of slaves in Rhode Island in 1790 stood at 952, the total black population of the state was 4,421, or 6.4 percent of the population, the highest proportion of blacks among New England states. Not surprisingly, Rhode Island's higher percentage of blacks resulted in harsher local slave laws than were generally found in the rest of New England.

Alone among New England states, Rhode Island had a land-and-labor system existing in what is today Washington County that somewhat resembled the plantation system of the South. These so-called "Narragansett Planters" had attempted to imitate Southern gentry, albeit on a much smaller scale when it came to the number of slaves they owned. Their farms, some of them very extensive in acreage and producing dairy products, livestock, and horses, utilized slave labor in the colonial period, but dependence on slaves, while not totally eliminated, peaked before the Revolution. The racial makeup of some of these Rhode Island slaves differed from other areas, as some displaced Narragansett Indians and blacks had intermarried years before.[31]

It was during the Revolutionary War that Rhode Island undertook an emancipation plan that allowed slaves to enlist in the Continental Army. Such recruits were to be freed unconditionally, with their owners compensated by the state. Furthermore, these slave recruits were to be entitled to all the benefits of white enlistees. This controversial emancipation law of 1778 was reversed after only four months, however, and involved fewer than ninety manumitted slaves at a large cost to the state government of more than 10,000 pounds. Furthermore, the veterans' benefits available to white soldiers never reached the emancipated black soldiers.[32]

The Rhode Island assembly approved a law in 1779 banning the sale of slaves to owners outside the boundaries of the state without the slaves' consent. The motive for this legislation appeared to be twofold; it mitigated the potential long-distance breakup of slave families, an often acknowledged evil, and prevented masters from avoiding financial loss by selling their slaves out of state before Rhode Island law might emancipate them at some future date. In late 1783, at the urging of Rhode Island Quakers, an assembly committee drafted a bill that would have ended slavery in the state and imposed large fines for involvement in the slave trade. When a vote was taken in the full assembly in early 1784, the bill was soundly defeated, reflecting in part the influence of Newport slaving interests. However, an alternate bill was crafted and passed that provided gradual emancipation for all slaves born after March 1, 1784, but did nothing to limit the slave trade.[33] As a result of this gradual emancipation legislation in Rhode Island, the last census to list slaves in the state was that of 1840, in which five slaves were reported.[34]

Pennsylvania, with its colonial Quaker background, would seem like an ideal place to find antislavery sentiment and laws in full force. However, while the rhetoric of emancipation was clearly evident during the colonial period, little or no progress was made legislatively until after American independence was declared. This is not to detract, however, from the outstanding abolitionist work of French-born Pennsylvania Quaker Anthony Benezet, an advocate for education for blacks and the distribution of abolitionist literature, a man who Benjamin Quarles calls "the leading antislavery propagandist in pre–Revolutionary War America."[35] While never friends of slavery, the Quakers took an approach to emancipation that was "less than satisfactory" to black communities, who were not even permitted to join the Society of Friends until the 1790s. According to Jean R. Soderlund, "Gradualist, segregationist, and paternalistic" aptly describe the Quaker attitude, which "set the tone for the white antislavery movement in America from 1780 to 1833."[36] While Quakers may have taken the lead in voicing antislavery sentiment in colonial Pennsylvania, their pacifist theological orientation lost them considerable public credibility during the Revolution, and even resulted in some persecution when they were mistakenly viewed as unpatriotic British sympathizers for their refusal to take up arms. As a result, the government of Revolutionary Pennsylvania fell into the hands of those largely unsympathetic to or ignorant of the Quaker heritage.

A ban on importation of additional slaves into the state was urged by Pennsylvania's Executive Council in 1778 as an incremental step on the way to emancipation, on the grounds that such a practice would be humane and at the same time make the new nation appear less hypocritical in European eyes which were "astonished to see a people eager for Liberty holding Negroes in Bondage."[37] However, such a suggestion could only be implemented by the Assembly, Pennsylvania's unicameral legislature. A member of the Assembly went a step beyond the council's initial recommendation and introduced a gradual emancipation bill that year, but it was tabled. The Executive Council pressed on with encouragement for the Assembly to act on a gradual bill, even going so far as to offer to draft such a bill for the Assembly. This approach backfired and produced a debate in the Assembly focused on the overstepping of political bounds by the Executive Council, rather than a debate on actual emancipation.[38]

After the members cooled down, the Assembly did appear ready to grapple with a gradual emancipation bill, and one was crafted in early 1779. The preamble of the bill condemned slavery as "highly detrimental to morality, industry, and the arts" and again raised the paradox of Pennsylvanians fighting for liberty while enslaving their fellow humans. Providing a bill for gradual emancipation was also seen as an appropriate gesture by which to show gratitude to God for the British evacuation of Philadelphia in June of 1778. The proposed bill would free all slave children born in the future; girls would receive their freedom at age eighteen and boys at age twenty-one. The bill also would ban the importation of new slaves while continuing the state's ban on interracial marriage. Faced with some public opposition to the proposed legislation, the Assembly stalled and took no action during that legislative session, delaying final consideration of the bill until the next session. The newly elected Assembly sent the bill to committee for substantial revisions, which removed the ban on interracial marriage but increased the length of service to twenty-eight years for slave children born after the bill's passage. In March of 1780, the Pennsylvania Assembly passed the bill on a vote of thirty-four to twenty-one.[39] While no slaves were immediately freed by this legislation, blacks who were already free felt the greatest immediate impact as several restrictive laws affecting their activities were lifted at once.[40]

Pennsylvania in 1780 thus became the first state to pass an abolition law, but due to its gradual nature, slavery continued in the state for decades. The Census of 1790 showed 3,737 slaves; by 1800 that number had been cut in half to 1,706. The 1840 Census was the last to record the presence of slaves in Pennsylvania—64 of them. By that year there were 47,854 free blacks in the state, compared with 1,676,115 whites.[41]

The various state legislative acts bringing slavery to an ultimate, if often gradual, end in these Northern states should not be interpreted as a public embracing of African Americans and a widespread belief in "liberty and justice for all." Genuine concern for the well being of the slave was matched or exceeded by racist views that made it difficult for whites to conceive of society implementing complete equality of the races. Even Abraham Lincoln would refute Stephen Douglas's insinuation in one of their 1858 debates that "because I do not want a black woman for a *slave* I must necessarily want her for a *wife.*" Though no doubt playing to the crowd with largely Southern roots in his debate with Douglas in Charleston, Illinois, Lincoln asserted, "I am not nor ever have been, in favor of bringing about in any way the social and political equality of the white and black races. . . . There is a physical difference between the white and black races which I believe will forever forbid the two races living together on terms of social and political equality."[42] Lincoln would eventually modify his views regarding blacks, primarily after he became acquainted with a few, including Frederick Douglass. But to think that in 1858 Lincoln, who was soon to become a national voice of reason and moderation in the antislavery cause, would hold such views is a good indication of just how racist nearly all whites would remain not only in the early Republic but throughout antebellum America.

ABRAHAM LINCOLN. *Illinois lawyer and politician who despised slavery yet believed it to be protected by the Constitution where it existed, while advocating its containment elsewhere. His views on African Americans evolved: as president, he signed the Emancipation Proclamation on January 1, 1863, and agreed to allow African Americans to fight as equals in the Union army. By the end of the Civil War, he had pushed forward the Thirteenth Amendment abolishing slavery and was openly talking about citizenship and voting rights for former slaves.*

Such views on the part of white America must have been discouraging to free blacks, as well as those yet yearning to be free. Being a free black was no guarantee of access to freedoms that whites possessed, much less to the equality proclaimed in the Declaration of Independence. The idea of removal to a colony where blacks would be empowered and be in the majority actually made sense to some African Americans, and had a great deal of appeal to many whites, including those with the best of intentions. Removal of blacks from America to colonies in Africa or elsewhere had been contemplated in the early eighteenth century, but resulted in nothing concrete. In the late 1700s there was a brief flurry of interest in Britain's West African colony of Sierra Leone as a possible haven for free American blacks, especially after Gustavus Vassa (as Olaudah Equiano was then known) was given a supervisory role in the project by the British government.[43] The Sierra Leone experiment, primarily involving freed slaves from the British Empire, did not go well from the beginning and failed to become a desired destination of resettlement for American blacks.

The idea of removing blacks to Africa or elsewhere was far from dead in America, however. The American Colonization Society was founded in 1816, shortly after a prosperous free New England black named Paul Cuffe transported fifteen African Americans to Africa at his own expense.[44] If prominent names guaranteed success, the American Colonization Society should have prospered. Francis Scott Key was one of the Founders, and Supreme Court Justice Bushrod Washington served as the society's president. Other prominent members included Henry Clay, Daniel Webster, John Tyler, and Andrew Jackson.[45] With financial assistance from the federal government, the American Colonization Society established its own colony of Liberia on the coast of West Africa, with its principal settlement named "Monrovia" for President James Monroe. However, the Liberian experiment failed to attract significant numbers of African Americans. In fact, Northern blacks demonstrated "almost universal opposition to colonization, particularly in Africa." There were exceptions; a few black leaders, including Martin Delany, thought non-African colonization might have merit and suggested locations as diverse as the Caribbean, Central and South America, Canada, and the American West. Opposition to colonization won the day. A group of free blacks in Lynne, Connecticut, labeled colonization "one of the wildest projects ever patronized by enlightened men."[46] While President Lincoln would speak in favor of voluntary colonization, none of these schemes worked; African Americans were here to stay, even if their freedom was still elusive.

Today, few Americans, including residents of the New England states and Pennsylvania, are aware that slavery existed in these regions after American independence was declared. And in at least three of these states, gradual emancipation represented a crawl, not a march, to freedom for African Americans. In 1840, nearly six decades after the passage of their gradual emancipation legislation, Connecticut, Rhode Island, and Pennsylvania still tolerated human bondage within their borders. If by then the numbers of slaves were miniscule, it was the Grim Reaper, more than compassion, that finally extinguished slavery in these states. The story of emancipation in the other Northern states, along with attempts to introduce slavery into the Upper Midwest, would demonstrate how the twists and turns on the road to emancipation would continue unabated. The colonization schemes would also continue. These events and movements were haphazard in nature, and none represented a coordinated consensus regarding emancipation. Meanwhile, the self-styled Cavalier Kingdom of the South, whose ideals were enshrined with the symbolic purity of lily-white cotton, went about creating its own mythology to buttress its rationale for slavery.

CHAPTER 4

FORWARD TO THE PAST:
THE SOUTH'S "CAVALIER KINGDOM"

In much of the South, labor and social standing were perceived quite differently from in the North. Just as colonial Puritan New England left a significant and enduring imprint on the culture and psyche of the North, including its views on slavery, the South was under the influence of a separate and fundamentally elitist worldview that can be traced back to early colonial Virginia. Sir William Berkeley's decades-long governorship (1642–76), which overlapped the English Civil War, transformed the struggling Virginia colony from a "military outpost or lumber camp" atmosphere of about eight thousand disorderly settlers into a viable, even prosperous colony of forty thousand inhabitants with "a coherent social order, a functioning economic system, and a strong sense of its own special folkways."[1] More than any other individual, Governor Berkeley, through laws and immigration policy, shaped early Virginia into his vision of a New World society of English gentry. Royalist Cavaliers were lured to Virginia in significant numbers and given extensive estates and important offices. Ironically, just as New England had attracted Puritans fearful of royal authority and religious conformity a generation earlier, Virginia now appealed to Cavaliers distressed over regicide, repressive Puritan control, and last but not least, lack of economic opportunity in England. Massachusetts had offered Puritans the chance to build a "New England" according to their specifications; now Virginia offered a similar way out for those fleeing Puritan heavy-handedness and economic woes back in the old country. These refugee Cavaliers would establish many of the first families of Virginia. Many of the Cavalier immigrants were younger sons of English gentry whose economic prospects at home, even without the detested Puritans in charge, were rather dismal. For example, John Washington, a younger son, arrived in Virginia in 1657 after his clergyman father lost his pulpit and income thanks to Puritan domination in England.[2]

A widely held belief, at least in the antebellum South, was that the aristocratic, agrarian heritage of that region was traceable to early settlement by members of the royalist (but defeated) Cavalier party in the English Civil War, and that the North had been infested by commercial and democratic elements thanks to settlement by those commoners, the Puritan Roundheads, whose temporary victory over the English throne degenerated into a Cromwellian catastrophe that was rebuffed by the good sense of the English people in the restoration of the monarchy.[3] In reality, while the Cavalier origins thesis has some validity in Virginia, even in that colony the vast majority of white settlers were indentured servants and otherwise landless whites. For other Southern states to look to Cavalier origins as proof of their gentrified social if not racial superiority over the democratic riff-raff of the North may have boosted their self-esteem, but it was not grounded in historical reality. Many of them realized it; as Elizabeth Fox-Genovese and Eugene Genovese have pointed out, "Much of Southerners' self-image derived from—and was intended to reinforce—the legend that they descended from [aristocratic, albeit lower nobility] Cavaliers. Virginians pretended to take for granted their aristocratic origins in England, and other Southerners pretended to believe them."[4] Some Southerners, however, scoffed at the Cavalier origins theory and took pride in their more plebeian English roots. Regardless of this disagreement, "both [Southern] promoters and detractors of the Cavalier legend agreed on the superiority of slaveholders as a class and on slavery as the foundation of southern civilization."[5]

The early nineteenth century was the age of Romanticism. The romantic novels of Sir Walter Scott were widely read in the South, which in turn adopted the imagery of chivalry to reinforce regional self-concepts. The Southern gentry relished their plantation social life of parties, balls, fox and deer hunts, and later in the antebellum period, jousting tournaments with participants assuming the names of medieval knights and competing for prize money and the affections of a designated "queen" presiding over the event.[6] Both the antebellum proslavery novels and the postwar "lost cause" literature employed the romantic myth of Southern manhood as virile knights and cavaliers, protectors of hearth and home, and defenders of Southern virtue.

D. W. Griffith's racist epic, *The Birth of a Nation,* praised by Southern-born-and-bred President Woodrow Wilson, stands out as one of the most glaring examples of this cultural identity. Ever since the end of the Civil War, the literature on Southern figures of the era has portrayed them as genteel cavaliers or knights. As Alan T. Nolan points out, the most popular Civil War novel and film of the twentieth century, Margaret Mitchell's *Gone With the Wind,* provides a more recent example: "An orthodox statement of the legend, contributing significantly to its popularity and survival, it explicitly idealized the men and women of the planter class, extolled the superior valor of Southern manhood, imputed gentility to the slaving planter aristocracy, exaggerated the relative material disadvantages of the South's armies, and characterized the Yankees as venal bushwhackers. Consistent with the legend's racist origins, most dramatic was the novel's portrayal of slaves as the simple, happy, and devoted companions of their owners."[7]

Historical accuracy has never been the criterion of greatest importance in capturing the public imagination, and as the nineteenth century progressed, the supposed Puritan-Cavalier origins theory grew, even finding a willing acceptance among some Northerners.[8] French visitor Louis Phillipe noted in 1835 that American regionalism could be explained by the fact that "You have the Puritans in the North and the Cavaliers in the South, Democracy with its leveling rod, and Aristocracy with slavery raising its haughty head in the other section and creating a social elegance, a superiority of breeding, and race." He found this dichotomy disturbing: "I do not wish to be a prophet of evil but you as a people have conflicting interests and ambitions and unappeasable jealousies."[9] Southern perceptions of the North's hostility toward them and their way of life were explained by continued belief in the Cavalier-Puritan dichotomy, with J. D. B. DeBow writing in 1851, "The odor of Puritanism surrounds much of the population of the North."[10]

Regardless of its validity from a historical point of view, the Southern Cavalier myth had a surprisingly powerful impact on the development of a Southern self-image that glistened with a false veneer of superiority requiring and justifying a feudal-like, slavery-dependent, planter aristocracy. In 1861, Confederate President Jefferson Davis, in a speech given not long after his inauguration, trotted out the Roundhead-Cavalier comparison and promised that those Puritan Roundheads of the North, descended from an inferior people "bred in the bogs and fens of Ireland and northern England" would never prevail over the South's "descendants of the bold and chivalrous cavaliers of old."[11] Even though many Southern leaders, including the beloved Andrew Jackson, were of Ulster Irish ancestry (known as Scots-Irish in America), people act on what they *believe* to be true, or even what they *wish* to be true, whether or not it is true in actuality. As one realist put it in 1911, "if only descendants of Cavaliers and heirs of Cromwellian Puritanism had materialized on the battlefields, the Civil War could have been fought under a circus tent."[12] As inaccurate and misleading as the Cavalier myth might have been, it provided an inspiration and a rationalization for a Southern society based on anything but equality. The old Puritan admiration of social inequality had dissipated by the nineteenth century; the "Cavalier" elitist position had, if anything, hardened.

Such an elitist Southern worldview did not align well with certain political and cultural trends of the early nineteenth century: popular government, upward mobility, and civic engagement and equality. And there was also a certain tension with religious commitments held at least nominally by many Southerners. As Bruce Levine has pointed out, "Aristocratic gentility and condescension, cavalier pride and swagger, libertine indulgence and gaming rubbed against evangelical tenets of equality, humility, austerity, sobriety, and propriety."[13] This "Cavalier" cultural orientation did not bode well for the promise of freedom for the region's slave population anytime soon.

Freedom's delay for America's slave population would be greatly extended as a convergence of factors dealt a severe blow to slave hopes and the Founders' earlier assumption that slavery in America would die out in the not too distant future. The huge growth in the demand for cotton to supply the developing textile mills of England, the technological advance, simple as it now seems, of the cotton engine or "gin," that efficiently separated cotton seeds from the fiber, the possibility of territorial expansion in the Deep South facilitated by the removal of Native Americans from ancestral lands, and advances in trade, transportation, and financial infrastructures resulting from the market revolution of the early nineteenth century all gave rise to a resurgence of interest in and demand for a mobile slave workforce in the new Cotton Kingdom of the Lower South.[14] "King Cotton," made possible by this convergence, was exactly what the "Cavalier Kingdom" needed to justify its existence. Planters at the apex of a hierarchical structure, like Roman patricians made wealthy by slave labor, ruled their world with its often undemocratic political arrangements where dissent was not tolerated either from the slaves or socially inferior whites. This "Cavalier" Cotton Kingdom went far beyond what the Founders could have envisioned in its internal controls and its territorial expansion.

The property of this Southern Cotton Kingdom was protected by the federal government through its role as national slave catcher. Some of the Founders, still very active during George Washington's administration, had supported the passage of the Fugitive Slave Law of 1793, signed by President Washington. This act, sanctioned in the Constitution, was even approved by many antislavery Federalists because it strengthened the power of the national government. The law involved the federal government in the fugitive slave controversy but did not require more than a sworn oral statement or other minimal evidence that the accused was indeed a runaway. Due process was denied accused fugitive slaves; they did not have the right to counsel, nor could they testify or provide witnesses on their behalf.[15] A few abolitionists, such as members of the Pennsylvania Abolition Society, saw real danger in the act and warned that it would "be productive of mischievous consequences to the poor Negro Slaves appearing to be calculated with very unfavorable intentions toward them."[16]

The cultivation of cotton made slavery more profitable than ever and the thought of emancipation more distant. The ascendancy of cotton was remarkable; in 1787 no American cotton was being exported to England. In the twenty years from 1787 to 1807, the American share of England's cotton imports jumped from zero to 60 percent. By 1860, 88 percent of the cotton imported by England came from the American South.[17] The unforeseen development of the New England textile industry by 1810 also increased the demand for cotton production. The constitutionally allowed 1808 end to the slave trade's protection had convinced many of the Founders in the North, and even some in the South, that slavery was clearly on the road to extinction in the United States. Another factor seeming to assure slavery's demise was the decline of the tobacco industry with its well-known tendency to deplete soil rapidly. But the demand for cotton and the unexpectedly high fertility of the American slave population dramatically changed the perception that slavery was on the way out. The congressional end to the slave trade that went into effect on January 1, 1808, was no longer a harbinger of freedom's arrival for the slaves, and the rapid expansion of the cotton kingdom destroyed the hope that the slowing of tobacco cultivation would lessen the demand for slave labor.

It is interesting to observe the dynamics at play in the congressional decision to end international slave importation as permitted by the Constitution. President Thomas Jefferson got the ball rolling in his message to Congress on December 2, 1806:

> I congratulate you, fellow-citizens, on the approach of the period at which you may interpose your authority constitutionally, to withdraw the citizens of the United States from all further participation in those violations of human rights which have been so long continued on the unoffending inhabitants of Africa, and which the morality, the

reputation, and the best interests of our country, have long been eager to proscribe. Although no law you may pass can take prohibitory effect till the first day of the year one thousand eight hundred and eight, yet the intervening period is not too long to prevent, by timely notice, expeditions which cannot be completed before that day.[18]

The following day, in response to Jefferson's call to action, Vermont Senator Stephen R. Bradley introduced legislation which successfully made its way into passage on March 2, 1807, as the act prohibiting the African slave trade. In some ways, the vote on this bill was an anticlimax, as all states had banned such slave importation on a state level prior to 1800. South Carolina was an exception, having banned slave imports but then reversing course and between 1803 and 1807 importing nearly forty thousand new slaves.[19]

While Jefferson could moralize over the "unoffending inhabitants of Africa," nothing was done to address the plight of the unoffending African Americans. Ending slave importation was one thing; ending the domestic American slave trade and slavery itself were altogether different. Some slaveholders, Jefferson likely included, were able to nuance the issue and enthusiastically support the new law for both humanitarian and racist reasons, while continuing to embrace slavery. Enslaving free people in Africa was more morally offensive than buying and selling Negroes who had been raised as slaves and knew nothing else. Prohibiting such trade would also reduce the rate at which the black population in America was expanding.[20] Gordon S. Wood has captured well the hopeful but naive Northern response to the end of the slave trade: "Northerners scarcely understood what was happening. They had little or no appreciation that slavery in the South was a healthy, vigorous, and expansive institution. As far as they were concerned, the Virginia and Maryland planters were enthusiastically supporting an end to the international slave trade as the first major step in eliminating the institution. This assault on the overseas slave trade appeared to align the Chesapeake planters with the antislave forces in the North and confused many northerners about the real intentions of the Upper South."[21]

In reality, the congressional vote to ban further importation of slaves into the United States after 1808 was less than the sum of its parts. On the surface, and in line with Jefferson's moralistic admonition to pass such a measure, the 1807 act was intended to shut down American involvement in the international slave trade, before any slave importation expedition that might enter American waters on or after January 1, 1808, could even get underway. As of that date it would "not be lawful to import or bring into the United States or the territories thereof from any foreign kingdom, place, or country, any negro, mulatto, or person of colour, with intent to hold, sell, or dispose of such as a slave, to be held to service or labor."[22] The law set forth enormous fines for its day (up to ten thousand dollars) as well as daunting prison terms (up to ten years) for American citizens caught in violation of the Act of 1807. The full power and authority of the U.S. Navy could be used to interdict ships entering U.S waters with foreign slaves aboard. Had the federal government actually funded enforcement of the act, and possessed a navy worthy of the name, the law would have been more impressive. For Jefferson, with his limited-government philosophy, the act seemed to be an uncharacteristically robust exercise of federal power. The act was never adequately funded, and the miniscule American Navy (reduced drastically after Jefferson took office) was not much of an impediment should slave importers wish to violate the law.

The Act of 1807 had further weaknesses. Much of the law's content focused on the disposition of innocent slaves victimized in violation of the law. One might assume that any slaves brought illegally into the country would either be freed or returned to Africa. Given the Jeffersonians' racial views and tight-fisted fiscal practices, neither of the above options was acceptable. The hapless slaves may have been brought to the United States illegally, but they would remain slaves, and treated according to the laws of the state into which they had entered (all assumed to be Southern slaveholding states since by this time gradual emancipation was being enacted in the North). Absolutely nothing in the law promised them their freedom, once they were brought to American shores. In fact, the states where the illegal slaves entered would actually profit financially from their sale. The 1807 Act may have sought to end the slave trade, but it did nothing to weaken the legitimacy of chattel slavery or the sale and transport of domestic slaves within the country. The act did require ships legally transporting domestic slaves within the United States (essentially a Northern transportation business) to more systematically register their "cargo" before setting out. Southerners, not just Northerners, largely favored the ban on slave importation. The Chesapeake region, which had supported such a ban at the time of the Constitutional Convention, was known to have a surplus of slaves, whose selling price to the expanding Lower South would be higher if future slave imports were banned. According to W. E. B. Du Bois, Southern desire to limit slave imports was really the only thing that made the Act of 1807 enforceable.[23] Finally, as a legislative enactment, it was vulnerable to repeal at any time, although proposals for repeal which continued throughout the antebellum period went nowhere.

Even at its Montgomery convention in 1861, the Provisional Congress of the Confederate States rejected proposals for reopening the international slave trade.

The ban on importation of new slaves into the United States after 1808 had virtually no impact on territorial expansion and growth of the slave population into the "Old Southwest" of Louisiana (1812 statehood), Mississippi (1817 statehood), and Alabama (1819 statehood). Slavery was not new to this region; Spain and France had established Caribbean-style slavery in the Lower Mississippi Valley, which was on the verge of expansion at the time of American acquisition. The authorization of slavery in this region was allowed by Congress initially as an accommodation to existing labor practice,[24] which in the process provided an open door to the arrival of thousands of American slaves and their masters just as the demand for cotton production was on the rise.

The Cotton Kingdom was expanding quite well without the importation of new slaves; Louisiana's slave population grew from 34,660 in 1810 to 168,452 by 1840, and 326,726 by 1860. In the case of Mississippi, the slave population grew from 17,088 in 1810 to 196,577 in 1840, increasing to 437,404 by 1860. Alabama, whose slave population was first counted separately in the 1820 Census, had 47,439 slaves that year, growing to 253,532 in 1840, and 435,080 in 1860. Despite selling surplus slaves to the Deep South, Virginia's slave population continued to expand through 1860, when the slave population numbered 490,685. Maryland also sold surplus slaves to the Deep South and was the only Southern state to experience a decrease in its slave population before the Civil War, declining from a high of 111,502 in 1810 to 87,189 in 1860. Throughout the slave states, the population of slaves grew more than 300 percent in a fifty-year period following the ban on slave importation. From 1,191,354 in 1810, the American slave population reached 3,953,760 in 1860.[25] Slavery was far from dying out, although there were those, North and South, who wished it would.

In the early nineteenth-century South, slavery was not yet being promoted as a positive good—rather, it was portrayed as a necessary evil. This reflected the conflicted views of Southern whites such as Virginia's Patrick Henry (of "give me liberty or give me death" fame), who said very honestly of slavery in the revolutionary era, "I will not, I cannot justify it," and who looked forward to the time "when an opportunity will be afforded, to abolish this lamentable evil." Yet at the same time he saw the necessity of slave labor and was, as he expressed it in a letter to a friend, "drawn along by the general inconveniency of living without them."[26] Too many slaves, as well as the presence of free blacks, were seen as problematic by the government of Virginia that in 1806 required blacks who were manumitted to leave the state within one year.

The self-styled Cavalier Kingdom with its hierarchical, antidemocratic social institutions and its large slave population grew dramatically and prospered during the half-century following the congressional ban on importation. Following the end of slavery in the British Empire in the 1830s, American slaves outnumbered all the combined slaves in the rest of the Western Hemisphere. While some illegal slave importation continued into the United States, the number was fairly small, and as Peter Kolchin has pointed out, was probably surpassed by the number of runaway slaves.[27] But the rapid growth of the slave population could not be easily controlled without two elements—internal controls and outward expansion. Slave (servile) insurrection was a nightmare that was a constant threat to the security and stability of the South. Territorial expansion was needed to spread the slave population to new regions and thus diminish slave-population pressures within the older states, while making healthy financial profits in the process.

The early specter of servile insurrection in the South was fueled in good measure by events that began in 1791 in Saint Domingue (modern Haiti), France's most valuable colony, whose slave labor force at the time outnumbered the combined slave populations of Virginia, Georgia, and South Carolina.[28] Tens of thousands of Napoleon's crack troops, many sickened by yellow fever in the tropical Caribbean climate, could not put down the slave rebellion led by Toussaint L'Ouverture that rocked that island colony, eventually resulting in the formation of an independent black republic in 1804. Napoleon, souring on the idea of a reinvigorated French empire in the New World by this humiliating setback, decided to cash in the Louisiana Territory by offering it to the stunned Americans in 1803—an unexpected bonus derived from the failed French struggle to maintain colonial slave status for Saint Domingue. American leaders dealt with this awkward situation of a former slave society turned black republic in various ways. Washington and Jefferson sympathized with the island's French planters, while Alexander Hamilton was more aligned with the cause of the black rebels. Northern Federalists generally backed the former slaves, while Southern Federalists feared the influence that such a revolt might have on their own slaves. Many French refugees from the Saint Domingue revolution sought a haven in the American South, especially Louisiana, where they were welcomed. The slaves they brought with them, however, were often suspect.[29] In 1811, the largest slave revolt in American history occurred near New Orleans, where it was brutally crushed. This revolt further heightened anxiety over servile war. All of this led to a more watchful white Southern stance and increased internal controls over the slave population.

To insure their "homeland security," Southern states put in place a number of repressive measures, affecting both blacks and whites. This was not difficult to accomplish since the political climate of the South was far less democratic (despite outward trappings of democracy) and more hierarchical than state and local governments in the North. Virginia provides a case study in the politics of the early nineteenth-century "Cavalier Kingdom," where the franchise required freehold ownership of fifty or more acres, voting was done orally rather than by ballot, and wealthy planters held a disproportionate number of seats in the state legislature. As Gordon S. Wood has pointed out, "Unlike in the Northern states, the only elected officials in Virginia were federal congressmen and state legislators; all the rest were either selected by the legislature or appointed by the governor or the county courts, which were self-perpetuating oligarchies that dominated local government. Thus popular democratic politics in Virginia and elsewhere in the South was severely limited, especially in contrast to the states of the North, where nearly all state and local offices had become elective and the turbulence of politics and the turnover of offices were much greater."[30] South Carolina was even more politically closed; it would be 1868 before the first popular vote for president would be cast in that state. Prior to that date, the state legislature selected the presidential electors.

In this oligarchical political climate, control of the slave population, and to some extent the white population, could be undertaken expeditiously and with minimal accountability. Harsh slave codes were imposed to insure the complete subjugation of slaves and the expulsion of free blacks in some communities. Mississippi laws prohibited teaching reading and writing to slaves, and no slave could work in a printing business. Religious services could not be held by slaves unless at least two white observers were present. If a slave were executed for a capital crime, the State of Mississippi would compensate the owner for half the slave's market value.[31]

Similar restrictive codes were in place throughout the South. Local whites were conscripted into night patrols that roamed through Southern communities looking for runaway slaves and signs of slave rebellions. Warrantless searches of private homes were allowed when hunting for runaway or rebellious slaves. Censorship of the press was imposed to prevent unfavorable discussions of slavery. Mail censorship was imposed to prevent abolitionist agitation. Free speech, when it pertained to antislavery sentiment, was prohibited, and whites who dared question the institution of slavery were silenced, forced to flee, or even killed. All of this was done to protect, strengthen, and perpetuate the institution of slavery and the related economic and social benefits of the planter class. As James Brewer Stewart has observed, "The disempowered blacks in the plantation South acted both as substitutes for and as a check on a restive white proletariat which might have otherwise applied revolutionary ideas about equality to a rebellion of its own against its slaveholding "betters." Throughout the antebellum period, lesser whites would continue to express racial solidarity with the planters, thereby muting social conflicts within the ruling race."[32]

Meanwhile, territorial expansion moved forward. Despite his theories of limited government, Thomas Jefferson authorized the purchase of the Louisiana Territory in 1803, a vast region where slavery already existed and the future slave states of Louisiana (1812), Missouri (1821), and Arkansas (1836) would be established. In 1810, West Florida was annexed after a filibustering expedition seized the territory and proclaimed an independent republic. The region was added to Louisiana in 1812. East Florida was seized in 1813 and ultimately was divided between Mississippi and Alabama. The rest of Spanish Florida was purchased in 1819 and became the slave state of Florida (1845). These events were the harbingers for the seizure of Texas, and the filibustering campaigns of William Walker and others in the 1850s. Some Southerners, including Jefferson Davis, began nurturing the concept of the "Golden Circle," a slave empire comprising the South, the islands of the Caribbean, and territories in Mexico and Central America. The necessity of slavery's expansion was becoming firmly entrenched in the Southern worldview.

While the "Cavalier Kingdom" of the South professed the ideals of liberty and republican government under the American Constitution, it was rapidly regressing into an oppressive, militaristic, separate world, closer in some respects to medieval European feudal structures than to the society and politics experienced by fellow Americans of the North. The dawn of freedom for the South's slaves seemed more distant than ever.

CHAPTER 5

THE ARITHMETIC OF EMANCIPATION: FROM THE PURCHASE OF LOUISIANA TO THE COMPROMISE OVER MISSOURI

Even as the political, social, and economic norms of the "Cavalier Kingdom" began to crystallize into an ideological justification for its peculiar institution of slavery, the early years of the nineteenth century witnessed events of great importance to the development of the new American Republic. These events highlighted the growing bifurcation of the nation into regions with populations dependent on slave labor and regions with populations far less dependent on slavery and taking steps to rid themselves eventually of this institution. Three events of major significance, providing both challenges and opportunities for the young nation and shaping the growing argument over the future of slavery, include the Louisiana Purchase of 1803, the War of 1812 with Britain, and the Missouri Compromise of 1820. Each event was tied in some way to the struggle between human freedom and slavery, and pushed the arguments about the future of slavery in the United States to a new level in the national conversation.

Three additional events further influenced the future of slavery and emancipation in the United States. The first of these was the slave revolt in Saint Domingue (Haiti), with its horrific slaughter and the flight of many of that colony's slave owners to Louisiana. The violence which attended the slave revolts of the late eighteenth and early nineteenth centuries seared the terrible consequences of slave uprisings into the Southern consciousness. These horrors were soon experienced firsthand in America's largest and most deadly slave uprising in the German Coast region of Louisiana in 1811. In this neglected episode in American history, a slave army of rebellion far larger than that of Nat Turner in 1831 threatened New Orleans and vicinity with murder and chaos, resulting in the largest loss of life of any American slave uprising. Another event of consequence was the oft-heralded 1808 congressionally legislated end of American involvement in the slave trade, which on the surface might appear to have struck the greatest blow for freedom. Unfortunately for the slaves themselves and for others desiring emancipation for the slaves, the end of the slave trade was not the harbinger of the institution's end as had been predicted. Rather than decreasing in numbers and importance as a labor supply, the native-born slave population was moving in exactly the opposite direction. The arithmetic of emancipation as envisioned by many of the Founders was not adding up. However, 1808, the year of the abolition of the legal Atlantic slave trade, can be seen as a turning point for the antislavery struggle, and for hardening regional identification on the slavery issue. Prior to 1808, regional identity concerning slavery was not yet firmly determined. For example, Virginia identified more with the mid-Atlantic states and with the Northwest. Some in the Northwest saw a future for slavery in their region. After 1808, as the first post-revolutionary generation emerged, a new era began.[1]

The Louisiana Purchase and slavery were inseparable when the trajectory of American cotton expansion and the motives for France's decision to part with this massive territory are understood. The available lands of the Old Southwest, where cotton thrived in the rich Mississippi soil, lured planters and their slaves in significant numbers from the Carolinas, Georgia, and as far away as Virginia and Maryland. By 1800, New Orleans cotton brokers were involved in highly competitive recruitment for contracts with the new cotton planters of the Southwest, which in turn drove up the value of slaves. Slaves worth well over one thousand dollars each became the norm on the new cotton plantations of the Mississippi Territory, and in the decade after 1800 the slave population of the region grew 500 percent from 3,500 to about 17,000[2] as many slaves found themselves sold or otherwise relocated to the Southwest.

New Orleans and its surrounding territory looked increasingly attractive to American expansionists, even as it was becoming increasingly less attractive to France, thanks to the tumultuous events in France's valuable but troublesome colony of Saint Domingue. Napoleon's inability to crush the slave rebellion in Saint Domingue made him focus all the more on European conquest. The decision by Napoleon to divest France not only of New Orleans but all of the Louisiana Territory seemed at the time to be mutually advantageous. Napoleon received $15 million with which to shore up his war chest for future European adventures while the United States, without bloodshed, doubled its land area with the stroke of a pen at a rock-bottom price and now possessed a large and crucial port city in the South near the mouth of America's greatest river highway. Though once a thorough Francophile, Jefferson had more recently come to fear any foreign power, including France, that controlled New Orleans and had the power to close that essential port to Western American shipping. The Louisiana Territory, and particularly New Orleans, now taken out of European hands once and for all, "removes from us the greatest source of danger to our peace," announced an exuberant Jefferson.[3]

The purchase of the vast Louisiana Territory held the promise, or threat, of a massive expansion of slavery into at least portions of the newly acquired 828,000 square miles of American territory. This was reason enough for Northern Federalists to condemn the purchase, but their criticism was leveled more after the fact, as Jeffersonians tightly controlled the Congress, enabling the Senate to pass the purchase treaty in three days with little substantive debate on its content. However, in the House of Representatives, which the Jeffersonian Republicans controlled by a majority of three-to-one, the purchase met some initial stiff resistance not so much over slavery, but over strict-constructionist constitutional concerns, although the "necessary and proper clause" eventually won the day, to Jefferson's relief. However, Federalists from the Northeast saw to it that the slavery issue did not go unnoticed. The Louisiana Territory was ridiculed by Federalist Congressman Fisher Ames of Massachusetts as "a great waste, a wilderness unpeopled by any beings except wolves and wandering Indians," and he believed it to be little more than an excuse to spread slavery under the leadership of Virginia, for whom Ames had a special dislike and mistrust.[4]

The Louisiana Purchase was viewed by Northern Federalists as creating a fundamental shift in power in favor of the South, causing a few of them to flirt with fantasies of a New England confederacy, an idea that would reappear later during President Jefferson's Embargo Act of 1807, which proved devastating to Northern shipping interests, and again during the War of 1812. Federalist opponents of the Louisiana Purchase were concerned about the expansion of slavery into numerous future states and the representation that such slave states would bring to Congress, tipping the balance of power forever against the Northeast. This was more of a Federalist political issue, however, than a hue and cry against the immorality of slavery. In the first decade of the nineteenth century, the majority of voters even in New England appeared to care little about the evils of the three-fifths federal ratio that gave the South such additional political muscle. This "avowed inequality . . . given in contempt of the rights of man," according to Fisher Ames, simply did not concern his constituents.[5] Sereno Edwards Dwight, a Northern Federalist polemicist, penned a scathing pamphlet entitled *Slave Representation* under the pseudonym of "Boreas," savaging not slavery, but the power of the slave states to make policy counter to northeastern interests. They were able to do so because of the added representation they received in Congress thanks to their slaves. Men of the North, Dwight maintained, were now in the humiliating position of having to follow national policy dictated by slave states, making the North "the slaves of slaves." Any real concern for the plight of slaves was overshadowed by concern about the political power wielded by the South, which Dwight liked to refer to as "THE SLAVE COUNTRY."[6]

Despite these sporadic attacks against slavery and the South, most Northerners were as yet unmoved, although the War of 1812 would redefine the issue to some extent. Matthew Mason has summed up the situation well:

> A key reason for most Northerners' acquiescence in slavery's expansion was their belief that slavery was a necessity in the Deep South. They believed in a doctrine of separate spheres for slavery and freedom that grew from two basic assumptions: first, that it would be fruitless or even dangerous to try to outlaw slavery where it had taken firm root; and second, that African slavery was best suited—or perhaps indispensable—to agricultural labor in the Southern climate. Subscription to these maxims made it possible for most white Northerners to concede that slavery was a necessary evil, indefensible in principle but only very gradually eradicable in the South. . . . [A]ntislavery for the vast majority of white Yankees consisted mostly of a desire to separate themselves from it. They had abolished slavery in their States, but only a few abolitionists concerned themselves beyond the state level.[7]

Haitian independence was declared on January 1, 1804, after nearly fifteen years of slave uprisings on the island. A feature of those years was the departure of some 10,000 French planters (some with their slaves) from Haiti to the United States. The Haitian slave uprisings terrified American slaveholders, and accounts of atrocities in the former French colony caused terror in the South along with fear that Haitian slaves brought into the United States would spread rebellion among American slaves. Consequently, Congress passed severe limitations on immigration from the West Indies in 1803. To prevent slave agitation and rebellion prior to the Louisiana Purchase, James Monroe had suggested to President Jefferson that all free blacks and unwanted surplus slaves in the United States be removed elsewhere. A colony somewhere in the West was considered, but rejected by Jefferson who did not want free blacks standing in the way of white American expansion. Haiti was considered, as well as West Africa. However, the growth in demand for slaves in the Mississippi Territory and the purchase of Louisiana helped solve the problem of where surplus slaves might be settled.[8]

The Louisiana Purchase was an enormously important milestone in American history and in the history of American slavery. The territorial expansion of the United States was not the only consequence of acquiring Louisiana. The first substantial European population not from the British Isles was added to the American body politic. Of French and Spanish origins, and overwhelmingly Catholic in religion, many were mixed-blood creoles who had intermarried with free blacks. Mixed-blood Metís of French and Indian origin lived as traders and trappers among the Native Americans. St. Louis, a village near the strategically important juncture of the Mississippi and Missouri rivers, had been founded in 1764 as a refuge for French exiles from the Illinois Country after the French and Indian War. African slavery was already well established within the European-settled areas of the Louisiana Purchase. While the purchase was geographically large, reaching westward to the crest of the Rockies and northward into present-day Canada, actual European-style settlements existed primarily in modern Louisiana, the Mississippi Basin, and the lower Missouri River Valley.

While the treaty of purchase was ratified in 1803, implementation of a government for the Louisiana Territory evolved from the congressional debates over the controversial Louisiana Ordinance of 1804. Ironically, even some Jeffersonian Republicans, such as Kentucky's Representative Matthew Lyon, criticized the autocratic ordinance which would appoint, not elect, a governor and a council of thirteen to rule the region. It was, stated Lyon, "probationary slavery" for the inhabitants of Louisiana.[9] The Jefferson administration countered that the inhabitants of Louisiana, long under French and Spanish rule, were not accustomed to self-government and must be brought gradually to a point of liberty, using arbitrary rule in the meantime as needed. Residents of Southern Louisiana and the New Orleans area were far more diverse in language, religion, legal tradition, and racial attitudes and amalgamation than inhabitants of the rest of the United States, which caused Fisher Ames to spread fear among more conservative Americans by warning that the region was populated with "savages and adventurers" with questionable morals not likely to "sustain and glorify our republic."[10] A Federalist named Abraham Ellery wrote from

Natchez to Alexander Hamilton in 1803 that New Orleans was populated by an unsavory element known for their "dissipated habits, unruly tempers, and lawless conduct," and this was in good measure explained by the fact that "the white population bears so small a proportion to the black."[11]

The Senate proved to be the stage for passionate debate over slavery while the Louisiana Ordinance of 1804 was being discussed. Facing the possibility, indeed the likelihood, of congressional action banning importation of foreign slaves after 1808, national leaders, including President Jefferson, were attempting to assess the impact of such action and its relationship to the newly acquired Louisiana Territory. The revolts in Haiti played into this situation as well; many Southerners were ready and willing to end the importation of new slaves for security reasons. In New Orleans, the city's mayor favored slaves coming into his region who were "domesticated" and "already acquainted with our habits and attached to our country" as opposed to West Indies slaves who might be more prone to insurrection. The end of the slave trade could only increase the value of existing slaves, a hope especially important to Virginians and Marylanders who "did the math" regarding their surplus slaves and who welcomed new opportunities to sell them at a handsome profit to planters in new territory now open to American settlers. Facing newly enacted gradual emancipation laws, some Northern slaveholders also saw the new territory as a market for their soon-to-be-banned property. Senator John Breckinridge of Kentucky argued the case for "diffusion," an idea that Jefferson had earlier agreed would benefit the Old South that needed to become "whiter." The redistribution of blacks throughout a wider territory would "disperse and weaken the race—and free the southern states from a part of its black population, and of its danger," according to Breckinridge.[12] The ongoing need for "diffusion" would play an important part in the future arguments over the spread of slavery.

Partly due to the concern over slave importation, Congress divided the huge Louisiana Territory into two regions. The Territory of Orleans was created in the south, whose Northern boundary corresponded to the current state line separating Louisiana and Arkansas, with New Orleans as the capital city. This region was the area most heavily populated by the existing French and Spanish residents. The huge area north of this line was designated as the District of Louisiana, and St. Louis was made its administrative center. Further action by Congress in 1804, with considerable Southern support, closed the Territory of Orleans to foreign slave importation four years ahead of the constitutionally approved limit for the end of the international slave trade throughout the United States. Another precedent had been established for congressional oversight on issues related to slavery in the territories.

In 1812, the State of Louisiana entered the Union as a slave state without significant controversy. In 1810 West Florida had been annexed to the United States as a result of a filibustering expedition. This territory was incorporated into the new State of Louisiana. East Florida was annexed in 1813, and Florida was purchased in 1819, adding more territory to the United States where slavery already existed. This territorial expansion of slavery between 1803 and 1819 caused increasing concern in the North. Subsequently, in 1819, when Missouri asked for admission to the Union as a slave state, it touched off the greatest controversy over slavery since the early days of the republic. This new, and for the first time truly sectional, agitation over the expansion of slavery into this vast territory was of great concern to Thomas Jefferson, living in retirement at Monticello. As proud as he was of the doubling of the nation's territory under his presidential administration, the aging Jefferson wrote to a friend in 1820, prior to passage of the Missouri Compromise, that the question of carving additional new states from the Louisiana Territory, "like a fire-bell in the night, [has] awakened and filled me with terror. I considered it at once the [death] knell of the Union."[13]

But between the purchase of Louisiana in 1803 and the great controversy over Missouri statehood in 1819, deteriorating relations with Great Britain would lead the young republic into a war that she was fortunate to survive. The war that Americans declared in 1812 was due in part to various unresolved issues from the end of the American Revolution and the 1783 Treaty of Paris, but also included the violation of human freedom—the impressment of American sailors on the high seas by the British Navy and the alleged agitation by the British of Native Americans against American frontier settlements. This violation of human rights and national sovereignty was sufficient to outrage enough Americans, including members of Congress, that it resulted in America's first declaration of war, authored by President James Madison in June of 1812. Any parallel to the violation of human rights perpetrated against African American slaves apparently was missed by prowar Republicans (as the Jeffersonian Democratic-Republicans were widely known in this era, not to be confused with the later Republican Party founded in 1854) in the furor against England and the desire of a new generation of political leaders to flex American muscle against the former mother country. White Southerners denounced the British hypocrisy of desiring to suppress the African slave trade while kidnapping Americans on the high seas. The War of

1812 brought partisan politics between Federalists and Republicans to new levels, and use of the slavery issue as a partisan weapon heightened sectional tensions all the more. As Matthew Mason has aptly observed, "American slavery was not the central issue of the day—the war was. But those contending over the war capitalized fully on the political value of slavery."[14] Thus the issue of slavery, far from retreating in the American consciousness, was raised to higher levels of awareness by this "second war for independence."

Prior to the actual war with Britain, Federalist ire had been kindled by Jefferson's Embargo Act of 1807, which made it illegal for American ships to sail to any foreign port, thus avoiding international conflict on the high seas. So misguided, inadequately justified, and economically devastating was the Embargo Act that many Americans wondered if the nation had declared war on itself. The New England economy was especially hard hit; exports from that region declined by 75 percent thanks to the embargo, and three-fourths of the sailors in America's merchant marine found themselves out of work. Shipyards (found largely in New England) reduced their construction of new vessels by two-thirds.[15] On August 11, 1808, Jefferson had to admit in a letter to his treasury secretary, "This embargo law is certainly the most embarrassing one we have ever had to execute."[16] The minority Federalist Party, stirring anew from its base in New England, was resuscitated for a time thanks to the Embargo Act, and would come out strongly against the war with Britain.

In the process of reloading for political war with the Jeffersonian Republicans, the Federalists made use of anti-embargo sentiment, making an analogy to slavery and using antislavery rhetoric to good effect. The Federalist Party experienced a resurgence in the elections of 1808 at the national and state levels, winning control of some state governments, racking up additional congressional seats, and making Madison's election in 1808 more difficult than Jefferson's election had been four years earlier. As had been the case during the Revolution, the slavery metaphor was again brought forth to explain what was happening to New England under the embargo policy of the proslavery Jeffersonian Republicans. Harrison Gray Otis stated that, without relief from the detested embargo, "our people are enslaved and our country ruined." Otis continued to urge a New England convention to discuss a regional response to abusive Jeffersonian economic policy, a suggestion not realized until near the end of the war.[17] The very fact that the Embargo Act could be enacted in Congress was proof enough for the Rev. David Osgood that the North was jeopardized by the "strange absurdity" [of the three-fifths slave population advantage] that enabled the predominantly Republican slaveholding South to exercise "an undue and baneful influence in our national counsels."[18]

Northern Federalists saw the Republican-initiated war with England as a grand scheme to undermine, and even destroy, Northern commercial and political advantages. When war came, it was easy to look backwards and see a Southern Republican conspiracy at work: the Louisiana Purchase, the admission of Louisiana as a slave state, the taking of West Florida, and the disruption of trade with Britain, followed by Madison's declaration of war in June 1812. However, the majority of the Congress, and the American people, favored the war and eventually came to view the New England Federalists as overly pious and self-serving alarmists, with their moral arguments against invading Canada and siding in European politics with Napoleon—who some New England clergy and politicians considered a prime candidate to be the Anti-Christ.[19] Even more extreme were Northern Federalist concerns about an expanding American Army (under Republican control) that might be used, in the words of Federalist Congressman Josiah Quincy of Massachusetts, to enslave the Northern population along "with negroes, chained to the car of a Southern master."[20] Then there were those such as New England Presbyterian pastor Nathan Strong, who urged Northern men to put away their alliance with the slaveholding South in the war with England. To do otherwise was to risk the wrath of God, and the judgments of the Book of Revelation. Thus did antislavery theology find its way into the Federalist antiwar argument, heighten sectional discord over slavery, and give further rationale for a possible New England break with the Union.[21]

While Northern Federalists had made political gains from the ill effects of the Embargo Act, their opposition to the war that followed ultimately proved to be the party's undoing. It is true that the war was among the least popular of America's conflicts (Madison's declaration of war passed in Congress on a less than resounding vote of 79–49 in the House and 19–13 in the Senate). However, the utter lack of enthusiasm for the war in the Northeast, to the point that New England militia stopped short of the Canadian border and refused to be part of the invasion, cast a cloud of "dubious patriotism, even near-treason" on these Yankees.[22] Much Federalist rhetoric during the war was aimed at the Slave Power made possible by the three-fifths ratio that gave Southern states additional congressional seats. New England Federalists even asserted that, without the additional power of slave representation, the war would never have been undertaken. The abuse of power on the part of prowar, proslavery Jeffersonian Republicans was seen as so severe that "the majority of articulate New England

Federalists repudiated the Constitution and insisted that the Union was not working as the Founders had hoped. Even as they invoked the revolutionary example of resistance to tyranny, many Federalists deemed the Founders' spirit of compromise with the South a product of, at best, the earlier generation's political naïveté."[23]

The Hartford Convention of December 1814, attended by twenty-six disaffected New England Federalist leaders in Connecticut's capital to discuss a range of possible antiwar actions, ranging from withdrawal from the Union (rejected by the group) to proposed constitutional amendments (including repeal of the Three-Fifths Clause), to refusal to collect federal duties, to a demand for President Madison's resignation, proved to be poorly timed. Following their deliberations, in early February 1815, the Hartford Convention sent three members to Washington to press their demands, only to learn the day after their arrival that a treaty had been signed in Ghent on Christmas Eve, thus ending the war.[24] After the War of 1812, the Federalist argument against slave representation was largely dropped as the party descended into obscurity.

The War of 1812 has been largely ignored in the broad sweep of American history, and certainly as it relates to slavery. While this war kept the issue alive in the national debate, once again "slavery" was used as a weapon to further a particular political agenda without becoming, in its own right, the actual cause of the day. At the time of President Madison's request for a declaration of war against Britain in June of 1812, the response of young Congressman John C. Calhoun, speaking for the House Foreign Relations Committee to which he had recently been appointed chairman, contains irony, coming as it did from a slaveholder. Attacking British impressment of American sailors on the high seas was an act worthy of war, since "Our Citizens are wantonly snatched from their Country, and their families; deprived of their liberty and doomed to an ignominious and slavish bondage."[25] When it became known that British naval officers were applying the lash to kidnapped white American sailors, it was more than many Southern members of Congress could bear. According to Alan Taylor, "Black slavery generated a hypersensitivity to corporal punishment among whites. That racial polarity accounts for the prominence of slave-state congressmen pushing for a military crusade to liberate white men from a bondage deemed fit only for blacks."[26]

During the war, while New England Federalists were attacking the prowar Republicans for being slaveholders, and chafing at the three-fifths ratio and at the thought of becoming slaves to Southern interests, few were interested in the well-being of the actual slave population, or of the free black population. Yet this was the very population that could have helped America win the war, had not racial prejudices against black troops hardened even since the Revolution. Secretary of War John Armstrong advocated arming free blacks, but President Madison and other Southern Republicans opposed it. Secretary Armstrong said of restrictions prohibiting black troops, "We must get over this nonsense . . . if we mean to be what we ought to be."[27] As for moving from slavery toward freedom, the War of 1812 had little if any impact, although some six hundred Virginia slaves did escape to British lines in the summer of 1813.[28] However, certain themes that would recur in the later national discourse regarding slavery emerged during this war. The unfairness of the three-fifths ratio and the imagery of the slave power dominating the national agenda would surface again in the coming years. The Treaty of Ghent also closed down the alliance between British and Native American forces in the Ohio River Valley that had discouraged, but not halted, the trek of American western migration. With the threat to their security greatly reduced, pioneers flooded west, and consequently six new states, three slave and three free, were added to the Union between 1816 and 1821.[29] One of these was Missouri, where the expansion of slavery became the central national issue.

It was as though Missouri's February 1819 application for admission to the Union as a slave state fanned all the quietly glowing embers of sectional division over slavery into a raging inferno with the potential to engulf the nation. While Southern migrants made up the majority of the territory's population, the geographical location of the proposed State of Missouri rankled many Northerners. It was too far north to be uncontested as obvious slave country, and in a related but perhaps more important consideration, Missouri bordered on the old, slave-free Northwest Territory, Illinois in particular. Northern states desired to be as far removed from slavery as possible. The Ohio River, seen as a natural division between slave country and free territory, could no longer be seen in the same light, as Missouri lay north of that river's junction with the Mississippi. Old paradigms were at risk, making many Northerners uncomfortable and fearful of the future of slaveholders' designs. The "diffusion" argument that whites would be better off as black populations scattered more widely now came into question. Pennsylvania's John Sergeant argued in Congress that the doctrine of diffusion "leads directly to the establishment of slavery throughout the world. The same reasoning that will justify the extension of slavery into one region of the country, will justify its extension to another."[30]

Missouri's application for statehood was met immediately with a startling and provocative proposal by New York Congressman James Tallmadge. An independent-thinking Republican, Tallmadge was suspected by some as being a secret Federalist, and his twin amendments to the Missouri Statehood Bill gave some credence to the allegation. Tallmadge's amendments would have prohibited any further importation of slaves into Missouri and would have freed all slave children born after admission to statehood upon their twenty-fifth birthday. In essence, Missouri would be admitted as an eventual free state. The Tallmadge amendments narrowly passed the House in two separate and very sectional votes; the provision barring additional slaves entering the region was approved 87–76, and the provision requiring emancipation at age twenty-five passed 82–78. In the Senate, the first of Tallmadge's amendments failed 22–16, and the second was rejected on a vote of 31–7. The Tallmadge amendments were a direct confrontation between North and South on the issue of slavery, although five free-state senators joined in the vote against them (four of these five were Republicans, and one was a non-affiliated independent).[31] Had these five free-state senators voted in favor of the first of the amendments, it would have passed, but would likely have been vetoed by President Monroe, a Virginia slaveholder. The extent of the controversy caused by Tallmadge's amendments is seen in the accusation made by Representative Thomas W. Cobb of Georgia that "You [Tallmadge] have kindled a fire which all the waters of the ocean cannot put out, which seas of blood can only extinguish." Tallmadge responded, "If a dissolution of the Union must take place, let it be so! If civil war, which gentlemen so much threaten, must come, I can only say, let it come!"[32]

Once the Tallmadge amendments were killed by the Senate, the debate over Missouri statehood entered a new and intense period lasting several months. Debates over slavery and Missouri statehood came to dominate the political stage, both in Congress and out, during 1819 and early 1820. Speaker of the House Henry Clay, more concerned in 1819 about the nation's economic downturn and foreign relations, had to acknowledge that the question over slavery and statehood for Missouri "monopolizes all our conversation. . . . No body seems to think or care about any thing else."[33] No issue seemed to inflame voters as much as the Missouri question, and members of Congress felt compelled to give their constituents what they wanted—speeches explaining their positions. Unlike the soaring rhetorical debates over the Compromise of 1850 some three decades yet in the future, the debates over slavery and Missouri resulted in "numbingly long and repetitive debates in Congress."[34] The stakes were high; admitting Missouri to the Union as a slave state would give the South two additional Senate seats, throwing the balance of that body in favor of slave interests. But the very fact that the Tallmadge amendments could pass in the House of Representatives reinforced the South's worries about the now-permanent Northern majority controlling that legislative body.

Maine (heretofore a district of Massachusetts) had applied for separate statehood as a non-slave state. Those favoring Missouri's admission as a slave state were pushing the idea that, if Congress had authority to ban slavery in Missouri, it also had the authority to link Maine's admission as a free state to Missouri's admission as a slave state. On January 3, 1820, the House voted to admit Maine as a free state. On February 16, the Senate on a vote of 23–21 took action to consider the Maine and Missouri statehood bills together. It was at that point that a new amendment to the statehood bill was introduced by Senator Jesse B. Thomas of Illinois. Thomas, seeking a win for both North and South, proposed that, in addition to the admission of Maine as a free state and Missouri as a slave state, slavery would be prohibited in future states carved from the Louisiana Purchase north of the southern boundary of Missouri—latitude 36 degrees, 30 minutes.

Under this compromise the North would allow Missouri's entrance as an unrestricted slave state, and the South would acknowledge that Congress could regulate slavery in the territories.[35] The Senate approved the Thomas amendment 34–10, then went on to approve the Maine-Missouri bill containing the amendment on a vote of 24–20, with senators from New England and the middle states casting 14 of the 20 negative votes. The House, however, rejected the Senate bill and on March 1, 1820, proceeded down a separate path of passing a bill admitting Missouri without slavery, on a vote of 91–82. To overcome this congressional deadlock, on March 2 House Speaker Henry Clay appointed key individuals to a House-Senate conference committee that agreed to accept the Senate version of the bill. Later that day the House narrowly approved by a highly sectional vote of 90–87 that Missouri be admitted as a slave state. Had not 14 free-state representatives voted in favor (only one being a Federalist), and another 4 abstained from voting, the measure would have lost. Without the additional representation given to the South by the Three-Fifths Clause, there would have been 17 fewer representatives to provide votes from that section.[36] The House then accepted the Thomas amendment (134–42) and passed the Maine-Missouri Enabling Act, more popularly known as the Missouri Compromise, which President James Monroe signed into law on March 3, 1820.[37]

There were yet more complications ahead, however. Once the Maine-Missouri Enabling Act became law, a constitutional convention was held in Missouri in 1820, in which proslavery delegates overwhelmingly dominated. Their zeal to draft a state constitution prohibiting free Negroes from entering the state nearly wrecked the Missouri Compromise. Congressional controversy was thus reignited as Northerners claimed that Article IV, Section 2, of the U.S. Constitution was violated by such a restriction. Free Negroes were citizens in some Northern states and were given the constitutional guarantee that citizens in each state are entitled to the same privileges as citizens in the rest of the states. Secretary of State John Quincy Adams warned that the proposed Missouri constitution "would change the terms of the federal compact—change its terms by robbing thousands of citizens of their rights." Henry Clay negotiated a second Missouri Compromise whereby Congress would approve the Missouri constitution if the new state legislature would promise to pass no law violating the Privileges and Immunities Clause in the federal Constitution. Missouri acted accordingly and entered the Union as the twenty-fourth state on August 10, 1821, but technically was able to exclude all free blacks who could not prove that they were actual citizens of another state. By 1847 the state dropped all pretenses of sorting out free blacks with citizenship in other states from those without such citizenship and simply banned all free blacks from moving to Missouri.[38] Yet the Missouri laws were no different from similar bans that existed in the state constitutions or statutes of several free states during the same time that likewise flouted the guarantees of the federal Constitution.

Two things were made clear by the debates over the Missouri crisis. First, the South was much more committed to maintaining slavery now than it had been during the revolutionary era and, therefore, the institution could not be expected to die a natural death anytime soon. This can be largely explained by the opening up of the Southwest to lucrative cotton cultivation, made possible in part by the development of the cotton gin, and the significant rise in the value of slaves on the domestic market. Closing Missouri to slavery, even though the region was not in a cotton-growing climate, would limit the market for new slaves. Second, growing numbers of Northerners were increasingly serious about limiting the extension of slavery, if not seeking to end the institution altogether.

With the Missouri crisis, the moral issue of slavery was beginning to take greater hold in the North, although Jefferson was among many Southerners failing to fully acknowledge it. Calling the crisis in a letter to Lafayette "not a moral question, but one merely of power,"[39] the former president seemed to deny the moral implications of his views expressed earlier that year that slavery was like holding a "wolf by the ear," and that the Missouri question was "like a fire bell in the night." The disappointed and disillusioned Jefferson lamented in 1820, some six years before his death, that "I regret that I am now to die in the belief, that the useless sacrifice of themselves by the generation of 1776, to acquire self-government and happiness to their country, is to be thrown away by the unwise and unworthy passions of their sons, and that my only consolation is to be, that I live not to weep over it."[40]

Looking back at the Missouri Compromise, it seemed to make sense both politically and geographically in 1821. It was still generally believed that most of the territory obtained in the Louisiana Purchase was part of the "Great American Desert" and largely unusable given the agricultural technology of the day. Many thought of the plains not as a place for white settlement and thus future states, but as a great reserve for Native Americans and the great buffalo herds that still existed at the time. Since no one anticipated expansion into the Great Plains, and there were no prospects in 1821 for further territorial expansion, the Missouri Compromise was thought to be the final national settlement of the slavery question in terms of its expansion within the United States, satisfactory to the political and territorial needs of both North and South. The compromise lasted for nearly three and a half decades, and under the principles established at the time, eight states, four free and four slave, were added to the Union. The Missouri Compromise serves as a watershed event for the slavery issue, bridging the early national and antebellum eras.

By 1850 the national situation had changed dramatically. Even with the three-fifths provision, Northern states had always enjoyed small but growing majorities in the House of Representatives. The surge in population growth in the North that included the tidal wave of Irish immigration starting in the mid-1840s wiped out any earlier advantage the three-fifths ratio might have provided the South in the House of Representatives or the Electoral College. Political equilibrium in the Senate and control of the presidency became paramount considerations. Technological advances in agriculture making farming on the Great Plains practicable, Americans leapfrogging the continent to Oregon and California, the annexation of Texas, and the Mexican Cession would unravel the assumptions that had made the Missouri Compromise possible. The repeal of the compromise in 1854 would usher in a new chapter for the debate on the future of slavery in the nation and cause a further recalculation of the arithmetic of emancipation.

CHAPTER 6

THE SUNSET OF NORTHERN SLAVERY: FREEDOM WITHOUT EQUALITY

The Northern states, grappling with decisions and actions to be taken regarding slavery, were each marching to their own drumbeat. While influenced to some degree by their neighbors, each state in the North acted as an independent, sovereign entity on this internal issue, influenced by local attitudes and conditions. While the U.S. Constitution had granted Congress the power to end American participation in the international slave trade, the federal government had nothing to say about slavery in the states where it existed. Only the territories and the District of Columbia were fair game for federal intervention when it came to slavery, and federal jurisdiction in those regions was questioned by many proslavery advocates. Beginning in 1799, three Northern states made momentous decisions regarding the future of slavery within their borders. New York and New Jersey opted for gradual emancipation. Illinois, subject to the Northwest Ordinance of 1787 which banned slavery, actually debated the legalization of slavery in a state whose southern half largely reflected the Southern roots of many of its settlers.

The importance of New York City and the general size and political impact of the state gave New York a very significant role to play in the national debate on slavery. Of all the states north of the Mason-Dixon Line, New York had the largest number of slaves in the period between the American Revolution and 1827. New Yorkers provided essential political support for the Southern Slave Power in national politics. This support was based on the many financial ties New York, especially New York City, had with the South and its peculiar institution. Many New York businessmen maintained regular commerce with the South in the form of loans and investments in the Southern economy as well as trade in finished goods in exchange for cotton and other agricultural commodities. Many of the ships that participated in the slave trade, before and after 1808, originated from New York Harbor with virtual immunity since these ventures were financed by the wealth of Wall Street. So tied was the city to the Southern economy that, following Lincoln's election and on into 1861, proposals were made by some leading New Yorkers, including Mayor Fernando Wood, to have New York City secede from the Union and declare itself an independent republican city-state joined neither to the United States nor the Confederate States. A growing pro-Union movement in the city prevailed, however.[1]

At the same time, other New Yorkers reacted against slavery and provided what David N. Gellman has called "a home and a critical base of operations to the antebellum abolitionist movement." Sojourner Truth was born into slavery in New York; *Freedom's Journal,* America's first African American newspaper, was established in New York; and Frederick Douglass made Rochester his home and headquarters for his abolitionist writings and other activities for many years.[2] Gerrit Smith—New York philanthropist, social reformer, congressman, and three-time presidential candidate of the Liberty Party—gave away thousands of acres of land to blacks and poor whites in upstate New York and befriended fellow abolitionists John Brown and Frederick Douglass. Upstate New York, especially the region of western New York stretching from Utica to Buffalo, was emerging as a stronghold of abolitionist fervor, being settled by children of New England yeomen. Despite the presence of leading abolitionist voices and the actions and attitudes of a substantial free black population, slavery in New York State in general, and New York City in particular, would die a protracted death.

The first legal action regarding emancipation of slaves in New York occurred in 1781 when the legislature voted to manumit slaves who served the patriot cause in the Revolutionary War. Four years earlier, after New York had thrown off British rule and needed a new government, the delegates to the 1777 state constitutional convention overwhelming supported a resolution made by Gouverneur Morris stating that "every human being who breathes the air of the state shall enjoy the privileges of a freeman."[3] While Morris's dream would remain unrealized, a gradual emancipation bill passed the New York legislature in 1785, but it was marred by provisions that made blacks ineligible to hold public office, serve as witnesses, vote, and marry outside their race.[4] Vetoed by the state's Council of

GERRIT SMITH. *Wealthy New York lardowner and abolitionist who served a term in Congress in the 1830s and declared himself a candidate for president three times. A noted philanthropist, he gave away thousands of acres of land in upstate New York to blacks and poor whites. Smith was one of a handful of secret supporters of John Brown's 1859 raid on Harper's Ferry.*

Revision for not granting freed blacks the franchise, the proposed emancipation law was excoriated as "repugnant to the principle on which the United States justify their separation from Great Britain."[5] The legislature was not yet ready for such a bold move as full citizenship, however, and another fourteen years would pass before gradual emancipation would be implemented.

In the meantime, the legislature added insult to injury, as far as abolitionists and slaves were concerned, by enacting a comprehensive new slave code for New York that strengthened the grip of slaveholders in the state. No longer could human bondage in New York be explained as an unfortunate vestige of British colonial rule; now "the independent state of New York had put its seal of approval on the institution." One provision of the new slave code, however, was welcomed by slaves and abolitionists; it became illegal to buy or receive a slave for purposes of exporting said slave, the penalty for such action being a fine and freedom for the slave.[6] Although intended to prevent the sale south of soon-to-be emancipated slaves, the law was basically unenforceable, though with the subsequent gradual emancipation act of 1799, it likely discouraged some slave owners from the practice and, like other gradual emancipation laws, encouraged a number of early manumissions.

Finally, in 1799, the Council of Revision approved, and antislavery Governor John Jay signed, the state assembly's bill that provided for New York's approximately thirty thousand slaves to be emancipated gradually. This Gradual Emancipation Law was made possible by the efforts of the New York Manumission Society along with other African Americans and white reformers who worked together in the 1790s to delegitimize slavery in New York.[7] While no slaves were freed immediately by the act, children born to slave women after July 4, 1799, would be freed at the age of twenty-eight for males, and twenty-five for females. This gradual act deliberately omitted any mention of the civil status of the to-be-freed slaves, however, to avoid the kind of political wrangling that had sidetracked the measure several years earlier. If a slaveholder failed to register any slave children born after the implementation date of the act, such children would be immediately freed. Slaveholders could waive their rights to slave children born after July 4, 1799, and would be relieved of any support for such children if they were properly assigned to the care of local almshouses where dependents could be bound out for service.[8]

In a legal and financial twist, New York slave owners could be compensated for their lost property when they turned over their slave children to the overseers of the poor, who then bound them to service and paid a $3.50 monthly maintenance fee to the caretaker, who was often the former owner of the slave child.[9] This became, in effect, a covert form of compensated emancipation that would discourage the breakup of African American families, further discourage the practice of selling slaves south, and encourage the manumission of parents not covered by the law. Financial responsibility for abandoned slave children had implications especially for New York City, where urban poverty had increased dramatically even before gradual abolition was enacted. As David Gellman has pointed out, "A swirl of mixed goals and messages surrounded the political economy of 1790's reform: doing good meant addressing embarrassing social anachronisms, extending the sympathetic boundaries of the public sphere, and accounting for financial resources."[10] Within five years, the State of New York had paid out over twenty thousand dollars in maintenance fees for slave children, enough of a financial burden that the state legislature ended the program in 1804.[11]

New York's Gradual Emancipation Law of 1799 had two fairly immediate impacts—it reduced the number of runaway slaves and increased the number of slave manumissions, especially in New York City. Records indicate that, of the 300 manumissions in New York City between 1783 and 1801, 260 of them occurred after passage of the Gradual Emancipation Law.[12] It is unlikely, however, that the increased number of manumissions was due to a rise in antislavery sentiment. Shane White has shown a correlation between manumissions in New York City and economic downturns, and has also suggested that the Gradual Emancipation Law gave slaves more bargaining power with their masters to negotiate manumission.[13] But, as Patrick Rael has noted, despite the Gradual Emancipation Law and the increased number of slaves able to obtain their freedom, in the early nineteenth century "free black New Yorkers confronted strictures that sharply curtailed their personal and community lives. Families remained sundered by slavery, as some black men and women gained liberty while their spouses, parents, children, and kin remained in bondage. Freed into a fiercely competitive economy with few if any resources, African Americans changed their occupations as often as they changed their places of residence. Hard pressed, some black New Yorkers turned to petty crimes of opportunity to make ends meet, fencing stolen goods and clothing, running small-scale confidence schemes, or operating hidden gambling establishments."[14]

An anti-abolitionist backlash of sorts created a climate in New York in the second decade of the nineteenth century whereby blacks were seen increasingly as flawed and irredeemable, as evidenced by their high incarceration rate, lack of education, and low skills—as if slavery and its constraints had nothing to do with the situation. In 1810 the number of free blacks living in New York City was 8,137, compared to 1,686 slaves.[15] The franchise previously given to free black men was severely curtailed by laws in 1811 and 1815 requiring a complex certification and registration process similar both in intent and effect to the Jim Crow laws of the post–Civil War South.

In his annual message to the legislature in January 1812, Governor Daniel Tompkins referred to "slavery, that reproach of a free people," and requested that the 1799 laws regarding gradual emancipation be revised to speed the process.[16] It had become clear that, by leaving out slaves born before July 4, 1799, slavery could continue to exist in New York until very late in the nineteenth century. Following a five-year effort, thanks in part to Tompkins, by now vice-president of the United States and a member of the New York Manumission Society, the New York legislature in 1817 finally set the year 1848 as the termination date for slavery in the state. This was accomplished by freeing all slaves not included in the Gradual Emancipation Law of 1799 as of July 4, 1827. The 1817 law also reduced the apprenticeship of children born of slave mothers prior to July 4, 1827, to twenty-one years for both males and females, thus arriving at 1848 as the last year slaves could legally be held in the state. The 1840 Census, the last to record slaves in New York, listed only four slaves in the state.

Accepting freedom for New York's black population was a far cry from advocating equality, as witnessed by the New York State Constitutional Convention of 1821. The original state constitution had required property as a condition for voting, but race was not an issue. However, in 1821, "New York's ambitious political leaders [including future president Martin Van Buren] ensured that as the state moved toward the vanguard of American democratic politics, race would be constructed as a presumptively disabling condition."[17] Compounding the irony is that the presiding officer of the New York State Constitutional Convention of 1821 was none other than former Governor Daniel Tompkins, who had pushed hard for an accelerated end to slavery in the state during his tenure as governor and again as vice-president in 1817. Now, four years later, Tompkins argued in favor of a double-standard for whites and blacks when it came to voting rights. Determined to expand dramatically the franchise to white male voters in an age of democratic exuberance, the convention came within a hair of disqualifying non-whites from voting altogether, based solely on views of black racial inferiority.

The new state constitution, as finally adopted and defended vigorously by Martin Van Buren, retained a higher bar for black males when it came to the franchise. White males could vote at age twenty-one if they served in the militia or paid any tax and had at least a one-year residency in the state. Black adult males were required to live in the state for a minimum of three years before being given the vote, and were required to own, debt-free, property worth at least $250 on which they paid taxes. Tompkins joined future president Martin Van Buren in arguing for this discriminatory policy.[18] The removal of property requirements for black voters was reconsidered twenty-five years later when the New York constitution was again revised in 1846 and slavery was a thing of the past in the state. The legislature decided to submit the issue of equal suffrage for black voters to a popular vote, where it was decisively defeated.[19] Freedom and equality continued to be two separate issues in New York, as in the North in general.

In neighboring New Jersey, the governor of that state had called for gradual abolition of slavery as early as 1778, calling the practice of slavery unchristian as well as "odious and disgraceful."[20] The legislature's response was to avoid controversy over slavery due to the precarious nature of the country during the Revolution, the war for independence creating "too critical a situation to enter on the consideration of it [emancipation] at that time."[21] That emancipation in New Jersey was nowhere in sight was evident when a January 1781 editorial in the *New Jersey Gazette* argued that, because of constitutionally guaranteed property rights, "The liberation of our slaves, therefore, without the concurrence of their possessors, we apprehend, is an object infinitely further distant from the legal attention of our assembly, than are the heavens above the earth."[22]

Indeed, no action was taken other than making the process of manumission somewhat easier, until years later when a bill for gradual emancipation was again introduced in the legislature in 1803. The bill inspired intense and protracted debate to the point that a vote was delayed until February 1804. At the crux of the matter was the issue of property rights of slaveholders versus the indefensibility of slavery "in a land of freedom, and by a people distinguished for reason and humanity."[23] The gradual abolition of slavery was approved by the New Jersey legislature in 1804 and became state law. Every slave child born on or after July 4, 1804, would be entitled to freedom upon reaching the age of twenty-one, if female, and twenty-five, if male. The birth of every slave child born after July 4, 1804, must be registered with the county clerk, and the slaveholder of the mother was responsible for the care of the child for one year, following which time the slaveholder could choose to abandon the child to the local township or county who, in turn, could bind the child out to service at an appropriate age.[24]

When the 1804 gradual abolition bill came to a vote, it easily passed in the New Jersey legislature with a large majority of thirty-four to four in the house, and twelve to one in the legislative council. Arthur Zilversmit has asked the intriguing question of how this bill passed so easily when "only a few months earlier abolition had been the subject of acrimonious debate and repeated postponements."[25] Zilversmit credits the lobbying efforts of abolitionists, who succeeded in getting opponents of the bill to abstain, or in some cases to change their views and vote for it, in order to give a stronger show of legislative unity and thus set an example that would sway public opinion more strongly in favor of the measure. According to Zilversmit, abolitionists agreed to the abandonment clause "to get the overwhelming vote essential to public acceptance of abolition." While arguments were made in favor of New Jersey's abandonment law (that were either deceptively false or badly misinformed) stating that New York's similar and earlier slave child abandonment law had resulted in an insignificant expense to that state, reality proved otherwise. Repeal of both the abandonment clause, and even the entire gradual abolition law itself, was actively sought by citizens' groups in various parts of the state. The impact of New Jersey abolitionists waned following the gradual emancipation bill's passage. The New Jersey Society for Promoting the Abolition of Slavery was unable to stem the tide of votes in the state legislature that disenfranchised blacks in 1807, two years before the society disbanded in 1809.[26] As had been the case with New York, New Jersey ended support payments for abandoned slave children in 1811 when the costs for this program in fiscal year 1808–9 exceeded 40 percent of the state's budget.[27]

The State of New Jersey adopted a new constitution in the year 1844 in which the first article stated, "All men are by nature free and independent, and have certain natural and inalienable rights, among which are those of enjoying and defending life and liberty, acquiring, possessing, and protecting property, and of pursuing and obtaining safety and happiness."[28] Unlike the Massachusetts judicial decision that abolished slavery based on a similar statement in the Massachusetts constitution, the New Jersey Supreme Court declared in a case brought before it in 1845 that the New Jersey constitution was merely setting forth the "general proposition, that men in their social state are free to adopt their own form of government and enact their own laws." The constitution's wording was not, according to the court, directed at "man in his private, individual or domestic capacity; or to define his individual rights or interfere with his domestic relations, or his individual condition." The court ruled that the new constitution of 1844 had neither abolished slavery nor changed the slave laws in effect at the time of its adoption. There is some irony here, given that in 1820 the New Jersey legislature had passed a resolution against the admission of Missouri as a slave state in 1820.[29]

New Jersey's slave population peaked at 12,422 in the Census of 1800. In 1810, New Jersey was the only Northern state in which the population of slaves (10,851) exceeded the population of free blacks (7,843). The number of slaves in New Jersey declined to 7,557 by 1820 and 2,254 by 1830. In 1846 an abolition act was passed which technically ended slavery in New Jersey, but in reality it merely reclassified the state's remaining slaves into "apprentices for life." There were still 236 such "apprentices" in New Jersey in 1850, and 18 remained in the state according to the Census of 1860.[30] The last of these "apprentices" likely received their freedom only as a result of the Thirteenth Amendment. New Jersey remained an intensely conservative state regarding slavery and African Americans. In the antebellum era, the state was often referred to as the northern-most Southern state. George McClellan, a New Jersey native who sought to save the Union while not disturbing the peculiar institution of the South, grew up in this environment.

The gradual abolition of slavery in New York and New Jersey proved to be both disappointing and encouraging for those opposed to slavery. The strength of the argument made in favor of property rights over human rights was appalling to some, and revealed, as Arthur Zilversmit has noted, "a fundamental division within the American creed."[31] The debates over slavery and the incremental approach to ending it in New York and New Jersey also demonstrated to abolitionists the difficulty of their task. If it had been this difficult to eradicate slavery in these two Northern states, how much more difficult would it be for abolitionist principles to take root in the South? Despite the frustrations of delay, the gradual emancipation laws of New York and New Jersey and the debates that preceded them signaled a new and fundamentally different attitudinal approach toward race and freedom that would eventually diverge greatly from that of the South. Open debates about the future of slavery were rare in the South and, when they did occur as in Virginia in 1831 and 1832, usually led to even more repressive measures rather than to a path toward eventual freedom.

Meanwhile, in the territories of the Northwest Ordinance, freedom and equality also remained separate considerations mixed with a heavy dose of what was then called "negrophobia." Illinois and slavery present a study in manipulation, appeasement, flexibility, hypocrisy, obfuscation, and other terms that explain the human capacity for rationalization and justification for behavior that contradicts what the law appears to mandate.

The Northwest Territory, from which Illinois was carved as a state in 1818, was closed to slavery by the Northwest Ordinance of 1787. That ordinance includes the following in Article 6: "There shall be neither slavery nor involuntary servitude in the said territory, otherwise than in the punishment of crimes whereof the party shall have been duly convicted: *Provided, always,* That any person escaping into the same, from whom labor or service is lawfully claimed in any one of the original States, such fugitive may be lawfully reclaimed and conveyed to the person claiming his or her labor or service as aforesaid."

This does not mean, however, that slaves were not present in Illinois, or for that matter in other states carved from the Northwest Territory, as the ordinance permitted settlers already living in the Northwest Territory to keep their slaves. While most of the early migrants into the Northwest Territory were antislavery New Englanders, they were not the only ones. In fact, the 1820 Census listed 917 slaves in "free" Illinois, and as late as the Census of 1840, 331 slaves were counted in the state.[32]

Once the United States began to function under the newly ratified Constitution in 1789, slavery was given an unexpected boost in the Northwest Territory when President George Washington, himself a large slaveholder, chose not to enforce Article 6 of the Northwest Ordinance, and allowed settlers essentially to ignore the ban on slavery, setting a presidential precedent that would be followed by the next fourteen presidents, through Buchanan's administration. Arthur St. Clair, who had served as the presiding officer of the Confederation Congress during the session when the ordinance was passed, was appointed by that same Congress as the first governor of the Northwest Territory. After the establishment of the federal republic, both presidents George Washington and John Adams retained St. Clair in this position. Like Washington, St. Clair was a slaveholder, and brought slaves with him, holding the governorship in the Northwest Territory until its reorganization and then serving as territorial governor of Ohio to 1802.[33]

When in 1800 the Northwest Territory was reorganized and divided into two parts, the Ohio Territory and the Indiana Territory, what would later become the state of Illinois fell within the Indiana Territory. At the time of the territorial reorganization, a petition was sent to the U.S. Senate by some slaveholding Illinois residents asking permission to keep their slaves, born outside of Illinois, for life but agreeing to emancipate their slaves born in Illinois at the ages of thirty-one for men and twenty-eight for women, ages significantly higher than those in gradual emancipation laws enacted in the Northern states. The Senate decided not to get involved in this issue and took no action on this request. Going to the Indiana Territorial Assembly a few years later, proslavery settlers received a major concession through passage in 1808 of "an act concerning the introduction of negroes and mulattoes into this Territory," which allowed slaves to be brought into the region under the age of fifteen years and held in service until the age of thirty-five (for males) and thirty-two (for females). As Christopher Lehman has pointed out, "The passage of the statute marked one of the first instances of popular sovereignty concerning slavery in the United States. The federal government permitted the people of Indiana Territory to decide how to define and enforce slavery and emancipation."[34]

In 1809 the federal government carved the Illinois Territory from the Indiana Territory. Slaveholder James Madison appointed Ninian Edwards, a Kentucky slaveholder, as territorial governor. In one of those historical coincidences, Edwards's son, also named Ninian, later married Elizabeth Todd, Mary Todd Lincoln's older sister. It was in their parlor in Springfield that Abraham Lincoln and Mary Todd were married in 1842. While governor of the Illinois Territory, Ninian Edwards Sr. spoke favorably of servitude, calling it "beneficial to the slaves, and not repugnant to the public interests." When another slaveholder, James Monroe, became president, Edwards was reappointed territorial governor. Edwards showed no interest in enforcing the federal ban on slavery in the region.[35] In 1826, eight years after statehood, Edwards was elected governor of the state and, like some other early governors of Illinois, continued to own slaves.

Illinois statehood came in 1818, and while the state's constitution banned slavery in Article 13, slavery was both sanctioned and openly practiced in the state, thanks to Article 14 which stated, "That all laws in force at the adoption of this constitution, and inconsistent therewith, and all rights, actions, prosecutions, claims and contracts of this State, individuals or bodies corporate shall continue, and be as valid as if this constitution had not been adopted."[36] Through this provision, alleged "contracts" between African Americans and their masters, some of which were set for as long as ninety-nine years, were deemed lawful. Since "slavery" had been banned in the Northwest Territory, slaves had been brought in as "bondsmen" or "indentured servants" who were under contract, even if such a bond or contract lasted a lifetime. Consequently, slavery existing before statehood was largely left alone. Hence, through a constitutional sleight of hand, Illinois banned slavery on one hand and affirmed its continuation on the other. Federal census takers ignored this legal ruse and counted these "indentured servants" for what they were, slaves. The Illinois constitution also prohibited anyone from bringing a slave into the state for the purpose of manumission, but was silent on any other purpose such as sale.

This ambiguity was clarified by an 1828 Illinois Supreme Court case, *Nance vs. Howard,* in which it was ruled that African Americans could indeed be sold in Illinois.[37] In 1819, pursuant to yet another anti-black provision of its constitution, the Illinois legislature enacted legislation discouraging African Americans from residing in the state and barring African Americans who nonetheless did reside in the state from bringing suit or testifying in Illinois courts. In another blow at freedom for African Americans in Illinois, slaves could be imported as "seasonal workers" as long as they departed the state at appropriate intervals.[38] Abraham Lincoln was hired as legal counsel in 1847 by Robert Matson, a slaveholder who had brought slaves into southern Illinois from Kentucky for a temporary work assignment. The slaves had run away and sought the help of abolitionists in obtaining their freedom, but Lincoln argued that the law sided with Matson's attempt to recover his lost property since the slaves were in Illinois on a transitory basis. Lincoln lost this case, as well as his legal fee since Matson disappeared without paying Lincoln for his services. As David Donald points out, this case "should not be taken as an indication of Lincoln's views on slavery: his business was law, not morality."[39]

Illinois became a popular destination for migrating Southerners in the first few years after statehood. While New Yorkers and New Englanders generally settled in the Northern part of the state, the central and southern sections of Illinois were populated largely by immigrants from Virginia, Tennessee, Kentucky, and the Carolinas, and they brought their folkways regarding slavery with them.[40] An attempt was made by proslavery forces in 1824 to call a convention to change the Illinois constitution to permit full-blown, Southern-style slavery in the state. By a slim margin of 1,668 votes, the idea of such a convention was rejected, thus effectively ending any likelihood that slavery would play a substantial role in the future of Illinois.[41] While slavery eventually disappeared from Illinois by the 1840s, the anti-black attitudes that tolerated and even encouraged slavery persisted in Illinois until after the Civil War, and is an important backdrop to an understanding of the Lincoln-Douglas debates.

Modern American sensibilities are offended by the practices of inequality in the antebellum North as well as the South. As Gary W. Gallagher has rightly stated, "Anyone remotely conversant with nineteenth-century U.S. history knows that democracy as practiced in 1860 denied women, free and enslaved African Americans, and other groups basic liberties and freedoms most white northerners routinely attributed to their republic."[42]

While the vast majority of Northern blacks enjoyed freedom from actual bondage, they nonetheless suffered discrimination in virtually every aspect of life, either through legal means or social practice reflecting prevailing white attitudes. Alexis de Tocqueville noted with surprise, following his grand tour of America in 1831, "The prejudice of race appears to be stronger in the states that have abolished slavery than in those where it still exists; and nowhere is it so intolerant as in those states where servitude has never been known. . . . Thus the Negro is free, but he can share neither the rights, nor the pleasures, nor the labor, nor the afflictions, nor the tomb of him whose equal he has been declared to be; and he cannot meet him upon fair terms in life or in death."[43]

Laws throughout much of the antebellum North attempted to restrict blacks from residency. Robert Dale Owen, Democratic Indiana Congressman and social reformer involved with the New Harmony utopian community among other projects, was a typical "liberal" exclusionist who saw it as in the black race's best interest to depart from a society in which "we are not willing to accord the most common protection [to them] against outrage and death."[44] Bans on interracial marriage existed throughout the North. Repealed in Massachusetts in 1843 after a decade of heated struggle, the point was, according to William Lloyd Garrison, not to encourage such amalgamation but rather "to establish justice, and vindicate the equality of the human race."[45] From restrictions on the use of public transportation, to lack of educational and employment opportunities, to seating restrictions in public meeting places, to overt discrimination against them, if not outright prohibitions, when it came to voting and property rights, African Americans in the North experienced anything but equality. Freedom and equality were indeed two very different things, even in the minds of some of the most ardent abolitionists. The sun may have been setting on Northern slavery, but it was still broad daylight when it came to inequality.

The decline and effective demise of slavery in New York, New Jersey, and Illinois brought an end to the era of emancipation by individual states. Starting about 1840, the debate about the future of slavery shifted from the arena of state legislatures to the halls of Congress. An emerging abolitionist movement fastened the Puritan ideas of communal sin and communal guilt to the institution of slavery. In response, the South would reinvent slavery as a "positive good" in part to answer the abolitionists but also to assuage its own guilt and fears of the proverbial wolf they held by the ear—the potential of their own slaves to revolt.

CHAPTER 7

THE WOLF BY THE EAR: SLAVE RESISTANCE, WHITE REACTION, AND THE GROWING ABOLITIONIST MOVEMENT

While slavery was coming to an end in the North in the early nineteenth century, there were many in the South who viewed the continued existence of slavery as a threat, and who feared the multiple forms of slave resistance, especially the ever-present possibility of slave uprisings if not all-out servile war. This deep anxiety was not without foundation, and had a long history including the horrific experiences in the French colony of St. Domingue (Haiti). When Thomas Jefferson wrote to John Holmes in 1820 concerning slavery and the Missouri question, he noted that, "as it is, we have the wolf by the ear, and we can neither hold him, nor safely let him go. Justice is in one scale, and self-preservation in the other."[1] Jefferson was giving voice to a very genuine concern and dilemma faced by the slaveholders of the South. Slavery required coercion, and coercion invited not only the desire for freedom, but for some, retaliation. Slave owners realistically could never feel completely safe.

The desire for freedom evoked a wide range of slave and free-black responses, legal and illegal, moral and immoral. Tactics used to oppose a state of bondage included self-purchase of one's freedom; taking flight and assisting other runaways; seeking legal redress; seeking white allies in the cause; using the power of religion and religious songs to inspire hope and deliverance; despite the odds, learning to read and write and, in some cases, producing literary output advocating freedom and/or rebellion; passive resistance using various forms of deception including feigning illness, ignorance, or incompetence; self-inflicted injuries; theft; sabotage; acts of murder committed against individuals or families; and most radical of all, but used only in a relatively few instances, armed rebellion.

The planter class of the South had its hands full dealing with myriad creative slave responses to their captivity and their desire to be free. While Southern planters tried to convince Northerners of their slaves' well-being, loyalty, and happiness, few believed it, especially slaveholders themselves, who lived in constant suspicion and dread of slave chicanery, escapes, and plots of the worst kind. Southern leaders privately expressed fears that, slave or free, African Americans would retaliate with wanton violence for the horrors inflicted in slavery. In early 1863, Jefferson Davis, an apostle of the "sunny" South with its happy slaves, discarded this fantasy in his response to the Emancipation Proclamation as he condemned Lincoln's measure "by which several millions of human beings of an inferior race . . . are encouraged to a general assassination of their masters" as "the most execrable measure recorded in the history of guilty man."[2] It was only in 1979 that noted historian of slavery Eugene Genovese wrote, "the extraordinary scholarship of recent years has finally laid to rest the myth of slave docility and quiescence."[3]

There is little evidence of slave insurrection during the Civil War, however, the slaves apparently having taken Lincoln's advice in the Emancipation Proclamation to refrain from acts of violence. While advocates of the South's Lost Cause seek to produce evidence of African American support for the Confederate cause, the historical record is replete with Southern fears that only absolute repression could save them and their families from racial genocide. One needs only to examine the debates over arming African Americans in the Confederate cause to see how many prominent whites feared black reprisals in the form of race war.

In this environment of pervasive fear, it is not surprising that the planter class determined to stifle as much criticism of their peculiar institution as possible with a full-blown assault against basic civil liberties, even for whites, which began in earnest in the 1820s. In the minds of the ruling class, the suppression of basic liberties was a reasonable and necessary step to prevent antislavery sentiments in the South. Blacks, free and slave, were further restricted by laws prohibiting them from learning to read or write, to have freedom of movement, or the right to assemble or even to pray in groups without white supervision.

The widespread public debate over slavery initiated by the sectional divide over Missouri statehood was certainly a factor in this growing Southern white insecurity, as was Gabriel Prosser's conspiracy in 1800 and a major slave uprising in New Orleans in 1811. An alleged massive uprising planned by free black Denmark Vesey in Charleston, South Carolina, in 1822 added fuel to the fires of Southern fear and panic. One can go further back to the Haitian revolts of several years before and the terror that this possible contagion caused in the South. During Thomas Jefferson's first presidential term, Gideon Granger, postmaster and presidential advisor, sent a confidential letter to Georgia Senator James Jackson, chairman of the Senate's Committee on the Posts, in which he stated,

> After the scenes which St. Domingo [Haiti] has exhibited to the world, we cannot be too cautious in attempting to prevent similar evils. . . . [I]n Virginia and South Carolina (as I have been informed) plans and conspiracies have already been concerted by them [slaves] more than once, to rise in arms, and subjugate their masters. . . . Every thing which tends to increase their knowledge of natural rights . . . or that affords them an opportunity of associating, acquiring, and communicating sentiments, and of establishing a chain or line of intelligence, must increase your hazard, because it increases their means of effecting their object.

Granger's letter culminated with his warning of the dangers of "employing negroes, or people of color, in transporting the public mails" because "By travelling from day to day, and hourly mixing with people, they must, they will acquire information." Most dangerous of all, "They will learn that a man's rights do not depend on his color" and they will "become teachers to their brethren."[4]

Slave revolts and liberation conspiracies in the nineteenth century began with the actions of Gabriel Prosser in 1800. Often referred to as Gabriel's Rebellion, an organized group of armed slaves was determined to march on Richmond and obtain their freedom. The movement was organized by Gabriel Prosser, an enslaved blacksmith in Henrico County, Virginia, who was sufficiently skilled in his trade that he was allowed at times to hire himself out. He apparently used some of his free time to forge weapons and a conspiracy to target the master class. He envisioned, with the help of his co-conspirator and brother, raising an army of some one thousand men armed with guns, knives, and clubs who would massacre enough whites to scare the planter class so thoroughly that they would be willing to negotiate terms of emancipation. The revolt was planned to begin at midnight, August 30, 1800. Unfortunately for Prosser and his followers, the weather proved highly uncooperative, sending torrential rains that flooded the rivers and creeks that the insurrectionists needed to cross. To make matters worse, the conspiracy was exposed by two slaves, and the ringleaders, including

Gabriel himself, were captured by six hundred troops sent after them by Governor James Monroe. Following a trial in October 1800, about thirty black men, including Gabriel Prosser, were found guilty of conspiracy and executed (with owners of the executed slaves being compensated by the Virginia government). The remaining captured rebels were sold to a slave dealer who removed them to Spanish-held New Orleans.

White relief at the foiling of Gabriel's conspiracy was tempered, however, by the scale and ideology of the undertaking. Apparently Prosser was counting on assistance from Haiti, and the American Revolution had provided the slogan for the rebellion: "Death or Liberty." Furthermore, religious passion had played a role in the uprising as recruitment for Gabriel's army had taken place at black praise meetings where Martin, Gabriel's preacher brother, let it be known that God would favor their actions and stated that "their cause was similar to the Israelites" who had been held in bondage in Egypt.[5] On a much smaller scale, two years later in 1802, the Sancho conspiracy in Mecklenburg County, Virginia, involved an alleged plot on the part of several slaves to poison whites. Although the supposed conspiracy thoroughly terrified the local white population, only two of the fifteen or so slaves arrested were found guilty of any misdeeds.[6]

In January of 1811, what was to be America's largest slave revolt in terms of lives lost began in the German Coast region of Louisiana near New Orleans. Originating several miles outside the city, a slave army under the leadership of slaves Charles, Kook, and Quamana made its way toward New Orleans, leaving in its wake death, destruction, and fear that this was to be another Haitian-style revolution. The terror felt by the white community resulted in a refugee traffic jam of carriages and carts some nine miles long on the muddy River Road leading to the city. Upon receiving word of the approaching slave insurrectionists, Governor William Claiborne of what was then the Orleans Territory ordered a strict curfew for male Negroes in the city of New Orleans after 6 o'clock beginning on January 9. With very little American military presence in New Orleans at the time, two volunteer militia companies and about thirty U.S. troops rode out to ascertain the nature and size of the threat, and were joined en route by several planters who were cheered by this show of force and decided to fight rather than flee. The number of slaves involved is difficult to discern; Daniel Rasmussen has identified 124 individual slaves in the revolt based on documentary evidence, although he acknowledges that eyewitness accounts put rebel slave numbers at between 200 and 500 persons. Using West African military strategy, the slave army appeared to retreat well outside the city, but this was a ruse to lure their enemies into a trap.

The militia prevailed, however, and on January 10, 1811, completely defeated the rebel slaves, killing and decapitating many and taking few prisoners. Over 100 severed slave heads were displayed on poles along the German Coast levees, along with their headless, decomposing bodies as an example of what rebel slaves could expect[7] in a grotesque mimicking of the Roman response to the Spartacus Revolt nearly two millennia before. This slave revolt was minimized by Governor Claiborne, with the goal of "covering up the revolt and saving face before an anxious nation." The result has been, according to Rasmussen, that "North America's largest antebellum slave revolt has languished in the footnotes of history for 200 years."[8]

In 1822 in Charleston, South Carolina, a free black carpenter named Denmark Vesey allegedly laid plans for a slave insurrection inspired by his own biblical interpretation of human freedom and the Haitian revolution of three decades before. An active churchman in the African Methodist Church of Charleston, Vesey was convinced that slavery was contrary to the law of God. Supposedly, the original plan was to seize the city arsenal on Sunday, July 14, 1822 (Bastille Day), burn Charleston, liberate slaves by force of arms in the surrounding countryside, and finally commandeer ships in Charleston Harbor and set sail for a life of freedom in Haiti. Word of the elaborate plot was leaked out weeks in advance of its implementation date, the authorities were ready, and a local military force moved in and captured Vesey and thirty-four others who were tried, convicted, and hanged.

There are questions about the extent of the Vesey plot, to what degree it may have been exaggerated for political purposes, or if it was even fabricated altogether to get rid of Vesey and other blacks who openly questioned white supremacy. The official report of the trial seems to bear witness of a major conspiracy, but Michael P. Johnson has concluded in a compelling analysis that

> Vesey, it appears, was the victim of a conspiracy of collusion between the white court and its cooperative black witnesses, both eager for their own reasons to pay homage to the enduring power of white supremacy. Unanswered questions about Vesey and his co-conspirators abound. But this much is clear: Vesey and the other condemned black men were victims of an insurrection conspiracy conjured into being in 1822 by the court, its cooperative black witnesses, and its numerous white supporters and kept alive ever since by historians eager to accept the court's judgments while rejecting its morality. Surely it is time to pay attention to the "not guilty" pleas of almost all the men who went to the gallows, to their near silence in the court records, to their refusal

to name names in order to save themselves. These men were heroes not because they were about to launch an insurrection but because they risked and accepted death rather than collaborate with the conspiratorial court and its cooperative witnesses.[9]

Whether the case against Vesey was real or fabricated by the court, it was highly influential in creating further dread and deep anxiety on the part of South Carolina whites, providing added rationale for greater state control over both slaves and free blacks. A citizens' guard of twenty-five hundred men was created to defend Charleston against any such future conspiracies; the state strengthened its slave code, restricted free blacks to the point of requiring all black gatherings to be under white supervision and required free blacks to be assigned white guardians, banned any free black who left South Carolina from ever returning, and required that all black sailors be jailed upon the docking of their ships, until the ships departed port.[10]

Nearly a decade later, in the summer of 1831, Nat Turner, a literate and religious slave in Southampton County, Virginia, organized a rebellion based on what he believed to be signs and visions from God. The revolt took place in an isolated region where most whites were not slaveholders, and those who were owned relatively few slaves. Turner and six accomplices murdered five whites at the Travis plantation, Turner's home, and moved on to a neighboring plantation, picking up slave recruits as they went. By late afternoon, Turner's army of rebels numbered over sixty, and several more plantations had been attacked. Most of the sixty or so whites slain by Nat Turner and his followers were women and children. By early the following morning, the militia had rounded up or killed nearly all the rebel slaves, but Nat Turner himself eluded them and hid out for nearly ten weeks. The revolt resulted in the mobilization of three thousand soldiers in Virginia who, along with vigilantes, killed over one hundred suspected insurgents. Thirty were actually brought to trial and convicted, of whom nineteen were executed with the remainder being removed from Virginia. As a result of the Nat Turner rebellion, many of Southampton County's free blacks, about three hundred in number, suddenly found resettlement in Liberia a desirable prospect. Turner was tried, convicted, and hanged on November 11, 1831, but before his execution he gave an interview to white attorney Thomas Gray who later published the account as *The Confessions of Nat Turner.*[11]

Slave revolts and the mere threat of such revolts placed a heavy emotional burden on the ruling class, and indeed on virtually all whites in the South. As James Oakes has aptly observed,

This is what made the prospect of slave rebellion so frightening in the Age of Revolution: its universal appeal to a slave culture and a liberal ideology that together transcended ethnic and local loyalties. Most of the major plots and insurrections fused traditional African conceptions of spirituality with Christian millennialism. . . .

Masters knew that the slaves could not influence American politics with their votes, petitions, speeches, and editorials. But . . . it was becoming apparent that slaves could affect the political system by intruding themselves into it as runaways, criminals, victims, or even witnesses. Any action that forced the legal system to recognize the slave as in any way independent of the master represented an implicit threat to the principle of total subordination.[12]

The reaction of Southern whites to slave revolts—actual, imagined, and potential—was paradoxically both predictable and surprising. The Nat Turner rebellion of 1831 created such a frenzy of fear and foreboding in Virginia, the state with the largest number of slaves at the time, that there was serious discussion in the legislature of whether slavery should be abolished in that state. Thomas Jefferson Randolph, grandson of Thomas Jefferson, got the debate started with a speech on January 16, 1832, in the Virginia House of Delegates that foresaw doom and gloom in years to come if slavery persisted, and offered a plan of gradual emancipation for slaves born after July 4, 1840, upon reaching adulthood, with deportation of the former slaves to Africa. Otherwise, Randolph prophetically envisioned the tragedy of "a dissolution of this Union" and ultimately, a Northern "invasion . . . in part with black troops."[13] Randolph's proposal received condemnation from those opposed to emancipation as well as those who believed emancipation should be implemented immediately. James Gholson expressed a conservative's shock in his speech to the House of Delegates that the possibility of ending slavery was even being debated: "When the distant reader shall discover, that the Virginia Legislature, in the year 1832, is engaged in solemn debate on the questions, whether 'private property can be taken for public use without compensation,' whether 'slaves are property,' and whether 'the increase of slaves is property;' he will be lost in amazement, and will be ready to exclaim of us, 'can these be the sons of their fathers?'"[14]

After much debate, the curious actions of Virginia's legislators produced a statement that simultaneously condemned the institution of slavery while proclaiming the inexpediency of emancipation. This paradoxical attitude was evident in Virginia's earlier revolutionary era history, as noted by Eva Sheppard Wolf, who concludes that "white Virginians, though sometimes disturbed by the existence of slavery, remained generally convinced of slavery's importance to their society as well as of the inferiority of the black people who were enslaved."[15] The debate in Virginia's legislative chambers was but a prelude to a larger public debate in 1831–32 in newspapers and other public forums. Central to the debate was not the human dignity and natural rights of the slave population, but rather, what was ultimately in the best interests of the white population. Nearly all those advocating abolition coupled this proposed action with removal of the black population from the state. Those favoring the retention of the peculiar institution were forced to rethink previous proslavery arguments that, despite its fundamentally immoral nature, slavery needed to be preserved for economic and social reasons. The new proslavery argument that ultimately emerged from the Virginia debate was that slavery was a positive good for slaves and whites alike.[16] Even those whites favoring emancipation moved "from being limited by racial fears to being motivated by them."[17]

In this ongoing environment where the fear of slave revolts was ever present, John Brown's attempt twenty-seven years later to start a servile insurrection throughout Virginia and the South symbolized a potent and fundamental threat to Southern security. On the night of October 16, 1859, John Brown led a small band that attempted to seize the federal armory at Harpers Ferry, Virginia, so that slaves in that region could be armed. The raid was financed by a group of Northern abolitionists, with the abolitionist philanthropist Gerrit Smith prominently among them. While area blacks failed to rally to Brown's call for revolt, if they ever received it, the raid was quickly suppressed by federal forces led by Col. Robert E. Lee. Ironically, the first person killed in the raid was a black station attendant going about his nightly duties. Brown was wounded, captured, tried, and convicted of treason against the United States and hanged on December 2, 1859, at Charles Town, Virginia. Several other members of Brown's band were also captured, tried, and executed.

Short of armed rebellion, the slave action most dreaded by whites and most risky to slaves was that of running away, a decision that cost slave owners significant financial loss and, when successful, inspired other slaves to attempt more escapes. Harsh treatment, deplorable and degrading working conditions, inadequate food and shelter, sexual abuse, lack of basic human rights, and complete lack of options for a better life for oneself and one's children were more than sufficient motives for slaves to escape and seek freedom, no matter how elusive. Unable to accept that their slaves were essentially unhappy with their lot in life, and with their masters, some Southerners went to great lengths to explain why their slaves sought to escape. Southern white rationalization for such behavior ranged from runaway slaves making a "childish mistake" to an alleged mental illness described and named in 1851 by New Orleans physician Dr. Samuel Cartwright as "drapetomania," derived from the Greek words for "runaway slave" and "crazy" or "mad."[18]

The Underground Railroad, an alliance of black freedmen and white antislavery activists, assisted in the transport of blacks to freedom, but not always in the Northern states. Many whites preferred that escaped blacks continue on to Canada rather than reside with them as neighbors. Famous black conductors like Harriet Tubman and Sojourner Truth slipped into the South numerous times, risking their lives to bring slaves north to freedom. Many tales depict harrowing moonlit journeys north with slave patrols and hunting dogs hot on their heels. Yet, there was no safety in the North

JOHN BROWN. *Fanatical abolitionist who fled Kansas after killing five proslavery neighbors. His failed raid on a U.S. arsenal at Harpers Ferry, Virginia, was designed to foment an armed slave rebellion, but it resulted in Brown's capture and hanging for treason. A martyr in much of the North, Brown sent convulsions through the South, convincing many that they and their peculiar institution were no longer safe in the Union.*

for runaways or freemen from the reach of bounty hunters armed first with the Fugitive Slave Act of 1793, and later with the draconian Fugitive Slave Act of 1850. Despite antebellum Southern angst and postwar Northern mythology, the few thousand slaves freed via the Underground Railroad made up a tiny fraction of the South's millions of enslaved souls. Even in the Deep South, where the Underground Railroad could not often reach, the possibility that a slave in that region could be assisted to freedom was anathema to the white population.

To assist runaway slaves, many Northern states enacted personal liberty laws forbidding even the transit of slaves through their territory. These laws actively sought to frustrate federal marshals in the enforcement of the congressionally enacted Fugitive Slave Law of 1850. Northern mobs also forcibly prevented enforcement of the law. These state-initiated personal liberty laws had the clear intent of nullifying federal authority, an action that was not unknown in the South. However, unlike South Carolina's response to the federal tariff in 1831, the Northern states were careful never to pass resolutions openly defying the national government or threatening secession.

Slaves were fleeing bondage long before the Underground Railroad or the Northern states with their personal liberty laws had come to the assistance of such fugitives. Despite state and federal laws aimed at stemming the flow of slave runaways, the self-theft (as Frederick Douglass would later express it) of human property was a major source of grief and irritation to slaveholders. Newspapers were constantly printing notices about runaway slaves, offering physical descriptions of the missing chattel, clues as to where they might be headed, and promising rewards for the fugitives' return. The following advertisement in the *Nashville Whig* of May 26, 1813, is representative:

TWENTY DOLLARS REWARD

Runaway from the subscriber living near Nashville, State of Tennessee, on the 27th of April, 1813, a negro man named SAM, about 25 years of age, nearly six feet high, stout, well proportioned, active and likely [pleasant, agreeable]; . . . is extremely proud; smokes segars, and walks with a considerable air—he is a good cook, an excellent waiter in the house, and carriage driver: he understands all kinds of farming work and the distillery . . . he is inclined to steal, and no doubt will soon provide himself with good clothing; his back and thighs, if examined, will shew the marks of the whip. It is most likely he will make for Cincinnati, and from thence for the Canada lines.[19]

Slaves used various methods to escape their bondage; disguising themselves and/or preparing or obtaining fraudulent documents allowing them

SOJOURNER TRUTH. *Born a slave in upstate New York before 1800, Isabella Baumfree learned Dutch before she learned English and took on the name "Sojourner Truth" after she became a powerful itinerant preacher and abolitionist. Her multifaceted work on behalf of African Americans before and after emancipation received wide recognition.*

to travel or to pass as free persons were among the most common. In a few cases, fugitive slaves made their escape by being transported as cargo. Henry "Box" Brown became famous for being successfully shipped for twenty-six hours in a wooden box from Richmond to freedom in Philadelphia.[20]

Several misconceptions about fugitive slaves have been corrected by more recent historical scholarship. John Hope Franklin and Loren Schweninger have demonstrated that the majority of runaways never left the South, few received assistance in their escapes, many fled with a sense of "terrible urgency," and it was not uncommon for slaves to go missing for periods ranging from days to months and then to return. Furthermore, not every slaveholder in the South was white. The Five Civilized Tribes of the old Southwest had slaves and brought them to the Indian Territory, where slavery existed until the end of the Civil War. There were also a few African American slaveholders in the South and Indian Territory. John Carruthers Stanly was a free black who, in the 1820s, owned three plantations in North Carolina worked by 163 slaves. Stanly suffered several slave escapes, despite the best efforts of his two white overseers. Though relatively few in number, such "black" slaveholders (usually of mixed black-white parentage) sometimes held their own children in bondage, as did many white slaveholders who had impregnated their slaves.[21]

As already noted, successful slave flight was at times dependent on the efforts of others who assisted them, and was enhanced by the growing free black population, particularly in parts of the Upper South. Free blacks, whether residing in or outside of slaveholding areas, were seen as threats to slavery. Southern concern over the presence and influence of free blacks in their midst prompted Georgia to propose an amendment to the federal Constitution in December 1824 that would allow states to ban such persons within their borders. In Ohio, a region on the receiving end of numerous fugitive slaves who managed to cross the Ohio River to freedom, there was also concern about the presence of free blacks. The Ohio plan would amend the Constitution to condemn slavery as a national evil and provide federal funds for colonization. Division even within the South prevented either the Georgia or Ohio plan from implementation. By the summer of 1825, eight state legislatures had endorsed the Ohio plan, while nine state legislatures had rejected the Georgia plan. The Ohio plan was rejected by Missouri and the cotton states of the Deep South, the Georgia legislature calling it a scheme "calculated to infringe the rights of the states" while other Upper South states were less hostile to the Ohio plan.[22] Even without the sanction of a provision in the federal Constitution, state constitutional provisions and laws in numerous free and slave states alike sought to pro-hibit free blacks from residing within their borders.

David Walker, a free black merchant of used clothing in Boston, authored a powerful pamphlet in 1829 entitled *Appeal to the Coloured Citizens of the World.* He called for freedom, condemnation of the idea of black inferiority, and an end to colonization schemes, stating that America "is more our country, than it is the whites'—we have enriched it with our blood and tears."[23] Walker urged blacks to seek education and solidar-ity, and to believe that the cause of the slave was a "glorious and heav-enly cause" sanctioned by God, who would certainly approve of armed resistance on the part of the oppressed. Walker attacked the hypocrisy of America's founding creeds and Founding Fathers, and called for immedi-ate action on the part of the slave population, boldly stating that hatred for whites was the only manly response open to them, given their degrad-ing treatment at the hands of white masters. Walker prophesied that the nation would be required to pay for the sin of slavery, and that a deliverer would soon be sent from God. Walker's *Appeal* made its way into the South, where whites read it in horror and responded with stronger anti-literacy laws for the slave population. When David Walker died suddenly in 1830, it was believed by many that he had been poisoned.[24]

The few political rights granted free blacks, mostly in New England, were also seen as a threat to slavery. To eradicate this expression of equal-ity, Stephen Douglas proposed a national constitutional amendment as a compromise measure in late 1860 stripping free blacks of any right to par-ticipate in the political life of their communities, regardless of the laws of their state of residence. Ironically, the measure would have stripped states of their right to determine their own political practices within their borders, the very cause for which the South claimed justification for secession.[25]

Successful slave flight was at times dependent on the efforts of others who assisted them, and was enhanced by the growing free black popula-tion, particularly in parts of the Upper South. One can see the worrisome dilemma facing slaveholders caused by the presence of free blacks, result-ing in frequent statements such as this in advertisements which promised financial reward for the return of runaway slaves: "It is probable this fel-low may endeavor to pass for a free man, as there are many free blacks passing about this country."[26] One can only imagine the inconveniences if not horrors facing free blacks in the South who may have been forced repeatedly to prove their free status.

The desire to reunite with family members inspired many slave attempts to flee to freedom, and inspired many heroic and risky acts, which far too

STEPHEN A. DOUGLAS. *The "Little Giant" whose ambivalent views on slavery and presidential ambition led to the authorship of the Kansas-Nebraska Act in 1854. Four years later, he opposed the proslavery Lecompton constitution of Kansas, earning the ire of Southerners. Though defeated by Lincoln for the presidency in 1860, he was a Unionist and stood behind Lincoln in the secessionist crisis. When Lincoln removed his hat to deliver his first inaugural address, Douglas, seated nearby, graciously offered to hold it.*

often ended in failure. As James and Lois Horton have pointed out, slave sales proved the greatest destroyer of slave family life, and not surprisingly, attempts by slaves to flee to freedom were made "at critical moments of change in their lives when their circumstances were likely to worsen significantly, such as when a master died or was about to sell them."[27] At the same time, family ties decreased the likelihood of runaways, assuming the slave family remained intact under one owner. Even after families were parted by sale, some masters moved quickly to pair up male and female slaves whose families had been sold. Such matchmaking might decrease the desire to chase after relocated family members, and would perhaps produce additional valuable slave children in the process. This recognition of family ties by many slaveholders, as James and Lois Horton note,

> contradicted the contentions of some slaveholders, that African Americans did not suffer from the family separation that was an increasingly common part of slavery with the ever-expanding internal slave trade. Many slaveholders answered charges that the trade was inhumane by arguing that slaves were limited in their ability to form human attachments and thus were not affected by being separated from other family members. Clearly their use of family as a means of slave control contradicted such assertions, and these claims were rendered ludicrous by plainly visible evidence to the contrary. Even casual observers who witnessed the reactions of slaves torn from their loved ones understood the absurdity of this rationalization.[28]

Though far less urbanized than the North, the few cities and sizeable towns of the South provided opportunities for slaves to experience far more autonomy than on the plantation. Though technically illegal, some slaveholders allowed their slaves to negotiate employment in the South's urban centers, where slaves found positions as construction workers, stevedores, gardeners, cooks, steamboat stewards, domestic servants, drivers of carts and carriages, laundry workers, along with other forms of employment. Sometimes slaves earned good wages, often with no questions asked, as long as the master received a profit from the arrangement. Such an environment also provided a haven for fugitive slaves, who were often successful at finding employment in larger Southern communities while convincing employers (who often asked no questions) that they had been authorized by their masters to find work.[29]

Owners who had a financial stake in healthy, working slaves were reluctant to maim or kill their captured runaways, although severe punishments were often inflicted. It was especially distressing to Deep South slaveholders who suspected that their runaway slaves had actually made it to the North, for the cost of retrieval could sometimes equal or exceed the monetary value of the slave. Out of sheer frustration and anger, a few slave owners offered a reward for their fugitive slaves, dead or alive. Recalcitrant slaves, some of whom attempted to flee multiple times, were sometimes physically maimed to hamper their further escape, or sold at discounted prices.

The political implications of fugitive slaves ultimately became more important than the actual loss of the slaves themselves and heightened the sectional tension between North and South. James Oakes has effectively laid out the case that

> [a]t the heart of the fugitive slave controversy rested a "conflict of laws" that could have political significance only if slaves actually ran away. Northern law presumed that black people, however "inferior" and however much discriminated against, possessed the basic rights of life, liberty, and property. Southern law presumed the opposite. To protect free blacks from kidnapping by fugitive-slave catchers, northern states established legal procedures for determining whether or not a slaveholder's claim of ownership was valid. These "personal-liberty laws" necessarily extended the presumption of freedom to fugitive slaves, flatly contradicting southern law. They thereby created a potential for sectional conflict every time a slave set foot on northern soil.[30]

Oakes has rightly concluded that "as the conflict between North and South intensified, acts of slave resistance had increasingly disruptive effects."[31] Those slaves who did run away to the North during and after the 1820s heightened sectional tensions at a time when antislavery literature was rising in output and influence, and more and more Northerners were becoming convinced that slavery and slaveholders were evil.

Increasing numbers of fugitive slaves, generally from the Upper South, found refuge in Ohio and Pennsylvania just across the border from slavery's legal limits. Unlike fugitives from Kentucky, Tennessee, or Virginia, slaves from Delaware, Maryland, or Missouri did not face any substantial geographical impediment in their flight to freedom. Slaveholders attempting to retrieve their vanished property ran into increased resistance, legal and otherwise, from hostile mobs as well as law enforcement and judicial officers. Especially irksome to slaveholders, who were always demanding greater protection for their slave property, were Northern judges who used legal technicalities to free runaway slaves.[32]

It was possible for slaves to secure freedom by fleeing to other parts of the South, by crossing into the North, fleeing across the Rio Grande to Mexico, or by going south into Seminole communities in Florida. While there were multiple reasons behind the federal government's Indian removal acts in the Southeast, the Seminole removal was centered more on the issue of slavery than on land acquisition. Slaveholders in Florida, Georgia, and South Carolina were troubled by Seminole willingness to harbor fugitive slaves, and indeed to welcome them, where they became known as "Black Seminoles." The Seminole Wars in Florida were the most violent and expensive attempts at Native American removal undertaken by the federal government. The Cherokee removal required $1.3 million to relocate slightly over 12,000 Cherokees, while the Second Seminole War removed 3,000 Seminoles at a cost to the government of $30 million and more than 1,500 military lives lost. When the somewhat inconclusive Second Seminole War was declared to be over in 1842, Florida had lost its haven status for fugitive slaves, and witnessed widespread expansion of slavery within its borders.[33]

Slave conspiracies and the many forms of resistance by countless individual slaves had an eroding effect on the slave society of the South. The slaves were not alone in their struggle. Their road to freedom was augmented by a growing abolitionist movement consisting of free blacks and whites in the North. The autobiography of a very literate eighteenth-century slave named Olaudah Equiano (also known as Gustavus Vassa) proved to be a valuable text in the British and early American antislavery movements, as it included a vivid description of the infamous "middle passage" between Africa and the Caribbean.[34] Even so, prior to 1830 the American antislavery cause was championed by individuals and small groups, often Quakers, who did not attract the attention of a wide audience. A few manumission societies in the Upper South encouraged owners, with meager results, to free their slaves. A journal with a small following dedicated to incremental, voluntary emancipation with compensation, *The Genius of Universal Emancipation* had been published by Quaker Benjamin Lundy in Baltimore since 1821. In 1828 Lundy met editor William Lloyd Garrison in Boston and inspired him with his antislavery rhetoric.[35] The antislavery movement in America was about to surge to a new level of intensity and public acceptance.

The 1830s marked the ushering in of an era of militant abolitionism on a national scale. The convergence of several factors helps explain the vigorous growth of the movement at this time, one being the very public debates of the British Parliament over emancipation in the British Empire that grabbed the attention of an American audience. William Wilberforce, an abolitionist member of Parliament for many years, led the fight to end the slave trade in the British Empire in 1807 and helped bring an end to slavery itself just before his death in 1833, making him a hero to many in America as well as in Britain. The British nation had struggled to reconcile the moral dimension of slavery with the perceived benefits to the British Empire long before the American Revolution, but according to Christopher Leslie Brown, the American Revolution was a pivotal point in the British struggle over slavery because the conflict with America "directed unprecedented attention to the moral character of colonial institutions and imperial practices."[36]

Combining Enlightenment values of liberty and intellectual virtue with Quaker and Evangelical Christian condemnation of violations of the law of love, the antislavery movement in Britain, although "marked by false starts, routes not taken, [and] initiatives that petered out," ultimately emerged in part as "an amalgam of secular principles and religious doctrine" but even more as a reaction against merely nominal Christianity by urging commitment to move from moral opinion to moral action.[37] Chief among British intellectuals pushing the abolitionist movement forward was Thomas Clarkson, who began urging commitment to the cause in 1786, and in 1808 published the movement's first history in his two-volume *History of the Rise, Progress, and Accomplishment of the Abolition of the African Slave-Trade by the British Parliament.* According to Christopher Leslie Brown, "Clarkson was the first to characterize the campaign as the working out of impulses deeply imbedded in the society from which it emerged, as the elaboration of principles essential to British Protestantism, as the expression of a distinctively British devotion to liberty and the rule of law."[38] Antislavery arguments based on both religion and reason from "across the pond" did not go unnoticed by American abolitionists, and indeed boosted the cause, yet it remained for Americans to create their own rationale and strategies to end slavery in the distinctive American social, cultural, and economic climate in which the institution was found.

The Second Great Awakening, an American religious revival of major proportions that seemed preoccupied with social reform as well as spiritual renewal, resulted in many converts to a Christianity emphasizing the eradication of evil in the world in order to prepare the way for the second coming of Christ. One of the many key leaders of the revival movement was lawyer-turned-theologian Charles G. Finney. Echoing old Puritan themes, Finney attracted a considerable following with his call to personal salvation as well as with his denunciation of slavery as "the national sin." He stated that ministers of the Gospel needed to speak out against public policy that was out of harmony with biblical Christianity, slavery being "Exhibit A." Finney, whose six-foot-three-inch frame, large head, and piercing gaze matched the intensity of his preaching, called on Christians

CHARLES G. FINNEY. *A formidable-looking, Connecticut-born theologian, evangelist, and educator, Finney became the spiritual father of many abolitionists. For many years he served as professor and president at Oberlin College in Ohio, a seedbed of abolitionist thought and one of the first higher-education institutions to admit blacks and women.*

"to expose and rebuke the national sins. We are all aboard the same ship. As a nation our very existence depends upon the correct moral conduct of our rulers. . . . [S]hall ministers be told, shall any man be told, that he is meddling with other men's matters when he reproves and rebukes the abominations of slavery?" Failure to speak out would carry dire consequences, Finney believed; "Christians have been very guilty in this matter [of slavery]," he asserted, and "the time has come when they must act differently or God will curse the nation and withdraw his spirit."[39]

For all his personal hatred of slavery, however, Finney did not advocate radical actions with abolitionist Christians seizing the reins of political power. Rather, he sought to influence the culture through moral persuasion. For many Americans, Enlightenment zeal may have started the abolitionists' race against slavery, but evangelical Christian zeal helped push them toward the finish line. As Simon Schama has pointed out, Enlightenment-based Founders such as Thomas Jefferson and Patrick Henry condemned slavery in principle, but Enlightenment values alone were insufficient to compel them to give up their slaves.[40]

One of Finney's most influential converts was Theodore Dwight Weld, who married the abolitionist-feminist Angelina Grimke, who had moved to the North to avoid the evils of slavery in her native South Carolina. Weld first wielded significant influence during his student days at Cincinnati's Lane Seminary, founded by Lyman Beecher (father of Harriet Beecher Stowe) to train converts, largely from Finney's revivals, for the ministry. As a fire-breathing abolitionist, Weld helped spark a series of discussions about slavery in early 1834 on the Lane campus (one mile from slaveholding Kentucky) that lasted for eighteen days and nights and became known as the Lane Debate. Two questions opened the debate:

1st.   Ought the people of the Slaveholding States to abolish Slavery immediately?

2d.   Are the doctrines, tendencies, and measures of the American Colonization Society, and the influence of its principal supporters, such as render it worthy of the patronage of the Christian public?[41]

When the debate was over, the answer to the first question was a resounding "yes" and to the second question, "no," and essentially the entire student body had signed on to the abolitionist cause. As to the question, "Can slaves take care of themselves if emancipated?" an emancipated slave by the name of James Bradley addressed the gathering. The unnamed editor of the record of the debate commended this "shrewd and intelligent black"

THEODORE DWIGHT WELD. *A disciple of evangelist Charles G. Finney, Weld became an early leader in the antislavery crusade, including his work with the American Anti-Slavery Society and his authorship in 1839 of* American Slavery As It Is *(published anonymously). Weld married another outspoken abolitionist, South Carolinian Angelina Grimke, in 1838.*

for his response: "They have taken care of, and support themselves *now, and their master, and his family into the bargain;* and this being so, it would be strange if they could not provide for themselves, *when disencumbered from this load.*"[42] The editor wished that "the slanderers of negro intellect could have witnessed this unpremeditated effort." The account of the debate ended with the admonition "'Lord, what wilt THOU have me to do?' is the question which every soul of us ought, in the premises, heartily to agitate at the throne of grace. . . . The cause of equity is the cause of God. . . . [I]f God be for us, who can be against us?"[43]

The endorsement of immediate emancipation by many of Lane Seminary's students and faculty and the antislavery society which was founded on campus led the local white population to express deep concerns about the "town-gown" relationship between Cincinnati and the seminary. This prompted the seminary's board of trustees to disband the antislavery society, a move that ultimately resulted in Weld and about forty Lane students departing Lane for Oberlin, Ohio, where the wealthy businessmen brothers Lewis and Benjamin Tappan agreed to fund a new college open to students without regard for gender and race.[44] Thus the first interracial, coeducational American institution of higher education was born out of the abolitionist movement. Charles G. Finney, Weld's spiritual father, joined the faculty of Oberlin College in Ohio in 1835, and later became the institution's president.

Under Theodore Dwight Weld's influence, the Tappan brothers also helped organize and bankroll the American Antislavery Society in New York in 1833. Weld, one of the true firebrands of the abolitionist movement, focused on the expanding prairie regions of the Midwest, preaching the evils of slavery and asking why the British had been able to end the nefarious institution while liberty-loving America had not yet done so. Through the influence of men like Finney, Beecher, and Weld, the antislavery message spread to many Northern pulpits and congregations, gradually leading the Northern branches of the major Protestant churches to reflect a more rigorous antislavery stance.

A pivotal point in the abolitionist movement came in 1831 when Bostonian William Lloyd Garrison, inspired in part by Benjamin Lundy, began publishing his own newspaper, *The Liberator,* which Garrison biographer Henry Mayer has called "a sterling and unrivaled example of personal journalism in the service of civic idealism."[45] Garrison took the radical and uncompromising stand that all slavery must end immediately throughout the United States. In his view, there was no room for gradualism or colonization. Garrison sharply denounced the U.S. Constitution as "a covenant with death and an agreement with Hell" and went so far as to call for *Northern* secession and a repudiation of any laws, such as fugitive slave laws, that contradicted the higher natural law of God. Should the South persist in its wicked ways, the North should open wide its arms to embrace every fugitive slave seeking freedom. Garrison quickly became one of the most controversial men in America.

In an Independence Day address delivered on July 4, 1829, at the Park Street Church in Boston, Garrison's words did not follow the usual patriotic pattern for the day as he proclaimed, "Before God, I must say, that such a glaring contradiction, as exists between our creed and our practice, the annals of six thousand years cannot parallel. In view of it, I am ashamed of my country. I am sick of our unmeaning declamation in praise of liberty and equality; of our hypocritical cant about the unalienable rights of man."[46] With his ceaseless hammering at the evils of slavery through

WILLIAM LLOYD GARRISON. *Boston-based radical abolitionist speaker and journalist whose newspaper,* The Liberator, *outraged Southerners and some Northerners with its progressive views of racial equality and condemnation of the U.S. Constitution for its protection of slavery.*

The Liberator and other antislavery activities, Garrison blended the secular natural rights philosophy of Enlightenment thought with the revivalist Protestant language of repentance and conversion to produce a powerful vision of American equality.

A prominent lecturer in the abolitionist movement and initially a close ally of Garrison, fellow Bostonian Wendell Phillips, with his law degree from Harvard, was among the most active and acclaimed speakers on the abolitionist circuit. Converted to the antislavery cause in part by the murder of abolitionist publisher Elijah Lovejoy in Illinois in 1837, Phillips often wrote articles that appeared in Garrison's *Liberator* and served as a delegate from Massachusetts at London's 1840 World Anti-Slavery Convention. Phillips was an immediatist when it came to emancipation, and proved to be one of President Lincoln's harshest critics when it came to Lincoln's reluctance to push for emancipation early in his presidency.

The abolitionist movement had an ally in the small but influential circle of Boston-area intelligentsia that came to be known as the Transcendentalists. Beginning in the 1830s, this group of men and women challenged what they perceived as the wrong direction for the American democratic experiment that had become, in their view, far too centered on materialism and lacking in a fully egalitarian vision for the nation. Searching for meaning through philosophical reflection and spiritual intuition rather than through evangelical theology, this group of reformers, led by Ralph Waldo Emerson, Henry David Thoreau, Margaret Fuller, and others, came down hard on slavery. Emerson was especially active on the antislavery speaking circuit in the 1840s, including a major address in the summer of 1849 at a New England antislavery convention held in Worcester, Massachusetts attended by over five thousand people.[47]

Too often overlooked by earlier generations of historians, free blacks were deeply involved in the abolitionist movement from the beginning, but not always allowed to take the leadership roles they desired. In many cases, blacks experienced significant racism and paternalism within the white antislavery movement, attitudes they found perplexing and discouraging. Partly in response to this, blacks had organized at least fifty antislavery society chapters of their own by 1830 and let their voices be heard in literary outlets such as *Freedom's Journal*, begun in 1827 in New York City, in which the inaugural issue declared, "for too long others have spoken for us."[48] The national Negro convention movement likewise became a major outlet for black self-expression and advocacy concerning antislavery thought and the future of free blacks in the United States.

Beginning in 1830, free blacks in the North borrowed the early nineteenth-century reformist tradition of holding national gatherings of delegates to advocate for various causes and debate various strategies for implementation. State conventions were often held as well. Several national Negro conventions were held between 1830 and 1864, with five of the first six gatherings occurring in Philadelphia. These meetings, while at times including white observers and invited white speakers, were organized and implemented by and for African Americans and provided a venue "for expression of Negro thought which would not have been possible in biracial assemblies" which Howard Holman Bell has likened to the need African Americans had to develop their own churches decades earlier.[49]

The first national convention, in which Bishop Richard Allen of the African Methodist Episcopal Church played a significant leadership role along with Hezekiah Grice, was convened in September of 1830 in the City of Brotherly Love. There, about forty delegates (only two of whom were women) representing seven states took up the issue of emigration of American blacks outside the borders of the United States, a topic already having caused considerable consternation over the proposed settlement of American blacks in Liberia. The 1830 convention concluded that emigration to Liberia would be "detrimental to the general welfare of American Negroes" but agreed to support blacks who felt the need to flee from Ohio to greater safety in Canada. Later conventions would vacillate on the idea of any black emigration; in 1832 it was concluded that departure of large numbers of American blacks would have a derogatory impact on those who remained in the United States. The schemes of the American Colonization Society to send American blacks to Africa were consistently opposed, at least until 1850.[50]

Early Negro conventions also took up the idea of establishing a black college, an idea promoted by William Lloyd Garrison until 1835, when he concluded that schools with liberal interracial admission policies would be a better option. The idea of separate black schools would reemerge in the 1850s. The national Negro convention movement itself experienced a hiatus from 1835 to 1843, with smaller state and local gatherings predominating during these years. During this time a major debate arose whether the focus of such gatherings should be the abolition of slavery or efforts to advance the situation of free blacks,[51] who found their rights increasingly restricted in many parts of the North.

New black leadership within the convention movement began to emerge in the 1840s, including Frederick Douglass and Henry Highland Garnet, both of whom helped shape a more militant black argument for equality. Garnet, in a speech at the national convention of 1843 in Buffalo, went so far as to encourage slaves to rise up against their masters, labeling it "SINFUL IN THE EXTREME" to submit to slavery without a struggle.[52]

So controversial was Garnet's address that, with a less militant Frederick Douglass arguing against it, the speech failed to be included in the official minutes of the 1843 convention by a single vote.[53] Passage of the Fugitive Slave Act as part of the Compromise of 1850 promoted both a sense of despair and of militant urgency, and also rekindled the thinking among some black leaders, including Garnet, that perhaps emigration might be a viable option after all. Debates over emigration continued to be heard at national Negro conventions in the 1850s. Garnet, in fact, later served as U.S. minister to Liberia, where he died in 1882.

The final national Negro convention was held in Syracuse, New York, in 1864 and, with 144 delegates, was the most significant gathering of African American leaders during the Civil War. Although Syracuse was known as an abolitionist stronghold, white opposition to the convention was evident even before it started; Rev. Garnet was physically assaulted, thrown to the ground, and had his papers stolen from him outside his hotel by a group of antagonistic Irish Americans.[54] Following ratification of the Thirteenth Amendment in 1865, it was optimistically assumed that the national Negro convention movement would no longer be needed.

A major cause for discouragement among black, as well as white, abolitionists was that initial resistance to their cause was as strong in the North as in the South. Abolitionism was very unpopular in much of the North, where entrenched racist views and practices were threatened by abolitionist activities, often perceived as radical, whether led by whites or blacks. Even in some circles where antislavery ideas were quite popular, there was fear that abolitionist agitation could further endanger the Union. Considered idealists, fanatics, or negrophiles in the North, and unwelcome outside agitators in the South, abolitionists were able to make only painstakingly slow progress in attracting followers to their movement in the 1830s and early 1840s. But the Mexican War, the Wilmot Proviso, the Fugitive Slave Act of 1850, and other events of the 1850s would ultimately give the movement a much greater following.

The most significant black voice in the abolitionist movement preceding and during the Civil War was that of Frederick Douglass, born to a slave mother and white father and raised as a slave in Maryland. Douglass largely taught himself to read and write, and made his escape as a young man in the 1830s to Bedford, Massachusetts. In 1841 he first attended a meeting of the Massachusetts Anti-Slavery Society and gave a powerful impromptu speech which caught the attention of white abolitionists, including William Lloyd Garrison. Douglass was recruited to work for the American Anti-Slavery Society as the organization's first ex-slave, full-time

FREDERICK DOUGLASS. *An articulate and highly literate runaway slave who became the best-known African American abolitionist, renowned for his impassioned speeches and the publication of his abolitionist paper,* The North Star. *John Brown tried to recruit Douglass for his 1859 raid at Harper's Ferry, but Douglass believed it was misguided and did not participate. Douglass and Lincoln came to appreciate and respect each other, despite Douglass's early criticisms of Lincoln's caution on the slavery issue.*

lecturer. His lectures were so eloquent that doubts were expressed by many of his hearers that he had ever been a slave, which prompted Douglass to write the first of three autobiographies which then put him in danger of recapture. After fleeing to England for two years, Douglass was able to purchase his freedom with the help of friends. His time in England, where he was able to live in a setting largely devoid of racism, persuaded him that America's greatest obstacle to abolitionism was intense racism, pure and simple. Douglass settled in Rochester, New York, and began publishing an abolitionist newspaper, *The North Star,* while in great demand as an abolitionist speaker. Years later, Frederick Douglass would be unsuccessful in his attempt to dissuade John Brown from carrying out the infamous raid at Harpers Ferry, Virginia. Douglass would eventually become one of the few African Americans whom President Abraham Lincoln came to know personally and whose viewpoints mattered to Lincoln. All told, Frederick Douglass was among the most important voices, black or white, in the abolitionist movement.[55]

One of Frederick Douglass's unique contributions to the causes of emancipation and human equality was his understanding of the power of photography. Mesmerized by the possibilities of "natural" image-making through the commercialization of the daguerreotype in 1839, Douglass became "enthused over photography's social and epistemological potential."[56] In a lecture titled "Pictures and Progress" given by Douglass in Boston on December 3, 1861, he praised the ability of photography to overcome some of the racial stereotypes that white illustrators had often employed to lampoon and dehumanize slaves and other black Americans. The camera would expose the full humanity of black men and women, emphasizing the similarity of the human condition and providing an image of the justness of emancipation. Photography, Douglass optimistically hoped, would help "bring the world into . . . brotherly kindness."[57] In reality, the horrific photographic images of death and destruction from Civil War combat made a stronger impression on most white Americans than did photographs used to create sympathy for emancipation and racial harmony at the time. But in grasping the importance of photographic images to further a cause, Frederick Douglass was well ahead of his contemporaries.

Despite discouragement at the slowness of change and the seeming intractability of human prejudice, in 1839–41 the cause of abolition witnessed a small, but significant, victory for freedom and justice in the court system of the United States. The *Amistad* case demonstrated the power of slaves to take matters into their own hands, as well as the struggle within the American legal system to cope with the problem of runaway slaves on both domestic and international levels. *La Amistad* was a Cuban ship chartered by two Cuban slave dealers to transport their fifty-three newly acquired slaves from Havana to a port about three hundred miles east. These slaves, newly arrived from Sierra Leone thanks to Portuguese slavers, were imported into Cuba illegally since Spain's involvement with the slave trade officially ended in 1820. However, the law was often regarded rather lightly by Cuban and Spanish officials. Cinque, who would become the leader of the revolting slaves, was able to pick the lock on his iron collar and those of several other slaves who then found and used sugarcane knives to kill the ship's captain and other crew members. Pedro Montes, one of the two slave owners on board, had once been a sea captain and was ordered by Cinque to sail the ship back to Africa, following the morning sun. Montes steered the ship north at night, hoping to land on American shores if they were not first rescued by another ship. Desperate for food and water, Cinque ordered the ship to land at Long Island, where an American revenue ship spotted and seized the foreign vessel and towed it to New London, Connecticut. The African captives were all placed in custody in a New Haven jail. It was determined that the legal status of the captives required that the case be handled under federal jurisdiction. The question now became whether the Africans should be tried for mutiny and murder.

Presidential politics and international relations complicated the case; Democratic incumbent Martin Van Buren was eager to avoid any controversy over slavery that might further weaken his dimming hopes for reelection in 1840. Some within the American government did not want to alienate Spain, or Cuba, as many Southerners hoped that eventually Cuba would be annexed as an American slave state. The Spanish government demanded that the ship and its cargo be sent to the Spanish consul in Boston, thence to be returned to Cuba where the slaves would be tried. Complicated legal maneuverings lasted for over eighteen months with former President John Quincy Adams eventually defending the Africans, while the surviving thirty-six of them endeared themselves to many Northerners. Members of the Yale faculty were paid by a donor to provide religious instruction to the captives. The New Haven District Court concluded that the Africans had been illegally enslaved and that their mutiny to secure their freedom was not a violation of the law. The Van Buren administration appealed the case to the Supreme Court, where in February 1841 John Quincy Adams argued a brilliant defense of the Africans' case. While asserting that American law sanctioned slavery, the Supreme Court's final decision was that the Africans on board *La Amistad* had been illegally enslaved and transported to the New World and had acted in self-defense. The eight-to-one decision of the Taney Court was read by Justice Joseph Story with only Justice Henry Baldwin, a Pennsylvania jurist, in dissent.[58] Even though the five Southerners on the court, including Chief Justice Roger Taney, voted with the majority, the South was enraged by the high court's decision. Nearly three years after their capture in Africa, the survivors of *La Amistad* returned to Sierra Leone as free men.

Southern politicians, concerned about alienating Spain and losing any opportunity to annex Cuba, introduced unsuccessful legislation in both the Senate and House of Representatives requesting compensation to Spain for the value of the freed slaves. Cinque and the other Africans of *La Amistad* became heroes to the growing abolitionist movement, and copies of a portrait drawn of Cinque were sold for one dollar to finance the group's legal defense. The portrait found its way into many African American homes. One New York newspaper celebrated the Supreme Court decision in the case as "a great and glorious triumph for humanity" while a Mobile, Alabama, newspaper decried the "insult" to Spain and "no small triumph" for the abolitionist cause.[59] The controversy dramatically highlighted the issue of slavery and the still existent international slave trade at a time when the fledgling abolitionist movement was seeking to find an identity in American politics. It was, as noted in Mobile, Alabama, and elsewhere in the South, a tangible victory for the abolitionist cause. Finally, the court's decision was a rare triumph of justice for blacks in nineteenth-century America.[60]

In a turnabout situation, the *Creole* case of 1841 demonstrated the federal government's commitment to protect the property rights of American slaveholders. Sailing from Virginia to New Orleans with a cargo of 135 slaves, the *Creole* was hijacked by a group of slaves on board who ordered the ship to Nassau, where British officers ordered the slaves freed, over the strong protests of the American consul in the Bahamas. Daniel Webster, as the American secretary of state, argued for the constitutionally protected property rights of the slaveholders, even though the slaves were now outside U.S. jurisdiction in British territory that outlawed slavery. The *Creole* episode sharpened debate in Congress and elsewhere about the national nature of slavery, or whether it was really a sectional or local institution. Ohio Congressman Joshua Giddings was censured by his colleagues for introducing nine resolutions (which were all tabled) clarifying slavery as a local institution that had no validity beyond the boundaries of the slave states.[61] The Supreme Court, and indeed the American people, would have much more to argue about in coming years concerning the peculiar institution of human slavery and its place in a nation and society based on Enlightenment ideals and Christian virtues.

Slave resistance found its ultimate expression in the Civil War. When war finally came, Lincoln eventually agreed to allow former slaves, liberated by the Emancipation Proclamation, and blacks already free, to fight, not as part of a slave army in servile insurrection but as free men in a national army following the rules of war. Approximately 180,000, mostly Southern, blacks fought for the North despite unequal pay (for a time), often degrading conditions and assignments, and frequent use as expendable cannon fodder for Union assaults. Ten thousand additional black Americans served with distinction on Union naval vessels. Other blacks, women as well as men, served as a willing and effective fifth column undermining the Confederate war effort. Despite the prejudice often shown toward blacks, even by their white officers, twenty-five African Americans were awarded the Medal of Honor during the Civil War.[62]

The Confederate leadership, Jefferson Davis, Robert E. Lee, and most especially Nathan Bedford Forrest among them, refused to accept these men as men and adamantly refused to make the distinction between blacks participating in servile insurrection and those participating in an organized national army. Jefferson Davis suppressed a petition signed by some of his own generals to enlist slaves in the Confederate cause, and then in late 1864 was, by dire necessity, compelled to push the idea forward. Lee refused to exchange Union soldiers who were former slaves and managed to bring captured blacks, free and runaway alike, back with the Army of Northern Virginia after Gettysburg to be sold on the auction blocks of Richmond. Forrest allowed the wholesale massacre of black prisoners at Fort Pillow, Tennessee. While black Union regiments marched through Georgia, fought on the Red River, or sacrificed their lives in the crater before Richmond, it was only in the desperate eleventh hour of the spring of 1865 that the Confederate Congress reluctantly accepted the evidence before them that blacks might make good soldiers. Had it not been for the orders of white commanders to prevent it, the first Union regiment into the center of Richmond would have been a black unit.[63] Indeed the words of Thomas Jefferson came back to haunt the South. The South did have the "wolf by the ear," and in the end the institution that Southerners sought to preserve was turned loose to fight against them for the cause of human freedom.

CHAPTER 8

FREEDOM'S FAITH:
SLAVERY SECTIONALIZES THE SACRED

In the two decades before the Civil War, signs of the fragility of national integration and the increasing possibility of sectional separation over the institution of slavery appeared on multiple fronts. The debate over the expansion of slavery and ultimately over its elimination through some form of emancipation would escalate as America reached mid-century. The debate over the future of slavery could no longer be limited solely to politics. The poisonous passions becoming evident in the political arena were also taking root and spreading into fundamental aspects of American life, including the religious sphere. In the process, America's two largest religious denominations would be torn asunder along sectional lines, and biblical interpretation would be used both to attack and support human slavery, heating moral passions to a new level.

In the overwhelmingly Protestant America of the 1840s and 1850s, two denominations stood out as exercising the greatest influence over the religious sensibilities of the American people, North and South. The Methodists and Baptists, whose numbers had grown substantially during the Second Great Awakening, became engrossed in debates over the morality of slavery, debates which were to have far-reaching consequences for the nation at large. The Methodist Episcopal Church was at this time the largest Protestant denomination in the country. According to a census taken for the 1844 General Conference of the Methodist Episcopal Church, actual membership in that body was numbered at 1,068,525, but total Methodist adherents were estimated to be 4,500,000.[1] This was in line with the assertion of church historian Robert Baird, who noted in his 1844 treatise that, within American Protestantism, "not only do persons who have not yet become members by formal admission as such attend our churches, they form a very large part of our congregations. In many cases they form two-thirds, three-fourths, or even more."[2] The Baptist Churches in America, although lacking the structural unity and hierarchy of the Methodists, made up the second largest denomination in the country in the 1840s. Baptist membership in 1844 was reported at 704,926, with an estimated 4,000,000 total followers.[3]

With an American population of slightly over 17,000,000, according to the 1840 Census, the extent of the Methodist and Baptist imprint on American life is evident as approximately half of all Americans identified themselves with those denominations. Both denominations extended their impact across the land not only through their congregations but also through numerous educational institutions, dozens of religious newspapers and journals, and church adherents in positions of political influence. As an example of the latter, Methodism was so pervasive in Indiana that in 1852, eleven of its thirteen congressmen were Methodists, along with one Senator, and the governor.[4] Due to the significant impact of the Methodist and Baptist denominations on American life, it was not surprising that ecclesiastical division in these two groups over slavery would sharpen sectional hostility and further push the issue into the national political spotlight.

Of course, not all Americans were Methodists or Baptists, or even Protestants. The nation's small but growing Roman Catholic population took a much more detached view of slavery regarding their church's involvement. Slavery was viewed by most Catholics as a political rather than an ecclesiastical matter, with the rightful concern of the church being to save the souls of slaves, not agitate for their emancipation. The predominant American Catholic view, while not necessarily proslavery, was one of hostility toward abolitionism. Pope Gregory XVI issued an apostolic letter in 1839 which was read at the church's Fourth Provincial Council in Baltimore in December of that year, condemning the slave trade but not slaveholding itself, a point stressed by Irish-born John England, bishop of Charleston.[5] Protestant churchmen, however, tended to see much more connection between their religion, the slavery issue, and politics.

The Methodist Episcopal Church provides the most striking example of what the moral debate over slavery could do to a national religious organization. In its early years, American Methodism had taken a strong stand against the institution of slavery. Methodist leaders Francis Asbury and Thomas Coke had circulated antislavery resolutions in the 1780s, and in 1784 called for an end to admission of slaveholders into the church as "contrary to the Golden law of God . . . as well as every principle of the Revolution."[6] However, as both the church and slavery prospered and with a large contingent of membership from slaveholding areas, North and South, official church convictions against slavery were significantly weakened. The growing specter of sectional schism over slavery had been feared, but was effectively repressed, prior to the 1840s. It was only as slavery died out in the North, paralleled by a heightened moral crusade against the institution, that fractures began to appear.

The schism within the Methodist Episcopal Church began in 1843 with the formal withdrawal and establishment of the Wesleyan Methodist denomination. At a meeting in February 1843 known as the Wesleyan Anti-Slavery Convention, it was resolved, "That a sense of duty to God; the obligation resting upon us to do what we can to preserve the purity of Christianity; a love for the enjoyment of true Christian liberty, and a desire to leave this blessing as an inheritance for our children, induces us to call upon all, of the same views and feelings to unite with us in the organization of a Wesleyan Methodist Church, free from Slavery and Episcopacy."[7]

While the total number of antislavery protesters joining the Wesleyan Methodist movement did not inflict a serious blow to the size of the large Methodist Episcopal Church, it did bring the slavery issue to the forefront of the larger body. The Wesleyan Methodist movement was met with sarcasm by some, but it caused genuine concern among Methodist leaders. A sectional split in the Methodist Church had been avoided by compromising on earlier antislavery principles, but now an unanticipated Northern walkout based on antislavery moral outrage had resulted.

When the 180 delegates of the quadrennial General Conference of the Methodist Episcopal Church convened at the Greene Street Methodist Church in New York City on May 1, 1844, the controversy stirred by the Wesleyan Methodist separation was very much on the minds of the delegates. The presiding bishop's opening address made no mention of slavery, but that subject could not be kept off the convention floor for long. One of the meeting's first items of business was the appointment of a standing committee to handle the multitude of antislavery petitions flooding into the conference.[8]

Some Northern conferences had prepared statements to present to the General Conference, such as the Boston convention which affirmed, "Slave-holding is sin; that every slave-holder is a sinner, and ought not to be admitted to the pulpit or the communion; that the Methodist Episcopal Church is responsible for slavery in its pale; and that nothing short of a speedy and entire separation of slavery from the church could satisfy the consciences of honest Abolitionists, and therefore reformation or division is the only alternative." The Claremont, New Hampshire, convention stated that "the only way to prevent an entire dissolution among us as a Church, is an entire separation from the South," and there was considerable talk of a separate New England Convention free from slavery.[9] One petition, bearing 10,000 Northern signatures, demanded that the rule against the testimony of colored persons be rescinded, that no slaveholding bishops be elected, and that the General Conference take action to completely separate the church from slavery.[10]

Southern delegates claimed that they could get an equal number of proslavery petitions and signatures, but they did not desire to stoop to insulting epithets and degrading remarks, in spite of their assertion that their position was not receiving a fair hearing.[11] These remarks paralleled contemporaneous comments by their political representatives in Washington regarding the antislavery petitions reaching Congress.

Things heated up when the case of the Reverend Francis Harding of the Baltimore Conference appeared on the agenda. During the course of his ministry, Reverend Harding came into possession of five slaves and would not manumit them. Although it was a border conference, the Baltimore Conference suspended Harding for refusing to emancipate his slaves. Harding appealed the decision to the General Conference. During the debate, which dragged on for five days, Southern delegates accused the Baltimore Conference of violating the *Book of Discipline,* the Methodist handbook of doctrine, rules, and procedures, which stated that ministers were required to emancipate their slaves only if practicable and if the freed slaves could enjoy their freedom. Under Maryland law, emancipated slaves had to leave the state but, in fact, few did. Despite this argument, the vote to reverse the decision and reinstate Harding failed by a vote of 56 ayes to 117 noes.[12] An ominous division was evident as all but two Southern delegates voted in favor of Harding's appeal, and most Northern conferences voted unanimously in favor of the Baltimore Conference's decision. The case revealed the presence of two irreconcilable views of slavery among Methodists. Also, for the first time Northern antislavery delegates held a clear majority at a General Conference.

Although the case of Reverend Harding was important, it paled by comparison to the case of a bishop that appeared later at the same gathering. Bishop James O. Andrew, from Georgia, acknowledged that he had indeed become a slaveholder, legally but not willingly, through inheritance and marriage. While the character of Bishop Andrew was never questioned, and his record as a churchman was impeccable, many Northern delegates were of the opinion that, if Harding had to go because of slave ownership, should not the same fate befall a bishop? On May 22, a concise resolution was introduced by two delegates from the Baltimore Conference: "*Resolved,* that the Rev. James O. Andrew be, and is hereby, affectionately requested to resign his office as one of the bishops of the Methodist Episcopal church."[13] While not every slaveholding Methodist was being castigated by the antislavery crowd, there existed a "subtle distinction between slaveholding in the membership and in the ministry, which implied that there was a contaminating vice in it, unfit for the purest Christian functions."[14]

But the outright removal of a bishop, unprecedented in American Methodism, seemed unduly harsh even to many Northern delegates. Consequently, two delegates from Ohio softened the resolution with a more lenient recommendation that would merely ask Bishop Andrew to desist from the exercise of his office until he no longer owned slaves. Rather than appeasing the Southern delegates, however, this new resolution triggered an argument over the right of the General Conference to dictate to a bishop.[15] It was this question of church polity, not slavery itself, which many Southern Methodists later blamed, rather ingenuously, for the resulting schism.

With the Wesleyan Methodist movement of the previous year very much on their minds, what concerned Northern members of the General Conference of 1844 was the threat of a mass exodus of antislavery Methodists who were offended by a slave-holding bishop. "Expediency" was the word frequently used to justify Bishop Andrew's proposed suspension. Southern Methodists argued that the North's plea for "expediency" was merely a cover for abolitionism. During a debate that raged for another ten days, Bishop Andrew, never a lover of controversy, tried to resign but was dissuaded by other Southern delegates who convinced him that for the good of the South he must remain a bishop.[16] Several eloquent and passionate defenses of Bishop Andrew were presented by Southern delegates, including one by Reverend Crowder of Virginia, who predicted that, if Bishop Andrew were suspended, "The division of our church might follow, a civil division of this great confederacy may follow that, and then hearts will be torn apart, master and slave arrayed against each other, brother in the church against brother, and the north against the south; and when thus arrayed, with the fiercest passions and energies of our nature brought into action against each other, civil war and far-reaching desolation must be the final results. My brethren, are you prepared for this? No, I am sure you are not. Then refuse to pass this resolution now pending."[17]

Delegate George F. Pierce viewed the controversy over the bishop as part of a conspiracy, increasingly obvious, to deprive Southern ministers of their rights and to disenfranchise the Southern church. New England, Pierce maintained, was at the heart of this conspiracy, and it would be preferable for New England to secede or be expelled from the Methodist Church than for the entire South to be alienated by Bishop Andrew's dismissal due to his ownership of slaves.[18] On Saturday, June 1, 1844, the vote to suspend (but technically not dismiss) Bishop Andrew from office as long as he remained connected to slavery was passed on a strongly sectional vote of 110 to 68. The General Conference did try to appease the South somewhat by leaving Bishop Andrew's name in the *Minutes, Hymn Book,* and *Discipline,* and by voting continued financial support for him as a bishop, albeit a nonfunctioning one. During these debates, the hard-core abolitionist delegates at the conference were strangely silent. Prior to the convention, the Northern delegates had agreed that moderate antislavery delegates should carry the antislavery banner.[19] Antislavery feeling in the Methodist Episcopal Church was not limited to a wild-eyed abolitionist faction but was much more widespread, as the South painfully discovered.

On Wednesday, June 5, 1844, a Committee of Nine was charged to attempt a final settlement between North and South, or to devise a plan for the division of the church. A day later, and before the special committee could agree to any recommendations, a scathing Southern declaration was placed before the conference which labeled that body's action against Bishop Andrew as "an attempt to degrade and punish, a lawless persecution, an illegal arrest, an anomalous quasi-suspension, imperative and mandatory in form." The declaration concluded that "the South cannot submit, and the absolute necessity of division is already dated."[20] Three days later, the Committee of Nine presented their recommendations, which called for a sectional division, with Christian charity and the strictest equity, between Northern and Southern segments of the church. Local conferences in the border areas could determine their preference by a majority vote, and individual ministers could choose with which conference they would affiliate. This "Plan of Separation," as it was called, encountered little opposition and was approved on a vote of 146 to 16.[21] Peaceful dissolution could not, however, mitigate the bitter fact that one of the nation's great religious bodies had just divided because of slavery.

Reactions to the steps taken at the 1844 Methodist General Conference were overwhelmingly negative in both the North and the South, but for different reasons. It was the Northern segment of the church that was forced to bear the brunt of the criticism; the South was embittered, and many Northern church members felt that the General Conference had over-stepped its bounds and acted hastily, while abolitionists severely thrashed the Northern delegates for not purging the church entirely of slavery.[22] The more robustly antislavery Wesleyan Methodists took a particularly dim view of the Methodist Episcopal Church's situation, blaming the South for the split but highly critical of the North's weak convictions, accusing them of failing to act against slaveholding within the entire church membership, not just the ordained leadership.[23] As for the South, a bitter verbal barrage was hurled at the alleged tyranny of the Northern majority at the General Conference. Southern Methodists denounced the North's "unprincipled" desire for "political power," "fanaticism and ignorance," and "reckless disregard for the rights of the slaveholding portion of the church." Numerous Southerners also took advantage of these harangues to include their resentment of Northern opposition to the acquisition of Texas.[24]

On May 17, 1845, the Methodist Episcopal Church, South, was officially born, comprised of 1,313 ministers and 433,200 members. Delegates meeting in Louisville asserted that no religious doctrine had separated them from their Northern counterparts, but rather the issue of human slavery had created hopelessly irreconcilable differences between brethren in the faith.[25] Almost immediately following the launch of the Southern church, battles began for the allegiance of the border conferences by Northern and Southern Methodists with both groups displaying unprecedented partisan aggressiveness. Un-brotherly strife ran rampant in the border conferences, where it was not uncommon for worship services conducted by one faction within a border area to be broken up by mobs representing the opposing faction.[26] As the acrimony deepened, litigation ensued over the ownership of the property and proceeds of the Methodist book concerns, an extensive publishing and distribution arm of the denomination. Eventually, the Southern branch prevailed in the civil courts.[27]

In 1860, a further splintering of Northern Methodism occurred with the founding in upstate New York of the small but dynamic Free Methodist Church. The "free" in Free Methodism referred not only to an adamant antislavery position, but also to the belief that all levels of society ought to be welcomed into their egalitarian fellowship without anyone having to pay pew rental fees.

A similar drama played out among the Baptists. Baptists, perhaps because of their strong feelings about local church autonomy and independence of thought and conscience, had often been involved in divisive controversies, such as debates over the compatibility of Free Masonry with biblical Christianity and the antics of the failed American prophet of the last days,

William Miller. However, never did an issue produce a division as significant among Baptist brethren as that created by the slavery controversy.

Although independence of the local congregation was a fundamental tenet among Baptist churches, it was often the practice of local bodies to voluntarily unite with cooperating state or national agencies. In the case of many Baptist churches in America, cooperation at the national level was focused on another basic tenet of Baptist belief—missionary activity to foreign lands. Delegates to a national Baptist convention in Philadelphia in 1814 had organized "The General Missionary Convention of the Baptist Denomination in the United States of America for Foreign Missions." At that time, slaveholding was not mentioned as a disqualifier for missionary service as that issue had not yet become highly controversial in most Baptist circles. A triennial convention was established and given ultimate authority in matters relating to the missions organization, although no claim was made to the right of interference in the affairs of individual church congregations.[28] In 1832 the Baptists established a sister agency to cooperate in the work of domestic missions, largely involving work on the American frontier and with Native Americans. It was agreed that the American Baptist Home Mission Society and the older foreign missions agency would meet jointly every three years in a General (Triennial) Convention.

In the early decades of the nineteenth century, large numbers of slaveholders, as well as slaves, became adherents to Baptist Christianity.[29] Early antislavery efforts among New England Baptists were aimed at supporting colonization movements, but around 1830 the focus shifted to immediate emancipation, with waning interest in colonization. By the end of the 1830s, most of the Baptist ministers in the North, and most especially in New England, were taking a strong antislavery stance. Those holding this position grew more vocal as slavery threatened to expand into new territories. Many Northern congregations passed resolutions against slavery, and Baptist clergymen were often found in the leading ranks of abolitionist organizations.[30] It was argued that increased European opposition to slavery, especially after the abolition of slavery in the British Empire, would hamper the activities of missionaries who held slaves.

Prior to 1840, serious discussion of slavery was not part of the Baptists' General Convention, where Southern men usually presided and where substantial Southern financial support was deemed vital to missionary work.[31] By 1840, however, some Northern Baptist churches were beginning to withhold contributions to the General Convention on the grounds that they did not wish their funds to mingle with those of slaveholders.[32]

The situation became more serious when, in 1840, delegates representing abolitionist sentiment among Northern Baptists held the first American Baptist Anti-Slavery Convention in New York City. Also represented was a small group of Baptist missionaries in Burma (now Myanmar) who had broken off relations with the General Convention and formed the Foreign Provisional Missionary Committee in order to minister without any association with slaveholders.[33]

Antislavery activities such as this caused deep concern among Baptists in the South. In November of 1840, the Alabama Baptist Convention appointed a committee to investigate antislavery activity among Baptists at the national level and to make recommendations. The committee concluded that abolitionism was unscriptural, that it violated the national constitution, that it worked against the peace and prosperity of the churches, and that it was dangerous to national union, arguments parallel to those being made in the political sphere. Specifically it was recommended that money be withheld from national mission organizations until assurance was received that these agencies maintained no connection with abolitionism.[34] Faced with this crisis, the Acting Board of the General Convention published a circular letter later that month which declared neutrality on the slavery question and indicated that any discussion of slavery was outside the scope of the mission society's operations.[35] The Home Mission Society, also under pressure from Southern churches, felt it would be prudent to follow with their own neutrality statement concerning slavery in 1841.[36]

In the meantime, the cause of emancipation was growing ever stronger among Northern Baptists. A Baptist Anti-Slavery Convention that met in Maine early in 1841 proudly declared that 180 of the 214 Baptist ministers in that state were abolitionists. National Baptist leadership, which was of moderate persuasion on the slavery issue, feared that the 1841 General Convention planned for Baltimore would likely become the scene of intense conflict over slavery. In order to avert this, a secret caucus was convened to hammer out a compromise statement before the convention actually got underway. The document produced and signed by 74 persons disclaimed any participation in abolitionist activities and discouraged the introduction of any new requirement for missionary candidates; that is, slaveholding should not be a factor in their selection. While the 1841 General Convention did not become the storm center that had been feared, the so-called "Baltimore Compromise" angered many Northern Baptists.[37]

A degree of national Baptist solidarity had been preserved in 1841, but the following year saw clear signs of deterioration in Baptist unity.

In 1842 a proslavery faction, sarcastically calling themselves "The Provisional Foreign Mission Committee of the American Baptist Anti-Slavery Convention" distributed a leaflet to all Baptist missionaries, critical of the humiliating attitude being displayed toward slaveholders and warning that a conspiracy was in the works to form a General Convention that was essentially antislavery. While the board of the General Convention denied these charges in a circular letter, the South was unconvinced, and financial support and attendance at committee meetings on the part of Southerners tapered off significantly.[38]

Alienated by what they perceived as the General Convention's pandering to Southern interests, a group of Northern Baptists established the "American Baptist Free Mission Society" in Boston on May 4, 1843, stating that "we hereby separate ourselves now and forever from all connection with religious societies that are supported in common with slaveholding. . . . This Society shall be composed of Baptists of acknowledged Christian character . . . who are not slaveholders, but believe that slavery, under all circumstances, is sin, and treat it accordingly."[39] This new association was declared illegal by the parent body, but the damage was done—further division over slavery had been encouraged, and the triennial meeting of the General Convention of 1844 promised to be fraught with danger to continued national Baptist cooperation. Several months before the 1844 meeting began, William Lloyd Garrison predicted big trouble for the Baptists in the pages of the *Liberator,* pointing out to his readers "many indications of the troubled state of the Baptist church, on account of slavery, which we have lately noticed" and concluding that sectional division in that denomination would be fully justified.[40]

Philadelphia's First Baptist Church hosted the 1844 national Baptist gathering, consisting of 460 delegates of whom only 80 were from the South.[41] Dr. Francis Wayland, the president of Brown University and a moderate on the slavery issue, was selected to preside over the convention. Early in the proceedings, a resolution on the issue of slavery was introduced that disclaimed any position for or against slavery on the part of the foreign mission agency itself but stated that the delegates, "as individuals . . . are perfectly free, both to express and to promote our own views on these subjects in a Christian manner and spirit." This resolution passed with unanimity and without discussion.[42] The *Liberator*'s response to this action was less than laudatory, denouncing the Baptist delegates in Philadelphia as a "brotherhood of thieves" for not taking a strong antislavery posture.[43] The smaller Home Mission Society portion of the Philadelphia meeting was not as harmonious as the foreign missions segment, however. In that portion of the convention, a neutrality resolution regarding slavery was approved on a vote of 123 to 61. Tension among delegates of the Home Mission Society ran high and, on the day of adjournment, "Brother" McGinniss of New York introduced a successful resolution calling for appointment of a committee to consider the dissolution of the agency unless their constitution could be altered to allow for peace and cooperation among those with opposing views over slavery.[44]

Challenges to peace and cooperation soon arose from the South. The Georgia Baptist Convention decided to pursue a test case using the application of slaveholder James Reeves as a home missionary candidate. The Georgians' challenge to the home mission agency was to demonstrate to the South that a slaveholding missionary could actually still be appointed. The board's response was a shrewd one which resorted to a technicality, not in rejecting Mr. Reeves as a candidate, but rather in refusing to process his application. Because the Georgia Convention had deliberately and rather publicly introduced this applicant as a test case regarding slavery, it would be a violation of the neutrality resolution passed in Philadelphia to consider the case![45]

Although no slaveholders had ever actually applied for Baptist foreign missionary service, the Alabama Baptist Convention demanded to know in 1845 if the appointment of a slaveholding foreign missionary would be possible. The foreign mission board's lengthy reply concluded with the statement, "If . . . anyone should offer himself as a Missionary, having slaves, and should insist on retaining them as his property, we could not appoint him. One thing is certain, we can never be a party to any arrangement which could imply approbation of slavery."[46] What was probably the strongest written protest over this decision came in the form of a letter to the Baptist churches of Virginia by that state's Board of Foreign Missions. Ultimately, the decision was "an outrage on our rights."[47] This decision not to hire slaveholding missionaries set off a vigorous debate in the South. Southerners began in earnest to justify slavery from their interpretations of the Bible, and many claimed that slavery was a commendable method of Christianizing the Negroes in their region.

For America's Baptists, 1845 proved to be the fateful year of separation over slavery. In May, 1845, 377 Southern Baptist delegates converged on Augusta, Georgia, and agreed to form the Southern Baptist Convention and draw up a constitution. Upon its formation, the Southern Baptist Convention included about 350,000 members of whom 125,000 were Negro slaves, and about 2,000 preachers.[48] In defending their separatist actions to "the Brethren in the United States; to the congregations connected with

the respective churches; and to all candid men," the new Southern convention explained, "A painful division has taken place in the missionary operations of the American Baptists. . . . [I]n the last two Triennial conventions,
slavery and anti-slavery men began to draw off on different sides. . . . These
brethren, thus acted upon a sentiment they have failed to prove—That
slavery is, in all circumstances, sinful."[49] In what would appear to be a
flurry of sectional pride, the Southern Baptist Convention was to prosper
as the national effort had never done. In the period from 1845 to 1861,
some 750 foreign missionaries were commissioned, 15,000 converts were
reported, and over two hundred new churches were constructed throughout the world.[50] There was far less bitterness among Baptists than had
been true of Methodists after their division over slavery. The Baptist division into Northern and Southern factions was accomplished without the
bitter quarreling and lawsuits that the Methodists endured.

The divisions of the two largest Protestant denominations over issues
rooted in human bondage were early fire bells in the night in the mid-
century crisis over slavery. Both divisions occurred contemporaneously
with the political debate over the annexation of Texas, but before the even
more contentious war with Mexico, annexation of the Southwest, and the
debate ignited by the Wilmot Proviso that would have prohibited slavery
in all territory acquired from Mexico.

The events of the 1844 Methodist convention foreshadowed events to
be played out in the political arena a decade and a half later. A newfound
Northern majority had asserted itself. The abolitionists had coalesced with
more moderate Northern sentiment. The South fought back, registering its
outrage, claiming its honor, denouncing the tyranny of the Northern delegates, and threatening division if it did not get its way. Each side engaged
in self-righteous posturing. The border-state congregations were left to
somehow find a middle path, resulting in a religious civil war among and
within their congregations. Finally, the South chose separation rather than
submission to the decisions of a democratically constituted majority. No
doctrinal issue separated them. The only differences would be that Southern ministers and bishops would now be able to own slaves, Southern
Methodists would no longer be confronted by their Northern brethren
regarding the immorality of slavery, and the Southern Convention would
be "right" on issues related to slavery. A divorce based on the premise of
"let them go in peace" turned into a contentious legal fight over money
and property. The Methodist experience of 1844 was a preview of what
the national government would experience in late 1860 and 1861. The
schism in the Baptist Convention, though less contentious than the split

in the Methodist Church, was also characterized by mutual self-righteous-ness, Southern determination to put their peculiar institution ahead of any other concern, and the coalescing of Northern abolitionists and moderates into a working majority against slavery.

Through these events, the abolitionists learned the importance of hav-ing moderate allies. The South learned that, through religious separation, it could set up its own institutions free of Northern interference and moral suasion. The border states learned the true meaning of a North-South split and perhaps gained their ardor for the compromises that some would advocate in the coming years.

With the division over slavery of the two largest religious denomina-tions in the United States, the war of words throughout the nation over the moral issue of slavery intensified, and the crisis among America's Protes-tants was viewed with dread by a broad spectrum of the nation's political and religious leaders. Moral conviction concerning slavery had led to reli-gious schism, and such a disruption could not be afforded by the delicately balanced Union. The theological stance of both the Northern and Southern churches as reflected in the Sunday sermons of their ministers provided the moral underpinning of the ideologies of both sections toward slavery. The resentment by Southerners of Northerners casting accusations of South-ern sinfulness would find expression in some of their later declarations of secession. These theological debates were no mere medieval exercise about counting the number of angels on the head of a pin, but a mutually serious and ultimately deadly divination of God's will.

As the churches split and the slavery debate heated up in the 1840s, the institution that was of such concern to Lincoln would become the sub-ject of a great battle over biblical interpretation. "Slavery and Christianity are eternal opposites, as separate from each other as vice is from virtue, or heaven from hell" is how one Methodist writer expressed his feelings against the institution that bound millions of Americans, some with but the slightest hint of African descent, in perpetual bondage.[51] Many Ameri-cans in the Protestant-dominated religious landscape following the Second Great Awakening turned to the pages of the Bible for guidance in either condemning or justifying slavery. Regardless of which side of the slavery issue one favored, the vast majority of Americans professed acceptance of the moral teachings of the Judeo-Christian Scriptures. "It is a fact that the Bible is generally felt to be the standard, by which the right or wrong of human conduct must be tested," stated Luther Lee in 1855. "The almost universal circulation of the Scriptures, the fact that all the truly religious and prayerful hold them to be given by inspiration of God, and the manner in which they are appealed to by all successful debaters in our legislative halls, and by advocates in our courts of justice, proves how strong a hold they have upon the public confidence."[52] Almost immediately, the theological debate over slavery reached a juxtaposition contrasting a broader, principle-centered interpretive view of God's revelation through Scripture and a highly literal approach to biblical precepts.

In attacking the immorality of slavery, the most objective Northern theologians realized that the problem with basing their attack squarely on Scripture was the Bible's ambiguity on the subject. Although some tried, they found it impossible to point to literal passages of Scripture, rightly interpreted, that specifically set forth the doctrine that slavery was inherently sinful. In the absence of clear statements to that effect, antislavery theologians depended heavily on interpretations of broader biblical principles to support their position. Aware that they were likely to be criticized by their Southern brethren, some antislavery clergymen tried to explain, as did one Methodist writer, "We admit that slavery is not specifically prohibited in the New Testament. Neither are murder, burglary, counterfeiting, and various other high crimes. Shall we conclude that these are consistent with Christianity, because they are not particularly specified among its prohibitions?"[53]

Francis Wayland, president of the Baptist Triennial Convention at the time of its division, explained that divine truth had been revealed only gradually to mankind so that we would be able to grasp it. The words of Jesus, "I have many things to say unto you, but *ye cannot bear them now,*" no doubt could be applied to the evils of slavery. The Scriptures could not be expected to be overly specific at such an early stage in human history, or else the universality of the Bible would have been undermined. Instead of a specific prohibition against slavery and other evils, "slavery is forbidden in the Scriptures just as almost every other sin is forbidden, that is, by the inculcation of moral principles which are utterly at variance with it. Is not this the almost universal method of the teaching of the New Testament?"[54] God could not possible countenance slavery, Northern theologians argued, when even the Old Testament contained passages such as

> For the oppression of the poor, for the sighing of the needy, now will I arise, saith the Lord; I will set him in safety from him who puffeth at him.
>
> Is not this the fast that I have chosen—to loose the bands of wickedness, to undo the heavy burdens, and to let the oppressed go free, and that ye break every yoke?[55]

Even a now-beloved Christmas carol, "O Holy Night," carried an anti-slavery message when in 1855 John Sullivan Dwight rewrote the words to an older French carol to include a third verse that assumed Christ was clearly in the antislavery camp:

> Truly He taught us to love one another;
> His law is love and His gospel is peace.
> Chains shall He break for the slave is our brother;
> And in His name all oppression shall cease.[56]

A common theme in antislavery rhetoric based on biblical argument was that the law of God took priority over civil law, even the Constitution of the United States. Christians were frequently reminded by antislavery voices that they were under obligation to obey the moral law of God as contained in the Bible, even if it stood at odds with the laws of the state: "The establishment of slavery by laws does not make the system right; because God's law, which is superior to all laws, condemns slavery as wrong; and God's laws can not be repealed by the laws of man. Is it right to steal human beings or—what is the same—rob them of their liberty, convert them into property, treat them cruelly, because human laws allow or authorize this outrage? . . . Where is the *right, authority,* or *warrant* from the word of God, by which one Christian holds another as property?"[57]

Theological arguments against the evils of slavery were widely circulated and accepted in the North. It was commonly believed that slavery violated God-given natural rights of men and that every man had a natural right to his own mind and body from the time of his birth. Christianity and liberty, it was maintained, were blessings that were intended to go hand in hand: "What is Christianity in its spurious form when it comes to us divested of liberty . . . ? Such a Christianity never goes from bad to good, but invariably from bad to worse."[58] The Enlightenment's natural rights philosophy was not viewed as contrary to Scripture, but rather in harmony with it: "The Bible recognizes and asserts the existence of the natural rights of men in the strongest manner, by denouncing and threatening with punishment those who violate them. . . . Now slavery annuls and tramples on all the natural rights granted to all men by their Creator. It is a tremendous sin. . . . It is a heathenish and barbarous cruelty, utterly inconsistent with enlightened and pure Christianity."[59]

Slavery was viewed as antithetical to the dignity and authority given to mankind in the Scriptures. Man was created just a little lower than the angels, and given dominion over the entire earthly creation. Humanity was "of one blood," and this "common nature is not affected, in any respect, by the color of the skin, and difference of the hair, or by any other variety of physical formation." Such a "common nature" remains intact regardless of "every degree of intellectual development." Thus did Baptist leader Francis Wayland argue for the unacceptability of slavery, which he concluded was "wrong, utterly and absolutely at variance with the relations which God has established between his moral and intelligent creatures."[60] The prophet Malachi (2:10) bore witness of this—"Have we not all one Father? Hath not God created us? Why do we deal treacherously every man against his brother?"[61]

The institution of slavery was also attacked because of its degrading effect on the humanity of the slaves. It tended to instill in slaves certain vices such as "disobedience, lying, purloining, and eye-service [working only while being watched]."[62] The humiliation of taking men and women, created in the image of God, and placing them on the level of animals, was denounced as a great evil: "How wicked, then, is it to degrade the image of God in man, by sinking man into the degradation of a brute! God made man only a little lower than the angels; but slavery associates him with the beasts. God 'crowned man with glory and honor;' but slavery tears off the crown of honor and glory, and places him under the *yoke*."[63]

The ways in which divinely ordained family relationships were destroyed by slavery were castigated by antislavery theologians. Slavery destroyed marriages through forced separation, rape of slave women by masters and overseers, and simply by stripping the slave husband's biblical right and duty to be the head of the family. "What therefore God hath joined together let no man put asunder," quoted Luther Lee from Matthew 19:6.[64] Relationships between parents and children under slavery were not as God intended them to be, according to antislavery theologians. Children could not always obey their parents because they were subject to their masters, and this was a clear violation of biblical precepts. The commandment exhorting children to honor father and mother could not be obeyed under slavery, which "directly violates as plain a command as there is in the book of God, and if this is not a sin, the ten commandments may all be violated without sin."[65]

Antislavery theologians also maintained that slavery interfered with the exercise of Christian worship and spiritual knowledge. Although some slaves were allowed to attend worship services, it often was not on a regular basis. While a few slaves were taught to read the Bible, most were not. Countering Southern arguments that the Bible did not condemn but in fact supported slavery, Northern antislavery voices challenged Southern masters to teach their slaves to read the Bible. Charles Elliott argued, "If the relation of the master and slave is one recognized in the Bible, then the Bible is the right book to put into the hands of the slaves; and the slave should immediately be taught to read, that he may read the Bible, which, they say, sanctions slavery. If the Bible never speaks of slavery as *sinful*, then the best thing that could be done to support slavery would be to teach all the slaves to read it, that slavery may have the *sanction* of the Bible, as some pretend to affirm that it has."[66] Another biblical argument against slavery that enjoyed wide circulation was that the institution violated the Bible's law of love and the Golden Rule. Since no person would willingly reduce himself or his family to slavery, one could not subject others to slavery and maintain that the Golden Rule was being followed.[67]

A less strident antislavery religious rhetoric in the mid-nineteenth century was based on the idea that slavery was a spiritual problem that could only be solved by spiritual regeneration, not merely by legislation. Both slaves and slaveholders, this argument stressed, needed redemption from their sins by the preaching of the gospel. Emancipation would then proceed naturally, and the slaves would be prepared for it. The general public needed spiritual rebirth as well, so that they might possess the moral insight and courage to cry out against the evil of human bondage. Such a radical change in public sentiment and engagement could only "be done by moral, and not by political partisan instruments."[68] While there was no disagreement expressed among antislavery voices over the authority of Scripture in its condemnation of slavery, there were arguments over how best to proceed in the crusade against the institution. *The Christian Observatory,* published in Boston, took a dim view of abolitionist attacks on Northern churches, although the paper was clearly antislavery. The meetings of abolitionists, it was reported, are full of unbiblical "railing, cursing, and blasphemy. . . . Their holy madness expends itself mostly on the American Union and the American Church. Meanwhile the good cause of liberty slowly and surely wins its way, in spite of the fanatics of reform, and the darker and more dangerous fanatics who stake all on the perpetuation of slavery and its abominable deeds."[69]

As might be expected, Northern attacks against the immorality of slavery met with a flurry of defensive literary activity in the South. Articles, pamphlets, sermons, and books were produced in great numbers by clergy and laity alike which not only defended slavery as a necessary evil approved by God, but also portrayed it as a positive good. To the outside world slavery may have been immoral, but to the slaveholding South it increasingly came to be seen as foundational to a proper social order, and therefore it was "the essence of morality in human relationships."[70] Zeal was required of the Southern defenders of slavery, for they faced the daunting task of not only refuting Northern antislavery voices loaded with righteous indignation, but also of convincing the vast majority of their own population that did not own slaves that the institution was desirable and even essential. Many of the literary apologies for slavery showed concern for the state of Southern opinion. George F. Holmes expressed anxiety in the *Southern Literary Messenger* of 1853 about "the weak minds and vascillating fancies of many . . . slaveholders." If the slaveholders were not strong in their convictions, how could the rest of the South stand the onslaught? Because of their "lukewarm, shilly-shally convictions," they had "armed . . . Abolitionist adversaries with firebrands" which "they were hurling into the South's combustible materials."[71] A proslavery professor at the University of Alabama wrote to John C. Calhoun in 1849 that, when it came to slavery, the "many religious people at the South who have strong misgivings on this" posed a greater threat to the survival of slavery than did Northern abolitionists.[72]

In developing a moral philosophy whereby slavery could be authoritatively supported, the Bible played a central role for Southern apologists. Most of the more systematic arguments were published after the division of the churches, which could be interpreted as the Southern churches sensing a strong need to justify the schism to others, if not to themselves. The Bible became the most widely used source for proslavery arguments, and a Scriptural defense of the institution was the most elaborate and systematic of all proslavery justifications. The tremendous amount of literature produced in favor of slavery was noted by a Southern clergyman in 1854 who observed, "Our table was crowded with pamphlets and sermons, with speeches in Congress and dissertations by clergymen and laymen, on the subject of slavery. The teachings of the Bible are the most effective weapons that are used."[73]

There was a seemingly genuine attempt on the part of proslavery writers to demonstrate that theirs was the true Christian position. They were not merely defending an institution, they believed they were defending God's will for the land. A prominent Methodist advocate of slavery wrote in 1845 that, if the South could be shown the errors of their ways from the pages of the Bible, they would abandon the institution: "Only convince us that God forbids the relationship of master and slave—nay, only give us a satisfactory answer to the arguments which we adduce from Scripture to show that he sanctions it—and all the wounds of our church will be healed in an instant. . . . What you believe to be sinful, we believe to be perfectly innocent."[74]

The views of abolitionists were scorned in proslavery writings, and abolitionism itself was equated with religious infidelity. Since, in Southern eyes, abolitionists could not support their views with literal passages in Scripture, it was charged that they "have turned away from the word [of God], in despondency; and are seeking, somewhere an abolition Bible, an abolition Constitution for the United States, and an abolition God."[75]

Abolitionists were charged with going beyond the literal interpretation of the Bible and basing their antislavery positions on intuition, natural law, or some other extra-biblical moral sense. The Bible, and the Bible alone, was considered the only infallible guide by proslavery theologians. Proslavery author John Fletcher, in response to Northern antislavery theological arguments, responded by writing in 1852: "shall we not be forced, with regret, to acknowledge that there are quacks in divinity?[76] Virtually all defenders of slavery on biblical grounds were of the opinion that the institution was either of God's own creation, or at least sanctioned by his permissive will. This was convenient and necessary, for if it could be proven true, no Christian antislavery argument could stand. To answer critics who denied that a loving God could perpetrate this arrangement on mankind, slavery was depicted as part of God's plan for effectively dealing with humanity's sinful nature. But the alleged sinfulness of slavery was vigorously denied, even though some Southern clergymen acknowledged that atrocities may result from the abuse of slavery, but not because of anything inherently wrong with the system.[77]

According to proslavery theologians, countless blessings were showered upon the Negro race through the God-ordained institution of "Christian" slavery. Comparisons of the Negroes' condition in America and Africa were frequently made, and Christianized American Negroes, albeit in a state of bondage, always came out superior to the "noble savage"; American slaves enjoyed unprecedented prosperity, tremendous population growth, and great moral and mental strides.[78] When the true benefits of slavery were properly understood, "slavery will be hailed by the good, the pious, and godly-minded, as an emanation from the Divine Mind, portraying a fatherly care, and a watchful mercy to a fallen world."[79] "We have never known a negro," wrote the Rev. Thomas C. Thornton, "who professed to be an Atheist, an Infidel, a Unitarian, or a Universalist, though we have been acquainted with at least one hundred thousand of these sable sons of Africa."[80] It was argued that, compared with apostasy in the North, the slave South had kept the purity of the faith. What better justification could a Christian have for the existence of slavery?

In reality, much of the proslavery theological argument was based on pure and simple racism. Some Southern theologians parted company with their Northern brethren on the origins of all humanity in Adam and Eve, proclaiming that Adam and Eve's history should be understood as producing the line of Christ and all white people, while other races had separate origins.[81] But the most commonly held view of the origin of the races was that the sons of Noah—Shem, Ham, and Japheth—were the fathers of the three primary races. Ham, the supposed father of the black race, was held responsible for reducing his people to a state of bondage by means of his disrespectful conduct toward his father. As a result, Noah proclaimed a God-inspired curse on the posterity of Ham, predicting that they would be servants of their brethren, as recorded in Genesis 9:25–27. This curse on Ham's descendants was the ultimate basis on which religious Southerners justified slavery.[82]

The schisms in the churches, often ignored or relegated to the back-waters of American ecclesiastical history, were recognized by contemporaries, North and South, as an early and significant division over slavery. North and South began to go different ways not merely over slavery's expansion or emancipation, but over the more fundamental question: is slavery morally and religiously justified? How one answered this question was fundamental to one's approach to slavery and to the political issues and events that swirled around it in mid-nineteenth-century America. Insufficient attention has been paid to the profound effect that these ecclesiastical schisms and theological debates had on contemporary religious thinking and their impact on American political thought.

Southern pulpits continued to ring out with their traditional viewpoint that slavery was biblically sanctioned. From the Presbyterian pulpit of Woodrow Wilson's father, the Rev. Joseph R. Wilson in Staunton, Virginia, to the preacher at a Baptist tent meeting at a Texas frontier outpost, slavery was praised as a moral good. In the South, there was no need for debate or handwringing over human bondage. On the other hand, free and open debate on the issue of slavery emerged in the churches of the North. These Northern churches, freed from the restraints of maintaining a national fellowship, became increasingly strident and unforgiving regarding slavery. While most pulpits were not yet abolitionist strongholds, ministers began to press the underlying abolitionist theme of slavery as intrinsically evil along with the old Puritan concept of communal sin and judgment. These moral concerns spread to the pulpits and pews of other Northern denominations, leading to severe division, if not outright schism, in America's other two major Protestant denominations, the Presbyterians and the Episcopalians.

These antislavery themes and the accompanying religiously charged rhetoric would reverberate in the Wilmot Proviso, the Free Soil Party, the struggle for Kansas, and John Brown's raid on Harpers Ferry. Harriet Beecher Stowe, the daughter of a Connecticut Presbyterian minister, Lyman Beecher, gave these ideas their most popular literary expression in her novel *Uncle Tom's Cabin*. Abolitionist ideas about the immorality of slavery, if not their calls for outright emancipation, were thus sanctified and spread to audiences well beyond the reach of Garrison's *Liberator* and other abolitionist tracts. Meanwhile, Southern clergymen continued to reassure Southern slaveholders that God had literally decreed perpetual bondage for the black man as part of a benevolent divine plan.

With opposing camps composed of faith-based believers, strong moral convictions would no doubt lead to growing political demands. The westerner Lincoln, the states' rightist Calhoun, the Northern Whig Webster, and

HARRIET BEECHER STOWE. *After the death of her young son, she recommitted her life to God, reflecting on the heartbreak that slave mothers experienced as their living children were taken from them. The resulting literary work was* Uncle Tom's Cabin, *an instant best seller reviled in the South and the most powerful piece of antislavery literature to emerge from the antebellum era.*

the border Whig Clay each rightly viewed these denominational fractures along sectional lines with genuine alarm. In April of 1845, Clay wrote regarding the Methodist division, "Indeed scarcely any public occurrence has happened for a long time that gave me so much real concern and pain as the menaced separation of the Church, by a line throwing all the Free States on one side, and all the Slave States on the other. I will not say that such a separation would necessarily produce a dissolution of the political union of these states; but the example would be fraught with imminent danger, and, in co-operation with other causes unfortunately existing, its tendency on the stability of the Confederacy would be perilous and alarming."[83]

In his final speech before the Senate in 1850, Calhoun decried the effects of the division of the churches as he noted: "It is a great mistake to suppose that disunion can be effected by a single blow. The chords which bound these states together in one common union are far too numerous and powerful for that. Disunion must be the work of time." Calhoun continued, "The first of these cords which snapped, under its [agitation over slavery's] explosive force, was that of the powerful Methodist Episcopal Church. The numerous and strong ties which held it together are all broken, and its unity gone. . . . The next cord that snapped was that of the Baptists, one of the largest and most respectable of the denominations. . . . If the agitation goes on, the same force, acting with increased intensity . . . will finally snap every cord, when nothing will be left to hold the states together except force."[84]

In his debate with Stephen A. Douglas in Alton, Illinois, on October 15, 1858, Abraham Lincoln asked, "But does not this question [slavery] make a disturbance outside of political circles? Does it not enter the churches and rend them asunder? What divided the great Methodist Church into two parts, North and South? . . . Has any thing ever threatened the existence of this Union save and except this very institution of slavery?"[85]

In the end, the sectional religious arguments based on divergent and contradictory views of God's will reinforced each section's self-assurance that God was on their side, a logical and theological impossibility that Lincoln later pointed out in his Second Inaugural Address.[86] God-fearing Americans on both sides would all too soon forget about the God of love and mercy, and commit and then justify the horrors of civil war in hundreds of incidents large and small across the land. It was no aberration that John Brown was revered by many in the North for attempting to ignite servile insurrection at Harpers Ferry, or that Nathan Bedford Forrest was defended in the South for his massacre of black Union troops at Fort Pillow, Tennessee.

The necessary intellectual precondition for change, the acceptance of the idea of slavery as a moral evil, was gaining momentum in the North while Southern pulpits reassured their congregations that slavery was a positive, divinely sanctioned good. As a result of the clarion call from Northern pulpits and presses, the conversation in the late 1840s and 1850s moved closer to, but short of, national emancipation, and focused on containing slavery in the states where it currently existed.

CHAPTER 9

SLAVERY AND MANIFEST DIVISION: THE MEXICAN CESSION, FREE SOILERS, AND THE COMPROMISE OF 1850

At the time when Northern churchgoers began to internalize the antislavery sermons delivered from their pulpits and published by their book houses, a new phase in the national debate over slavery was commencing. While segments of the still marginal abolitionist movement were calling for slavery's immediate end, the main national political debate centered on the question: would slavery be contained where it existed, or would it expand into new territories? The annexation of Texas, America's subsequent war with Mexico, and the treaty that followed became the catalysts for this debate. The Mexican War, instead of uniting the American people against a common enemy, proved highly divisive because, in the minds of many, North and South, the war's purposes were linked to the future of slavery. Many Northerners found the war distasteful, even abhorrent, both for its insufficient moral justifiability and the potential for slavery's expansion. Hoping for slavery's eventual demise, they viewed the opening of newly obtained territory to slavery as a giant step in the wrong direction. Many Southerners were equally convinced that the future of their way of life depended on just such an expansion of slavery into new territories, allowing for the opportunity to "diffuse" their ever-growing slave population. Some Americans, North and South, opposed any expansionist designs on more heavily populated Mexican territory for racist reasons of feared amalgamation with large numbers of "the half-breeds and mongrels of Mexico," the thought of which was "revolting."[1] Religious animosity toward Catholicism by Protestant America also played a role in the opposition to expansion and absorption of Catholic populations.

The expansionist platform of the Democratic Party aided the election of James K. Polk, a Tennessee slaveholder and expansionist protégé of Andrew Jackson, in 1844. The party's platform called for a favorable settlement of the Oregon boundary with Britain and the annexation of Texas, but did not mention California or other Mexican territory. Neither did Polk mention California in his inaugural address, although he soon sent scouts, including John C. Fremont, to check out conditions, including reported insurrections, in that remote and relatively unpopulated region of Mexico.[2] Relations between the United States and Mexico deteriorated precipitously, especially given Polk's oft-stated goal of "re-annexing" Texas and his not so secret obsession with acquiring California. Furthermore, Polk asserted that the Rio Grande, not the Nueces River as claimed by Mexico, was the border recognized by the United States between Texas and Mexico. Polk's claim was based in part on the treaty that Sam Houston and the Texas Republic had forced the Mexican president, General Antonio Lopez de Santa Anna, to sign under duress in 1836, and also on the debatable claim of some Southerners that Texas as far as the Rio Grande should have been included in the Louisiana Purchase.[3] The Adams-Onis Treaty of 1819 with Spain, however, had given up any American claim to Texas. Polk felt this had been a highly unfortunate surrender of American interests; thus he called for the "re-annexation" of Texas.[4]

American citizens' claims against Mexican piracy and other damages totaled millions of dollars, and new American claims against a succession of essentially dysfunctional and unstable Mexican governments were piling up fast, providing another source of friction between the two nations. President Polk envisioned acquisition of sparsely inhabited California as part of a bargain in exchange for the United States assuming these Mexican obligations. This was not a new idea, having been initially floated by the American ambassador to Mexico in 1842.[5] Both of Polk's objectives in the Southwest, acquisition of California and annexation of the former Mexican province of Texas, now an independent republic run by American expatriates, were totally unacceptable to the Mexican government.

As late as May 1846, President Polk continued to state publicly that all he wanted from Mexico was to secure the Texas–Mexico border. However, Southern leaders, especially John C. Calhoun, saw tremendous opportunity for the expansion of slave territory as a result of both the already consummated annexation of Texas and further territorial concessions that might be wrung from a defeated Mexico, aspirations of which President Polk was

JAMES K. POLK. *Tennessee slaveholder elected president in 1844, whose aggressively expansionist "Manifest Destiny" policies greatly increased American territorial holdings, including much of Mexico. As a result, the issue of whether to allow the expansion of slavery into new American territories significantly escalated North-South tensions.*

not unaware. The South believed it needed more territory and additional slave states to maintain political power within the federal government and for greater security in the event of a sectional break with the non-slave states. The annexation of Texas and the acquisition of additional territory through conquest in the Southwest could fulfill both objectives. Governor James Hammond of South Carolina predicted, "With Texas the slave states would form a territory large enough for a *first rate power* and one . . . that would flourish beyond any on the Globe."[6] Some leaders, such as former Texas President Mirabeau Lamar, had envisioned a Texan Empire stretching west to the Pacific and deep into Mexico. One of the South's greatest fears was that, if the United States did not annex Texas, the British, now opposed to slavery but ever on the prowl for empire and influence, might hold sway over the Lone Star Republic and eventually seek to abolish slavery there in exchange for financial assistance. Despite repeated British denials of any such plan, some Southern politicians continued to be suspicious.[7] Towards the end of the Mexican War, many Southern leaders would put aside racial and religious concerns about the Mexican population and advocate the annexation of all of Mexico to advance slavery's expansion.

Northern Whigs, including Daniel Webster and Abraham Lincoln, had grave misgivings about the annexation of Texas and a war with Mexico, as did Henry Clay, a Kentucky Whig with presidential ambitions. But James K. Polk had a better sense of public opinion on the matter, and won the presidency in good measure because of his stand favoring Texas annexation. For Polk, annexation would be the fulfillment of a campaign promise, and good for the country. The American annexation of Texas was actually arranged under departing President John Tyler (a Virginia slaveholder) and implemented early in Polk's term. This action became in no small way responsible for the eventual outbreak of hostilities between the United States and Mexico. It was not surprising that war was declared in the spring of 1846 after Polk proclaimed that American blood had been shed on American soil during an April 26 attack by Mexican forces in the disputed border region, provoked by a large American troop concentration (ordered into this provocative position by Polk) on what Mexico considered its sovereign territory.

In the meantime, Polk abandoned his slogan of "54°40' or fight" over Oregon, which he had used to garner Northern votes. He signed a treaty with the British that split the region the North coveted at the forty-ninth parallel. He instead pushed a more vigorous expansion program to benefit the South. In the summer of 1846, after a few months of war and disingenuous policy statements that the government had no plans for postwar territorial expansion into Mexican territory, President Polk sought an appropriation of two million dollars from Congress in hopes of encouraging the Mexican government to cease hostilities sooner rather than later, and for the purchase of territory from Mexico. This appropriation measure ultimately failed, but it provided the kindling for the fiery debates over the expansion or containment of slavery that raged during the next decade and a half. Concerned by Polk's apparent duplicity regarding Oregon and the acquisition of additional Mexican territory and its implications, Democratic freshman Congressman David Wilmot of Pennsylvania saw in the president's appropriation bill an opportunity to strike a blow against the extension of slavery.

Wilmot was no abolitionist, but he and growing numbers of other Northerners feared the Southern "Slave Power conspiracy."[8] One historian has noted that "his motivation was not over black bondage but rather a reverence for the free toil of his own kind."[9] Wilmot had initially supported President Polk's war policy, but was determined that the war with Mexico should not turn into a proslavery land grab. His proviso stated that slavery would not be allowed in any territory acquired from the war with Mexico, a nation where slavery had ostensibly been abolished in 1829. The appropriation bill with Wilmot's proviso attached won narrow passage in the House, but predictably failed to win approval in the Senate. President Polk, a proslavery man possessing a broader national outlook than many of his Southern colleagues, was irked by Wilmot and his proviso less for the ban on slavery than because it slowed the process of ending the war with Mexico. The Wilmot Proviso would be raised up again in December 1846 as the war was coming closer to an end. This time, New York Democratic Congressman Preston King picked up the banner initially raised by Wilmot, with the same result of passage in the House and defeat in the Senate.[10]

National political parties were strained by the Wilmot Proviso and its antislavery implications. As the 1848 presidential election approached, cracks appeared in both major parties along sectional lines after the Proviso's resurrection in late 1846. Some Northern Democrats, seeing presidential aspirant John C. Calhoun as so extremely proslavery as to be unelectable, attempted to distance themselves from his expressed opinion in the Senate in opposition to the Wilmot Proviso that all new territory should be open to slavery and every new state should potentially be a slave state.[11] In sharp contrast, Van Buren Democrats in the North became increasingly obsessed with stopping the spread of slavery as their top priority, and as a consequence came to be known as "Barnburners" by their political rivals, the "Hunker" Democrats. The Barnburners, it was charged, would risk burning down the Democratic barn to eliminate the proslavery rats.[12]

Mainstream leadership in both parties saw the necessity of remaining nationally viable, and turned to presidential candidates in 1848 who would be as noncontroversial as possible on the issue of slavery. Michigan Senator Lewis Cass, waving the banner of "popular sovereignty" (later picked up by Stephen Douglas) to determine the future of slavery in newly won territories, claimed the Democratic nomination. The Whigs, bypassing political veterans Henry Clay and Daniel Webster, chose as their candidate Mexican War hero and slaveholder General Zachary Taylor, an amazingly nonpolitical candidate for such high office with no known political views about anything who had, in fact, never voted in his life. Thus did both Democrats and Whigs attempt to appeal to a national constituency in 1848, hoping to keep the future of the Mexican Cession and its relationship to slavery from splintering the country, as well as their respective parties.

The political dynamics of 1848 were shaped by antislavery politics from earlier in the decade. The antislavery movement, while certainly maintaining a moral dimension after the 1830s, turned increasingly to the political arena for achievement of its objectives. In the 1840s, abolitionists had formed alliances with moderates to oppose slavery in the debates that split the churches. Meanwhile, the abolitionists began to look for similar coalitions in the political arena. As Eric Foner has aptly noted, "Although the transition [from moral to political crusade] was painful for many antislavery men, the movement turned almost entirely to political action in the 1840's and 1850's."[13] As an example of this change in strategy, the first serious abolitionist political party, the Liberty Party, was founded in New York in 1839. While committed to political action, the new party initially persisted in the moralizing ways of earlier abolitionists, containing in its leadership more preachers than politicians. The Liberty Party succeeded in attracting a mere 7,000 votes for James G. Birney, its presidential candidate in the 1840 election, but it was a start. However, the Liberty Party did make some inroads with Yankee Whigs as well as with some Northern Democrats, to Martin Van Buren's consternation in 1840.[14] Though not ready for prime-time presidential politics, the Liberty Party aided, in a small way, the Whig Harrison's victory over Van Buren. In 1844 the Liberty Party again nominated Birney as their standard bearer, and this time he garnered 60,000 votes, doing well enough to rob Whig candidate Henry Clay of the presidency by taking 15,000 votes in New York, allowing Polk to take that state narrowly and thus win the presidency for the Democrats.

Salmon P. Chase, two decades later a member of Lincoln's cabinet and later still chief justice of the U.S. Supreme Court, was an early member of the Liberty Party and was instrumental in guiding it to more effective political actions. The practical Chase sought to deflect the party from a zealous moralistic crusade for immediate abolition and to refocus on a more strategic political agenda of legally challenging slavery wherever it could be challenged—not in individual states where it currently existed, but in areas where the federal government held sway—in the nation's capital and the territories, as well as the interstate slave trade and the national fugitive slave law. Chase even went so far as to suggest, without success, that the Liberty Party disavow public identification as an "abolitionist" party, even though eventual abolition was the hope of virtually every party adherent.[15] Despite Chase's ultimate failure to remake the Liberty Party into something less extreme and more effective, it was his voice and pen "which gave body and popular consistency to the doctrines of the Liberty party" according to one New England newspaper.[16]

One key Liberty Party strategy was to hammer away at the existence of the "Slave Power"—thought to be between 250,000 and 350,000 slaveholders in the South, perhaps 1 percent of the nation's population, whose views, it was claimed, completely dominated Southern life and politics, and whose influence was far too strong in the national government. This slaveholding oligarchy, with a few Northern politicians under their spell, had, in the eyes of a Liberty Party paper in Michigan, achieved "an overwhelming political monopoly . . . which by holding the balance of power in the nation, has long rigidly controlled its offices, its finance and all its great interests, and has thus tyrannically subverted the constitutional liberties of more than 12,000,000 of nominal American freemen."[17]

But in the early and mid-1840s, it would take more than the Liberty Party to place slavery on the center stage of national politics. The two major parties, Whigs and Democrats, would have their own internal debates, and the whole political spectrum would be reconfigured with the issue of slavery emerging more and more at the center of controversy. The selection of General Zachary Taylor as the Whig presidential candidate in 1848 was more than many antislavery Whigs could bear. He may have been a military hero, but Taylor also owned slaves and a plantation in Louisiana. Zachary Taylor's nomination shocked Horace Greeley, a Clay supporter, who called the Whig convention "a slaughterhouse of Whig principles."[18]

Antislavery Democrats were having struggles of their own in 1848. New York "Barnburner" Democrats, unhappy with the nomination of Lewis Cass at their party's Baltimore convention, had walked out and returned to New York City to the cheers of thousands of antislavery supporters. In June of 1848 at Utica, New York, the state's antislavery Democrats, along with a few antislavery Whigs and other antislavery Democrats from as far away as Wisconsin and Massachusetts, met to nominate their own presidential candidate—the old political warhorse and former president, Martin Van Buren. These renegade Democrats and others aligned with them wrote a platform that supported the Wilmot Proviso and attacked slavery as "a great moral, social, and political evil—a relic of barbarism which must necessarily be swept away in the progress of Christian civilization."[19]

The Liberty Party, meanwhile, had nominated John P. Hale for the presidency. However, seeing opportunity in the formation of a larger political coalition of antislavery forces, New York antislavery Democrats, some antislavery Whigs, and Liberty Party faithful met in Buffalo, New York, in August of 1848. The Liberty Party withdrew their candidate and joined in the formation of the Free Soil Party with Martin Van Buren as their presidential nominee. For vice-president, the Buffalo convention nominated Charles Francis Adams, son of former President John Quincy Adams. Hale would again have his chance as a presidential candidate in 1852, the "last hurrah" of the Free Soil Party before it amalgamated with the new Republican Party a couple of years later.

The centerpiece of the Free Soil Party platform was support for the Wilmot Proviso, banning extension of slavery into any of the territory obtained from Mexico. The result of the 1848 election was almost predictable—"Old Rough and Ready" Zachary Taylor, the Whig candidate, kept his political opinions (assuming he had any) to himself and won the presidency rather easily. The Free Soil Party made its mark by assuring the defeat of mainstream Democrat Lewis Cass, and it also elected a few members to Congress, including Salmon P. Chase as a U.S. senator from Ohio. Hence, the Free Soil Party represented the first major political unification of antislavery sentiment across the political landscape of the free states, another fire bell ringing in the darkening political debate.

A convergence of events presented Congress with an intensified crisis between proslavery and antislavery camps in the period 1848–50. The Treaty of Guadalupe Hidalgo ending the war with Mexico in February 1848, the presence of a substantial free population in New Mexico, the territorial claims of Texas to much of eastern New Mexico, the 1846 settlement of the Oregon question opening up that region for future free states, the discovery of gold in California, the population boom in that region triggered by the Gold Rush, and the subsequent California request for statehood as a free state all worked to create an atmosphere of animosity and crisis that threatened the very fabric of the Union. All of these issues brought debate over the future role of slavery to the forefront.

The Congress that met in 1849 was somewhat transitional in nature and still contained a few of the giants of the early Republic nearing the end of their political careers. Henry Clay, Daniel Webster, Thomas Hart Benton, Lewis Cass, and even the strident states' rights advocate John C. Calhoun, born and raised in the post-Revolution era of nation-building, were men who had dedicated their lives to the success of the young nation. Alongside of them, younger partisan sectionalists including Jefferson Davis, Robert Barnwell, David Atchison, Salmon P. Chase, Charles Sumner, William Seward, Hannibal Hamlin, and the ever-ambitious Stephen A. Douglas made their way into the political limelight that they would dominate in the coming decade. These younger men had received their political tutoring not from Madison and Monroe, but rather from the divisiveness of Jackson, the chicanery of Van Buren, and the uncompromising duplicity of Polk. The giants of accommodation and compromise were being replaced by the ideologues of confrontation.

Compromise regarding slavery played a significant role in American national politics, going back to the Constitutional Convention of 1787. That body found grounds for sectional compromise on the continuation of the slave trade, the counting of slaves for representational purposes, and a policy toward fugitive slaves. Later, Congress found a way to compromise regarding slavery and new territories; lands acquired from France in 1803 and Spain in 1819 were affected by the Missouri Compromise of 1820. From that compromise, both free and slave states had emerged.

Now it was time to divide up the territories and their resources derived from Polk's settlement of the Oregon question and the Mexican Cession. The Oregon Territory would unquestionably evolve into free states, tipping the political balance of power further on the side of the North. Yet when a wealthy black named, coincidentally, George W. Bush, attempted to settle in Oregon in 1844, he was denied residency and forced to move north of the Columbia River. While slavery was banned from the territory, free blacks were not legally admitted to Oregon until 1861.[20] California not only claimed the mineral rich Sierra Nevada but also the great harbors of San Francisco and San Diego, blocking the emergence of slave states on the Pacific Coast. The Mormons occupied lands in the northern Mexican Cession, and Hispanics who opposed slavery lived in the Southern portions of the territory. Technology, in the form of the Deere plow and the McCormack reaper, was suddenly turning the plains north of the

Missouri Compromise line into useful farmland. Where the new territories did not have arable land for farming, they had vast mineral resources to be exploited. A new territorial division between free and slave states was now necessary. Southern survival, many held, depended on Southern expansion to counter Northern free-state expansion.

Meanwhile in the North, there were those wishing to justify their forefathers while ignoring their own involvement both in the enslavement and trading of Africans. A Northern myth involving half-truths was being created that their forefathers had been compelled to accept evil bargains with the Slave Power for the sake of national unity. In reality, the Founders were generally men of considerable probity and, while some objected to the continuation of slavery in light of the principles of the Revolution, most accepted the constitutional arrangements as supportable, albeit amoral, political deals that were essential to creating a nation. The myth suited the commercial and industrial interests of the North that saw the mineral wealth of the West as the needed capital to fuel its expansion.

All of these factors turned the slavery debate in a more rancorous direction. Henry Clay, the "Great Pacificator" who had been instrumental in the Missouri Compromise nearly thirty years earlier, was determined to do all he could to save the Union from being again "at the edge of the precipice"[21] over the issue of slavery. When Clay arrived back in Washington to take his Senate seat at the start of the Thirty-first Congress on December 3, 1849, congressional politics were highly divisive and chaotic with sectional division over slavery at the center of the maelstrom. As a result of the 1848 elections, no party held a majority in the House of Representatives, with twelve Free Soilers and one Nativist holding the balance of power. Membership in the House now included 139 free-state representatives and 90 slave-state representatives, and contained an unusually large group of young freshmen legislators. Third-term Representative Robert Toombs of Georgia made a dismal assessment of the new Congress, which he said contained "the worst specimens of legislators I have ever seen here, especially from the North on both sides [regardless of party]. There is a large infusion of successful jobbers, lucky servingmen, parishless parsons and itinerant lecturers among them who are not only without wisdom or knowledge but have bad manners, and therefore we can have little hope of good legislation."[22] When Daniel Webster returned from Massachusetts to take up his Senate seat in the new Congress, he was surprised at all the "excitement & inflammation on the subject of Slavery [and] Dissolution [of the Union]" but concluded that "All this agitation, I think, will subside, without serious result. . . . [T]he Union is not in danger."[23] There were those, including Henry Clay, who thought otherwise.

HENRY CLAY. *A Kentucky Whig politician with a national following and presidential ambitions, Clay held moderate antislavery views, including colonization, which had a great influence on Abraham Lincoln. Known as "The Great Compromiser," Clay's efforts were foundational for the Compromise of 1850.*

The opening of Congress had been prefaced by two significant and virtually simultaneous events on opposite sides of the continent. Just as the delegates to California's Constitutional Convention were completing their free-state document in Monterey and preparing for a ratification vote, Southern state representatives were convening a meeting on October 1, 1849, in Mississippi, largely at the instigation of South Carolina Senator John C. Calhoun, designed to create Southern unity and a strategy to protect Southern interests. At the heart of its agenda, the gathering known as the Mississippi States' Rights Convention was concerned about the Wilmot Proviso, or some similar measure, eventually being approved by a Northern-dominated Congress. Calhoun had warned on the floor of the Senate earlier in 1849 that "the agitation of the subject of slavery would, if not prevented by some timely and effective measure, end in disunion." But such division was not inevitable if Northern men would "do justice by conceding to the South an equal right to the acquired territory."[24] While initially stating their devotion to the Union, the delegates denied that Congress had the right to prohibit slavery in any American territories, or the right to abolish slavery in the District of Columbia, or in any way support the emancipation of slaves. The possibility of secession was eventually put on the table if slavery were to be barred from any territory won from Mexico. The group called for a larger meeting of all the slave states to be held in Nashville in June of 1850.[25]

Within this atmosphere, the election of a Speaker of the House of Representatives in December 1849 became tumultuous and bitterly sectional, with neither Democrats nor Whigs in their own caucuses able to transcend North-South tensions and reach a consensus. The front-running candidate for Speaker on the Democratic side, Georgia Representative Howell Cobb, concluded after his own party's three-day caucus that "the slavery question . . . so completely alienated north from south" that Democratic Party unity was now "utterly impossible."[26] After three weeks of debate, thirty nominated candidates, and sixty-three ballots, Howell Cobb was finally elected as Speaker of the House on a vote of 102 to 99.[27]

The three-time unsuccessful presidential aspirant Henry Clay, now at age seventy-two still highly respected throughout most of the country and beset by his status as a political celebrity wherever he went, felt responsible for doing something to prevent this impending national train wreck over slavery. Clay's strategy was to craft a set of proposals dealing with post–Mexican War issues which Clay believed were connected to each other and inextricably related to slavery. His proposals included eight resolutions, which can be condensed to six major components: (1) the creation of a territorial government for Utah, (2) the settlement of territorial claims against New Mexico by Texas in exchange for the assumption of that state's debt, (3) the admission of California as a free state with the boundaries established by the Monterey convention in 1849, (4) the creation of a territorial government for New Mexico, (5) the passage of a stronger fugitive slave act, and (6) the abolition of the slave trade in the District of Columbia. Each component of the package had its peculiar challenges.

The Salt Lake City area had been settled by disaffected Mormons who willfully entered Mexican territory to escape the jurisdiction of the mistrusted United States. Founded in upstate New York, the Mormon faith (officially known as the Church of Jesus Christ of Latter-Day Saints) contained beliefs that placed it outside the pale of other established Christian churches, as well as the law. Their supplemental scriptures, the Book of Mormon, the practice of polygamy, their communal exclusiveness, their theocratic and hierarchical practices in political and religious spheres, and their claim to the territory of Deseret which took in a wide swath of the Southwest from the Rockies to the Sierras and deep into the province of New Mexico all served to cause concern among non-Mormons and Mormons alike when the territory of Utah became part of the United States. Geographically, Utah was not favorable to slavery, and Mormons did not practice it. However, Mormon belief at that time (and since revised) saw blacks as inferior to whites and thus unable to enjoy the benefits of the priesthood shared by all white male Mormons. The Utah territorial bill was silent on the subject of slavery, but this was not unusual in such legislation. The difference was that, prior to 1850, it was assumed that territories would be slave or free as determined by the provisions of the Northwest Ordinance or the Missouri Compromise, and neither statute applied here. While most of the Utah territory was located north of the Missouri Compromise line separating free and slave territory, the line had not been extended that far west.

Generous territorial claims also affected the issue of the boundaries of Texas. In 1836, the Texas Congress laid claim to all the territory between the Sabine River and the Rio Grande. The United States went to war with Mexico in part to assert this claim. Texans, however, claimed the land east of the Rio Grande all the way to its source. Many Southerners claimed that Texas was part of the Louisiana Purchase and should have never been ceded by the Adams-Onis Treaty of 1819. A northern boundary of the Texas Panhandle would eventually be set at 36° 30', the Missouri Compromise line, where it remains to this day. That left eastern New Mexico in dispute—an area that Texas had attempted to conquer but had failed.

To complicate matters, the proud and defiant Comanche people controlled a large swath of territory in West Texas known as Comancheria, making Texan control of New Mexico impractical.[28] Texas had incurred debts during its period of independence, which under Clay's proposal would be assumed by the United States government if Texas would give up its claims to eastern New Mexico. Such an assumption of state debt, however, ran contrary to stated Democratic Party principles.

Generous territorial claims also played a role in California's application for statehood. The Monterey convention that drew up a state constitution in the fall of 1849 drew extensive boundary lines from the Oregon territory to the newly drawn Mexican border and east beyond the Sierra Nevada. The only reason Baja California was not included is that, during the Mexican War, American scouts had visited Baja and determined it to be worthless desert that Mexico might as well be allowed to keep. A key feature of California's proposed 1849 constitution was the prohibition of slavery. California's miners did not want to be humiliated at the prospect of laboring for gold alongside slaves who were doing the same work for their masters. Beyond that, blacks, whether they were slave or free, were simply not wanted by much of California's white population. Racism again trumped justice, although the end result produced a "free" state— initially largely "free" of persons of African descent. If California became the nation's thirty-first state, however, it would upset the exact balance of fifteen slave states and fifteen free states, a situation causing grave concern among Southern leaders, especially without a new slave state on the horizon. Southern proposals to divide the state into a free Northern California and slave Southern California were not well received by either most Californians or the Northern states' representatives in Congress. A geographically large free California would balance out a geographically large slave Texas, and so the proposed California boundaries were left alone.

New Mexico was now ready for territorial status or statehood. While the largely Hispanic population of the region desired immediate statehood as a free state, a move favored by President Taylor,[29] Congress was unready to grant the region more than territorial status without mentioning the issue of slavery. Although a few Texans had settled with their slaves in the Mesilla Valley, New Mexico's geography was generally hostile to an economy based on slavery. In the final territorial bill, for Utah as well as New Mexico, no mention was made regarding slavery, either allowing it or prohibiting it. The Missouri Compromise line was not extended westward.

The fifth element in Henry Clay's set of proposals was an amended and tougher fugitive slave law. Fugitive slave laws were nothing new in

1850—the young nation had such legislation generations earlier; Article IV in both the Articles of Confederation and the Constitution of the United States authorized Congress to pass such laws on a national level, and indeed the Congress had done so with little debate in 1793. The rise of the antislavery movement in the North had resulted in the passage of personal liberty laws which attempted to undermine and/or nullify federal authority. The South wanted a tough fugitive slave act which would allow federal officials to impress Northern citizens into fugitive-slave-catching activities. Since many Southern whites were already required to participate in night patrols to catch runaway slaves, this provision was not offensive to them. Northern politicians, however, knew how offensive such a plan would be among their constituents. Furthermore, the proposal stripped what scant rights blacks had in the courts to challenge their extradition south, resulting in their re-enslavement. And it wasn't always *re*-enslavement; Northerners were convinced, with good reason, that many a free Northern black had been captured and sent to a life of slavery in the South under already existing and less harsh fugitive slave laws.

Senator William Seward rejected the Fugitive Slave Act by saying, on March 11, 1850, on the Senate floor, "I am opposed to any such compromise in any way, and in all the forms in which it has been proposed. They involve the surrender of the exercise of judgment and conscience." He further condemned the Fugitive Slave Act "because you cannot roll back the tide of social progress."[30] The Fugitive Slave Act was clearly written to favor the slaveholder over the alleged runaway, first by appointing low-level, quasi-judicial officers to preside over fugitive slave cases and to provide them with authority normally exercised by federal judges. There was no trial by jury and no appeal. While neither alleged fugitive slave nor alleged slave owner could directly testify in the proceedings, the slave owner had resources and witnesses on which to call, while the alleged fugitive slave generally had no such thing. The crowning insult to justice was that commissioners were paid different commissions for their rulings—ten dollars when the alleged slave was given over to the supposed owner via a "certificate of removal" and five dollars when the ruling acknowledged the freedom of the alleged slave. The rationale for this discrepancy was the increased paperwork in the former cases.[31]

Finally among Clay's action items in his package of proposals, the slave trade in the District of Columbia was to be ended. The subject of Northern petitions to the Congress for over twenty years, the trade had continued, to the consternation of Northern members of Congress having to witness the sale of human beings almost literally within the shadow of the Capitol building. The South had sought to block this agitation by a so-called gag rule in the 1830s and 1840s to keep slavery out of the national political debate in the House of Representatives, but former President John Quincy Adams, a member of the House from 1831 until his fatal stroke in that chamber in 1848, successfully led the fight against the gag rule and was a relentless thorn in the side of proslavery Congressmen.[32]

Clay's proposals were handicapped by a relationship of mistrust with the administration of President Zachary Taylor, even though Clay and Taylor were both Whigs. While Clay was too old and tired to have further presidential ambitions, the president was wary of what he perceived as Clay's attempt to once again become the Whig Party leader.[33] Doing everything possible to garner support in the Senate for his series of resolutions without any support from the administration, Clay even suggested to key supporters that they organize "spontaneous" rallies of public support throughout the country, as long as it did not appear that these public meetings had been "prompted from any exterior source."[34] On January 29, 1850, Clay introduced his resolutions on the floor of the U.S. Senate. The initial reactions in the Senate to Clay's proposals were largely negative. North and South each felt that they would gain little, and that the other side would benefit much more. New York's William H. Seward called Clay's plan a "magnificent humbug."[35] Mississippi Senator Jefferson Davis, who had nothing but contempt for most of Clay's ideas, denounced the resolutions in the bill as "dangerous doctrines" and called on defenders of the Constitution to defend the property rights of slaveholders to take their slaves into "any part of the United States where some sovereign power [that is, the state government] has not forbidden it."[36] Clay spoke for over four hours on February 5 and 6 defending his ideas, ending with an emotional appeal "to pause—solemnly to pause—at the edge of the precipice, before the fearful and disastrous leap [of secession] is taken into the yawning abyss below." As an emotional appeal, Clay brandished a small piece of wood said to be a fragment of George Washington's coffin in an attempt to invoke memories of the patriot price paid for the Union. Clay's depiction of the disastrous war that he prophesied would follow secession made such an impression on Abraham Lincoln that in 1861 Lincoln re-read Clay's speech as he prepared his first inaugural address.[37] A staunch Unionist, Clay closed by declaring that, if secession were to tear apart the Union, it was his prayer that he "not survive to behold the sad and heart-rending spectacle."[38] His prayer would be answered; Henry Clay succumbed to tuberculosis in 1852.

Public reaction to Clay's compromise proposals was much more positive. Even former President Martin Van Buren sent his congratulations

to Clay, although on the surface it did appear that the South might benefit more than the North as the Wilmot Proviso would be rejected, thus
alienating the staunchest Northern antislavery voices. At the same time,
Clay seemed to reject the Southern view that slavery was a positive good
that deserved to expand into new territory; in fact Clay did not actually
defend slavery at all. The moderate, border-state slaveholder Henry Clay
had become an "equal opportunity offender" in order to find a compromise that would save the Union, the Whig Party, and his own reputation
as a great statesman. The dying John C. Calhoun, the gold standard of
hard-line proslavery, had prepared a speech in response to Clay's proposed resolutions. Although Calhoun was present at his desk on the Senate floor, he was too ill to deliver the address. On March 4, 1850, Virginia
Senator James Mason read Calhoun's speech to the Senate. The essence
of Calhoun's speech was that the North was the aggressor and had for
too long forced legislation unfavorable to Southern interests (including
the Missouri Compromise) through the Congress, the political balance
between the North and South must be restored by some sort of Constitutional amendment, the attacks on slavery must end, and new western
territories must be accessible to the South and her institution of slavery.
Furthermore, if California entered the Union as a free state through Clay's
proposals, it would no longer be possible for slave states to remain in the
Union.[39] It was a speech that Sean Wilentz has accurately characterized
as "devious" since Calhoun had been a supporter of the Missouri Compromise and other legislation for which he now castigated the North, and
that in reality, "if any portion of the Union enjoyed an artificial subsidy of
federal power, it was the slave states, whose representation in the House,
the Electoral College, and the parties' national nominating conventions
was greatly inflated thanks to the three-fifths clause."[40]

Criticism of the Clay proposals rose in the debate, which continued
for days. Missouri's Senator Thomas Hart Benton was critical of Clay,
but for different reasons from those Calhoun had expressed. What was
especially upsetting to Senator Benton was Clay using California's request
to enter the Union as a pretense for attempting to settle the issue of slavery
in the United States. In Benton's words, "I am opposed to this mixing of
subjects which have no affinities."[41] Senator Henry Foote of Mississippi
recommended that President Taylor's plan for California statehood and all
of Clay's proposals be sent to a special Senate committee that would merge
everything into one piece of legislation requiring a single up-or-down vote.
This is not what Clay intended or wanted, and he expressed his displea-
sure on the Senate floor, using the term "omnibus" (a new form of urban
public transit) to ridicule Foote's proposal. Clay explained that "My desire

was that the Senate should express its sense upon each of the resolutions.
. . . I never did contemplate . . . bringing them all into one measure."[42] As
Robert Remini has pointed out, the word "omnibus" later became popu-
larized in reference to all of the Clay proposals of 1850, although this was
clearly erroneous in terms of Clay's intentions.[43]

On March 7, 1850, Daniel Webster of Massachusetts gave one of the
most famous speeches in the history of the U.S. Senate. He had reversed
his earlier assessment that the South was bluffing about secession, and
concluded that he must do what he could to save the Union. Public expectations were high that Webster's speech might work a miracle of sectional
compromise and reconciliation, and the Senate gallery was packed with
spectators who had arrived early to obtain a seat. Webster did not disappoint. He spoke as a nationalist pro-Union man, not as a Northerner,
and he blamed North and South alike for the present atmosphere of crisis.
Webster turned his back on the Wilmot Proviso, and blamed some in the
North for not doing their constitutional duty to return fugitive slaves. He
then blamed the South for not understanding the North's befuddlement
at the Southern transition from viewing slavery as a necessary evil on the
road to extinction to seeing slavery as an expansive, positive good that
now compared favorably (in Southern eyes) with Northern free laborers.
This comparison was offensive to the North, Webster asserted. He warned
both abolitionists and secessionists of the dangers of their positions. When
he came to the topic of secession, he asserted that no such thing was possible by peaceful means. Webster's emotions showed most clearly as he
blasted the thought of Southern secession, which, if it were to occur, would
bring "rebuke and reproach" from earlier generations and "shame" in the
eyes of future generations. What was needed was "liberty and union."
Webster did not refer specifically to Clay's proposals in this speech, and it
was not clear how he stood on President Taylor's ideas about California
statehood. Webster made it clear, however, that compromise in some form
was urgently essential if the nation were to be preserved.[44]

Senator William Seward of New York delivered a speech four days after
Webster's oration that did little to soothe sectional tensions over slavery.
Seward was a shadow of the orator that Webster was, but his words had
a devastating effect on Southern sensibilities, and earned him the harshest
rebukes as he denied the validity of compromise in the present situation
and invoked the condemnation of God on slavery. Sounding more and
more like an extreme abolitionist, Seward did his presidential ambitions
no good with such rhetoric, which would rebound to Abraham Lincoln's
benefit a decade later. Stephen A. Douglas, Democrat of Illinois and chair-

man of the Senate Territorial Committee, proved to be a conciliatory voice of calm, favoring the Clay program and optimistic that a way out of the crisis would yet be found. His was one of several senatorial voices heard in support or opposition to the Clay proposals as the debate continued throughout March. In the midst of these debates, John C. Calhoun died, on March 31, leaving the South without its stalwart and eloquent champion and punctuating the congressional debate with a somber pause.

Several senators, including the Free Soil Party's only member of the Senate, Salmon P. Chase, were now clamoring for a vote on California statehood completely removed from any of Clay's other proposals. Clay vehemently countered that a separate vote on California would end any chance of overall compromise. In April, with no end to the debate in sight, Clay began to rethink Senator Foote's "omnibus plan" that he had initially berated as now perhaps an expedient in reaching some sort of conclusion. The Senate went along, and appointed a Committee of Thirteen, six slave-state senators, six free-state senators, and Henry Clay as chairman. In reality the committee never actually met, and Clay did all the work, presenting his report to the Senate on May 8, 1850.[45] What he devised was a series of three bills—a fugitive slave bill, a bill to end the slave trade in the District of Columbia, and a third bill, properly called an "omnibus bill"—that dealt with all issues pertaining to the Mexican Cession, including admission of California as a free state. President Taylor, meanwhile, threatened to veto any bills that he interpreted as concessions for California's admittance to the Union as a free state. Clay then gave another speech in the Senate on May 21, denouncing the president's obstructionism. As June came, Clay's discouragement grew as he calculated vote projections in the Senate and worried that his plan would fail. Clay's sense of urgency was increased as the promised Southern states' conclave met in Nashville on June 3. Although delegates announced that their intent was to "preserve unimpaired the Union," speeches hammered the theme of Northern discrimination and oppression, and resolutions were passed stopping just short of urging secession.[46]

The unanticipated death of President Taylor on July 9, 1850, was a game changer. Millard Fillmore, the new president, was much more cordial and consultative with Henry Clay than Zachary Taylor had been. Daniel Webster swung around to full support for Clay's efforts, and believed that President Fillmore would sign the legislation if Congress passed it. On July 22, Henry Clay rose to his feet for the seventieth time in the Senate since his proposals had been introduced and gave an impassioned closing statement. But things did not go as Clay intended; the omnibus bill collapsed on July 31 as components of it were pulled apart by various adversaries and even some friends with good intentions, and Clay saw months of work seemingly go down the drain.[47] Highly discouraged, Clay left Washington on August 5 for Philadelphia, New York, and Newport, Rhode Island, where he sought a rest for his health's sake, and found himself greeted at every turn by appreciative crowds.

Back in Washington, Senator Stephen Douglas, a man with presidential ambitions, came to the rescue and with the help of fellow Democrats carved up Clay's omnibus bill into individual bills, hoping for "shifting majorities" to enable each of the separate bills to pass.[48] On August 13 the Senate passed the bill providing California's admission into the Union as a free state. The remainder of the now individually packaged Clay proposals, tweaked here and there, passed in amazingly rapid succession. By the time Henry Clay returned to Washington, Douglas had masterfully steered all the Clay proposals through the Senate except the one ending the slave trade in the nation's capital. Clay personally shepherded that final bill through to Senate passage on September 16, 1850. The House of Representatives, with much wrangling of its own, passed their versions of the same bills between September 6 and 16. President Fillmore signed each bill as it became available, and on September 20, the several bills that made up the Compromise of 1850 became the law of the land. Senator Douglas characterized the success of the compromise as "one grand scheme of conciliation and adjustment" in which "neither section has triumphed over the other."[49]

The preservation of the Union for the next decade despite the divisive, central issue of slavery has served to mask the reality that the Compromise of 1850 was less a compromise than what Sean Wilentz has called the "Evasive Truce of 1850." Rather than each side agreeing to give up something to make an accord possible, the Compromise of 1850 witnessed a series of laws being passed with "the majority of congressmen from one section voting in each case against the majority of congressmen from the other."[50] David M. Potter refers to the legislative package as "The Armistice of 1850."[51] In the Senate, only four members supported all six measures comprising the compromise, eight voted for five, nine voted for four, eleven voted for three, nineteen voted for only two, and ten voted for only one of the six measures. One senator did not vote on any of the measures. Only three of the six measures were supported by a majority of the Senate: the admission of California (thirty-four votes), the abolition of the District of Columbia slave trade (thirty-three votes), and the Utah territorial bill (thirty-two votes). These bills were passed by three very different coalitions. The Texas boundary and compensation bill passed with thirty votes, thanks to ten abstentions. The New Mexico territorial bill and the Fugitive Slave Act each garnered twenty-seven votes, and passed thanks to twenty-three and twenty-one abstentions respectively. More ominously, for both the Democratic Party and the nation, many Northern Democrats abstained on the Fugitive Slave Act, allowing it to pass without a majority of the Senate, knowing full well the probable response of their constituents to its requirements. There was, in reality, no real consensus to the provisions of the so-called Compromise of 1850. It was less of a compromise than a realization that neither side was yet prepared for separation and civil war over slavery. The day the nation would confront a final solution regarding slavery was delayed again. More ominously, the age of compromise was at an end.

CHAPTER 10

RUSHING TOWARD DISUNION:
SLAVERY AND THE FACTIOUS 1850s

The Missouri Compromise of 1820 and the Compromise of 1850 witnessed political leaders seeking common ground and willing to yield on some points to sustain the Union despite serious sectional differences over slavery. But in the eventful, chaotic, and unpredictable decade of the 1850s, rising sectional tensions over slavery made compromise increasingly difficult and improbable as opposing sides dug in and solidified their positions. More of the cords holding the Union together began to snap. In relentless succession, events of national significance, all essentially focused on slavery, washed over the increasingly fragile Union, where a cycle of mutual recrimination and violence replaced dialogue as the decade moved on.

Each side began to react instinctively to what it felt was a threat to its position. The new, harsher Fugitive Slave Act provoked Northern outrage and virtual nullification of federal law, followed by Southern outrage that the law was not adequately enforced, and by Southern demands for additional protections for slavery. Fugitive slave Harriet Tubman began a series of daring runs that brought between two hundred and three hundred slaves to freedom as the Underground Railroad continued to provoke the South, despite the miniscule number of slaves that were freed in proportion to the region's total slave population. Harriet Beecher Stowe wrote a novel about slave life that brought Northerners to tears and infuriated Southerners, followed five years later by a book detailing the devastating effects of slavery by Hinton Rowan Helper, a North Carolinian who owned no slaves.

CHARLES SUMNER. *A staunchly antislavery Massachusetts senator, he delivered an intemperate speech in the Senate attacking South Carolina Senator Andrew Butler for his views on slavery while mocking Butler's physical infirmities. In retaliation, Butler's kinsman, Representative Preston Brooks, savagely caned Sumner on the floor of the Senate. Sumner survived, and sectional passions were further inflamed as both men became sectional heroes.*

Both of these works, one fiction, the other nonfiction, produced an out-pouring of Southern literary efforts to prove that slavery was a positive good. The democratic-sounding but divisive concept of popular sover-eignty (which included the repeal of the Missouri Compromise) was cham-pioned by Stephen A. Douglas as a stepping stone to the presidency, but it became a millstone around his neck and further ruptured national unity. A dress rehearsal for the Civil War broke out in Kansas as both North and South supplied and armed their partisans. Massachusetts Senator Charles Sumner was beaten within an inch of his life in the Senate chamber after giving an antislavery speech that included provocative personal attacks on a Southern colleague. The coalescing of antislavery forces into a new and robust regional political party signaled the beginning of a new era of high-stakes sectionalized politics. Proving the old adage that the law has little to do with justice, a Supreme Court case involving a slave named Dred Scott resulted in a decision that could be defended constitutionally if not morally, even as it tossed earlier political compromise out the window. As a result, the South rejoiced, while the North hardened its opposition to slavery for fear it might be imposed on free states as well as the territo-ries. As the decade ended, John Brown demonstrated the extreme to which antislavery zeal could be taken as he attempted to launch an armed insur-rection of slaves in Virginia. These momentous events, as well as many others more localized and less known, signaled the beginning of the final countdown toward national disintegration. At the heart of it all was the institution of slavery, which the Founders had hoped and assumed, incor-rectly, would be gone by this time, but was in reality flourishing as never before.

Northern reaction to the Fugitive Slave Act was highly negative in gen-eral, and vehemently, if not violently, opposed in many specific instances. The purpose of the 1850 act was to placate the South by amending, in fact replacing, the 1793 Fugitive Slave Act with legislation that supplanted state authority with a federalized process for dealing with fugitive slaves. Just weeks after the passage of the new law, a case presented itself in Boston involving George and Ellen Craft, runaway husband and wife slaves from Georgia who had been living in freedom for two years. Prior to the 1850 Fugitive Slave Act, Massachusetts law made it impractical for the Crafts' owner, Robert Latimer, to retrieve them even though he had learned of their location. Empowered by the new federal legislation, Latimer hired two slave catchers to retrieve his runaway property. Finally obtaining the necessary court documents to proceed with the Crafts' capture, the slave hunters were met with fierce resistance by Boston's abolitionist community, who sheltered the Crafts in separate and well-guarded locations, and saw that the slave catchers were threatened and arrested multiple times on various charges to the point that they finally gave up in despair. When President Millard Fillmore, appalled at the flouting of federal authority in Boston, offered to help Robert Latimer if he would try again to capture the Crafts, the fugitive couple prudently departed for England.[1]

Fillmore was determined to enforce the Fugitive Slave Act and maintain the Compromise of 1850 at all costs. In his State of the Union address in December 1850, Fillmore declared that the compromise was the "final and irrevocable" solution to sectional tensions.[2] Instead of leading the nation to a "final and irrevocable" solution, the Fugitive Slave Act was the one part of the compromise that pushed the nation closer to the "irrepressible conflict" described in an 1858 speech by New York Senator William Seward: "Shall I tell you what this collision [between slavery and antislavery] means? They who think that it is accidental, unnecessary, the work of interested or fanatical agitators, and therefore ephemeral, mistake the case altogether. It is an irrepressible conflict between opposing and enduring forces, and it means that the United States must and will, sooner or later, become either entirely a slave-holding nation or entirely a free-labor nation."[3] Abraham Lincoln came to precisely the same conclusion, in the same year, in his "House Divided" speech in which he stated that the Union would not endure half-slave and half-free; it would become all one thing or the other.[4]

The Fugitive Slave Act failed to stem the tide of fugitive slaves heading north and may have increased such activity. Northern newspapers, such as the *Detroit Democrat,* made a connection between the fugitive slave law of 1850 and the increased number of slave escapes after passage of the act, reasoning that Northerners were now more outraged with the South and sympathetic to runaways, making it more difficult for slaveholders to recapture their property. The *Baltimore Sun,* serving a region more invested in the success of the act, claimed that the law was not responsible for the increased runaways; blame was instead placed on the growing population of slaves, access to "facilities of rapid conveyance," and "increased numbers of free colored people at the North, who may be supposed to sympathize with the fugitives."[5] While the prospect of runaway slaves irritated all Southern slaveholders, the Fugitive Slave Act of 1850 was most appealing to owners of slaves in the border states, where most of the escapes originated. Some in the Deep South saw relatively little value in the act. In the words of Mississippi's Senator Henry Foote, his region was far less interested "in this matter as are those slave states which border on the free states." But the ease with which runaway slaves might escape to the

North did become an issue for all the South, for as William Freehling has pointed out, "the overriding problem was whether slavery on the fringes could remain in place or whether the South would gradually shrink to fewer and blacker black belts."[6] Other slaveholders residing in the middle and Deep South rightly feared that, if slavery were at risk on its Northern boundary, it would ultimately be disastrous for the entire South.

A wave of slave escapes in August of 1850 from northern Virginia, the District of Columbia, and Maryland coincided with a "fugitive slave convention" held in Cazenovia, New York, that same month, featuring thirty fugitive slaves and several hundred abolitionists who affirmed the righteousness of aiding fugitive slaves on the soil of slave states. The law in the Southern states, as well as American Constitutional legal precedents at that time, recognized slaves as property, as they had been considered since the founding of the Republic. Their theft, by the slaves themselves or aided and abetted by others, was a criminal act. Frederick Douglass admitted it when he told Northern audiences that he was a thief who had stolen himself.

These activities prompted the *Richmond Enquirer* to editorialize that Virginians must be "on their guard against the designs of the Abolitionists, who may venture even into the slave States, to carry out their hellish designs."[7] By including in the 1850 Fugitive Slave Act a provision whereby Northern men could be required to function like Southern slave patrols, Northern sentiment was convinced that the victims of Southern despotism now included whites as well as blacks, further stiffening Northern resistance. Thus, legislation that had been presented as part of a plan of compromise and national unity became a serious point of sectional conflict, and had, unintentionally, "actually transferred the controversy from remote, and barely settled, territories to the population centers of the East, potentially entangling the federal government in every escape, warrant, seizure, rescue, and trial until the advent of the Civil War."[8]

Despite the Fugitive Slave Act, the Underground Railroad continued to be very active in the 1850s, although its symbolic meaning was more significant than the actual number of slaves brought to freedom through its contacts and resources. In reality having nothing to do with railroads (although a few slaves, like Frederick Douglass, made it to freedom by traveling incognito or as cargo on trains), the "Underground Railroad" system of clandestine activities that brought a very small proportion of the slave population out of bondage in the South utilized railroad terminology; "conductors, stations, routes, cargoes, packages, and passengers" proved to be "a fitting, and tantalizing, way to describe its activities."[9] If one counts the "Underground Railroad" as coming into existence when the very first American slave ran away, the number of successful escapes may number as many as 100,000. But slaves had been escaping since they first reached North America, and the Underground Railroad only had a coherent organizational existence in the two or three decades prior to the Civil War. Although documentation is sketchy as few records exist, it has been estimated that in the late antebellum period perhaps 1,000 to 2,000 slaves per year escaped to freedom. After 1850, increasing numbers of whites contributed to or participated directly in Underground Railroad efforts, and several influential lawyers offered their services in the defense of fugitive slaves and those arrested for assisting them.[10] The very fact that Northerners, and former slaves, were deliberately encouraging and assisting runaway slaves was galling to the South and further eroded North-South relations. This illegal network of freedom seekers and those who helped them was not only despised in the South, but also was an activity against which most Southerners could unite. Many Northerners also disapproved of the activities of fugitive slaves and their allies; some were fearful of what such actions might do to the fragile Union; others wished that all blacks could be freed, but were loath to have them as neighbors.

Harriet Tubman became perhaps the best known "conductor" on the Underground Railroad after she escaped from slavery in 1849 by making her way to Philadelphia. She then returned to Maryland about twenty times to rescue members of her own family as well as others in bondage. The State of Maryland offered a $40,000 reward (an immense sum in those days) for Tubman's capture, but she successfully eluded Southern authorities. When not rescuing slaves in Maryland, Tubman could be found on the Northern abolitionist speaking circuit. In 1859, Tubman supported and encouraged John Brown's raid at Harpers Ferry.

In the year 1852, a remarkable book was published that did more to arouse antislavery sentiment in the North than anyone would have ever thought possible. Claiming that God had authored the book and provided her with "visions, one after another, and I put them down in words," Harriet Beecher Stowe wrote *Uncle Tom's Cabin,* which historian David Reynolds does not hesitate to call "the most influential book written by an American."[11] Harriet was one of eleven children born to New Englander Lyman Beecher, a Presbyterian theologian in the Puritan tradition, and a reformer whose antislavery views were moderate, taking a back seat to his main targets of rum, Catholicism, Sabbath-breaking, and gambling. Lyman Beecher was an emancipation gradualist, a believer in African colonization, and greatly concerned that radical abolitionism might destroy the American Union. All seven of Lyman's sons became clergymen, Henry Ward Beecher becoming in his day perhaps the most well-known preacher and one of the most ardent antislavery voices in America. Harriet's younger sister was the founder of the Women's National Suffrage Association, and her older sister became a pioneer of educational opportunities for women. The entire family was to some degree affected by the influence of evangelist Charles Grandison Finney. Clearly this was a family wanting to make a difference in their world, and Harriet's literary efforts did not disappoint. Harriet Beecher was one of the best educated women of her day, enrolling at Hartford Female Seminary, founded by her sister Catharine, where she honed her writing skills and concluded that her purpose in life was to write. After one of Harriet's best friends, Eliza Stowe, died of cholera in 1834, Harriet and widower Calvin Stowe, a professor of biblical theology at Lane Seminary where Harriet's father was the president, fell in love and were married in 1836.

HARRIET TUBMAN. *Among the most famous and successful black "conductors" on the "underground railroad," Tubman repeatedly risked her life to guide runaway slaves to the North. Southerners put a price on her head, but she successfully eluded capture.*

Uncle Tom's Cabin, the two-volume novel published in 1852, began as a series of articles in *The National Era* published in weekly installments over ten months. The work was inspired in part by the death from cholera of Harriet's young son Charley in 1849, causing her great grief that made her reflect on the sufferings of Christ and slave mothers. The volume reflects the reforming zeal and deep Christian spirituality of the author, to the point that *Uncle Tom's Cabin* was used as a Sunday School text and stimulated sales of the Bible throughout the world. David Reynolds has concluded that *"Uncle Tom's Cabin* went a long way toward winning Christianity for the antislavery cause."[12] The novel was a huge best-seller, with 10,000 copies sold in the first week of its release in the United States, and 300,000 copies sold in the first year. In Great Britain, 1.5 million copies sold in one year.[13] Countless others were exposed to the content of *Uncle Tom's Cabin* through a stage play adopted from the novel. David Potter's analysis of the novel concludes that the book

> lacked the standard qualifications for such great literary success. It may plausibly be argued that Mrs. Stowe's characters were impossible and her Negroes were blackface stereotypes, that her plot was sentimental, her dialect absurd, her literary technique crude, and her overall picture of the conditions of slavery distorted. But without any of the vituperation in which the abolitionists were so fluent, and with a sincere though unappreciated effort to avoid blaming the South, she made vivid the plight of the slave as a human being held in bondage. . . . Men who had remained unmoved by real fugitives wept for Tom under the lash and cheered for Eliza with the bloodhounds on her track.[14]

While a few Southerners may have taken small comfort in the lack of blame assigned to the South by Mrs. Stowe for the evils of slavery, most came to despise *Uncle Tom's Cabin,* especially as its influence increased abolitionist sentiment in the North and in other parts of the world. Virginia lawyer and planter George Fitzhugh assumed the task of providing the South's premier literary rebuttal to Mrs. Stowe's frustratingly popular opus. Fitzhugh's *Sociology for the South; or, The Failure of Free Society* was published in 1854 and was followed up in 1857 by *Cannibals All! Or, Slaves without Masters.* Fitzhugh's argument largely lies in the horrible conditions of the industrial North where the working class (the slaves without masters) were oppressed while living and working in wretched situations. This sad state of affairs, Fitzhugh explained, was due to the unfortunate belief in human equality that had sucked the hope out of the inferior people of the North and made them the victims of exploitation and misery, while in the South, the inferior slave class had found its natural level and all was well. Finally, Fitzhugh dwelt on current theories "proving" the substandard nature of Africans, whose blood, even in the tiniest proportion, would taint even the most white-looking person with inferiority.[15] Henry Hughes, a social theorist from Mississippi, held to common views about the intellectual inferiority of women and dismissed *Uncle Tom's Cabin* with the denunciation, "That book is womanish & I am afraid absurdly unprincipled; written by a woman clearly."[16] These views reflected the antiquarian, pastoral, paternalistic, and anti-capitalist attitudes of the South, attitudes that eschewed internal improvements, not only for the nation, but most especially for itself. The "Cavalier Kingdom" was all about the status quo, fearful of the economic, social, and political changes swirling in the world around it.

President Abraham Lincoln was far more impressed with Mrs. Stowe's literary abilities and more attuned to social change than was Henry Hughes. Recognizing the importance of Mrs. Stowe's contribution to the antislavery movement, he greeted her at the White House in December 1862. Harriet Beecher Stowe had been somewhat skeptical of Lincoln's antislavery commitment because of his initial support for the Fugitive Slave Act, and for his desire to preserve the Union at all costs, even if it meant that slavery was not brought to an end. Stowe's visit with Lincoln just days before he signed the Emancipation Proclamation reassured her of his heartfelt antislavery commitment, and following the signing of the proclamation on January 1, 1863, Lincoln became "the brightest star in Stowe's constellation of American heroes."[17] Stowe became a steadfast female voice in support of Lincoln. She would stand by Lincoln even in the dark days of 1864, describing him as one to whom "Almighty God has granted . . . that clearness of vision which he gives to the true-hearted, and enabled him to set his honest foot in that promised land of freedom which is to be the patrimony of all men, black and white—and from henceforth nations shall rise up to call him blessed."[18]

African American literary contributions to the cause of emancipation were considerable. Frederick Douglass's speeches (often receiving wide notice in printed form), his autobiography, *My Bondage and My Freedom*, and his prolific writings in *The North Star* and other journals built a strong and strident case for an end to slavery. At least three other slave autobiographies deserve recognition for their importance. William Wells Brown wrote *Narrative of William W. Brown, a Fugitive Slave,* published in 1848, and in 1861 Harriet Ann Jacobs's *Incidents in the Life of a Slave Girl Written by Herself* was published. Jacobs's opening words set the tone for reaching her readership in the free states before emancipation had become part of the national agenda:

"Northerners know nothing at all about Slavery. They think it is perpetual bondage only. They have no conception of the depth of degradation involved in that word, SLAVERY; if they had, they would never cease their efforts until so horrible a system was overthrown."[19]

A best-selling autobiographical volume, *Twelve Years a Slave,* appeared in 1853 written by Solomon Northup, a free black from New York who was deceived by a job offer that resulted in his being kidnapped and sold into slavery, spending about twelve years in bondage on several plantations in Louisiana before he was able to secure his release through legal means and return to his wife and children. His writings of life as a slave in Louisiana include the observation that

> It is a mistaken opinion that prevails in some quarters that the slave does not understand . . . the idea of freedom. Even on Bayou Boeuf, where I conceive slavery exists in its most abject and cruel form—where it exhibits features altogether unknown in more northern States—the most ignorant of them generally know full well its meaning. They understand the privileges and exemptions that belong to it—that it would bestow upon them the fruits of their own labors, and that it would secure to them the enjoyment of domestic happiness. They do not fail to observe the difference between their own condition and the meanest white man's, and to realize the injustice of the laws which place it in his power not only to appropriate the profits of their industry, but to subject them to unmerited and unprovoked punishment, without remedy, or the right to resist or remonstrate.[20]

In the political climate of the day, the extent of disagreement in the U.S. Senate, which reflected the national mood of sectional division over slavery, can be seen in its debate over yet another land acquisition treaty in 1853, the same year Northrup's autobiography was published. Often overlooked as playing a role in the battle over slavery, the Gadsden Purchase deserves recognition as a barometer of sectional tensions at that time. Initially negotiated as a Pennsylvania-sized territory comprising today's southern Arizona and a small portion of New Mexico, the land involved in the Gadsden Purchase was desired by Jefferson Davis and other Southern leaders as a route for a transcontinental railroad from the South to California. This southern route for a rail line would commercially link the Pacific Coast with the South rather than with the North, quite different from what Illinois Senator Stephen Douglas intended as he schemed for a railroad connecting California with Chicago, assuming that the vast Nebraska region could become organized and settled. It was an interesting convergence: Southerners wanted a Southern railroad; Douglas wanted a

Northern railroad; Mexican President Santa Anna needed money; many Americans, particularly in the North, felt guilt over the seizure of half of Mexico in the 1848 Treaty of Guadalupe Hidalgo—all while the nation was increasingly experiencing a rancorous division over slavery.

James Gadsden, appointed by President Franklin Pierce as minister to Mexico with Jefferson Davis's strong endorsement, was a railroad corporate executive from South Carolina. He succeeded in negotiating a treaty with Mexican President Santa Anna that would have ceded about 45,000 square miles of territory to the United States for a payment of $15 million. The treaty initially received a simple majority of votes in the Senate, but failed to receive the two-thirds majority required for approval, and was later reintroduced as a 29,000-square-mile acquisition costing $10 million. But even the scaled-down treaty met resistance for several reasons. Some senators felt the treaty did not provide a large enough territory; others were upset over the United States accepting responsibility for claims against the Mexican government in the region. But the greatest opposition was from Northern senators who were against acquisition of any new territory into which slavery might expand. However, on the second attempt, the treaty passed and was signed by President Pierce on June 8, 1854.[21] Slavery, it seemed, was affecting nearly every aspect of governmental decision-making, and for the first time in its history, as David Potter has noted, the U.S. Senate refused (at least in its first vote) to accept land ceded by treaty to the United States.[22]

As the 1850s progressed, it became increasingly clear to many Southern expansionists that, under the political arrangements of the day, when combined with the realities of climate and geography, there were no future states within present American boundaries where slavery could anticipate expanding its reach. Attention turned to a renewed interest in filibustering, an extreme form of Manifest Destiny making use of private and unofficial military expeditions to intervene in the affairs of nations with which the United States was officially at peace. One such episode was William Walker's invasion of Nicaragua, where the Tennessee slaveholder hoped, but failed, to establish a slave territory dominated by American Southerners. Franklin Pierce sought to purchase Cuba from Spain as an alternative to the filibustering plans of John Quitman to seize the island which Pierce realized would result in a colossal antislavery Northern backlash against the supposed Southern Slave Power. But plans for Cuba's purchase went awry when American negotiators at the Ostend, Belgium, conference in October 1854 put their names to an arrogant internal memorandum stating that, if negotiations with Spain over the purchase of Cuba failed, the

United States should simply seize the Spanish colony. Among the signatories of this ill-advised document was James Buchanan, a seasoned diplomat whose long-standing presidential ambitions may have gotten ahead of his diplomatic good sense. When exposed publicly, the whole "Ostend Manifesto" episode proved to be a serious embarrassment to the Pierce administration, resulting in immense criticism at home (especially in the North) and abroad, with the *London Times* bemoaning the fact that American diplomacy insisted on engaging in "the habitual pursuit of dishonorable objects by clandestine means."[23] Cuba remained in Spanish hands.

While the Ostend Manifesto was an embarrassment, the greatest disaster during the Pierce administration was the Kansas-Nebraska Act. As David M. Potter has insightfully observed, both the Ostend Manifesto and the Kansas-Nebraska Act managed to take the previously respectable American ideas of Manifest Destiny and popular sovereignty, and sully them through association with shameless aggression and the extension of slavery.[24] Initiated by sectional competition over the location of a transcontinental railroad, the Kansas-Nebraska Act was an attempt by Senator Stephen Douglas to establish a territorial government for the vast area between the Missouri River and the Rockies in the hope that a railroad could be built through that region and that Chicago, Douglas's hometown, would be its eastern terminus. One problem was that in 1830 Congress had declared this unorganized territory as a permanent reserve for Indians. Douglas, as chairman of the Senate's Committee on Territories, knew that if the region, which he suggested be called "Nebraska," could be organized as a territory it could then be opened to white settlers who could purchase land and establish settlements. More importantly for Douglas, Nebraska included the projected railroad route along the Platte River. With settlements in the Platte Valley, the desired railroad route would be more attractive. During the legislative process, the bill was modified to divide the proposed huge Nebraska Territory in two; the southern portion, well below the Platte River Valley, would become the Kansas Territory.

By the provisions of the Missouri Compromise of 1820, this area was closed to slavery. Douglas soon realized that adequate legislative backing for his proposal required Southern support, as New England had little interest in a transcontinental railroad that would aid further westward expansion. Missouri Senator David Atchison joined forces with several Southern senators to convince Douglas and President Pierce that, without a repeal of the Missouri Compromise's ban on slavery in the region, Southern support for the proposed legislation would not be forthcoming. Stephen Douglas wanted a transcontinental railroad with Chicago as a terminus, and above all he wanted to be president of the United States. The man who was instrumental in winning passage of the Compromise of 1850 was now willing to risk the sectional firestorm that he assumed his proposed repeal of the Missouri Compromise would elicit. Reintroducing the concept of "popular sovereignty," which had actually been used successfully in the Compromise of 1850 regarding Utah and New Mexico, Douglas argued that the settlers of the region should themselves determine whether slavery would be allowed.

Douglas was convinced that the future residents of Kansas/Nebraska would not want slavery, and that by pursuing a program that had something to offer both North and South (a railroad for the North along with a low risk of slavery entering Kansas/Nebraska; an end to the official ban on slavery through "popular sovereignty" for the South), he would become the Democratic candidate for the presidency in 1856. What Douglas failed to predict was the intensity of the fight over the status of the Kansas Territory and the extent of the divisive sectional fallout that the "popular sovereignty" policy would have on his own party. Neither could Douglas envision the impact on national politics in general. Introducing popular sovereignty into an area previously closed to slavery meant repealing the ban previously approved by both sections in 1820, a situation that had not been present when popular sovereignty was applied to the Utah and New Mexico territories in 1850.

As anticipated by Douglas, there was considerable Northern outrage at the repeal of the Missouri Compromise. Despite stiff opposition, Douglas was able to steer his legislation through the Congress with the full support of the Pierce administration in May of 1854, although he lost considerable Northern support within his own Democratic Party. While Southern senators got the repeal of the Missouri Compromise line, Douglas did not get his railroad in return. The Pacific Railroad Act was not passed by Congress until 1862, the year after the South seceded and Douglas had died.

The Kansas-Nebraska Act, becoming law on May 30, 1854,[25] had a profound impact on the nation's political climate and ushered in an era of sectional party realignments, eventually replacing national political parties with regional ones. Lincoln later stated that the repeal of the Missouri Compromise left him "thunderstruck and stunned."[26] Senators Salmon P. Chase of Ohio and Charles Sumner of Massachusetts drafted a document approved by other antislavery members of Congress calling the repeal of the Missouri Compromise "a gross violation of a sacred pledge; as a criminal betrayal of previous rights; as part and parcel of an atrocious plot to exclude from a vast unoccupied region immigrants from the Old World and free laborers from our own States, and convert it into a dreary region of despotism, inhabited by masters and slaves."[27]

While the fledgling Free Soil Party had arisen a few years before, the Kansas-Nebraska Act galvanized increasing numbers of Northern Whigs and Democrats to oppose what seemed to be a growing proslavery national political climate. The New York *Tribune's* Horace Greeley editorialized repeatedly that the time was right for a new Northern political party[28] while Gamaliel Bailey, editor of the *National Era,* proclaimed that the era of the old political parties was over and called for a meeting of antislavery Whig and Democratic members of Congress in May 1854, at which time about thirty Kansas-Nebraska opponents came together in Washington to call for a new party, and suggested "Republican" would be a good name. The Michigan Republican Convention met "under the oaks" at Jackson, Michigan, on July 6, 1854, a week before a similar event was held in Ripon, Wisconsin, demanding an end to compromises with proslavery factions, the repeal of the fugitive slave law, and an end to slavery in the nation's capital. Initiated primarily by radical antislavery voices such as Salmon P. Chase, Charles Sumner, and Benjamin Wade, the new party's various state organizations at times struggled to construct a large enough policy tent to maintain a powerful voice against slavery while not alienating more moderate factions, such as in Indiana where more conservative voices led the coalition that came together to oppose the Kansas-Nebraska bill.[29] When the Illinois Republican Party officially organized in Bloomington on May 29, 1856, one of the 270 delegates present was Abraham Lincoln, making a public and final break with his earlier Whig Party affiliation. It proved to be one of the most important decisions in his life, and in the life of the nation.

The greater part of Liberty Party voters joined in the Republican cause, as well as thousands of Whigs. The new party was clearly antislavery, although the focus was on the prohibition of slavery's expansion into the territories, rather than on any comprehensive plan for national emancipation. While the racial prejudices of the age were largely shared by Republicans, especially its "Know-Nothing" element (the popular name given to the anti-immigration, anti-Catholic American Party), there were divergent opinions within the new party as to exactly how far equal rights should be extended to free blacks, as well as what role, if any, colonization of free blacks should play in the nation's future. Republicans were also divided over nullification and repeal of the Fugitive Slave Act of 1850, and conservative Whigs became especially alienated by radical Republican threats of nullification. In the midwestern states of Ohio, Indiana, Illinois, Wisconsin, and Iowa, Republicans were divided on extending the franchise to blacks, and such attempted reforms generally went down to defeat, as was the case in Iowa's 1857 referendum denying blacks the right to vote by an overwhelming majority of 49,387 to 8,489.[30] When the Republicans fielded their first presidential candidate, John C. Fremont, in 1856, he carried eleven of the sixteen free states, but lost enough of the conservative Whig vote to lose the election to the Democrat Buchanan. Republicans with their candidate Fremont, perceived as too radical by conservatives, realized they must polish their image of being absolutely committed to the preservation of the Union. One can see in the results of the 1856 election the seeds being sown for the 1860 Republican convention's rejection of the more radical Seward in favor of the more conservative Lincoln. It was all about electability.

Passage of the Kansas-Nebraska Act, as is often the case with complex and controversial legislation, resulted in unintended consequences. One such consequence was the desertion of their party by a larger number of Northern antislavery Democrats than anyone would have predicted. The divisiveness of the bill among free-state Democrats when it was up for consideration in the House of Representatives showed a near-even split; forty-four voted for it while forty-three voted against it.[31] Another surprise was the extent of Democratic losses in the mid-term election of 1854. Northern Democrats in the House fell precipitously from ninety-one to twenty-five, while Southern Democrats suffered much less of a defeat, dropping from sixty-seven to fifty-eight seats. The Southern wing of the Democratic Party thus had the dominant voice and could clearly guide party policy in the new Congress.[32]

Another unintended consequence of the Kansas-Nebraska Act was the warfare that erupted between proslavery and antislavery factions in what came to be known as "Bleeding Kansas." Almost as soon as the act was passed, rivalry broke out to see which faction could introduce the most immigrants into Kansas, and thus decide which populace under "popular sovereignty" would win out—those in favor of, or opposed to, slavery. Missouri slave holders, already flanked by the free states of Illinois to the east and Iowa to the north, feared for the future of slavery in Missouri should their western neighbor also become a free state. Funds were raised on both sides, and immigrants were encouraged and aided in making Kansas their "home," even if just in time for the November 1854 election. The New England Emigrant Aid Company sponsored hundreds of antislavery Kansas settlers, but they could not compete with proslavery interests who lured more settlers, including hundreds of Missourians encouraged to cross the border into Kansas by Missouri Senator David Atchison. This was no friendly rivalry; the future of Kansas, and perhaps the future of American slavery, was at stake, and violence flared. While proslavery voters won control of the territorial legislature in the fall of 1854, antislavery forces were not willing to accept the "rigged" outcome, and the Free Soil Kansans elected their own antislavery legislature that banned slaves, as well as free blacks, from the Kansas Territory. Kansas thus had two rival territorial legislatures, each supported by armed partisans. In the town of Lawrence, an antislavery stronghold, hostilities broke out on May 21, 1856, when about eight hundred proslavery men entered the town, burned the Free State Hotel to the ground, and killed one man, enraging much of the North. Many Northerners came to view the fraudulent elections and threatening actions perpetrated by proslavery Kansas settlers as an assault on the liberties and political rights of free-state white settlers that far outweighed any concern for actual slaves in the territory.[33]

John Brown was one antislavery zealot who decided to act. Five of Brown's adult sons had left Ohio for Kansas in 1854 to farm homesteads in the new territory, and they had been dismayed at the danger posed by proslavery "border ruffians" crossing over from Missouri. Their father decided to come to their aid, and the aid of all who desired a Free Kansas. A failure at several business ventures and a man of intense religious beliefs derived from his Puritan New England ancestors, John Brown became a major player in the radical antislavery movement who saw it as a religious crusade. Preacher Henry Ward Beecher also saw the crusade for a Free Kansas as a divine enterprise, and sent crates of Sharps rifles, thereafter known as "Beecher's Bibles," to the antislavery forces. "There are times when self-defense is a religious duty," Beecher proclaimed.[34] Three days after the attack on Lawrence, John Brown and his sons exacted revenge by killing five proslavery neighbors who were likely innocent of any involvement in the raid. These revenge killings came to be known as the "Pottawatomie Massacre." This incident ignited further hostilities, and in Kansas over the next two years perhaps two hundred people were killed, and property worth two million dollars was destroyed.[35]

As Kansas prepared for statehood, conflict over slavery manifested itself in January of 1857 when the proslavery territorial legislature proposed a constitutional convention to be held in the eastern Kansas town of Lecompton despite the refusal of territorial Governor John W. Geary to authorize such an event. Delegates to the Lecompton convention were elected in June, but free-state voters stayed home in protest of the Lecompton gathering, thus assuring that the constitution hammered out at the meeting would be a proslavery document. When Governor Geary resigned in protest, he was replaced by a hand-picked Buchanan appointee, Robert J. Walker of Mississippi, who President Buchanan believed would ably maintain the principle of popular sovereignty in the Kansas Territory. During a recess in the Lecompton convention in October, elections were held for a new territorial legislature, but the voting was again rife with fraud. Shortly after Governor Walker disallowed some of the bogus proslavery ballots, the proslavery Lecompton gathering completed their constitutional draft. Both Governor Walker and President Buchanan demanded a public referendum on the Lecompton Constitution, which was set for December 21, 1857. But the Lecompton conventioneers had a disingenuous plan; voters would be given the choice between "the Constitution with slavery" or "the Constitution with no slavery." The "Constitution with no slavery" option was not the harbinger of a free state, however. A vote for this version of the Constitution simply meant that no further slaves could be imported into Kansas, but the slaves already in the proposed state could stay (as well as their offspring), and no constitutional amendment would be possible to disallow ownership of these slaves. Thus, there would be no option on the ballot for Kansas to be truly a free state.

While Governor Walker was horrified by this turn of events, he was even more outraged, as were most antislavery Kansas residents, when President Buchanan came out in favor of the Lecompton Constitution in his annual message to Congress on December 8, 1857. Stephen Douglas and other Northern Democrats broke with the president over this issue, creating further sectional division within the Democratic Party. Douglas's Senate seat was up for reelection in 1858, and Douglas knew that Republicans were likely to win control of the Illinois legislature over the Kansas furor if he did not oppose the Lecompton Constitution. Douglas was correct in his strategy; the Democrats were able to hold on to a slim majority in the Illinois legislature after the 1858 election, thus depriving Republican senatorial candidate Abraham Lincoln of a Senate appointment, despite Lincoln's solid showing in a series of seven debates with Douglas throughout the state. Douglas fought unsuccessfully against the U.S. Senate's vote to admit Kansas as a state under the Lecompton Constitution, but with Douglas's help, the House was able to prevent Kansas statehood under the dubious cloud of the Lecompton document. Kansas remained a territory, and a new referendum concerning statehood under the Lecompton Constitution was set for August 1858, at which time antislavery Kansans turned out in droves to defeat the proposal. By 1860 there remained but two slaves in Kansas, and free statehood was not far off.[36] "Bleeding Kansas" essentially destroyed the viability of popular sovereignty as a solution to the slavery issue and further hardened sectional animosity.

Meanwhile, violence over slavery reached the halls of Congress. In May 1856, during a debate over Kansas, Charles Sumner, a staunch abolitionist senator from Massachusetts, launched into a three-hour, two-day antislavery speech known as the "Crime Against Kansas."[37] In his speech, delivered on the Senate floor on May 19 and 20, Sumner attacked the authors of the Kansas-Nebraska Act, senators Stephen Douglas of Illinois and Andrew Butler of South Carolina. Douglas was present to hear Sumner's tirade, but Butler, increasingly infirm and in failing health, was absent from the Senate floor. Much of Sumner's speech was a heated discussion of the issue of slavery as it related to Kansas. The speech also contained particularly vicious personal attacks against Douglas and Butler, even mocking the physical infirmities, honesty, and integrity of Sumner's South Carolina colleague. Using the images of chivalry often found in the South and comparing the senator to Cervantes's Don Quixote, Sumner said, "The Senator from South Carolina has read many books of chivalry and fancies himself a chivalrous knight, with sentiments of honor and courage. Of course, he has chosen a mistress to whom he has made his vows, and whom though ugly to others, is always lovely to him; though polluted in the sight of the world; is chaste in his sight, I mean, the harlot Slavery. For her, his tongue is always profuse in words. Let her be impeached in character or any proposition made to shut her out from the extension of her wantonness, no extravagance of manner or hardihood of assertion is then too great for this Senator."[38]

Such imagery was not unusual for Northern Senators who often pricked the consciences of their Southern colleagues with the sexual aspects of slavery. Rather, it was the intemperate, even venomous, personal remarks Sumner made against Butler toward the end of his harangue that resulted in outrage:

> With regret I come again upon the Senator from South Carolina [Mr. Butler], who, omnipresent in this debate, overflows with rage at the simple suggestion that Kansas has applied for admission as a State, and, with incoherent phrase, discharges the loose expectoration of his speech, now upon her representative, and then upon her people. There was no extravagance of the ancient Parliamentary debate which he did not repeat; nor was there any possible deviation from truth which he did not make,—with so much of passion, I gladly add, as to save him from the suspicion of intentional aberration. But the Senator touches nothing which he does not disfigure—with error, sometimes of principle, sometimes of fact. He shows an incapacity of accuracy, whether

in stating the Constitution or in stating the law, whether in details of statistics or diversions of scholarship. He cannot ope[n] his mouth, but out there flies a blunder.

Not content with this personal attack, he renewed his castigation of Senator Butler and his native state of South Carolina:

> But it is against the people of Kansas that the sensibilities of the Senator are particularly aroused. Coming, as he announces, "from a State,"— ay, Sir, from South Carolina,—he turns with lordly disgust from this newly formed community, which he will not recognize even as "a member of the body politic." Pray, Sir, by what title does he indulge in this egotism? Has he read the history of the "State" which he represents? He cannot, surely, forget its shameful imbecility from Slavery, confessed throughout the Revolution, followed by its more shameful assumptions for Slavery since. He cannot forget its wretched persistence in the slave-trade, as the very apple of its eye, and the condition of its participation in the Union. He cannot forget its Constitution, which is republican only in name, confirming power in the hands of the few, and founding the qualifications of its legislators on "a settled freehold estate of five hundred acres of land and ten negroes." And yet the Senator to whom this "State" has in part committed the guardianship of its good name, instead of moving with backward-treading steps to cover its nakedness, rushes forward, in the very ecstasy of madness, to expose it, by provoking comparison with Kansas.[39]

The tone and tenor of Sumner's speech went well beyond the pale of anything that had been heard in the Senate. The language directed toward Senator Butler was deliberately provocative, and it encouraged the reaction it received. Many in the Senate were stunned by the extent of Sumner's venomous, personal remarks, and Stephen Douglas was heard to say, "That damn fool will get himself killed by some other damn fool."[40] Prior to the speech, William Seward had unsuccessfully urged Sumner to delete the most inflammatory remarks. Following Sumner's speech, Michigan Senator Lewis Cass rose to his feet with a few choice words for Mr. Sumner. Cass, the losing Democratic candidate in the presidential election of 1848 and a strong proponent of the doctrine of popular sovereignty, had returned to the Senate to represent Michigan the year after his defeat for the presidency. In Cass's words, Sumner's speech was "the most un-American and unpatriotic that ever grated on the ears of this high body" and was riddled with "personal assaults" made even more objectionable because they did not arise from a spontaneous debate but rather were "written with cool, deliberate malignity, repeated from night to night in order to catch the appropriate grace."[41] News of the speech was greeted with disdain in the South and mixed reviews in the North. Two well-known voices from Massachusetts, Henry Wadsworth Longfellow and Edward Everett, differed widely in their critique of Sumner's words. Longfellow gushed in a letter, "Your speech is the greatest voice on the greatest subject that has ever been uttered," while Everett's response was that "from a man of character of any party I have never seen any thing so offensive."[42]

Warned by Republican colleagues to watch for his safety after this speech, Sumner brushed off any fear of danger. Two days after the controversial oration, Representative Preston Brooks of South Carolina, a kinsman of Butler's, entered the Senate Chamber on May 22, 1856. Accompanied by Representatives Laurence Keitt, a fellow South Carolinian, and Virginian Henry A. Edmundson, Brooks approached Sumner, who was sitting at his desk. As Brooks spoke to Sumner, the senator began to rise. Brooks then viciously beat the senator with a gold-headed walking cane. Sumner struggled to resist but was trapped at his desk, which was bolted to the floor. The beating, lasting no more than a minute, was so savage that the walking cane finally broke, but even that did not stop the fury of Brooks's attack. Finally, the Southern representatives walked out of the chamber. Sumner, beaten, bloodied, and semi-conscious, was held in a colleague's arms. He survived, but did not return to a regular schedule in the Senate until 1859, carrying with him both the physical and emotional scars the trauma had inflicted for the rest of his life. As for Brooks, the congressman was arrested for assault but freed on a five-hundred-dollar bond, and on July 14 survived a motion that, if passed by a two-thirds vote, would have expelled him from the House of Representatives. Only one Southern Congressman joined the majority who voted for Brooks to be ousted.[43]

Reactions were ominously predictable and sectional. The North turned the verbally provocative and abusive senator into a near-martyr for the cause of free speech and free men. To the North, the South had again shown its violent and repressive nature. The Massachusetts legislature, ignoring Sumner's inflammatory rhetoric,

> *Resolved* That the Legislature of, in the name of her free and enlightened people, demands for her representatives, in the National Legislature entire freedom of speech, and will uphold them in the proper exercise of that essential right of American citizens.

> *Resolved,* That we approve of Mr. Sumner's manliness and courage in his earnest and fearless declaration of free principles, and his defense of human rights and free territory.[44]

Meanwhile, the South excused the near-murder of a U.S. senator in the

Senate Chamber. Preston Brooks wrote to his brother the day after the caning, "Every Southern man is delighted and the Abolitionists are like a hive of disturbed bees."[45]Brooks was hailed as a hero for upholding the honor of his kinsman and state and became the recipient of dozens of new canes from admiring gentlemen. To a Southern gentleman, honor was everything, and anything that touched on perpetuating and expanding their peculiar institution was, as the Southern senators and representatives repeated over and over again, a "matter of honor." Brooks had demonstrated that, for the South, violence was an acceptable remedy when honor was impugned. "Bleeding Kansas" and "bleeding Sumner" riveted the nation's attention and further divided the ever-precarious Union. But no one from Franklin Pierce down called for a cooling-off period. No one who controlled the strings of power, or hoped to, could afford to let the embers of their constituents' passions cool. After all, 1856 was an election year. Three and a half years later, many in the North would transform another provocateur into a martyr. But with John Brown, they would not be upholding a foolhardy brandisher of words like Sumner, but an antislavery zealot who brandished the sword and wanted to wash his hands in the blood of the South.

Further intensifying the debate over slavery's future was the publication of a highly controversial and influential book, written by a twenty-eight-year-old North Carolinian, Hinton Rowan Helper, in 1857. *The Impending Crisis of the South: How to Meet It* was surpassed only by Harriet Beecher Stowe's *Uncle Tom's Cabin* in its literary impact favorable to the abolitionist cause. The son of a slaveholding father, Helper claimed that his purpose in writing this book to his fellow Southerners was "to elevate the South to an honorable and powerful position among the enlightened quarters of the globe."[46] Helper compared the free states and the slave states and concluded that the North was "rising to a degree of almost unexampled power and eminence" while the slave South was "sinking into a state of comparative imbecility and obscurity."[47] And this conclusion was reached on only page 2 of the volume—small wonder that most Southerners found the work objectionable!

Helper asserted that there was something "socially, politically and morally wrong, in the policy under which the South has so long loitered and languished" which left the South "standing before the world, an object of merited reprehension and derision."[48] Convinced that the South was approaching an "inevitable crisis," Helper believed that "the sooner it comes the better; may heaven, through our humble efforts [his book], hasten its advent." Mincing no words, Helper was convinced that the "salvation of the South depends upon the speedy and unconditional abolition of slavery."[49]Helper was an abolitionist, but out of compassion for whites, not blacks. He described the slaveholding class of the South as "the lords of the lash" who are "not only absolute masters of the blacks . . . they are also the oracles and arbiters of all non-slaveholding whites, whose freedom is merely nominal, and whose unparalleled illiteracy and degradation is purposely and fiendishly perpetuated."[50] Slavery, Helper explained, can never equal "the triumphant achievements of free labor," and it was "preposterously false" to believe otherwise.[51] "There, friends of the South and of the North, you have the conclusion of the whole matter. Liberty and slavery are before you; choose which you will have; as for us, in the memorable language of the immortal [Patrick] Henry, we say, "give us liberty, or give us death!" In the great struggle for wealth that has been going on between the two rival systems of free and slave labor . . . the struggle on the one side has been calm, laudable, and eminently successful; on the other, it has been attended by tumult, unutterable cruelties and disgraceful failure."[52]

In words that few Southern whites could read without revulsion, Helper maintained that "no man can be a true patriot without first becoming an abolitionist," and "every person who has read the Bible, and who has a proper understanding of its leading moral precepts, feels, in his own conscience, that it is the only original and complete anti-slavery textbook."[53] The Southern response was to ban *The Impending Crisis* throughout the South as false and inflammatory, adding yet another title to its index of forbidden books. Republican Party campaign strategists published excerpts from Helper's book as a campaign document, and Helper was given credit for helping Lincoln's election bid in 1860, for which he was rewarded by the sixteenth president with the American consulship in Buenos Aires, Argentina, in 1861.

The year 1857 also produced a landmark Supreme Court case bearing heavily on the future of slavery in America. Dred Scott had been born a slave in Virginia, and was sold in 1832 or 1833 to Dr. John Emerson, a physician trained at the University of Pennsylvania. Not long after acquiring Scott, Emerson accepted an appointment as an army surgeon and was assigned to Fort Armstrong, located on an island in the Mississippi River that was part of Illinois, a free state but often ready to allow for exceptions. When in 1836 Dr. Emerson was transferred to Fort Snelling in the Wisconsin Territory (in present Minnesota), Dred Scott found himself a slave in land that had been part of the Louisiana Purchase and, at this time, closed to slavery by the Missouri Compromise. In this new setting, Dred Scott met a young slave woman named Harriet Robinson, and the two of

DRED SCOTT. *A slave who sued for his freedom, only to have his case rejected by the U.S. Supreme Court in 1857. In a decision characterized by an unusual number of concurrent opinions, the Taney Court ruled that the right of property in a slave was clearly affirmed by the Constitution, that Congress did not have the right to regulate slavery in the territories, and that, as a black man, Scott was ineligible for U.S. citizenship and could not bring suit in a federal court.*

them were married sometime in 1837 in a civil ceremony presided over by Harriet's owner, who was a major in the army, an Indian agent, and a justice of the peace. Scott's wife Harriet then became the property of Dr. Emerson. A few weeks after Dred and Harriet were married, Dr. Emerson received a reassignment to St. Louis, but chose to leave his slave couple at Fort Snelling where they were hired out to others. Within a month of being assigned to St. Louis, Emerson was given another assignment in Louisiana, where the doctor married in February 1838 and decided that Dred and Harriet Scott should join the newlyweds in April of that year. Apparently dissatisfied with his appointment at Fort Jesup in Louisiana, Dr. Emerson sought and received reassignment back north at Fort Snelling. En route up the Mississippi River to Fort Snelling, Harriet Scott gave birth to a daughter, presumably somewhere north of the line where slavery was prohibited by the Missouri Compromise.[54]

In May 1840 Dr. Emerson was ordered to Florida during the Seminole War, but his wife and the Scotts went to live with Mrs. Emerson's father in St. Louis until Dr. Emerson's military discharge in 1842. When the Emersons moved to Iowa, they left Dred and Harriet Scott behind in St. Louis in the service of one of Mrs. Emerson's relatives. Three years after Dr. Emerson's death in 1843, Mrs. Emerson hired out the Scotts to Samuel Russell. It was at that point that Dred Scott initiated legal proceedings in the Missouri state circuit court in St. Louis to free his wife and himself from slavery.[55] Thus, a case that commenced in April 1846 would not be ultimately resolved until the U.S. Supreme Court rendered its verdict in 1857, eleven years later.[56]

The Dred Scott case was initially argued before the Supreme Court in February 1856. Introduced early into the case by the legal team for the defendants was the contention that Congress lacked authority to exclude slavery from territory purchased from France in 1803. According to Earl M. Maltz, "The introduction of this argument fundamentally changed the nature of the *Dred Scott* litigation. By challenging the constitutionality of the Missouri Compromise, Johnson and Geyer were doing nothing less than inviting the Court to involve itself directly in the political crisis that was deeply dividing the country. Not surprisingly, for the first time the popular press began to take notice of the case."[57]

In essence the high court was, willingly or not, turning this case into a referendum on the federal government's right to exclude slavery from the territories. Acutely aware of the controversy surrounding the 1854 Kansas-Nebraska Act and repeal of the Missouri Compromise, the court in its delay in rendering a final decision in *Dred Scott* demonstrated its aversion to jump headlong into the sectional powder keg of slavery's territorial expansion. The court, comprised of nine justices, seven appointed by Southern proslavery presidents and five who were or had been slave owners, deliberated and did not render a decision until March 6, 1857, just after James Buchanan had been sworn in as the nation's fifteenth president. Chief Justice Roger B. Taney was both a staunch defender of the Union and eager to defend slavery. His hope was that, if the issue of slavery could be put out of the bounds of Congressional action, then sectional hostilities over the issue would subside.[58]He would be sadly disappointed.

The ruling of the court had multiple parts.[59] As an African American, Dred Scott, it was ruled, was not a citizen of the United States and could not bring a suit in a federal court. Two of the high court's justices offered strong dissenting views of this ruling, but did not prevail. While this decision could have put an end to the matter, Chief Justice Taney and the court's majority did not let it rest there. Stating that the Constitution's power given to Congress to regulate U.S. territories "applied only to those territories the United States owned in 1787" and that the Fifth Amendment protected the rights of slaveholders to maintain their property anywhere in U.S. territory, Taney's conclusion was that "the right of property in a slave is distinctly and expressly affirmed in the Constitution."[60] Pushing its judicial activism even further, the court finally ruled that African Americans were not citizens and could not enjoy the privileges of citizenship even if granted by the free states. While Chief Justice Taney wrote the majority opinion, there was an unusually high number of written concurring opinions as these justices, perhaps with an eye to the judgment of history as well as the politics of their section, sought to justify their votes.

Reaction to the *Dred Scott* ruling was swift and heated. Predictably, the Northern and Southern press differed widely in their opinion of the decision. Horace Greeley immediately charged that the court had deliberately delayed a decision until after the 1856 election. Northern opinion condemned the decision as anything from treason to proof that the Supreme Court could not be trusted and that perhaps the great American experiment in republican government was a failure. Slavery's defenders accused Northern dissenters of fomenting disunion. Indeed, Garrison and other radical abolitionists saw in *Dred Scott* the opportunity to advocate for disunion with the slaveholding South, and now looked increasingly at the federal government as the enemy under the influence of the Slave Power. Any chance that the *Dred Scott Case* would serve to lower the intensity of sectional hostility over slavery was gone with the wind. But the decade, with its many surprises, was not over yet.

John Brown's attempt to start a servile insurrection throughout Virginia and the South symbolized a potent and fundamental threat to Southern

ROGER B. TANEY. *Chief justice of the U.S. Supreme Court whose decision in the 1857 Dred Scott case stated that slaveholders had the right to take their slaves into American territories and that African Americans were not citizens and could not bring suits in federal courts. Taney hoped that, by taking the slavery issue out of the hands of Congress, tensions would cool over the issue; the exact opposite resulted.*

security that more than made up for Southern euphoria over the *Dred Scott* decision. On the night of October 16, 1859, Brown led a small band to seize the federal armory at Harpers Ferry, Virginia. The raid was financed by a group of Northern abolitionists. Brown was seriously wounded, captured, tried, and convicted for treason against the United States and hanged on December 2, 1859, at Charles Town, Virginia. Even before his death, John Brown became transfixed upon the cross of martyrdom. On November 18, 1859, Ralph Waldo Emerson stood before a meeting for the relief of the families of John Brown and the other conspirators at Tremont Temple in Boston. Linking Brown to his Mayflower ancestor, Emerson noted that Brown "joins that perfect Puritan faith." Extending his praise of Brown, Emerson waxed:

> It is easy to see what a favorite he will be with history, which plays such pranks with temporary reputations. Nothing can resist the sympathy which all elevated minds must feel with Brown, and through them the whole civilized world; and if he must suffer, he must drag official gentlemen into an immortality, most undesirable of which they must suffer most disagreeable forebodings. Indeed, it is the *reductio ad absurdum* of slavery, when the governor of Virginia is forced to hang a man whom he declares to be a man of the most integrity, truthfulness and courage he has ever met. Is that the kind of man the gallows is built for? It were bold to affirm that there is within that broad commonwealth, at this moment, another citizen as worthy to live, and as deserving of all public and private honor, as this poor prisoner?[661]

Many other intellectual and literary figures of the North, including Henry David Thoreau, turned a blind eye to their personal abhorrence of violence and the contemporary record of the raid itself to praise Brown's actions as both justified and praiseworthy.[62]

John Brown, having no doubt about his ultimate fate, actively participated in the fashioning of his legacy. His address before the court after his conviction was designed to assist in the metamorphosis before a generation of Northern congregations who had become well versed from the pulpit regarding the evils of slavery. Attempting to cloak himself in the mantle of righteous innocence and martyrdom, he made the following statement to the court on November 2, 1859:

> I have, may it please the court, a few words to say. In the first place, I deny everything but what I have all along admitted, the design on my part to free the slaves. I intended certainly to have made a clean thing of that matter, as I did last winter, when I went into Missouri and there took slaves without the snapping of a gun on either side, moved them through the country, and finally left them in Canada. I designed

to have done the same thing again, on a larger scale. That was all I intended. I never did intent [*sic*] murder, or treason, or the destruction of property, or to excite or incite slaves to rebellion, or to make insurrection. I have another objection; and that is, it is unjust that I should suffer such a penalty. Had I interfered in the manner which I admit, and which I admit has been fairly proved (for I admire the truthfulness and candor of the greater portion of the witnesses who have testified in this case), had I so interfered in behalf of the rich, the powerful, the intelligent, the so-called great, or in behalf of any of their friends, either father, mother, brother, sister, wife, or children, or any of that class, and suffered and sacrificed what I have in this interference, it would have been all right; and every man in this court would have deemed it an act worthy of reward rather than punishment. This court acknowledges, as I suppose, the validity of the law of God. I see a book kissed here which I suppose to be the Bible, or at least the New Testament. That teaches me that all things whatsoever I would that men should do to me, I should do even so to them. It teaches me, further, to "remember them that are in bonds, as bound with them." I endeavored to act up to that instruction. I say, I am yet too young to understand that God is any respecter of persons. I believe that to have interfered as I have done as I have always freely admitted I have done in behalf of his despised poor, was not wrong, but right. Now, if it is deemed necessary that I should forfeit my life for the furtherance of the ends of justice, and mingle my blood with the blood of my children and with the blood of millions in this slave country whose rights are disregarded by wicked, cruel, and unjust enactments, I submit; so let it be done!

Brown, further protesting his innocence, attempted to put a benign (and not very convincing) spin on his recent activities: "Let me say one word further. I feel entirely satisfied with the treatment I have received on my trial, considering all the circumstances. It has been more generous than I expected. But I feel no consciousness of guilt. I have stated from the first what was my intention and what was not. I never had any design against the life of any person, nor any disposition to commit treason, or excite slaves to rebel, or make any general insurrection. I never encouraged any man to do so, but always discouraged any idea of that kind."[63]

He then went on to state that everyone who had participated in the raid had done so voluntarily. In a note handed to his jailers on the day of his death, Brown echoed the teaching of the old Puritan theology, invoking divine judgment and prophesying that the end of slavery would only occur in a sea of blood: "I, John Brown, am now quite certain that the crimes of this guilty land will never be purged away but with blood. I had as I now think vainly flattered myself that without very much bloodshed, it might be done."[64] With these words, Brown may have been referring to the apocalyptic imagery in the New Testament Book of The Revelation where it states that the robes of the saints will be washed in the blood of the Lamb.[65]

The Harpers Ferry raid crystallized the fears of the South regarding Northern abolitionism. Although the raid turned out to be a quixotic adventure, the men who financed John Brown were cool headed and calculating. The South realized that there were now men in the North who were quite willing to unleash the horrors of race war on the South for the advancement of their abolitionist agenda. With these men, the abolitionist movement had moved from essentially peaceful and lawful agitation, in itself sufficient to stir Southern wrath, to funding bloodshed on a massive scale upon the Southern hearth and home. Although a failure, the raid raised the stakes exponentially in the struggle for black freedom. An abolitionist-inspired and -funded slave revolt was no longer an imaginary threat conjured up by fire-eaters. Now the very real potential existed for other perhaps more successful attempts toward the same end. The Northern response of metamorphosing John Brown into a martyr and protecting those of his little army that escaped to the North in order to evade prosecution for armed rebellion only accentuated and legitimized the fears, not only of slaveholders, but of non-slaveholding Southerners as well. In the words of Henry Mayer, John Brown's raid on Harpers Ferry "irrevocably moved the slavery controversy from the sphere of constitutional and moral abstraction to the visceral realm of feelings intensified beyond measure or reason."[66] In its later *Declaration of Causes for Secession,* Mississippi referenced Brown and his raid as part of the rationale for abandoning the Union: "It [the North] has invaded a state, and invested with the honors of martyrdom the wretch whose purpose was to apply flames to our dwellings, and the weapons of destruction to our lives."[67]

The decade before the Civil War was a time of troubles, a time of severe testing, and a time when the painful birth pangs of freedom for all Americans were keenly felt, without any real hope that a healthy delivery was even possible. Each side of the slavery issue had shown its willingness and capacity to resort to political maneuvering, provocation, vilification, and ultimately violence in pursuit of its agenda. The slender cords of Union described by a dying John C. Calhoun were quickly being rendered asunder. The tumultuous election of 1860, fought over the issue of slavery, would lead the nation to bloody civil war.

CHAPTER 11

PRESIDENTIAL POLITICS AND THE WAR FOR SLAVERY: THE SOUTHERN DECISION TO SECEDE

The turbulence of the 1850s now spilled over into the election of 1860. This election demolished the remnants of Southern control over the federal government as the Republicans with their agenda for the containment of slavery captured the presidency with a purely sectional vote that effectively blocked the extension of slavery into the territories. In Congress, although the Republicans had a minority in the House, the 1860 election returns would give any Northern Democrat pause about voting against prohibiting slavery in the territories. With control of the presidency, the Republicans possessed the dual weapons of patronage and the veto. Only the Supreme Court was beyond their grasp, until the Republican president had an opportunity to fill vacancies on the aging court.

In the twenty years prior to Lincoln's election the national political landscape had changed dramatically, leading to the demise of the Whig Party and the establishment of several transient antislavery parties culminating in the emergence of the Republican Party. As American churches had divided North and South over slavery in the 1840s, so it would be with the realignment of political interests along sectional lines based largely on the peculiar institution. With the election of Abraham Lincoln, the first Republican president, Southern secession would soon follow as many in the South not only feared that slavery's expansive days were over, but that the institution itself was now at great risk. It would become, to a considerable extent, a self-fulfilling Southern prophecy.

In 1840 the two national political parties, Whigs and Democrats, each had bastions of strength in different parts of the country as well as followers to be found in all regions. Ironically, the Whigs, with greater strength in the North, were led in Congress by Henry Clay, a Southerner, while the Democrats, with greater strength in the South, were led by Martin Van Buren, a Northerner. Given the growing disparity of population, bolstered by immigration, free-state representation in the House of Representatives had reached a forty-two-seat majority over the slave states. Consequently, the free states held a sizeable Electoral College advantage.[1] By 1840, the states where slavery no longer existed or was being phased out were capable of electing a president on their own any time that they could coalesce around a candidate or an agenda. That did not happen until 1860; instead, each president from 1840 to 1856 was elected with a combination of free- and slave-state support.

In 1840, William Henry Harrison was elected president by 52.9 percent of the national vote. This percentage would not be exceeded until Grant's second election in 1872 with 55.6 percent of the vote, and then not again until Theodore Roosevelt was elected in his own right in 1904 (56.4 percent). Harrison, the first president to die in office, was succeeded by John Tyler, whose title to the presidency and credibility with politicians of either party was marginal. Thus a president with a national majority was quickly succeeded by one who had no mandate at all. James Polk was a minority president who garnered 49.5 percent of the popular vote. He was followed by Zachary Taylor, who tallied a lower 47.3 percent of the popular vote due to the candidacy of Martin Van Buren's Free Soil Party.[2] Taylor was viewed initially as a weak president, but by the time of his death he had taken a strong stand for the Union. Taylor was followed by another vice-president, Millard Fillmore, who reversed the policies of his predecessor and, like Tyler before him, was denied nomination to a term in his own right. Fillmore was followed by the only president after Harrison to garner a majority of votes in this period, Franklin Pierce. Pierce garnered a slim national majority of 50.8 percent, even though he achieved a massive victory in the Electoral College. He, in turn, was followed by another minority president, James Buchanan, who managed a popular vote of only 45.3 percent even though his chief opponent, John C. Fremont, was excluded from the ballot in eleven of fourteen slave states, South Carolina not having a popular vote for president until 1868. Lincoln, who like Fremont was excluded from the ballot in nine of fourteen slave states, won the presidency while garnering only 39 percent of the national popular vote.[3]

Hence, the only two presidential popular-vote mandates to govern between 1840 and 1860 included Harrison's comfortable but not overwhelming tally in 1840, and Pierce's narrow majority in 1852. Due to his Jacksonian personality, Polk governed as if he had a majority, while Pierce was one of the nation's weaker presidents. In 1844, both presidential candidates, Polk and Clay, were from slave states. This was the last time both major candidates were slaveholders. Table 1 shows the pattern of nominations from the major parties regarding free and slave "home" states of candidates.

TABLE 1

SLAVERY STATUS OF HOME STATE OF PRESIDENTIAL CANDIDATES, 1840–1860

Year	Democrat	Whig/Republican	Other[a]
1840	Van Buren—Free	Harrison—Free[b]	
1844	Polk—Slave	Clay—Slave	
1848	Cass—Free	Taylor—Slave	Van Buren—Free
1852	Pierce—Free	Scott—Slave	
1856	Buchanan—Free	Fremont—Free	Fillmore—Free
1860	Douglas—Free	Lincoln—Free	Breckenridge—Slave

[a]1848 Free Soil; 1856 Fillmore, Whig/American; 1860 Breckenridge, Southern Democrat.
[b]Harrison, a native Virginian and slaveholder, was elected from Ohio.

The volatility of the electorate, the bane of politicians, was also a factor in these decades. Third parties became a feature of this era. Starting with the small Liberty Party in the 1840s, the period also saw the rise and fall of the Free Soil Party and the American (Know-Nothing) Party. The Liberty and Free Soil parties attacked slavery and advocated its containment by its prohibition in the territories. The American Party's focus was primarily an anti-immigrant, anti-Catholic agenda, but it did not oppose the expansion of slavery into the territories. While the American Party received only eight electoral votes in 1856, these minor parties forced the major party candidates to scramble for pluralities rather than majorities nationally as well as in individual states. Consequently, only one of the five men elected between 1844 and 1860 had a popular vote majority, and then only by a hair.

Yet, the American electoral system with its antiquated but surprisingly effective Electoral College produced for each of the elected presidents a clear mandate in the Electoral College, the true path to the presidency. Table 2 shows the majority percentage of each Electoral College vote from 1840 to 1860.[4]

TABLE 2

ELECTORAL VOTES OF PRESIDENTIAL WINNERS, 1840–1860

Year	President	Electoral Votes Available	Electoral Votes Received	%
1840	Harrison	294	234	80.0%
1844	Polk	275	170	61.8%
1848	Taylor	290	163	56.2%
1852	Pierce	296	254	85.8%
1856	Buchanan	296	174	58.78%
1860	Lincoln	303	180	59.4%

Lincoln's electoral victory in 1860 was greater than Taylor's in 1848 or Buchanan's in 1856. A further analysis will show how significant Lincoln's victory really was. Table 3 shows the electoral vote of the winner, *only showing states in which the victor had a popular majority* of 50 percent or more.[5]

TABLE 3

ELECTORAL VOTES RECEIVED BY WINNING PRESIDENTIAL CANDIDATES FROM MAJORITY-VOTE STATES, 1840–1860

Year	President	Electoral Votes Available	Electoral Votes Received from Majority-Vote States	%
1840	Harrison	294	234	80.0%
1844	Polk	275	129	46.9%
1848	Taylor	290	103	35.51%
1852	Pierce	296	222	75.0%
1856	Buchanan	296	152	51.35%
1860	Lincoln	303	169	55.78%

Polk and Taylor both failed to win a majority of popular votes in enough states to secure an electoral majority. Both depended upon third-party votes (the Free Soilers both times) to deliver them sufficient electoral votes to win the White House. Both Harrison and Pierce secured hefty electoral wins, but Buchanan's winning margin slipped significantly while Lincoln's margin of victory surpassed Buchanan's.

It is instructive to note the gradual sectional polarization of presidential politics in this period, culminating in the election of 1860. The electoral majority shifted from 1840 to 1860 away from the Democrats to the Republicans, successors to the Whigs. Between 1801 and 1861 the Democrats controlled the presidency for forty-eight of those sixty years. Only John Quincy Adams,[6] Harrison-Tyler, and Taylor-Fillmore interrupted the Democratic presidential hegemony. Historically, whoever controlled the Democratic Party had a virtual, though not guaranteed, lock on the presidency. For the party of Jefferson and Jackson with deep roots in the South, it meant dominance if not outright control by Southern slaveholders. Southern Democrats insisted that their Northern colleagues follow the Southern agenda regardless of the consequences to the viability of the party in the North. As the 1850s progressed, this agenda had a devastating effect upon Northern Democrats, significantly reducing their number and weakening the party everywhere.

As is the case today, each party had its loyal states which could normally be counted on for support. For the Democrats these included seven slave states, Alabama, Arkansas, Mississippi, Missouri, South Carolina, Texas, and Virginia, and four free states, California, Indiana, Illinois, Pennsylvania, and until 1856, New Hampshire. In the meantime, the Whigs could normally count on the support of the New England states with the exception of New Hampshire. The party had additional strength in the mid-Atlantic region, including New Jersey, Delaware, and Maryland. North Carolina was another state that leaned toward the Whigs. Beginning in 1852, New Jersey shifted to the Democratic column. The rest of the states, especially the electoral behemoth of New York, would swing between the parties with each election.

Thus, prior to 1856, the electoral maps did not show any regional solidarity. There was no solid North or South, politically speaking. Only New England, in the elections of 1824 and 1828 when the candidate was John Quincy Adams, acted as a sectional grouping. But in 1856, the electoral Solid South appears on the map for the first time. Every slave state except Maryland, which voted for Fillmore, voted for a single candidate, James Buchanan. However, this was not sufficient to elect Buchanan. The dependably Democratic states of Illinois, Indiana, New Jersey, Pennsylvania, and California gave Buchanan their 62 electoral votes and the margin of victory. Yet California (48.4 percent), Illinois (44.1 percent) and New Jersey (47.1 percent) could only muster pluralities for the Democratic nominee. Nonetheless, the overall Democratic vote in the free states dropped to an anemic 41 percent. Fremont, the first Republican presidential standard bearer, who by any measure was a flawed candidate, swept New England with majorities ranging from Connecticut's 53.2 percent to Vermont's 78.1

percent. Heretofore dependably Democratic New Hampshire also went solidly for Fremont. New York and Ohio gave Fremont pluralities while Michigan, Wisconsin, and Iowa garnered majorities for the Pathfinder. Overall, Fremont had a 45 percent plurality of the free state vote with a solid 114 electoral votes, 65 percent of the free-state electoral votes. Fremont's electoral vote was 35 short of the then requisite 149, a very impressive showing for the first candidate of a new, and clearly sectional, party. The fledgling Republican Party had come very close to electing a president on its first attempt and was immediately recognized as a major threat by many leading politicians of the South. The 1856 election had turned out to be closer than the electoral count indicated, and the decline of the Democratic Party in the North was apparent for all to see.

The election of 1856 signaled a major electoral shift and set the stage for Lincoln's election in 1860. The days of various Northern and Southern states forming electoral combinations were over. Northern reaction to the Kansas-Nebraska Act, first evident in the Congressional elections of 1854–55, expressed itself on the presidential level in 1856. Although the slave states had given Buchanan 56 percent of its popular vote and all but Maryland's 8 electoral votes, it was not enough. It was now evident to the entire country that the slave states did not have sufficient electoral votes to either elect or block a president if the North united behind a candidate.

After 1856, Southern success in national elections would depend upon retaining the electoral votes of states like Pennsylvania, Illinois, Indiana, and New Jersey. However, a profound shift was occurring in Northern public opinion that would affect the 1860 election in these states. This electoral shift had its beginnings with the presidential ambitions of Stephen Douglas. With his Kansas-Nebraska Act, he unknowingly sowed the seeds for the collapse of the Democratic Party. The Lecompton controversy in Kansas, popular sovereignty gone wrong, placed Douglas and the Northern Democrats in a no-win situation. If Douglas supported the proslavery Lecompton Constitution, he risked losing reelection to the Senate in 1858 and Northern support for his planned presidential run in 1860. As a result of the Lecompton fiasco, the ranks of the Northern Congressional Democrats, whose party had not recovered from the elections of 1854, were again reduced in the 1858 elections. As fallout from the Lecompton controversy of 1858 spread, nearly everyone came to blame Douglas's unpopular "popular sovereignty" position for their troubles. Looking ahead to 1860 there was, however, no other viable Northern Democrat to supplant Douglas. As unpopular as they had become, the discredited philosophy of popular sovereignty and the repeal of the Missouri Compromise could not be abandoned by Northern Democrats because to do so would be to admit that these were terrible mistakes for which Douglas and the party bore responsibility. At the same time, a Southern standard bearer for the Democrats would have great difficulty retaining those crucial Northern states since strident proslavery views were increasingly anathema in the North.

Thus, the Democratic Party, already damaged by disagreement over the situation in Kansas, disintegrated as a national body. In February 1860, Southern leadership abandoned the doctrine of popular sovereignty, and while claiming Congress had no power to regulate slavery in the territories, pressed a new demand for the protection of slavery. Led by Senator Jefferson Davis of Mississippi, the South now demanded that Congress pass a federal slave code that would guarantee slavery in the territories until a territory asked for admission as a state. Quite possibly, the timing of the proposal was meant to sabotage Douglas's presidential bid while promoting Davis's ambitions. Douglas, already out of favor with many Southern Democrats after his opposition to President Buchanan's support for the admission of Kansas as a slave state, now opposed the slave code as well. The Senate passed the code, but a coalition of Republicans and Northern Democrats desperate to retain their seats in Congress defeated it in the House.

When the Democrats met at their presidential nominating convention in Charleston in April 1860, a serious rift erupted over a proposed platform plank calling for a federal territorial slave code—a measure opposed by Northern Democrats, including Douglas. When the slave code failed to gain inclusion into the party's platform, the entire delegations from six Cotton Kingdom states walked out, as well as a portion of the Delaware and Arkansas delegations. South Carolina Congressman John Ashmore blamed the debacle on "the obstinate & offensive course of the friends of Douglas . . . [who] damn the South with great fury, saying that they can go to Hell."[7] Southern honor had been slighted again. The Charleston convention eventually adjourned without reaching closure on either a platform or a candidate. Convention rules demanded a two-thirds majority vote of delegates to secure the nomination, and while Douglas had a majority, he could not muster the required two-thirds.[8]

This whole scenario was not good news for Douglas, who won a rather hollow victory to become the Democratic standard bearer at a reconvened convention in Baltimore in June. Disaffected Southern delegates nominated Vice-President of the United States John C. Breckinridge of Kentucky as their candidate, and approved a platform that called for a federal slave code and freedom for slaveholders to bring their slaves into the territories.

Douglas and the Northern Democrats held onto the concept of popular sovereignty as envisioned in the Kansas-Nebraska Act, but threw the final decision of the issue to the Supreme Court. After Dred Scott, this would not be an acceptable solution in the North. Both Northern and Southern factions of the Democratic Party called for the annexation of Cuba to extend the Slave Power to the Caribbean. While previous Democratic plat-forms had contained this land grab, it is difficult to imagine why, when the campaign was being fought over the extension of slavery into the existing territories, Northern voters would endorse the annexation of another slave territory in 1860. The Democratic Party now had two presidential candi-dates, each with a regional following. The new Republican Party, mean-while, could hardly have asked for a greater gift than the disintegration of the Democrats into Northern and Southern factions.

Surprising everyone, Republican delegates passed over their front-runner, the abolitionist Senator William H. Seward of New York. The fact that the 1860 Republican convention was held in antislavery Chicago and that Abraham Lincoln was a "favorite son" candidate of Illinois and accept-able throughout the state, whereas Seward's more strident abolitionist posturing made him unpopular in much of Southern and Central Illinois, all worked in Lincoln's favor. Neither did it hurt that the *Chicago Press & Tribune* headline on the day before the convention opened read, "The Winning Man—Abraham Lincoln."[9] While Seward entered the conven-tion as the favorite, there were others close behind; Salmon Chase, Simon Cameron, and Edward Bates each had their supporters—but also their detractors (and surprisingly all would end up in the Lincoln cabinet).[10] Lincoln, on the other hand, was perhaps the favorite of relatively few del-egates, but neither did he carry the weighty baggage of numerous detrac-tors. Moderation was a virtue to many of the delegates, especially after the fanatical John Brown raid of a few months before, and Lincoln seemed to fit the bill. Seward failed to obtain a majority on the first ballot, his sup-port slipped, and Republicans nominated the more conservative and less controversial Lincoln on the third ballot at the "Wigwam" in Chicago on May 18, 1860. In addition to its platform provision banning slavery in the territories, the Republicans enhanced their electoral appeal with proposals for cheap land in the West (a proposed homestead act), a transcontinen-tal railroad, federally sponsored internal improvements, and a stronger protective tariff. Republicans, after nominating the moderate Lincoln and presenting a platform with broad appeal in the North, were now buoyed by great optimism that their party stood an excellent chance of winning

WILLIAM H. SEWARD. *Expected to win the Republican presidential nomination in 1860, Senator Seward held abolitionist views that proved too radical, and the more moderate Lincoln captured the nomination on the third ballot, naming the New Yorker as his secretary of state. Seward became a staunch Lincoln supporter during the war. Although seriously injured, Seward narrowly escaped assassination on the same night Lincoln was shot.*

the general election given the sectional rift in the Democratic Party. A fourth candidate in 1860, John Bell (a Tennessee slaveholder) of the Constitutional Union Party, offered a nondescript platform of platitudes and a vague call for national reconciliation.

With four parties in the contest, it would seem that confusion would reign everywhere. But this was not the case. Two of the parties, the Republicans and the Southern Democrats, rejected popular sovereignty, still a mainstay of the Douglas Democrats. More significantly, the Republicans and the Breckenridge Democrats offered clear visions as to what kind of future they wanted for the country. The Republican future was a country where slavery was banned from the territories and restricted to where it already existed, hopefully gradually to become extinct through individual state action. The Breckenridge Democrats wanted an America which not only allowed slavery to spread in the territories under the protection of a federal slave code but also was willing to continue expanding the country's borders to include more slave territory such as Cuba.

From the perspective of the Northern electorate, the failure of the popular sovereignty movement had already resulted from the violence in "Bleeding Kansas" and the debate on the proslavery Lecompton Constitution. Bleeding Kansas demonstrated that both sides on the issue of slavery's extension would use violence and extralegal means to get their way. From the Northern viewpoint, the South had overreached with its failed attempt to force Kansas into the Union as a slave state. Now, the South was making a new demand, a federal slave code to guarantee slavery in the territories. Popular sovereignty had lost its attractiveness, and Douglas, both as author and political midwife to the Kansas-Nebraska Act, suffered as a result. By presenting only a warmed-over version of popular sovereignty, the Douglas Democrats offered nothing new to either section.

Likewise, the Southern electorate was not in the mood for compromise. From the Southern perspective, slavery was now in mortal danger. Popular sovereignty had failed. The attempt to admit Kansas as a slave state had been rejected. Slavery, which needed to expand, was not taking root in Utah and only had a very tentative hold in parts of New Mexico. John Brown's raid had highlighted the eagerness of some Northern abolitionists to bring servile war to the South. Rumors and reports of slave violence in faraway Texas accentuated these fears. The Constitutional Unionists only offered a vague form of unity in their platform, and had appeal in some border states. However, like the North, the South wanted a solution, not a sugar pill, for the slavery question.

The Republicans, confident of victory with the split in the Democratic Party, proceeded to collect the 152 electoral votes they needed from the free states. With their electoral base from the 1856 election, reinforced in New England by the nomination of Maine's Hannibal Hamlin for vice-president, they could count on the electoral votes of these staunchly anti-Southern (and less-so antislavery) states. By then having Seward secure New York's continued electoral support, and counting on Fremont's 1856 wins in the Upper Midwest, along with the newly admitted state of Minnesota, a stronghold of free-soil Scandinavian farmers, a base of 118 electoral votes could be garnered. The next two states to look at were Indiana (13 votes) and Illinois (11 votes). Fremont had polled 40 percent in both states in 1856, and in 1860 there would not be an American Party candidate to divide the opposition. Republicans had done well in Illinois in the election of 1858, although the Democrats retained a slight edge in the state legislature, preventing Lincoln from taking Douglas's Senate seat. Buchanan had carried the Hoosier State by a bare majority, but again, Bleeding Kansas, Lecompton, John Brown, and immigration had changed the political character of the state. If things worked out, the Republicans would now have 136 electoral votes.

California and Oregon were geographically too far away to organize much of a campaign. California had voted Democratic in the past, and Oregon, while a free state, was exceedingly anti-black. New Jersey, with its Southern sympathies, would likely vote Democratic. The four electoral votes Lincoln got out of the Garden State on election night were icing on the electoral cake. The key for Lincoln was holding on to New York and winning Pennsylvania, producing either an electoral victory or, at the least, a fight in the House of Representatives between Lincoln and John Breckenridge, with Douglas as potential king-maker. Pennsylvania Democrats largely detested the Little Giant, so for all intents and purposes, Breckenridge, Buchanan's vice-president, would be the standard bearer of the Democratic Party in their eyes. So in Pennsylvania, the choice came down to the two extremes of the election—Lincoln and Breckenridge. In the end, Lincoln won an impressive 56.3 percent of the vote, a margin unknown in Pennsylvania presidential voting. Early on, Lincoln made the shrewd decision to concentrate on the free states and ignore the border states as hopelessly lost, which they were. That decision paid off on election day.

When the votes were in, Lincoln carried seventeen out of the eighteen free states. While Douglas carried the Garden State's popular vote, he managed to lose 4 of New Jersey's 7 electoral votes since Lincoln won slim majorities in four of the five congressional districts. Of the remaining seventeen free states, Lincoln received absolute majorities in fifteen of them for an electoral victory of 169 votes. The Democratic factions split the vote in California, leaving Lincoln with a plurality of 32 percent. Likewise, Oregon gave Lincoln a 36 percent plurality over his Democratic rivals. Nationally, Lincoln had carried 39 percent of the popular vote, even though nine states refused to put his party and his name on the ballot. However, Lincoln garnered 55 percent of the popular vote in the free states. The electoral vote of the free states for Lincoln was 180 to 3. Adding the electoral votes of the border states that would remain in the Union, the electoral vote was 180 to 29. Lincoln was the undisputed and constitutionally elected president. Significantly, he won a popular and electoral vote mandate of landslide proportions from the portion of the country that he would lead during the Civil War. The free North had united around an agenda to contain slavery where it existed and send it on a path to gradual extinction. Meanwhile, the South rallied around an agenda for the expansion of slavery in the territories and abroad.

In reality, there were two national elections in 1860. Each section held its own election without much reference to the other. In the North, the election was between prohibiting slavery in the territories versus popular sovereignty. Only in Pennsylvania was the election fought primarily between the forces of Lincoln and Breckenridge. There Lincoln achieved an overwhelming victory. In the slave states the contest was between guaranteeing slavery in the territories versus Bell's promises of normalcy and reconciliation. Each section had rejected popular sovereignty for its own solution to the slavery question. Meanwhile, the border states returned a mixed message, but popular sovereignty did not fare well there, either. Nonetheless, like the ecclesiastical world of the 1840s, the body politic of 1860 had now broken apart into two divergent camps.

The election returns emboldened the radicals, North and South. Abolitionists and fire-eaters alike believed that their hour had come. Early and radical Southern secessionists, known as "fire-eaters" in the North, had re-emerged as a potent political force in Southern politics by 1860. Unlike the abolitionists who were now celebrating their great electoral victory, the fire-eaters did not want electoral victory; they wanted disunion. They initially thought they could derail Douglas's nomination and perhaps replace him with an unpopular Southern candidate that would be readily rejected by the North. The third-party option only seriously developed after the second Democratic convention in Baltimore nominated Douglas. Perhaps a divided party on the ballot could deliver pluralities to elect Lincoln, weakening his stature in the North, while assuring secession in the South. While acknowledging the legitimacy of Lincoln's election, fire-eaters would claim that he was a sectional president and therefore unfit to rule and that they would not accept this situation. The fire-eaters thought they had won. But what they failed to discern, to their regret, was that Lincoln was indeed a sectional president but also the overwhelming choice of that powerful section.

The fire-eaters also ignored some other bad news on election night. If one considers Breckenridge the candidate of secession and Bell the candidate of reconciliation, the results were not promising for the future Confederacy. In Missouri, Breckenridge could only muster a distant third in a four-man race, polling a paltry 18.9 percent. Douglas and Bell combined for 71 percent of the vote while Lincoln picked up another 10 percent, foreshadowing Missouri's Unionist sympathies. Kentucky rejected her popular favorite son, John Breckenridge. He received 36 percent, with Bell receiving a substantial 45 percent plurality. In its congressional elections held in early 1861, nine of its ten Congressional districts went heavily for Union Party candidates. Only the district around Paducah voted for a secessionist candidate. Kentucky, the home of the Great Compromiser, Henry Clay, wanted reconciliation or neutrality and ultimately opted for the Union for which a substantial majority of her sons fought. Maryland split its vote 45.9 percent for Breckenridge and 45.1 percent for Bell. Like Kentucky, Maryland voters elected a congressional delegation favorable to the Union—five Union Republicans and a Peace Democrat. Maryland would not leave the Union, either. Like Maryland, Delaware also voted for Breckenridge, by a margin of 45.5 percent but elected a Unionist candidate to the House. However, Delaware was the only border state to give Lincoln a substantial vote count (23.7 percent) along with 24 percent for Bell, indicating that the vote for Breckenridge did not necessarily portend secession. When war came, Delaware, despite some opposition, steadfastly remained with the Union.[11]

If the votes in these states foretold problems for the South, the electoral results in the future Confederacy also hinted at dark days ahead. All the Southern states that made up the Confederacy voted for Breckenridge except for Virginia and Tennessee, which voted for Bell, 44.6 percent and 47.1 percent respectively. These latter votes represented a strong vote for compromise and gave these states pause in the initial round of secession. North Carolina did muster 50 percent for Breckenridge and 46 percent for Bell, foreshadowing civil strife in that state. North Carolina, like Virginia and Tennessee, would wait until the second round before seceding from the Union. The political divide between the planter tidewater and the yeoman-dominated hill country appeared everywhere, foreshadowing the differences that would split these states during the war.

Alabama and Arkansas gave their votes to Breckenridge, but their Democratic majorities dropped by nearly ten points from the 1856 totals amassed by the Buchanan-Breckenridge ticket to barely over 50 percent. In each case, Bell drew a third of the vote (30 percent in Alabama, 37 percent in Arkansas). Georgia and Louisiana could only muster pluralities for Breckenridge, with Bell receiving 40 percent in each of these states. Florida, Mississippi, and Texas were the only Southern states that provided large majorities for Breckenridge and future secession. Yet even in these states, Bell garnered a substantial minority.[12] The South Carolina legislature, of course, voted for Breckenridge. The November election results in the South reflected hesitancy, in fact an unwillingness, of many Southerners to break apart the Union. While the secession votes of January and February 1861 would result in decisions for secession, the overall vote was smaller than it was in November 1860, and intimidation was widespread. The fundamental underpinning of the Confederate South rested on coercion, not only of its slaves but of its white population as well. The South was about to pay a terrible price for both.

In 1860–61, the seceding states, which proclaimed their adherence to the letter of the Constitution of 1787, sought by their actions to nullify not a piece of legislation, but a free election following the process described in the Constitution. In essence, the seceding states sought to nullify the very Constitution they claimed they were defending. None of the declarations of secession questioned the legitimacy of Lincoln's election. Lincoln, albeit a sectional candidate, had won a national election premised on the electoral votes of the sovereign states. No threat had been made by Lincoln to the peace or tranquility of the South. In fact, he had openly acknowledged the federal government's duty to return fugitive slaves and to protect slavery where it existed. The rationale for secession was, in reality, far more complicated than the election of Lincoln, but his victory was a gauntlet thrown down by the North to the defenders of slavery and the way of life it made possible.

Lincoln's election on November 6, 1860, sent shock waves through the South. In a Thanksgiving Day sermon delivered on November 29, Rev. Benjamin Palmer, minister of the First Presbyterian Church of New Orleans, viewed the Republican victory as nothing short of the "spirit of atheism" which has selected the South "for its victims, and slavery for its issue," and was waiting "to inaugurate its reign of terror. To the South the high position is assigned of defending, before all nations, the cause of all religion and of all truth." Resistance—that is, secession and even war—is a "duty to ourselves, to our slaves, to the world, and to Almighty God."

It was nothing short of doing God's work "to preserve and transmit our existing system of domestic servitude, with the right, unchallenged by man, to go and root itself wherever Providence and nature may carry it. This trust we will discharge in the face cf the worst possible peril. Though war be the aggregation of all evils, yet should the madness of the hour [the election of Lincoln] appeal to the arbitration of the sword, we will not shrink even from the baptism of fire."[13] While most Northerners believed that the country was the "shining city on a hill," an example for freedom throughout the world, the Reverend Palmer envisioned a confederacy that would not only propagate slavery, but do so virtually without limits. Despite Palmer's heated rhetoric, even he had to acknowledge that Lincoln had been elected fairly and had pledged not to disturb slavery where it currently existed. But to Palmer, Lincoln was not to be trusted—his opposition to the extension of slavery and the reopening of the slave trade was a sure sign that eventually Lincoln would seek an end to slavery everywhere.[14]

Senator Robert Toombs of Georgia, among that state's most popular politicians in 1860, gave a pro-secession speech at the invitation of the Georgia General Assembly on November 13, 1860, in which he stated that the presidential election of a week earlier

> demands resistance to the rule of Lincoln and his Abolitionist horde over us; he comes at their head to shield and protect them in the perpetration of these outrages against us, and what is more, he comes at their head to aid them in consummating their avowed purposes by the power of the Federal Government. Their main purpose, as indicated by all their acts of hostility to slavery, is its final and total abolition. His party declare it; their acts prove it. He has declared it; I accept his declaration. . . . They declare their purpose to war against slavery until there shall not be a slave in America, and until the African is elevated to a social and political equality with the white man. Lincoln endorses them and their principles, and in his own speeches declares the conflict irrepressible and enduring, until slavery is everywhere abolished. . . . Then strike while it is yet today. Withdraw your sons from the army, from the navy, and from every department of the Federal public service. Keep your own taxes in your own coffers—buy arms with them and throw the bloody spear into this den of incendiaries and assassins, and let God defend the right.[15]

Secession would come for seven states even before Lincoln took office, while the nation was still under the leadership of the feckless Buchanan administration. William W. Freehling has rightly identified secession as "profoundly a preventative strike, to preclude natural rights violations that had not yet occurred."[16]

The issues that led to Southern secession were varied and complex, but they had a central thread running through them—the preservation of slavery and a desire for its expansion. Underlying the justification of slavery were white-supremacist racism and the social order that it allowed. The alleged inferiority of the black race was not only implied, it was openly discussed in the South, as articulated by Palmer and thousands of others, generally with the faulty assumption that most Northerners disagreed and sought complete equality of the races, a position that Lincoln himself only approached very near the end of his life. While Confederate leaders such as President Jefferson Davis and Vice-President Alexander Stephens insisted in their postwar reflections on the conflict that slavery was the "question" or the "occasion" on which larger conflicting principles, most notably states' rights, were at play,[17] an examination of secessionist documents and arguments makes it difficult to deny the foundational role of slavery, and belief in black inferiority, in the secessionist movement. The postwar architects of the lost-cause myth ennobled their sacrifice as solely a struggle for states' rights rather than for the discredited institution of slavery.

It began on December 20, 1860, when South Carolina's secession convention declared that "the Union heretofore existing between this state and the other States of North America is dissolved, and that the State of South Carolina has resumed her position among the nations of the world, as a separate and independent state." Four days later, on Christmas Eve, in its "Declaration of Immediate Causes for Secession," South Carolina stated that at the heart of the matter was the perception that the North

> assumed the right of deciding upon the propriety of our domestic institutions; and have denied the rights of property established in fifteen of the States and recognized by the Constitution; they have denounced as sinful the institution of Slavery; they have permitted the open establishment among them of societies, whose avowed object is to disturb the peace of and eloign the property of the citizens of other States. They have encouraged and assisted thousands of our slaves to leave their homes; and those who remain, have been incited by emissaries, books, and pictures, to servile insurrection. . . .

> A geographical line has been drawn across the Union, and all the states north of that line have united in the election of a man to the high office of President of the United States whose opinions and purposes are hostile to slavery. He is to be intrusted with the administration of the common Government, because he has declared that "Government cannot endure permanently half slave, half free" and that the public mind must rest in the belief that Slavery is in the course of ultimate extinction.[18]

Mississippi's *Declaration of Immediate Causes* resembled that of South Carolina, and included the statement that "Our position is thoroughly identified with the institution of slavery. . . . There was no choice left us but submission to the mandates of abolition, or a dissolution of the union, whose principles had been subverted to work our ruin." The Republican ascendancy under Lincoln "advocates negro equality, socially and politically, and promotes insurrection and incendiarism in our midst. . . . Utter subjugation awaits us in the Union, if we should consent longer to remain in it."[19]

Georgia and Texas issued similar declarations defending their peculiar institution. The Georgia "Report on Causes for Secession" proclaimed that the North had outlawed "our property in the common territories of the Union, put it under the ban of the Republic in the States where it [slavery] exists, and out of the protection of Federal law everywhere . . . because their avowed purpose is to subvert our society, and subject us, not only to the loss of our property but the destruction of ourselves, our wives, and our children, and the desolation of our homes, our altars, and our firesides."[20] In the case of Texas, which revolted against Mexico in part over the issue of slavery in 1835, history was to a degree repeating itself. Twisting the words enshrined in the Declaration of Independence, the Texas secession convention declared:

> We hold as undeniable truths that the governments of the various States, and of the confederacy itself, were established exclusively by the white race, for themselves and their posterity; that the African race had no agency in their establishment; that they were rightfully held and regarded as an inferior and dependent race, and in that condition only could their existence in this country be rendered beneficial or tolerable.
>
> That in this free government all white men are and of right ought to be entitled to equal civil and political rights; that the servitude of the African race, as existing in these States, is mutually beneficial to both bond and free, and is abundantly authorized and justified by the experiences of mankind, and the revealed will of the Almighty Creator, as recognized by all Christian nations; while the destruction of the existing relations between the two races, as advocated by our sectional enemies, would bring inevitable calamities upon both and desolation upon the fifteen slave-holding States.[21]

Eleven states would soon leave the Union and form the Confederate States of America. Seven of these seceded between Lincoln's election and his inauguration. In chronological order they were South Carolina, Mississippi, Florida, Alabama, Georgia, Louisiana, and Texas. Of these seven

states, two (South Carolina and Mississippi) had more slaves than freemen, and four had slave populations averaging 45 percent of their total
population. Only Texas, with a slave population of 20 percent, did not have
those in bondage either exceeding or approaching a majority of its population. Virginia, Arkansas, Tennessee, and North Carolina, with proportion-
ally fewer slaves than the states of the Deep South, left the Union in April
and May of 1861 following Lincoln's call for volunteers to put down the
rebellion that had begun with the attack on Fort Sumter on April 12, 1861.

Various theories about the reasons for secession and the historical interpretations surrounding these reasons have provided a great many scholarly
debates. While there were many factors involved, the preservation of slavery and its need to expand and continue to "diffuse" its ever-growing slave
populations were foundational in the eyes of the Southern ruling class.

The election of Lincoln did not make secession inevitable; indeed,
Alexander Stephens, later vice-president of the Confederacy, argued
before the Georgia legislature on November 14, 1860, the day after Robert
Toombs's secessionist speech, that everything possible should be done to
preserve the Union. "In my judgment," Stephens proclaimed, "the election
of no man, constitutionally chosen to that high office, is sufficient cause
for any State to separate from the Union."[22] But clearly, Southern misper-
ceptions of Lincoln's intentions fueled secessionist fires. What has often
been overlooked is the degree of debate and division within the South itself
over secession. As Michael P. Johnson has shown, in the case of Georgia, "secession was necessary because of the internal divisions within the
South, divisions which focused on the degree to which the slaveholding
minority could have its way in a government ultimately based on manhood
suffrage." Johnson sees in secession a "double revolution: a revolution for
home rule—to eliminate the external threat; and a conservative revolution for those who ruled at home—to prevent the political realization of
the internal threat. Men with conservative social and political ideas were
instrumental not only in creating the small electoral margin the secessionists enjoyed in Georgia, but also in the definition and direction of the second revolution."[23]

Further evidence of the centrality of slavery to the secessionist movement can be gleaned from the farewell addresses of Southern members
of the U.S. Senate as they left Washington for their new Southern Confederacy, as well as from the work of the secession commissioners whose
job it was to convince slave states not yet seceded that they should do so.
Senator Robert Toombs of Georgia had strong words for his fellow senators in his farewell address of January 7, 1861. President-elect Lincoln,

Toombs maintained, was "an enemy of the human race, and deserves the execration of mankind." Toombs went on to quote and attack the Republican Party's 1860 platform declaring that the territories should be free of slavery, and that Republicans thus "seek to outlaw $4,000,000,000 of property of our people in the Territories of the United States. Is that not a cause of war?" Toombs demanded. He again attacked Lincoln, who "ignorantly puts his authority for abolition upon the Declaration of Independence, which was never made any part of the public law of the United States. It is well known that these 'glittering generalities' [regarding human equality] were never adopted into the Constitution of the United States." Lincoln was further castigated by Toombs: "you not only want to upturn our social system; your people not only steal our slaves and make them freemen to vote against us; but you seek to bring an inferior race in a condition of equality, socially and politically, with our own people. . . . [W]e want no negro equality, no negro citizenship; we want no mongrel race to degrade our own."[24] Senator Jefferson Davis of Mississippi withdrew from the U.S. Senate after delivering his farewell speech on January 21, 1861. In it, he attacked those who used the "sacred Declaration of Independence" to "maintain the position of the equality of the races." In the Declaration, asserted Davis, the Founders "have no reference to the slave" and, in fact, railed against George III for the same thing the North was currently attempting—"to stir up insurrection among our slaves."[25] Alabama Senator Clement Claiborne Clay included the following remarks in his departure address on January 22, 1861:

> It is now nearly forty-two years since Alabama was admitted into the Union. She entered it, as she goes out of it, while the Confederacy was in convulsions, caused by the hostility of the North to the domestic slavery of the South. Not a decade, nor scarce a lustrum, has elapsed, since her birth, that has not been strongly marked by proofs of the growth and power of that anti-slavery spirit of the Northern people which seeks the overthrow of that domestic institution of the South, which is not only the chief source of her prosperity, but the very basis of her social order and State policy. . . . It denied us Christian communion, because it could not endure what it styles the moral leprosy of slaveholding; it refused us permission to sojourn, or even to pass through the North, with our property. . . . [I]t violated the Constitution and treaties and laws of Congress . . . designed to protect that property. . . . The platform of the Republican Party of 1856 and 1860 we regard as a libel upon the character and a declaration of war against the lives and property of the Southern people. No bitterer or offensive calumny could be uttered against them than is expressed in denouncing their system of slavery and polygamy as "twin relics of barbarism."[26]

After Lincoln's election in late 1860, five Deep South states appointed men to act as agents to travel throughout the other slave states to convince them of the merits of secession. Known as secession commissioners, fifty-two men took on this task, many of them relatively unknown beyond a local level, but articulate individuals having the ability to persuade with the spoken and/or written word. These men spoke to state legislatures, state secession conventions, and general public meetings about the merits of disunion. They also wrote letters to leading state political figures.[27] Their arguments are a vitally important source of information about what motivated secession. Governor John J. Pettus of Mississippi and Governor Andrew B. Moore of Alabama named commissioners shortly after Lincoln's election. According to Moore, the Republican agenda was "the destruction of the institution of slavery," and without disunion, "the peace, interests, security and honor of the slaveholding states" was in jeopardy.[28] Stephen Hale, an Alabama secession commissioner who had been born in Kentucky, was sent to his native state, but arrived at a time when the legislature was not in session. Instead of speaking to Kentucky lawmakers, Hale penned a remarkable letter to the state's governor, Beriah Magoffin. In his letter to Governor Magoffin, Hale makes disparaging reference to Lincoln's vice-president, Hannibal Hamlin of Maine, who according to the *Charleston Mercury,* "had negro blood in his veins and . . . one of his children had kinky hair." Hale went on to say that a Lincoln administration was

> nothing less than an open declaration of war, for the triumph of this new theory of government destroys the property of the South, lays waste her fields, and inaugurates all the horrors of a San Domingo servile insurrection, consigning her citizens to assassinations and her wives and daughters to pollution and violation to gratify the lust of half-civilized Africans. . . . The slave-holder and non-slave-holder must ultimately share the same fate; all be degraded to a position of equality with free negroes, stand side by side with them at the polls, and fraternize in all the social relations of life, or else there will be an eternal war of races, desolating the land with blood, and utterly wasting all the resources of the country.

What white Southerner, queried Hale, "can without indignation and horror contemplate the triumph of negro equality, and see his own sons and daughters in the not distant future associating with free negroes upon terms of political and social equality?"[29] According to Charles Dew's study of the secession commissioners, Hale's comments were "representative" of the messages given by other commissioners "almost simultaneously in

places as distant as Maryland and Missouri."[30] Dew's analysis of the secession commissioners' work was that they repeatedly prophesied the South's
worst three-part nightmare of their world to come in a Lincoln-Republican
administration: racial equality, race war, and racial amalgamation.[31]

On March 12, 1861, Alexander Stephens, life-long friend of Robert
Toombs and now vice-president of the Confederate States, gave the most
infamous and forthright speech dealing with slavery as a fundamental principle of the new republic. In an oration that became known as the "Cornerstone Speech," Stephens asserts that "the new [Confederate States] Constitution has put at rest *forever* all the agitating questions relating to our
peculiar institutions—African slavery as it exists among us—the proper
status of the negro in our form of civilization. This was the immediate
cause of the late rupture and present revolution." Stephens then acknowledged that the American Founders in 1787 believed that slavery was "an
evil they knew not well how to deal with" and that "the institution would
be evanescent and pass away." Stephens went on to say, "This was an
error. It was a sandy foundation, and the idea of a Government built upon
it; when the 'storm came and wind blew, it *fell.*'" Vice-President Stephens
then made it perfectly clear on what grand idea the Confederacy rested
(despite his postwar statements to the contrary): "Our new government
is founded upon exactly the opposite idea; its foundations are laid, its
cornerstone rests, upon the great truth that the negro is not equal to the
white man; that slavery—subordination to the superior race—is his natural and moral condition. (Applause.)"[32] Jefferson Davis criticized Stephens
for this speech, but he did not disagree with its content, only its timing in
light of the Confederacy's desire to secure European recognition as early as
possible.

It was the political genius of Lincoln to understand that he did not have
a mandate for war with the South. Some Northerners voted for Lincoln,
not out of support for the candidate or his party's agenda, but out of
abhorrence for the machinations of Douglas or the continued subservience
of the remnants of the Northern Democrats to the Southern agenda. The
political agenda of the free states, expressed by the election of Lincoln, was
that slavery would be prohibited in the territories. The consensus agenda
was only about the containment of slavery, not its abolition. Some Northerners who supported Lincoln in the election welcomed the departure of
the first seven Southern states. Let them and their slaves go in peace! The
territories would be theirs and open to free settlement. However, this view
did not take into account what would then be done by the remaining eight
slave states that initially stayed in the Union. Some Northerners did not

believe that secession would last or that the South would really leave the Union. Accustomed to ever-petulant Southern demands, many, including Lincoln, believed that the South would eventually come to its senses and find an accommodation with the national government.

The final proof that the North was neither voting for war nor expecting war to come was the Northern reaction to the Fort Sumter crisis. It clearly was a wake-up call. Lincoln, in his inaugural address, had said it best: "In *your* hands, my dissatisfied fellow-countrymen, and not in *mine,* is the momentous issue of civil war. The Government will not assail *you.* You can have no conflict without being yourselves the aggressors. *You* have no oath registered in heaven to destroy the Government, while I shall have the most solemn one to "preserve, protect, and defend it." Lincoln then used Southern political necessity, Southern ego, Southern bellicosity, and the political weakness of Jefferson Davis to push the South to attack Fort Sumter and force the North into war. Southern political necessity required that Fort Sumter be surrendered. No entity claiming to be an independent and sovereign state can allow a "foreign power" to hold a military installation in one of its chief ports. The martial ardor of the South, combined with their sense of honor, ultimately demanded that Fort Sumter *not be surrendered* but *taken* after Anderson's defiant stand in the harbor. The Southern authorities knew that Anderson would be starved out in a matter of days, but they wanted a victory. Davis knew that Lincoln was maneuvering him into a corner. But, as the newly elected president in convention, Davis was politically weak and ordered Beauregard to attack Sumter anyway. Only then did the North decide that it would have to go to war.

Both sides assumed naively that the war would last only a few months at most, and that they would win handily. At the outset, the North, far from pushing racial equality, pursued the war to prevent disunion rather than to end slavery, while the South went to war to preserve its "rights," although the chief "right" the South sought to defend was the freedom to hold human property in a white supremacist society and to take that property wherever the master class so chose. Abraham Lincoln made it clear in his second inaugural address that "slaves constituted a peculiar and powerful interest. All knew that this interest was, somehow, the cause of the war." As Ronald White has surmised, in choosing to use the word *somehow,* "Lincoln hinted at his own brooding and painful journey to grasp the true meaning of the war." He had progressed from a war to preserve the Union to a war to secure liberty for all.[33]

Twenty-nine years after the Civil War ended, Johnson Rossiter wrote in the 1894 *Annual Report* of the American Historical Association that,

When the Southern people entered upon the attempt at secession, they committed themselves to four capital absurdities: First, they went out with ten millions to meet those who could come against them with twenty millions, Second, they proposed to divide a great country along a line where there was no natural barrier—a line, moreover, that was crossed by great arteries of commerce, Third, they attempted to reverse the economical and political tendencies of a thousand years and divide instead of uniting. Fourth, to save an institution from gradual destruction they undertook a task, that, if accomplished would only have accelerated its decay.[34]

Mr. Rossiter's fourth point is especially significant. The Civil War brought a far quicker end to slavery than anyone would have expected in 1860. By attempting to create a Southern Confederacy, the South achieved the very containment of slavery that Jefferson Davis dreaded. Without Southern political resistance in the Senate, the Republicans banned slavery in the territories, abolished it in the District of Columbia, passed confiscation acts that were the legal justification for the president to emancipate the slaves in the rebellious South as a war measure by means of the Emancipation Proclamation, and eventually passed a constitutional amendment banning slavery throughout the country while Missouri and Maryland were convinced to get rid of the institution on their own. Who, on December 20, 1860, would have thought that, when South Carolina proclaimed the death knell of the Union, the bells tolled not for the Union but for the South's peculiar institution? Several members of the Virginia secession convention expressed fears that the coming war would result in the abolition of slavery. Needless to say, they were correct. As to the ultimate purposes, length, attendant violence, and consequences of the war, neither side had any idea what detours and devastations lay ahead.

The protection of slavery was foremost in the mind of the South. Secession had not come over the tariff, or the funding of internal improvements, or the government's opposition to filibustering adventures in the Caribbean and Central America. It came over the one issue that had split the churches in the 1840s, the political parties in the 1850s and, finally, the Union in 1860–61, that is, slavery. In each instance, the pattern was the same. If the South could not control, its honor was threatened. Therefore, it first sundered the churches, so it could control interpretation of the highly influential word of God. In the political arena, it smashed first the Whigs and then the Democrats so that it could control the presidential party. When the Northern Democratic party would not sacrifice itself on a platform calling for a federal slave code, anathema in the North, it destroyed any chance of the Democratic Party winning the 1860 election. Finally, after the Republicans won the election, the South rejected the verdict of a free election and moved to destroy the Union and set up a commonwealth of their own. In adopting their own constitution, they modified the old one so that slavery was explicitly enshrined and protected as a permanent institution. In such a republic, the South could have a gag rule; censor the press and the mails; limit free speech, free thought, and free association; maintain its slave patrols and otherwise continue to repress its own people, white as well as black, for the sake of the peculiar institution. The South fought, not for the idea that "all men are created equal," but rather that all white men are created equal and all others are inferior. While the Southern yeoman was convinced he was fighting for his "rights," the Southern elite planter class desperately scrambled to retain what they had always enjoyed, ownership and control of their fellow human beings in an elitist, white-supremacist society, for which they were willing to fight to the death.

CHAPTER 12

THENCEFORWARD, AND FOREVER FREE: ABRAHAM LINCOLN'S JOURNEY TO EMANCIPATION

In the same heroic and legendary way that George Washington is revered as "the Father of our Country," so Abraham Lincoln is regarded as "the Great Emancipator." Lincoln's opposition to slavery, his daring, brilliant, and often misunderstood executive order known as the "Emancipation Proclamation," his persuasive guidance of the Thirteenth Amendment through the Congress, and his martyrdom at the hands of a white supremacist Southern sympathizer days after the Civil War had been won have surely earned him highest honors in the struggle for emancipation in America—an end to freedom's delay for nearly four million Americans. Yet the presidential Lincoln of the Emancipation Proclamation and the Thirteenth Amendment is a great distance removed from the Lincoln whose views about African Americans, slavery, and the Constitution's protection of slavery reflected the realities and prejudices of the age. From the time of his boyhood years until his death, Lincoln underwent a significant transformation both in his political philosophy and his attitude toward black Americans. This journey, tempered through experience, introspection, and circumstances, was not an easy one for the fundamentally conservative Lincoln. After consecrating Lincoln with the halo of martyrdom and civil sainthood, many, including some historians, have failed to avoid the temptation to expect too much of Lincoln for his own time and culture, or to understand or appreciate his capacity for growth and change, not only on the issues of slavery and emancipation, but on a whole host of issues and ideas that make Lincoln such a fascinating and central character in our national history.

Abraham Lincoln was born into the poor frontier farm family of Thomas and Nancy Hanks Lincoln in 1809 and raised in a log cabin in the backwoods of slaveholding Kentucky until the family's move to southern Indiana during Lincoln's early childhood. His eventual rise to the upper-middle class through self-study, hard work, and marriage into a wealthy family should not obscure the importance of these formative, humble origins, although Lincoln generally avoided discussion of his impoverished upbringing. His childhood years, including the death of his beloved mother when Lincoln was nine, his father's remarriage to a loving and supportive stepmother, and the family's views on religion and slavery could not help but make deep impressions on the future lawyer and politician. The Lincoln family's move across the Ohio River into Indiana in 1816, shortly after Indiana became a free state, was due in part to Thomas Lincoln's dislike of slavery, as well as his desire for a more secure land title. The frontier Baptist groups with which the Lincolns affiliated also shared their distaste for slavery. Lincoln's childhood was nearly devoid of systematic education, and he once calculated that his actual time spent in school amounted to only about one year. Fortunately, the young Lincoln did not allow lack of formal schooling to stand in the way of his education. An avid reader despite his father's criticism of his bookishness, Lincoln came to epitomize the spirit of self-taught, lifelong learning.

As a young man of nineteen, Lincoln had the opportunity to travel down the Ohio and Mississippi rivers as a hired hand on a flatboat loaded with goods to be delivered in New Orleans. While Lincoln as a young boy likely saw slaves being marched along the main road near the family's Kentucky cabin, it was on this trip that Lincoln was probably first exposed to the full brutality of slavery as well as to the actual sale of human beings in the slave markets of the South's largest city. It was also during this trip that he and his fellow crew member successfully fought off a gang of seven black men attempting to rob them of their cargo.[1]

After helping his family move west to Illinois in 1830, Lincoln set out on his own for New Salem and within two years made his first, although unsuccessful, attempt at winning a seat in the state legislature. He campaigned successfully for the legislature as a Whig in 1834 and began a period of public service that would see him eventually move to Springfield, the new state capital. At this time, Lincoln began a serious study of law, encouraged and assisted by a well-educated attorney and fellow member of the legislature, John Todd Stuart, a cousin of Lincoln's future bride, Mary Todd.

Although Abraham Lincoln was a young legislator in a theoretically "free" state, many of the residents of central and southern Illinois had Southern roots and attitudes when it came to slavery.[2] William Lloyd Garrison's *Liberator* reported that in 1837 only 3 of the 607 antislavery societies within the United States were in Illinois.[3] Since the Illinois constitution of 1818 had banned slavery, but did not free any slaves already living there, some three hundred slaves were still residing in Illinois in 1840. At the same time, the state's black codes worked to bar free blacks from entering. As a state legislator, Lincoln did not seek to enact legislation that would counter either of these situations, realizing the politically inexpedient nature of such actions at the time.[4] However, while keeping his distance from abolitionism, Lincoln had acted with courage and conviction when, in early 1837, he cast one of only six "no" votes against a resolution in the Illinois legislature that asserted that Congress had no Constitutional right to deprive slaveholders in the District of Columbia of their property by ending slavery in the nation's capital. It was on this occasion that Lincoln publicly denounced the institution of slavery as being "founded on both injustice and bad policy."[5] Later that same year Elijah P. Lovejoy, an abolitionist editor, was murdered in Alton, Illinois, as an anti-abolitionist mob ransacked his office and destroyed his printing press, an event that captured Lincoln's attention and concern.

Lincoln's views against slavery, as well as his concerns about the radical views of abolitionists, were influenced by his admiration for national Whig leader Henry Clay, a Kentucky slaveholder. Clay accepted the full humanity of the slave and acknowledged that slavery was an evil. However, he was convinced that emancipation needed to be gradual and coupled with colonization since Clay was certain that whites, especially in the South, would never accept a large population of free blacks living in their midst with rights equal to those of whites. Clay believed that radical abolitionism had set back the cause of emancipation and, if unchecked, could lead to sectional warfare.[6] Lincoln largely shared Clay's perspective on these topics during much of his political life.

Lincoln's interest in politics was enhanced by the unwavering support of his wife, Mary Todd Lincoln. Lincoln's 1842 marriage to the daughter of a wealthy banker and slaveholder from Lexington, Kentucky, proved both a blessing and a bane. A highly educated, politically aware, and affectionate partner, Mary also had her darker side of emotional insecurity, disregard for living within one's means, a bad temper, and lack of social sensitivity. But when it came to supporting her husband politically, including his opposition to slavery, and having a driving ambition for him to make it all the way to the presidency, Mary was Lincoln's greatest champion.

Abraham Lincoln rose to prominence in Illinois state politics as a Whig legislator, believing that the Democratic Party under Andrew Jackson had strayed from the order and tradition of Jefferson's day that made for good government. Lincoln's reputation was also enhanced by his work as an attorney, first as a junior partner and eventually as head of a two-man law firm with a junior partner of his own, William "Billy" Herndon.[7] In 1846 Lincoln received his party's nomination for a politically safe Whig Congressional seat in predominantly Democratic Illinois. Since by prior agreement among the state's Whigs the seat would rotate to a different party leader every two years, the fact that Lincoln served only one term would not hurt his political standing within state politics. However, Lincoln was critical of Democratic President James K. Polk concerning the war with Mexico, a position that did not resonate with most of his constituents. Had not a one-term stint in Congress been prearranged, it is questionable if Lincoln could have been reelected had he so desired. His term in the House of Representatives was a good learning experience, but was not particularly distinguished.

Returning home to Springfield after his term in Congress that ended in early 1849, Lincoln resumed his law practice, which became increasingly lucrative as he took on cases for the railroad in Chicago in addition to his circuit-riding casework throughout central Illinois. Politics seemed to hold nothing but disappointment for him, and Lincoln focused on his legal career. When Henry Clay died in June 1852, Lincoln was asked to deliver a eulogy at the Illinois capitol in Springfield, which he was pleased to do for his old Whig hero. Among other virtues, Lincoln praised Clay's willingness to serve as president of the American Colonization Society, which Lincoln believed would assist free blacks in the future to carry back to Africa "religion, civilization, law and liberty." Colonization would be "a glorious consummation" to the process of "freeing our land from the dangerous presence of slavery; and at the same, in restoring a captive people to their long-lost fatherland, with bright prospects for the future."[8] Lincoln's belief in colonization would persist well into his presidency.

Other than his eulogy for Henry Clay and a handful of unremarkable campaign appearances for the unsuccessful Whig candidate Winfield Scott in the 1852 presidential contest, Lincoln had concluded that his political days were over. This was a premature assessment, however, as Lincoln was again motivated to enter the political arena when U.S. Senator Stephen A. Douglas of Illinois introduced the Kansas-Nebraska Act in 1854, which advocated the concept of popular sovereignty. Douglas's proposal would allow settlers to choose for themselves whether their territories and future states would be open to slavery. Such legislation, if approved, would also repeal the provision of the Missouri Compromise that had banned slavery in the territories formed out of the Louisiana Purchase north of Missouri's southern boundary. Lincoln, disliking slavery but believing that the Constitution protected it in the states where it existed, was thoroughly opposed to any legislation that could allow for slavery's expansion. Lincoln acknowledged that "I was losing interest in politics, until the repeal of the Missouri Compromise aroused me again."[9]

Lincoln was also concerned that the Kansas-Nebraska Act could be the start of a series of events that would seek to legitimize slavery nationally, a theme that would resonate in his 1858 "house divided" speech and again in his 1860 Cooper Union speech in New York. In mid-1854, Lincoln scrawled out some revealing thoughts on logic and slavery intended only for himself:

> If A. can prove, however conclusively, that he may, of right, enslave B.—why may not B. snatch the same argument, and prove equally, that he may enslave A?—You say A. is white, and B. is black. Is it color, then; the lighter, having the right to enslave the darker? Take care. By this rule, you are to be a slave to the first man you meet, with a fairer skin than your own.
>
> You do not mean color exactly?—You mean the whites are intellectually the superiors of the blacks, and therefore have the right to enslave them? Take care again. By this rule, you are to be slave to the first man you meet, with an intellect superior to your own.
>
> But, you say, it is a question of interest and, if you can make it your interest, you have the right to enslave another. Very well. And if he can make it his interest, he has the right to enslave you.[10]

After considerable hesitation, due largely to Mary Lincoln's objections, Lincoln finally consented to run for the Illinois legislature once again in the fall election of 1854. Prior to that contest, he gave a speech in Peoria, Illinois, that proved to be a turning point in Lincoln's political career and in his expressed views on slavery. This speech, along with an address given in Springfield two weeks prior, brought Lincoln to the nation's attention for the first time and placed him at the center of the popular debate over slavery that would dominate politics in Illinois and the nation for the next several years. The essence of Lincoln's Peoria speech of October 16, 1854, can be summed up in his own words from that address: "Slavery is founded on the selfishness of man's nature—opposition to it in his love of justice. These principles are an eternal antagonism; and when brought into collision so fiercely, as slavery extension brings them, shocks, and throes, and convulsions must ceaselessly follow. Repeal the Missouri Compromise—repeal all compromises—repeal the declaration of independence—repeal all past history, you still cannot repeal human nature. It still will be the abundance of man's heart that slavery extension is wrong; and out of the abundance of his heart, his mouth will continue to speak."[11]

Modern critics of Lincoln's position against equal rights find ammunition for their cause in his Peoria speech, as they would also find in later speeches from the debates with Douglas in 1858. At Peoria, Lincoln did make it clear where he stood at that time regarding black equality: "Let it not be said I am contending for the establishment of political and social equality between the whites and blacks. I have already said the contrary. I am not now combating the argument of NECESSITY, arising from the fact that the blacks are already amongst us; but I am combatting what is set up as a MORAL argument for allowing them to be taken where they have never yet been—arguing against the EXTENSION of a bad thing, which where it already exists, we must of necessity, manage as best we can."[12]

Lincoln's growing reputation as an articulate opponent of the expansion of slavery was made possible by the intense political and personal rivalry that developed between the lesser known Lincoln and the nationally known Douglas. After careful study of the issues involved in the Kansas-Nebraska Act, Lincoln felt compelled to respond to Douglas's viewpoints and speeches. Lincoln's 1854 Peoria speech, the longest speech he ever delivered, was given within hours of Douglas's oration in the same city.[13] Lincoln's oratory moved to a new level of condemnation of slavery in the Peoria speech, in which he expressed his hatred for the spread of slavery due to the "monstrous injustice of slavery itself." Lincoln had come to understand that the Founders had made necessary compromises that protected slavery while at the same time believing that the institution was on the road to extinction. As Lincoln saw it, somewhat anachronistically, for slavery now to be given free rein to expand in the territories would be a direct violation of the wishes and expectations of the nation's early leaders. Furthermore, allowing slavery to expand into the western territories would lessen the opportunities for free whites to "better their condition" with a fresh start—a valued possibility and hope, as exemplified in his own family's experience, at least in the North.[14] And, perhaps most important for Lincoln, the expansion of slavery would be a moral wrong. As Lincoln explained in his October 4 speech at the state fair in Springfield, local laws were appropriate in many cases, but slavery was too important an issue to be legislated locally, as the Kansas-Nebraska Act would allow. At stake was the real issue, "whether a Negro is *not* or *is* a man." And "If the Negro is a man," Lincoln continued, "there can be no moral right in connection with one man's making a slave of another."[15] Lincoln's views were placing him increasingly in alignment with the emerging Republican

Party, which was founded that same year, and with which he affiliated in 1856.

On November 7, 1854, Abraham Lincoln was again elected to the Illinois legislature. While keeping the seat in Whig control, he soon resigned in order to seek a seat in the U.S. Senate later that same year, a move necessitated by the fact that no sitting legislator was eligible for election to another office. Lincoln campaigned hard for this Senate seat, and nearly won as the Illinois legislature made its decision. Leading after the first ballot, but not quite winning, Lincoln could see that, unless he withdrew and threw his support behind another candidate, Lyman Trumbull, the Douglas Democrats would win the seat. Lincoln did his duty, but was "disappointed and mortified" and told a friend he would never run for public office again.[16]

An organizational meeting of the Illinois State Republican Party was held on May 29, 1856, in Bloomington. Whigs, Democrats, Know-Nothings, German immigrants, and abolitionists made up the 270 delegates forming the new party, a disparate group united by opposition to Douglas's Kansas-Nebraska Act with its threat of expanding slavery. The final speech at the convention was delivered by Abraham Lincoln, whose uncharacteristically extemporaneous remarks were not fully recorded. It is known that in this speech, perhaps one of the finest he ever gave, Lincoln put slavery squarely at the center of the nation's problems and said that he was "ready to fuse with anyone who would unite with him to oppose slave power." Lincoln's law partner, Billy Herndon, who usually made an effort to write down Lincoln's remarks, was carried away by "the inspiration of the hour" and failed to record his boss's words. Herndon noted, however, that the speech was "justice, equity, truth, and right set ablaze by the divine fires of a soul maddened by the wrong."[17] Lincoln had found his political voice through his antislavery rhetoric, and a new political home in the emerging Republican Party.

In his most significant speech of 1857, Lincoln attacked the Supreme Court's decision in the Dred Scott case, and attacked Stephen Douglas's defense of the court's ruling, which concluded that blacks were not eligible for citizenship and Congress could not prohibit slavery in the territories. This speech gives clear evidence of Lincoln's growing convictions about not only the moral, but also the legal, unacceptability of slavery. Siding with dissenting Justice Benjamin Curtis, Lincoln pointed out that free black men had the vote in five of the original states, and therefore they "had the same part in making the Constitution that the white people had." As for the words in the Declaration of Independence that "all men are created equal," Lincoln stated, "I think the authors of that notable instrument intended to include all men, but they did not intend to declare all men equal in all respects. They did not mean to say all were equal in color, size, intellect, moral developments, or social capacity. They defined with tolerable distinctness, in what respects they did consider all men created equal—equal in 'certain inalienable rights, among which are life, liberty, and the pursuit of happiness.' This they said, and this [they] meant." While he may not want a black woman for a wife, and "in some respects she is certainly not my equal," Lincoln asserted that "in her natural right to eat the bread she earns with her own hands without asking leave of anyone else, she is my equal and the equal of all others." Lincoln went on to assert that "the spread of the black man's bondage" was assured by the "erroneous" Dred Scott decision, a decision to which he would, as a respecter of the court, "offer no resistance" other than to "do what we can to have it [the Supreme Court] to over-rule this."[18] Congressional power to restrict slavery in the territories was a key doctrine in the new Republican Party; thus, for Lincoln the decision of the Taney Court was all the more reprehensible. Lincoln's speech was, as could be predicted, assailed by the Douglas Democrats, and yet found to be too conservative by some in his own party.

Despite his disappointing loss in 1854, four years later Lincoln was more interested in a seat in the U.S. Senate than ever. In 1858 Stephen Douglas's term was expiring, and he was eager to be reelected. While the selection of U.S. senators was up to the state legislature, the electorate determined the makeup of the legislature, and hence at least indirectly determined who the winning senatorial candidate would be. Lincoln coveted the Senate seat held by Douglas, and the debates that resulted between Douglas and Lincoln would rekindle the rivalry between the two men, hone Lincoln's debate skills to a higher level, and give Lincoln a wide national audience on the issues of slavery and its expansion. Prior to engaging Douglas in their seven agreed-upon debates, to which Douglas reluctantly consented, Lincoln accepted his party's senatorial nomination with his "house divided" speech on June 16, 1858. In that carefully crafted speech he made it clear that the Kansas-Nebraska Act's concept of popular sovereignty had not kept its promise of putting an end to agitation over slavery, but had greatly increased it. Such agitation "will not cease, until a crisis shall have been reached, and passed. 'A house divided against itself cannot stand.' I believe this government cannot endure, permanently half slave and half free. I do not expect the Union to be dissolved—I do not expect the house to fall—but I do expect it will cease to be divided. It will

become all one thing or all the other. Either the opponents of slavery, will
. . . place it where the public mind shall rest in the belief that it is in the
course of ultimate extinction; or its advocates will put it forward, till it
shall become alike lawful in all the states, old as well as new—North as
well as South."[19] Lincoln was laying the foundation for future speeches,
hinting that Douglas was engaged in a nefarious plot to make slavery legal
throughout the United States.

It is difficult to overstate the drawing power of the political debates
between Stephen Douglas and Abraham Lincoln that occurred between
August 21 and October 15, 1858. Thousands of people were attracted
from all over Illinois to these debates, and the texts of the candidates'
remarks were given wide press coverage. Douglas began the first debate
by accusing Lincoln and the Republican Party of being nothing but abolitionists, a charge that Lincoln denied. Throughout the debates, Lincoln
opposed slavery on both moral and political grounds. Douglas, on the
other hand, strongly advocated states' rights and the belief that the people
of each state or territory knew what was best for them regarding slavery.
While Lincoln's message was essentially consistent, he did shrewdly play
to his audience at times, saying things in the southern half of Illinois that
he did not emphasize in the northern half of the state. In the fourth debate
at southern-oriented Charleston, Illinois, on September 18, Lincoln chose
to address issues of racial equality at the outset of his opening remarks:

> I am not, nor ever have been, in favor of bringing about in any way the
> social and political equality of the white and black races; that I am not,
> nor ever have been, in favor of making voters or jurors of negroes, nor
> of qualifying them to hold office, nor to intermarry with white people;
> and I will say, in addition to this, that there is a physical difference
> between the white and black races which I believe will forever forbid
> the two races living together on terms of social and political equality.
> And inasmuch as they cannot so live, while they remain together there
> must be the position of superior and inferior, and I as much as any
> other man am in favor of having the superior position assigned to the
> white race. I say upon this occasion I do not perceive that because the
> white man is to have the superior position the negro should be denied
> everything.[20]

Remarks such as these have been blasted by Lincoln critics such as
Lerone Bennett Jr., whose controversial book, *Forced Into Glory: Abraham
Lincoln's White Dream* concludes that Lincoln was "a man who defined
himself and chose himself as a racist committed to the subordination of
nonWhites" and who "talked out of both sides of his mouth and who
carried the American sin, the divorce of principle and practice, word and

deed, to its highest octave." Lincoln's views favoring the removal of freed slaves through colonization seems to have reached full flower by 1858, another source of irritation to Bennett, who refers to Lincoln and his presidential cabinet as "ultraconservatives, deportationists, and racists."[21] It is true that Lincoln was known as a colonization advocate by 1858, serving in that year as a board member of the Illinois Colonization Society, a group he had previously addressed on two occasions. In an 1857 speech, Lincoln made a comparison between American blacks and the biblical Children of Israel who "went out of Egyptian bondage in a body." Lincoln never advocated mandatory resettlement, but believed that many free blacks and future freed slaves would find it a welcome relief to go to a land, in Africa or elsewhere, where they could truly be free and in control of their own affairs. This viewpoint was by no means unique to Lincoln; it represented, according to Eric Foner, "a plan for ending slavery that represented a middle ground between abolitionist radicalism and the prospect of the United States existing forever half-slave and half-free."[22]

From today's perspective, it might seem reasonable to condemn Lincoln's views on the social and political equality of blacks as expressed in his speeches from the 1850s. However, Lincoln was a man of the nineteenth century, not the twenty-first. Like his contemporaries, Lincoln was infused with the concept of black inferiority from the cradle. In an age when the Know Nothing movement spread hatred not only of blacks but of any American who was not a native-born white Anglo-Saxon Protestant, Lincoln's ability to listen, to reflect, to change the viewpoints of a lifetime —and to act on them—sets him apart from most of his contemporaries. Lincoln chose to read proslavery literature at times, to reflect on such viewpoints and sharpen his own arguments against them. Sermons and lectures by Rev. Frederick A. Ross were published in book form in 1857 as *Slavery Ordained by God,* and Lincoln read this work, which became a proslavery best-seller.[23] In a note penned to himself in October 1858, Lincoln reflects on some of Ross's assertions:

> Suppose it is true, that the negro is inferior to the white, in the gifts of nature; is it not the exact reverse justice that the white should, for that reason, take from the negro, any part of the little which had been given him? "Give to him that is needy" is the Christian rule of charity; but "Take from him that is needy" is the rule of slavery.
>
> The sum of pro-slavery theology seems to be this: "Slavery is not universally *right,* nor yet universally *wrong,* it is better for *some* people to be slaves; and, in such cases, it is the Will of God that they be such."
>
> . . . But, slavery is good for some people!!! As a good thing, slavery is strikingly peculiar, in this, that it is the only good thing which no man ever seeks the good of, for *himself.*

Nonsense! Wolves devouring lambs, not because it is good for their own greedy maws, but because it [is] good for the lambs!!![24]

It must be recognized that Lincoln surpassed nearly all of his white contemporaries by the end of his life in his acceptance of at least the possibility of equality, and in his determination to move beyond emancipation toward that goal. William Lee Miller has aptly noted that Lincoln's "racial prejudices were conventional, opportunistic—and changeable."[25] Lincoln's journey of personal growth should not be forever faulted for starting at point "A" when later on he arrived at destination "B." Every intellectual journey has a beginning. It is more important to judge a person for where that journey ends.

While Lincoln won a large popular following in his race for the U.S. Senate, he lost the vote where it most counted, in the Illinois legislature. A Democratic majority was again elected to that body in November 1858, which essentially assured that Douglas would be reelected to his Senate seat in January. Within a month of Lincoln's defeat, the *Chicago Tribune* was suggesting the possibility of endorsing Lincoln for president in 1860. Republican candidates in other states now clamored for Lincoln to make campaign appearances on their behalf, which he did in Indiana, Wisconsin, and Ohio throughout 1859. The Lincoln-Douglas debates were published in book form in the spring of 1860, and in three months had gone through four printings.[26] Lincoln's reputation as a reasoned, moderate, and articulate antislavery voice was now national in scope.

One sign of his growing nationwide reputation was Lincoln's invitation to speak at New York City's Cooper Union on February 27, 1860. In the assessment of Harold Holzer, without this speech, "Lincoln would never have been nominated, much less elected, to the presidency that November." The Cooper Union speech was a way of ascertaining whether Lincoln could expand his appeal as a reasonable antislavery advocate "from the rollicking campaigns of the rural West to the urban East, where theaters, lecture halls, and museums vied with politics for public attention. Cooper Union held the promise of transforming Lincoln from a regional phenomenon to a national figure. Lincoln knew it, and rose to the occasion." Not only did Lincoln's speech prove to be a great success, the Mathew Brady photograph taken in New York on the morning of his speech may be the most flattering portrait ever made of Lincoln, and it transformed his image, perhaps even in his own mind. The photograph was copied extensively in his presidential campaign, and Lincoln is supposed to have said shortly after his election that "Brady and the Cooper Union made me president."[27]

What Lincoln had to say about slavery and the future of the nation at Cooper Union was important and persuasive. Lincoln argued that the Constitution contains nothing that prevents the federal government from restricting the expansion of slavery. In fact, "the fathers" had banned slavery in the old Northwest Territory under the very limited national government of the Articles of Confederation. Lincoln carefully outlined how many of the Founding Fathers had voted one time or another to limit or prohibit slavery in the territories. In fact, he sought to make Republicans out of the Founders of the republic.[28] Lincoln then focused on and refuted Southern charges of Republican extremism and sectionalism. He outlined the moderate Republican belief that, while slavery must not be allowed to spread, it can be tolerated where it currently exists, although the hope is that it will ultimately cease to exist. Lincoln refuted any connection between John Brown's raid on Harpers Ferry and Republicans—"John Brown was no Republican" Lincoln stated, to loud applause. Lincoln accused the South of being willing to "destroy the Government, unless you be allowed to construe and enforce the Constitution as you please, on all points in dispute between you and us. You will rule or ruin in all events."

In addressing his fellow Republicans, Lincoln's moderation was evident: "It is exceedingly desirable that all parts of this great Confederacy shall be at peace, and in harmony, one with another. Let us Republicans do our part to have it so. Even though much provoked, let us do nothing through passion and ill temper. Even though the southern people will not so much as listen to us, let us calmly consider their demands and yield to them if, in our deliberate view of our duty, we possibly can." Lincoln then got to the heart of the matter: "Wrong as we think slavery is, we can yet afford to let it alone where it is, because that much is due to the necessity arising from its actual presence in the nation; but can we, [Lincoln rhetorically asks] while our votes will prevent it, allow it to spread into the National Territories, and to overrun us here in these Free States?"

Lincoln ended his speech with the now-famous words, "Let us have faith that right makes might, and in that faith, let us, to the end, dare to do our duty as we understand it."[29] The *Evening Post* reported that Lincoln received a standing ovation with "waving of handkerchiefs and hats, and repeated cheers."[30] Lincoln's position argued first for containment of slavery where it already existed and second, as had been the hope from the beginning of the Republic, that once contained, slavery would gradually be extinguished. Lincoln's view would allow the slaveholding states to fashion the timing and the details of emancipation within their borders. It was meant to be a hard-hitting, yet conservative, antislavery message that had broad political appeal across the North in 1860. Lincoln's stance was in sharp contrast to the more radical agenda of the leading Republican candidate for president, Senator William H. Seward of New York, who argued for immediate emancipation.

From the rousing success of the February 27, 1860, Cooper Union address in New York City, to the presidential nomination at the boisterous Republican convention in Chicago in May, Lincoln's hoped-for path to victory was far from certain. After the Cooper Union speech, his star was clearly rising while William Seward was raising doubts about his electability with his more radical, essentially abolitionist viewpoints. Lincoln was indeed eager to win the nomination, but realized it would be an uphill battle that would require skillful strategy. Lincoln's moderate, reasoned antislavery position paid off, and on the third ballot Lincoln won the Republican Party's presidential nomination as it became clear that frontrunner Seward did not have the support needed to carry the day. With the Democrats self-destructing through their sectional division over slavery, and a third-party candidate siphoning off additional Democratic votes, winning his party's nomination was actually more challenging for Lincoln than winning the presidency in the general election. The Republican platform, which Lincoln now personified, was fairly moderate on issues of slavery, although it did not embrace colonization. The platform condemned John Brown's raid (while Lincoln sympathized with Brown's hatred of slavery, he labeled him "insane" for his actions), and it declared that freedom was the natural and normal status of the territories. Whereas four years earlier, the Republican platform had referred to human slavery as "barbarism," this wording was omitted in 1860. While the Republican Party was clearly based in the North, 20 percent of the delegates to the 1860 Republican convention were from slaveholding states, and there was a desire in 1860 to broaden the appeal of the party as much as possible.[31]

Abraham Lincoln was elected the sixteenth president of the United States on November 6, 1860, with 39 percent of the national popular vote, but with a decisive majority of electoral votes. In many Southern states, his name was not even on the ballot. The 39 percent national vote for Lincoln hides the fact that, among four serious presidential contenders, Lincoln garnered 55 percent of the popular vote in the states where he was on the ballot, carrying every free state except New Jersey. While basking in the glory of election victory, this was also a sobering time for Lincoln, who knew that his Republican Party, of which he was now nominal head, was still in its infancy and was in reality more a collection of rival interest groups with common causes related to antislavery than it was a well-organized political party.

The public life of President-Elect Lincoln between his election and his inauguration was a contradictory whirlwind of exuberance and despair as seven Southern states, beginning with South Carolina, seceded from the Union. While Lincoln was powerless to act in any official capacity until his inauguration, he nonetheless articulated two momentous policy positions. First, he would not compromise by allowing the expansion of slavery into the territories. Secondly, he would not permit secession to go unchallenged.[32] Pressed on many sides to compromise, Lincoln noted that the time had come to stand firm.

In an attempt to assuage Southern panic about his election and his antislavery views, Lincoln drafted a statement for Illinois Senator Lyman Trumbull to use in a speech at a Republican victory event in Springfield two weeks following the election. In this statement, Lincoln expressed his view that "each and all of the States will be left in as complete control of their own affairs respectively, and as at perfect liberty to choose, and employ, their own means of protecting property [read "slavery"] and preserving peace and order . . . as they have ever been under any administration."[33] Unfortunately for Lincoln, this policy statement was viewed as overly conciliatory by some in the North, and did virtually nothing to calm Southern anxieties about what a Republican president was going to do to the Southern way of life.[34] The Lower South had already made up its mind, despite Lincoln's assurances, that an antislavery Republican president was to be neither trusted nor tolerated. The Lower South believed that the containment of slavery where it already existed, and thus that region's inability to diffuse its growing slave population geographically, was a mortal threat to their peculiar institution and their way of life. In this assessment, they were correct.

The president-elect embarked on a long, 1,900 mile, twelve-day circuitous train route from Springfield to his inauguration in Washington, designed by advisors and party leaders to give him maximum exposure to Northern audiences. During this tour, Lincoln experimented with differing tones regarding the South and its secession in his speeches. Talking about a response to secession in terms of "invasion" and "coercion" in Indianapolis and being castigated by segments of the press for it, Lincoln softened his tone and appeared less aggressive regarding what to do about secession in subsequent appearances in Pittsburgh and Rochester. He then took a stronger stance in Trenton, New Jersey, where the state assembly wildly cheered his comment that "it may be necessary to put the foot down firmly." Lincoln now realized that a good part of the North wanted a hard-line position against secession and that he could be less hesitant to express such a view, which in reality reflected his own preference.[35] Yet, the issue being addressed by Lincoln was not the fundamental issue of slavery, but rather of union.

Lincoln's initial draft of his inaugural address, while not actually discussing slavery, took a hard legalistic line toward Southern secession and can be summarized as follows: the Union cannot be dissolved, secession is not lawful, the Lincoln administration will enforce the laws of the land and maintain the property of the United States government, and finally, the burden of deciding war or peace rested with the South. Ironically, the abolitionist hard-liner William Seward told Lincoln the speech was overly provocative and he would risk losing Maryland to secession. Lincoln incorporated most of Seward's suggested revisions. The focus of the speech was on union, not slavery, and certainly not on invasion or coercion. The concluding paragraph, largely the work of Seward in concept, speaks of being friends with the South rather than enemies, of the shared mystic chords of memory stretching from battlefields and patriot graves, and of the better angels of our nature yet swelling the chorus of the Union. The fact that his defeated opponent, Democrat Stephen A. Douglas, held Lincoln's hat for him during the inaugural address and vehemently defended the speech is indicative of the widespread bipartisan support that Lincoln received among Northerners who were ready in early 1861 to link arms to preserve the Union.[36]

Reaction to the inaugural address was predictably negative in the South and mostly positive, although not without criticism, in the North. Abolitionist Frederick Douglass, however, was near despair over the president's remarks. In the speech, Lincoln mentioned an amendment to the Constitution that had recently passed Congress in the hope of bringing secessionists back into the Union. This "original" Thirteenth Amendment, never ratified, would have made it forever impossible for the federal government to interfere with slavery in the slave states. Lincoln stated that "I have no objection to it being made express, and irrevocable."[37] Yet this same statement that gave Frederick Douglass fits of despair caused no softening of the South's views toward Lincoln. David Herbert Donald has concluded that "in the Confederacy it [Lincoln's inaugural address] was generally taken to mean that war was inevitable."[38] On April 12, 1861, Fort Sumter was bombarded, Lincoln called for seventy-five thousand volunteers to suppress the rebellion, and the Civil War was underway.

Historians have debated for generations concerning the causes of the Civil War. However, it is irrefutable that slavery was a foundational factor in the conflict, as noted in the declaration of secession of several Southern states, and that Abraham Lincoln saw it as such. At the beginning of the war, the only Northerners who saw the conflict as a crusade to end slavery were the abolitionists. Devotion to the Union and its preservation is what motivated the states that remained loyal to do battle against the breakaway Confederacy, which proclaimed itself in its constitution to be a republic founded on slavery. Above all other issues and concerns, Abraham Lincoln cherished the Union and concluded that it must be preserved.

It must not be overlooked that, in 1861, four slave states remained in the Union—Delaware, Maryland, Kentucky, and Missouri. Slavery also existed in the western portion of Virginia until shortly after its admission as a free state in 1863, and officially or unofficially in a number of so-called free states and territories. Lincoln was sworn to protect slavery where it *already existed within the Union,* and he was acutely aware of the potential political, diplomatic, and military consequences if any of the four border states joined the Confederacy. It was especially important that Maryland not secede, as the nation's capital would then be entirely surrounded by Confederate territory. He understood the practical limits of his political maneuverability concerning these states and acted with due caution, although with a strong hand to keep Maryland secessionists from prevailing.

During his presidency there were many encounters and events that helped reconfigure and solidify Abraham Lincoln's views toward slavery and African Americans in general. Prior to taking office, he had some well-developed opinions and perspectives about slavery, slaves, and free blacks, and he had argued forcefully for these ideas, but his views were largely theoretical and not based on first-hand knowledge of African Americans and their actual situations. Lincoln's personal contacts with Frederick Douglass, beginning in 1863, would have a positive impact on both men as they came to understand and appreciate each other. According to John Stauffer's double biography of Lincoln and Douglas, "In 1860 Douglass helped elect Lincoln as president. At a time when most whites would not let a black man cross their threshold, Lincoln met Douglass three times at the White House. Their friendship was chiefly utilitarian: Lincoln needed Douglass to help him destroy the Confederacy; Douglass knew that Lincoln could help him end slavery. But they also genuinely liked and admired each other."[39]

When he entered the White House, Lincoln believed the institution of slavery morally bankrupt and contrary to his most basic beliefs and preferences, but he was no abolitionist. He strongly desired to contain slavery and not allow it to spread, but his constitutional duty, as he saw it, was to preserve the Union and to protect property rights (slaves being the greatest financial asset in the South), not to abolish slavery in the states where it currently existed. If slave states could be persuaded to engage in emancipation through legal rather than coercive means, as the Northern states had already done, Lincoln would be delighted, and he stood ready to encourage such actions with federal money as compensation to compliant slaveholders, an offer, however, that had no takers.

Lincoln's reputation among some Northerners suffered after he rescinded the August 30, 1861, order by General John C. Fremont that the slaves held by secessionists in loyal Missouri were to be emancipated. Lincoln knew instinctively that the fullness of time had not yet arrived for such action. Exactly one year after writing a letter to his good friend Senator Browning defending his rescinding of Fremont's proclamation, President Lincoln would, on September 22, 1862, issue his own preliminary Emancipation Proclamation involving not Missouri, but designated areas in rebellion against the United States as of January 1, 1863.

The situation on the ground had moved the agenda of emancipation forward as early as May 1861, with Benjamin Butler's designation of fugitive slaves at Fort Monroe as contraband of war. The issue of slavery continued to surface since slaves were "property" being used to advance the rebel war effort. Under the rules of war, such slaves could be seized and held. In fact, they were immediately put to work on behalf of the Union, and soon their families began showing up as well. Congress eventually passed two confiscation acts legalizing the seizing and holding of slaves of rebel masters. These acts only applied to the slaves of those states in rebellion and therefore left the status of slavery untouched in the border states.

Other events were also highlighting the issue of emancipation. In April 1862, Congress passed and Lincoln signed a bill abolishing slavery in the District of Columbia and providing compensation for slaveholders. Shortly thereafter, Lincoln signed a bill prohibiting slavery in the territories. In Utah, New Mexico, and the other territories, there was to be emancipation without compensation. The voters of the western counties of Virginia were told that, even though they were loyal unionists, they would only be granted admission to the Union after they agreed to free their slaves.

On July 22, 1862, five days after signing the second confiscation act, Lincoln shared a startling document with his cabinet. It was not read to them for their approval, but rather for their advice on timing and wording. He had made up his mind that emancipation must become part of the strategy to bring the war to an end. Two members of the cabinet voiced their reservations. Montgomery Blair feared such a proclamation would

BENJAMIN BUTLER. *Massachusetts attorney, Democratic politician, and Union general who, as commander of Fort Monroe, Virginia, declared escaped slaves as contraband of war in May 1861, the first step leading to the Confiscation Acts and ultimately to the Emancipation Proclamation.*

hurt Republican candidates in the fall mid-term elections, a concern that Lincoln dismissed. He had determined to issue an emancipation proclamation whether it was politically popular or not. On the other hand, William Seward's concern captured Lincoln's attention and won his approval. Seward liked the proclamation, but felt it was important that it be issued publicly following a significant Union military victory; otherwise it might look like a last, desperate war of words prompted by weakness rather than strength. Lincoln put the draft of his proclamation back in his desk and waited for the Northern armies to bring him a victory.

Just a month prior to going public with the Preliminary Emancipation Proclamation, but after he had made his decision to issue it, the politically astute Lincoln feigned wariness of emancipation while laying out the rationale for one of his greatest achievements, giving primacy to the overriding war aim of the North, the restoration of the Union. In his August 22, 1862, response to Horace Greeley's New York *Tribune* editorial called "The Prayer of Twenty Millions," in which Greeley urged the president to attack slavery, the very cause of the rebellion, Lincoln stated:

> I would save the Union. . . . My paramount objective in this struggle *is* to save the Union, and is *not* either to save or to destroy slavery. If I could save the Union without freeing *any* slave I would do it, and if I could save it by freeing *all* the slaves I would do it; and if I could save it be freeing some and leaving others alone I would also do that. What I do about slavery, and the colored race, I do because I believe it helps to save the Union; and what I forbear, I forbear because I do *not* believe it would help to save the Union. . . . I shall try to correct errors when shown to be errors; and I shall adopt new views so fast as they shall appear to be true views. I have here stated by purpose according to my view of *official* duty; and I intend no modification of my oft-expressed *personal* wish that all men every where could be free.[40]

Unknown to Greeley or anyone outside his cabinet, Lincoln was already moving to destroy slavery as a national institution.

On September 22, 1862, five days after General George McClellan had halted Lee's Confederate advance into Maryland at Antietam Creek, President Lincoln informed his cabinet that the time had come to issue his Preliminary Emancipation Proclamation. Treasury Secretary Salmon P. Chase recorded Lincoln's remarks in his diary:

> Gentlemen: I have, as you are aware, thought a great deal about the relation of this war to Slavery: and you all remember that, several weeks ago, I read to you an Order I had prepared on this subject, which, on account of objections made by some of you, was not issued. Ever since then, my mind has been much occupied with this subject,

and I have thought all along that the time for acting on it might very probably come. I think the time has now come. I wish that we were in a better condition. The action of the army against the rebels has not been quite what I should have liked best. But they have been driven out of Maryland, and Pennsylvania is no longer in danger of invasion. When the rebel army was at Frederick, I determined, as soon as it should be driven out of Maryland, to issue a Proclamation of Emancipation such as I thought most likely to be useful. I said nothing to any one; but I made a promise to myself, and (hesitating a little)—to my Maker. The rebel army is now driven out, and I am going to fulfill that promise.[41]

While McClellan failed to take this opportunity to pursue and destroy Lee's army, the battle at Antietam was nonetheless seen as a Union victory, and it gave Lincoln the chance he was looking for to make the preliminary proclamation public. The proclamation gave rebel states until January 1, 1863, to declare loyalty to the government of the United States; otherwise, the slaves within their borders would be freed as of that day. Neither the preliminary nor the final proclamation contained the eloquent, inspiring language that Lincoln was so capable of producing. Lincoln's purpose was to use emancipation as a war measure, in his capacity as commander-in-chief. It was not used as an opportunity to showcase the moral high ground or to otherwise risk irritating the still-loyal border states. Emancipation gave an additional meaning to the war—a fight for human freedom that was not altogether accepted in the North or in the Union Army. Lincoln would concisely and eloquently explain this new meaning of the war in his brief remarks at Gettysburg in November 1863.

Lincoln stated in the opening paragraph of the Preliminary Emancipation Proclamation that "hereafter, as heretofore, the war will be prosecuted for the object of practically restoring the constitutional relation between the United States, and each of the states, and the people thereof, in which states that relation is, or may be suspended, or disturbed." When Congress next convenes, Lincoln continues, he will recommend that it approve financial assistance to states not in rebellion against the United States if they will voluntarily adopt "immediate, or gradual abolishment of slavery within their respective limits; and that the effort to colonize persons of African descent, with their consent, upon this continent or elsewhere, with the previously obtained consent of the Governments existing there, will be continued." Lincoln also mentioned the possibility of compensating Southerners who remained loyal to the Union for the loss of their slaves. The heart of the proclamation then follows: "That on the first day of January in the year of our Lord, one thousand eight hundred and sixty-three, all persons held as slaves within any state, or designated part of a state, the people whereof shall then be in rebellion against the United States shall be then, thenceforward, and forever free; and the executive government of the United States, including the military and naval authority thereof, will recognize and maintain the freedom of such persons, and will do no act or acts to repress such persons, or any of them, in any efforts they may make for their actual freedom."[42]

News of the preliminary proclamation was mixed throughout the country. European reaction was initially largely negative. In both Britain and France, Lincoln's banning the military from any intervention as slaves took steps to secure their freedom was seen by conservatives as an invitation to servile war.[43] On the other hand, despite tens of thousands of British textile mill workers who were let go once supplies of cotton had been exhausted, resulting in a huge increase in public relief on the part of the British government, public sentiment was so antislavery that no movement ever resulted in a call for British intervention in the war or recognition of the South.[44] Lincoln, however, desired to ward off any chances that the British might decide to intervene.

The final draft of the Emancipation Proclamation as signed by President Lincoln on January 1, 1863, differed in significant respects from the Preliminary Emancipation Proclamation. These changes were no doubt influenced by reactions to the preliminary proclamation of a little over three months before, and reflected Lincoln's ability to grow, change, and be flexible while maintaining his basic principles. The final version of the Emancipation Proclamation omitted any reference to either colonization or compensation, points on which Lincoln was no longer insistent. It also indicated that former slaves would be eligible to enter the armed services, and fight for their own freedom. The final proclamation also enjoined the freed slaves to "abstain from all violence, unless in necessary self-defence; and I recommend to them that, in all cases when allowed, they labor faithfully for reasonable wages."[45] On learning that the president had signed the proclamation, free blacks and abolitionist groups celebrated wildly in Northern cities and in Union-occupied parts of the Confederacy. Norfolk, Virginia, saw ten thousand or more blacks take to the streets in jubilation on New Year's Day of 1863.[46] Meanwhile opponents, North and South, saw the proclamation as a call to servile insurrection. New York and New Jersey had recently elected new Democratic governors who took the opportunity to use their inaugural addresses to denounce the Emancipation Proclamation as "bloody, barbarous, revolutionary, unconstitutional," and to predict insurrection and massacre. Democrats in Kentucky openly discussed secession until their convention in February 1863 was shut down by federal troops.[47] A few in the Union Army deserted rather than fight for "the Negro." But other Union troops saw the value of the services provided them by friendly slaves and viewed the proclamation as undermining the South's ability to prosecute the war. Many Union troops also understood that, unless slavery was extinguished there would be no peace in a reunited nation. Karl Marx wrote that Lincoln's Emancipation Proclamation was "the most important document in American history since the establishment of the Union."[48]

Two questions about the Emancipation Proclamation have often been debated: Was the proclamation legal? And did it really free the slaves? As commander-in-chief, Lincoln had the authority to give orders to his troops, and under American jurisprudence since early colonial days, slaves were considered property. By the Confiscation Acts, Congress authorized the seizure of property of those in rebellion against the government. When such property was seized or otherwise controlled by Union forces, the government became the owner of said property, even if it were human, and was free to dispense with that property as it saw fit. By passing the Confiscation Acts, Congress authorized piecemeal emancipation as Union forces took control of rebel areas. Lincoln was careful to cite the Second Confiscation Act as a basis for his actions, but he turned the act on its head. Congress had said that the slaves would be free *whenever Union forces might reach them,* but in the Emancipation Proclamation, Lincoln declared the slaves were free *now.* Union forces would simply enforce that freedom. Slaves even in those areas specifically exempted from the proclamation considered themselves already free by virtue of Lincoln's action. All the slaves had to do was either flee to the Union lines or wait for the Union troops to come and effectuate their freedom—and the slaves knew these soldiers were on the way. The slaves believed that they were now free, and the Union forces believed that they were effectuating that freedom. Whatever legal arguments can be made to the contrary, the Emancipation Proclamation had the effect of freeing the slaves in the Confederacy and bringing the institution to an end in the South before the ratification of the Thirteenth Amendment.

With the Emancipation Proclamation, Lincoln did not free all the slaves. He only freed the slaves in specified areas of the Confederacy. For political reasons, Lincoln exempted Tennessee, even though it was still a rebellious state. He exempted areas of the Confederacy already under federal control and slave states that were loyal to the Union, and therefore was not interfering with slavery *where it already existed within the Union.* Lincoln was a savvy politician and a talented lawyer who had no difficulty in making these fine distinctions. The president wisely saw the Emancipation Proclamation as an extraordinary action necessitated by violent rebellion against the government of the United States, and therefore, as a war measure, it had to be limited in scope and could not apply to the Union or territory securely under Union control. The proclamation was not hypocritical or merely an empty threat—it was stark political and constitutional reality, played out with great skill. Throughout the Confederacy, slaves understood and believed that Lincoln had granted them their freedom, an idea readily proclaimed by former slaves upon Lincoln's arrival in Richmond at the end of the war. The slaves now knew that they had an ally; the Union blue was an army of deliverance. Escape became more common, passive resistance grew even stronger, and the economic underpinning of the slave republic disintegrated further.

Clearly, the Emancipation Proclamation directly led to the abolition of slavery throughout the United States. While the proclamation only freed slaves in designated areas of the Confederacy, the border states along with Tennessee and the other areas exempted by the Proclamation would continue to have slavery after the war in a strip cutting across the middle of the country. If, after the Emancipation Proclamation, the war aims of the North changed from preservation of the Union to the preservation of the Union with human freedom, how was one to deal with the existence of slavery in these areas? The answer was in abolition movements within these states and a new Thirteenth Amendment to the Constitution, this time not protecting slavery but abolishing it. Lincoln would play a leading role in these efforts.

The decision to arm and train African Americans was a giant step for a man who had once considered African Americans inferior in all things. Following the Union victories at Gettysburg and Vicksburg in July of 1863, Lincoln turned increasing attention to the essential role of blacks in the military. General Grant had written the president about the "heaviest blow yet given to the Confederacy"—the arming of blacks and the issuance of the Emancipation Proclamation.[49] Lincoln's response showed the importance the president now gave to black troops: "I think at least a hundred thousand [black troops] can, and ought to be rapidly organized along its [the Mississippi River's] shores. Such black soldiers would serve the Union as "a resource which, if vigorously applied now, will soon close the contest."[50] "It was an astonishing statement," comments John Stauffer; "blacks can win the war for us and assure their own freedom, he [Lincoln] was saying."[51] Nearly 180,000 African American soldiers and another 10,000 sailors, many of them former slaves, would bear arms and in many cases shed their blood and give their lives to win the war for the Union.

Lincoln's journey to emancipation had been a long one. Raised on the frontier, he was immersed in a culture of white supremacy and accepted it. He hated slavery and viewed blacks as human beings, but inferior ones. His hatred of slavery was a constant throughout his life. Lincoln's exposure to the brutality of the institution on his trips to New Orleans as a young man had an impact which never left him. He believed that the Founding Fathers had acknowledged the existence of slavery and continued its legal status looking forward to a day when the institution would die out. It did not do so. Lincoln came to believe that slavery should be contained where it already existed and by doing so it would in time gradually be extinguished.

As late as 1864, Lincoln continued to believe that colonization was a viable solution for freed blacks, both for their sake and the sake of white America, although South America was seen by Lincoln as a more likely relocation site than Africa after some African colonization schemes had not gone well. Lincoln's friend Frederick Douglass knew that colonization would not be acceptable to the overwhelming majority of freed slaves and pressed Lincoln to give up on the idea. Eventually, Lincoln came to understand that there had to be a new framework based on the old words of the Declaration of Independence that "all men are created equal," and that this horrific civil war must result in a "new birth of freedom" that included a place for black as well as white Americans.

By April 1865 Lincoln began to argue that blacks deserved some form of political equality. The first step was giving the vote to African American veterans who had risked their lives and shed their blood for the Union and freedom. Lincoln was pointing the way to black equality. John Wilkes Booth was present on the White House lawn when Lincoln made his first public remarks about what Booth knew was a path to black citizenship, and he promised that this would be the last speech Lincoln would ever make. Tragically, he made good on that promise. By the end of his life, Lincoln had largely rejected the bigotry of his era. He counted former fugitive slave Frederick Douglass as his friend, and accorded him access to the White House that other blacks would not experience for the better part of a century. In the end, Abraham Lincoln understood that the new birth of freedom he so eloquently advocated at Gettysburg would mean political equality, which in turn would bring social equality. It had been a remarkable journey for a nineteenth-century white man born into frontier poverty in a slave state.

CHAPTER 13

SLAVERY'S DEATH THROES: EMANCIPATION DURING THE CIVIL WAR

The call to arms by President Lincoln following the attack on Fort Sumter was designed to crush a rebellion against the United States that, if not suppressed, would mean disunion. While slavery was at the heart of the sectional antagonism that led to armed hostilities, the North was not initially engaged in a war to end slavery. Rather, it was a war to preserve the Union. It is difficult for the modern reader to understand the impact that the word "Union" had on Americans in the mid-nineteenth century. Gary W. Gallagher has rightly linked the term "Union" with "Nation" in that era; "Union" created powerful imagery that, Gallagher eloquently asserts,

> represented the cherished legacy of the founding generation, a democratic republic with a constitution that guaranteed political liberty and afforded individuals a chance to better themselves economically. From the perspective of loyal Americans, their republic stood as the only hope for democracy in a western world that had fallen more deeply into the stifling embrace of oligarchy since the failed revolutions of the 1840's. Slaveholding aristocrats who established the Confederacy, believed untold unionists, posed a direct threat not only to the long-term success of the American republic but also to the broader future of democracy. Should armies of citizen-soldiers fail to restore the Union, forces of privilege on both sides of the Atlantic could pronounce ordinary people incapable of self-government and render irrelevant the military sacrifices and political genius of the Revolutionary fathers.[1]

The South was willing to engage in a war causing disunion in order to preserve slavery. For years prior to 1861, zealous factions in both the South and the North had used the threat of disunion to further their proslavery or antislavery agendas. As Elizabeth Varon has stated, "from the very founding of the United States, the "question of Union or Disunion" was inseparable from the issue of slavery's destiny. The central premise of American political culture, in the North and South alike, was that the republic was fragile—beset by external and internal enemies, and in perpetual danger of moral decline."[2] The failure of compromise and the intensity of sectional conflict over union and disunion can be well summed up in the words Lincoln carefully chose for his second inaugural address: "Both parties deprecated war; but one of them would *make* war rather than let the nation survive; and the other would *accept* war rather than let it perish. And the war came." There was little doubt in Lincoln's mind what was behind the war: "These slaves constituted a peculiar and powerful interest. All knew that this interest was, somehow, the cause of the war."[3]

The war itself would create new circumstances which, intended or not, moved emancipation ever closer to reality. In a reversal of historic roles, the South, in its war for independence, had as the fundamental feature of its agenda not the overthrow but rather the protection of an *ancien regime* and its peculiar institution through the destruction of the Union. Conversely, as a means to suppress the rebellion and preserve the Union, the North, at first fitfully and sporadically, but eventually with purpose, adopted and implemented the heretofore radical agenda of immediate emancipation, whether compensated or not, in the rebellious states. Meanwhile, as the Northern agenda regarding the future of slavery slowly evolved, slavery in those slaveholding regions that remained loyal to the Union—the border states, western Virginia, and the District of Columbia—would undergo great challenges and changes.

Lincoln, while maintaining his focus on union rather than emancipation as the fundamental aim of the war, needed to weigh carefully the options regarding slavery and then choose those options that would be least disruptive to the slave states still loyal to the Union, not enlarge Copperhead (antiwar Northern Democratic) resistance, especially in the Old Northwest, and not jeopardize the loyalty of Union troops. And he needed to do this while developing a Northern consensus on the future of slavery not only in the rebellious South but throughout the country. Any leader faced with these challenges needed the wisdom of Solomon and the patience of Job to navigate these uncharted political waters. Yet, for his reasoned caution, Lincoln would be severely criticized by many in his own Republican Party, and by some historians since, for acting too slowly. Eventually, emancipation would be used as a military strategy to help end the war, and even the Confederacy would debate the possibility of freeing some of its slaves if it would help their cause of independence.

Shortly after the start of military hostilities between the North and South, another battle was underway—this time over the status of slaves seeking freedom by escaping to Union forces. It started with an unlikely figure— Union General Benjamin Franklin Butler, a politically astute Democrat who had been defeated for the governorship of Massachusetts in 1859. Butler, who had proslavery leanings and had favored John Breckinridge for president in 1860, now served under a Republican commander-in-chief. Butler's high rank reflected his status as a highly successful Massachusetts lawyer and public figure and masked the fact that he had been an appointed professional soldier for less than two months.[4] Butler was stationed with a Massachusetts regiment at Annapolis, Maryland, when rumors of a planned slave insurrection in that state surfaced. General Butler wrote to assure Maryland's governor on April 23, 1861, that his forces would "promptly and effectively" assist in suppressing any slave insurrection and that they would not "in any way" interfere with the property rights of slaveholders.[5] There was nothing exceptional in this support for Maryland slaveholders since Maryland was a loyal state and Lincoln had promised to protect, not interfere with, slavery in states where it already existed.

What proslavery Union General Benjamin Butler did next, like secession itself, was one of the many events during the Civil War that brought profound and unforeseen consequences to both sides. This event set the nation on the road to emancipation. On May 23, 1861, exactly one month after Butler had written to the governor of Maryland pledging to protect slavery, three fugitive slaves entered Union-held Fort Monroe, Virginia, seeking sanctuary. The slaves, property of Colonel C. K. Mallory of the 115th Virginia Militia, had been informed that they would soon be sent further south to work on projects for the Confederate Army. Not wanting to be assigned so far from home, they decided to take a risk and seek sanctuary by rowing a boat to Fort Monroe. Having taken command of Fort Monroe just the day before, General Butler interviewed the fugitive slaves and put them to work without compensation. The three runaways also shared important military information regarding Confederate activity. General Butler telegraphed his superiors seeking direction in the matter, but a response was a week in coming, and when it did, Butler was told to continue what he was doing and to keep an account of the value of the work done by the runaway slaves.

The following day, Major M. B. Carey of the 115th Virginia Militia presented himself to General Butler under a flag of truce. On behalf of Colonel Mallory, Major Carey demanded the return of the slaves as provided for in the Fugitive Slave Act. General Butler refused on the grounds that Virginia had severed its ties with the Union and that, unless Colonel

Mallory came to Fort Monroe and swore allegiance to the United States, he now claimed to be a member of a supposed foreign state and thus was not eligible for protection under the laws of the United States. Butler declared that, as property, slaves who performed military support functions for the enemy fell under the rules of war as contraband. Although now under Union protection, these slaves were not free. They were catalogued as property, the disposition of which would be determined at the end of the war, the same status slaves held in the Revolutionary War when they had fled to British lines.

Within days, other slaves made their way to Fort Monroe, including wives, children, and elderly persons. Slaves who had worked on Confederate military projects were easily classified as contraband, but field hands, house slaves, and the elderly could not be so easily defined except by making the generalization that slave labor in all its manifestations provided essential support for the Southern war effort. Logistical problems were raised by the need to feed, house, and otherwise provide for this growing number of runaway slaves. General Butler, not wanting to be swamped with this "onerous business," appointed a "commissioner of negro affairs" at the fort to handle the extra workload. As many slaves as possible were put to work providing support for the fort's garrison.[6] By August, Butler, to his dismay, had nearly a thousand runaway slaves under his authority. In a letter to Secretary of War Simon Cameron on July 30, 1861, General Butler was still seeking answers to basic questions about these people in his care: "Are these men, women, and children, slaves? Are they free? Is their condition that of men, women, and children, or of property, or is it a mixed relation? What their *status* was under the Constitution and laws, we all know. What has been the effect of rebellion and a state of war upon that *status*?"[7]

Those first three runaway slaves arriving at Fort Monroe represented a trickle of what by the end of the war would be an overwhelming flood of slaves making their way to freedom under the protection of the United States.[8] Eventually, hundreds of thousands of slaves would actively participate in their own emancipation by passive resistance, by ceasing to contribute to the Southern war effort, and/or by finding their way to Union lines, where they often enthusiastically aided the Union cause. As slaves abandoned Southern fields, barns, workshops, and kitchens, their white masters and mistresses were often left helpless without them. These fugitives from bondage provided the Union with valuable military intelligence, guided Union troops through Southern territory, spied for the Union Army, and in many cases died for the Union cause and their freedom. The

Confederacy was eventually brought to its knees in significant measure by the resistance and flight of its slaves.

One of the most daring and famous of slave escapes during the war was that undertaken by Robert Smalls, a South Carolina slave who had been allowed by his master to work on the docks and live independently in Charleston. Such urban slaves had much more autonomy, access to free blacks, and opportunities to escape.[9] Smalls rose through the ranks and ended up as a boat pilot in Charleston Harbor and vicinity at the time the Civil War began. Confederates used Smalls and a crew of other slaves to man a refitted steam-powered vessel, the *Planter,* for use as a gunboat. The vessel was docked in Charleston and guarded at night by the slave crew, who decided to make their escape, with their families, on the night of May 12, 1862. Knowing the appropriate signals, and flying the Confederate flag,

ROBERT SMALLS. *A South Carolina slave who was assigned to guard a Confederate gunboat in Charleston Harbor but instead commandeered it safely to the Union fleet. He aided the Union cause by enlisting other blacks into the army and was elected to Congress during Reconstruction.*

Smalls safely moved the boat past Confederate guards and out to sea, knowing that Union vessels were in the vicinity. Replacing the Confederate flag with a white sheet that Smalls's wife had brought along, Smalls and his crew then turned the vessel over to Union authorities. Smalls reportedly told the Union commander, "I thought the *Planter* might be of some use to Uncle Abe." Smalls and his crew not only stole a well-armed Confederate gunboat for the Union, they also brought valuable information about Confederate defenses in the region. Smalls joined the U.S. Navy and was eventually named captain of the *Planter*.[10] After the war, Smalls went on to serve in the South Carolina legislature and was elected to the U.S. Congress for five terms during Reconstruction. In 2007, Smalls became the first African American to have an Army ship named in his honor, the 5,412-ton USAV Major General Robert Smalls.[11]

Cognizant of the blow that would be dealt to the Confederacy by seizing slaves and harboring runaways used in the war effort by the rebellious states, the Republican-controlled Congress took action. On August 6, 1861, Congress passed *An Act to Confiscate Property Used for Insurrectionary Purposes,* more popularly known as the First Confiscation Act.[12] This law essentially stated that any person who allowed his or her slaves to work on military projects in support of the rebellion would forfeit such laborers—that they would be "lawful subject of prize and capture wherever found."[13] Opposition in Congress came from Unionists in the border states, as well as Democrats throughout the North. President Lincoln signed the bill into law in part because he became convinced that the Confederate victory, and Union humiliation, at Bull Run on July 21, 1861, was due in part to thousands of slaves pressed into service for the Confederacy.[14] This matter of slaves and what to do for and with them during the war would require much reflection and deliberation, resulting in great controversy on both sides of the conflict. There were few, if any, simple or obvious solutions. Any false step could prove deadly to the very Union the North was desperately attempting to preserve.

At the forefront of Lincoln's thinking was how to keep additional slaveholding states from leaving the Union. By the time of his inauguration in March, 1861, seven states had seceded. Four more joined the Confederacy after Lincoln's call to arms following the attack on Fort Sumter. This left four slaveholding states still loyal to the Union—Missouri, Kentucky, Maryland, and Delaware. While Delaware was essentially Unionist, its population tended to consider themselves as "Southerners,"[15] and Lincoln could not take their loyalty for granted. Maryland, Kentucky, and Missouri were divided in their loyalties, and each was strategically important to the Union. Lincoln could not afford to let any of them go, and thus had to tread with exceptional caution regarding his policy toward the slave populations of those states. It was critically important to keep Maryland in the Union, for if Maryland were to throw in with the Confederacy, the District of Columbia would be totally surrounded by enemy territory and Washington would be untenable as the capital city of the United States. The government of the United States would have to flee and relocate; how would that look to European powers who might be contemplating recognizing and perhaps materially aiding the Confederate States of America? If Kentucky seceded, the Northern boundary of the Confederacy would be on the strategic transportation artery of the Ohio River. If Missouri were lost, Kansas and the gold fields of Colorado to the west, critical to financing the war, would be in jeopardy. Finally, when the western counties of Virginia broke away and petitioned for admission as a slave state within the Union, a new and unforeseen set of political variables was added to Lincoln's political calculations.

One of Lincoln's biggest problems early in the war consisted of officers in the Army of the United States who thought they knew best regarding when to emancipate slaves, and who assumed they had the power to take such action unilaterally. Lincoln had no problem with Benjamin Butler's decision to harbor slaves coming to Fort Monroe from Confederate territory, although Butler was soon relieved of his command of the fort and sent back to a temporary assignment in New England for reasons entirely unrelated to his slave policy.[16] Butler's action occurred prior to the First Battle of Bull Run, and it did not alter the legal status quo regarding the slaves or slavery, issues to be left to a negotiated settlement which some still believed might include peaceful sectional reunion. Although the opponents of the First Confiscation Act said that the bill would lead to emancipation, many of its proponents viewed the bill as a war measure, not an emancipation scheme. The act did not discuss what would become of the confiscated "property," nor did the act free a single slave. Not atypically, legislators deferred the controversial implications of what they had done to a later date. Meanwhile, out west in Missouri, the actions of General John C. Fremont were highly problematic for President Lincoln.

An early and difficult test for the president came on August 30, 1861, when John C. Fremont, the "Pathfinder" and the 1856 Republican standard bearer whom Lincoln had placed in command of the Department of the West with headquarters in St. Louis, unilaterally issued an emancipation proclamation freeing the slaves of all secessionists living in Missouri. Fremont, an abolitionist, had taken this action after an early Confederate victory at Wilson's Creek in which Nathaniel Lyon became the first Union general to die in battle. Fremont, aware of it or not, was by this action broadening the aims of the war to include emancipation. The Pathfinder had not consulted his superiors in the army or the administration; rather he had discussed this move only with his wife and a Quaker abolitionist. Fremont cut through the proverbial Gordian Knot of the rebellion and went directly to the heart of the problem. He had touched upon the fundamental cause of the war, slavery. But neither Lincoln nor the country was ready for this, and Lincoln was correctly concerned that the loyal border states could bolt for the Confederacy if Fremont's emancipating actions were allowed to stand.

There were, however, a few Republican leaders, including Vice-President Hannibal Hamlin of Maine, and senators Zachariah Chandler of Michigan and Charles Sumner of Massachusetts, who had met with Lincoln shortly after the Union loss at Bull Run in July to urge the president to expand the war's aims beyond saving the Union to include an end to slavery. They argued that freeing the slaves in the South would create such disarray that the Confederacy would collapse. Lincoln's polite but firm response was that public opinion would not allow such measures at that time.[17] Lincoln, the political leader of the nation, knew that he could not lead where the nation was not prepared to follow. Lincoln was warned by his Kentucky commander, General Robert Anderson, that if the Missouri emancipation order were not immediately rescinded, "disastrous results" would follow and "Kentucky will be lost to the Union."[18] Even before this warning from General Anderson, Lincoln had concluded that Fremont was acting for political rather than military reasons, which made his decree unconstitutional. Furthermore, such an action was so significant in its implications that it was a decision that only the commander-in-chief should make in the context of the entire war effort, rather than being implemented piecemeal, with or without authorization, by local commanders.

Now that Fremont had actually issued a limited emancipation proclamation, Lincoln acted quickly to "caution," not "censure," Fremont about the dangers of such a policy that "will alarm our Southern Union friends, and turn them against us."[19] An irritated and offended Fremont sent his outspoken wife Jessie to Washington to defend his actions to his commander-in-chief. It was to no avail; Lincoln ordered Fremont to change his proclamation to conform with the provisions of the Confiscation Act, which fell short of actual emancipation. Lincoln's refusal to support Fremont's proclamation may have saved Kentucky for the Union, but it angered Northern abolitionists, including Frederick Douglass, who editorialized, "Slavery is the bulwark of rebellion—the common bond that binds all slaveholding rebel hearts together. Cut that bond, and the rebellion falls asunder. If the Government does this, it will succeed, and if it does not, it will not deserve success."[20] But Douglass did not stop there. He went on to denounce the "weakness, imbecility and absurdity" of Lincoln's countermanding of Fremont's proclamation.[21] To Lincoln's dismay, Fremont was given heroic status as an antislavery activist while the president's own stock was falling within the Republican Party. Even Secretary of War Simon Cameron was so impressed with Fremont's proclamation that he telegraphed congratulations to him.[22]

Lincoln's friend, conservative Republican Senator Orville H. Browning of Illinois, caught the president off guard with his critical letter stating that "Fremont's proclamation was necessary, and will do good. It has the full approval of all loyal citizens of the west and North West."[23] Lincoln expressed astonishment at Browning's letter and called Fremont's actions "dictatorship" that might mean that "Kentucky would be turned against us. I think that to lose Kentucky is nearly the same as to lose the whole game."[24] Lincoln struggled to keep the focus on the "big picture" of winning the war, preserving the Union, and preventing the permanent establishment of a Southern republic which had as its cornerstone the principle that African slavery was a positive good sanctioned by God. Fremont's abrasive personality, political tone-deafness, and inappropriate actions in other arenas led to him being relieved of his command by the president in early November, after strong encouragement from others who knew of Fremont's somewhat erratic and inept leadership style. Lincoln, however, paid dearly for this whole episode. Severe criticisms of his presidency began with the Fremont affair, and the attacks would only get worse.

There would be other embarrassments for the commander-in-chief, including unauthorized statements by the president's own secretary of war, Simon Cameron, about arming the slaves. On December 1, 1861, Secretary Cameron issued an advance copy of his annual report, not yet reviewed by the president, to the press that included the statement, "Those who make war against the Government justly forfeit all rights of property. . . . It is as clearly the right of the Government to arm slaves, when it may become necessary, as it is to use gun-powder taken from the enemy."[25] This action, coupled with corruption within the War Department, soon caused an aggravated and worried Lincoln to send Cameron packing as America's new minister to Russia. By removing Fremont, and then Cameron, Lincoln attempted to reassure the border states, but at the same time such actions placed him increasingly at odds with the more radical abolitionists within his own Republican Party.

Lincoln was again faced with a Union commander exceeding his authority relative to slavery when, on May 9, 1862, General David Hunter declared that the slaves in his military Department of the South (Georgia, Florida, and South Carolina) "are therefore declared forever free." Lincoln's response was a proclamation on May 19, 1862, in which he stated:

> I, Abraham Lincoln, president of the United States, proclaim and declare, that the government of the United States, had no knowledge, information, or belief, of an intention on the part of General Hunter to issue such a proclamation; nor has it yet, any authentic information that the document is genuine. And further. That neither General Hunter, nor any other commander, or person, has been authorized by the Government of the United States, to make proclamations declaring the slaves of any State free; and that the supposed proclamation, now in question, whether genuine or false, is altogether void, so far as respects such declaration. I further make known that whether it be competent for me, as Commander-in-Chief of the Army and Navy, to declare the Slaves of any state or states, free, and whether at any time, in any case, it shall have become a necessity indispensable to the maintenance of the government, to exercise such supposed power, are questions which, under my responsibility, I reserve to myself, and which I can not feel justified in leaving to the decision of commanders in the field.[26]

At the other end of the opinion spectrum on emancipation stood General George B. McClellan, until late 1862 Lincoln's greatest hope for Union victory and in 1864 Lincoln's Democratic opponent for the presidency. It was McClellan who, in July of 1862, took it upon himself to instruct his commander-in-chief with a paper in which the top Union general pontificated about the relation of the war to slavery. The power of the Union Army "should not be allowed to interfere with the relations of servitude," the general warned, and "not even for a moment" should the "forcible abolition of slavery" be contemplated. McClellan tried his best to convince Lincoln that a "declaration of radical views, especially on slavery, will rapidly disintegrate our present Armies." That same month McClellan's staff actually discussed, quite likely with the general's approbation, the possibility of marching on Washington to "intimidate the president." McClellan even shared with his wife that there were those who believed he should "assume the Government."[27]

In reality, a significant portion of Lincoln's own party was moving faster toward emancipation than the president felt was prudent. Republican radicalization on the issue of slavery can be seen in response to the

Crittenden-Johnson resolution (sponsored by senators John Crittenden of Kentucky and Andrew Johnson of Tennessee), which was passed in the House and Senate just days before the First Battle of Bull Run. The resolution stated that armed hostilities by the United States against the seceded states was not being undertaken for the purpose of "overthrowing or interfering with the rights or established institutions of States," but rather to "maintain the supremacy of the Constitution and to preserve the Union with all the dignity, equality, and rights of the several States unimpaired."[28] While three radical abolitionists voted against the resolution in the House and several abstained, after the loss at Bull Run the abolitionist wing of the Republican Party began to assert itself more aggressively.

In his annual message to Congress on December 3, 1861, Lincoln stated that it was his hope that the war "shall not degenerate into a violent and remorseless revolutionary struggle."[29] The very next day, political caution was thrown to the wind as the Crittenden-Johnson resolution (and by extension Lincoln) was repudiated by the House, thanks to a strong Republican majority.[30] The radicalization of Congress was further evidenced in March of 1862 when arch-abolitionist Wendell Phillips gave three lectures in the nation's capital, and was given a rare introduction on the floor of the Senate. The New York *Tribune* followed Phillips's Washington visit, noting the "violent contrasts" from reactions to earlier abolitionist activities, concluding that the "deference and respect now paid to him by men in the highest places of the nation, are tributes to the idea [of abolitionism] of which he, more than any other one man, is a popular exponent."[31] Emancipation was beginning to enter the public consciousness of the Union in ways not before experienced. Lincoln and many Republicans were clearly not, at this point, on the same page. While Lincoln detested slavery and had wished for its abolition since his youth, he knew that there was more at stake than his personal wish, as he later expressed it, that all men everywhere could be free. He would bide his time, doing what was most necessary in his opinion to pursue the war and keep the loyal border states in the Union, while never abandoning his hope for the extinction of slavery.

As if fighting a war to preserve the Union were not enough, four loyal states, the breakaway region of another state, and the District of Columbia were faced with questions of when and how, and initially even "if," to emancipate their slave populations. President Lincoln needed to be extremely careful what was said and done on the part of the federal government that would affect these critically important areas. Delaware, Unionist in sentiment and having barely seventeen hundred slaves within its borders, provided Lincoln with irritation but not issues of paramount importance, even though the state clung to slavery to the bitter end. But Maryland, Missouri, Kentucky, and the counties of western Virginia were problematic in many respects for the Union's president. What to do about slavery within the nation's capital was also vexing. Many possibilities had to be considered. What would befall the Union if any one or all three of the problematic border states were to abandon their allegiance to the government of the United States? How should Lincoln handle questions of slavery's constitutionality and the perennial question of states' rights? When should Lincoln take control of state militias, and if it became necessary to take military action to counteract secessionist tendencies in these states, how should it be done? What would the border states' reactions be to the possibility of armed blacks serving the Union cause? As if these questions were not weighty enough, Lincoln also faced the stark reality that Unionist supporters in these states were often not in agreement over methods and outcomes. Supporting the Union was well and good, but such support meant different things to different individuals and factions. All of these questions swirled around the issue of slavery and its future.

Kentucky, President Lincoln's birthplace, had not left the Union, but it did declare itself militarily neutral early in the war. While not happy with this situation and believing neutrality to be a form of rebellion, Lincoln nonetheless tolerated it as necessary to secure Kentucky's ties to the Union. The Confederate invasion and occupation of the town of Columbus by General Leonidas Polk in the summer of 1861 provoked Kentucky into abandoning neutrality and providing troops for the Union. But there was a catch; Kentucky's loyalty was contingent on the national government keeping its hands off slavery.[32]

Lincoln and the Republicans were looking to promote emancipation through two separate policies, one for states in rebellion and one for the loyal slave states. Immediate emancipation through military means was the original policy aimed at the seceded states, and it involved no compensation to slaveholders. A voluntary, compensated, and gradual emancipation policy for the loyal slave states was suggested and offered when, on March 6, 1862, Lincoln sent a message to Congress that he had been pondering for some time. While such a plan would be voluntary for each loyal slave state, Lincoln gave a gentle warning that the future of slavery could not be predicted as the war continued. In other words it was, Lincoln believed, in the best interests of the border states to act now to end slavery with compensation rather than to face the uncertainties of what might follow at the end of the war.[33] The day before Lincoln's announcement, Postmaster General Montgomery Blair, the most conservative member of Lincoln's cabinet, sent a written plea to the president urging him to include a plan of colonization as the only way to win over the border states. Blair may have been right about public support for emancipation in the border states at that time, but Lincoln had made up his mind to exclude a colonization provision. While the Congress cooperated in passing Lincoln's proposal offering compensated, gradual emancipation, the border states wanted no part of it, in large measure because, without a plan of colonization, the border states feared a large free black population in their midst.

Lincoln argued that, if the loyal slave states voluntarily emancipated their slaves, it would end any hope on the part of the Confederacy that these states would join them, thus shortening the war. Lincoln had also done the math, or at least his version of it; he calculated that the total cost of compensated emancipation for the slaves, at four hundred dollars a person[34] in Missouri, Kentucky, Maryland, Delaware, and the District of Columbia would equal the cost of waging the war for eighty-seven days, and surely the war would be shortened by more than eighty-seven days were the plan to be implemented, thus saving lives and money. Despite Lincoln's assurances about the voluntary nature of his plan, fear of federal interference made the border states skittish. Lincoln was disappointed with their response, but his moderate proposal had succeeded in placing the president firmly in control of the slavery issue and, for the moment, toned down the radical abolitionists while reassuring conservative loyalists in the border states.[35]

Despite rejection of Lincoln's compensated emancipation offer in 1862, Maryland became the first of the border states to end slavery. Pro-Union newspapers such as Chestertown, Maryland's *Kent News* blamed secessionists for the fact that slavery was on the way out. More damage had been done to the future of the peculiar institution by Southern rebels "than the crazy fanatics of the North could have done in one hundred years to come."[36] Charles Lewis Wagandt's study of Maryland slavery concludes that Lincoln's emancipation offer was rejected because "Conservatives saw in congressional offers of financial help ominous overtones of bribery and federal intervention, indignities insufferable to their pride. Yet some of them tried to give the impression that the state would abolish slavery if it stood in the way of the Union. The catch lay in the qualifications with which the conservatives encompassed the statement. Those debatable congressional funds must be provided for emancipation, deportation, and colonization before the border states would consider the proposal."[37] Perhaps Montgomery Blair had been right. When the House of Representatives approved the Second Confiscation Act of July 17, 1862, with its promise of freedom for slaves of rebels who came within Union lines, the Maryland congressional delegation was counted among the fifty-four nay votes who lost out to the eighty-two aye votes. One Maryland Senator opposed the measure, and the other was too ill to vote.[38] President Lincoln signed the bill into law.

Two years later, the demise of slavery in loyal Maryland was affected by an important election held on April 6, 1864, which would determine whether a convention would be called to write a new state constitution. The election, carefully monitored by the Lincoln administration, went smoothly, with roughly 60 percent of voters in support of a constitutional convention. Sixty-one of the ninety-six delegates selected for the convention were in support of emancipation, although the issue of immediate or gradual emancipation was not settled. Lincoln paid a visit to Baltimore shortly before the convention to encourage the emancipationists, telling them, "Recently, as it seems, the people of Maryland have been doing something to define liberty." Lincoln also used this occasion to defend his contentious decision to bring blacks into the Union Army. Although as yet unconfirmed, rumors of the slaughter of hundreds of black Union troops at Fort Pillow, Tennessee, by Rebel forces had caused further murmurings within the border states. Lincoln stated that he had enabled blacks to fight for the Union as "a clear conviction of duty" and that he saw the decision as his responsibility "to the American people, to the christian world, to history, and on my final account to God."[39]

The Maryland constitutional convention debated and then approved, on a vote of fifty-three to twenty-seven, a new article to the state's constitution that approved immediate emancipation. A series of unanticipated Confederate raids into Maryland in July of 1864 disrupted the convention. General David Hunter, who Lincoln had chastised in 1862 for a premature emancipation order in the South, again caused problems for his commander-in-chief with an overzealous response to these Confederate incursions. Hunter ordered the arrest and deportation to the Confederacy of all presumed Maryland secessionists and anyone who had given aid to the enemy in the recent raids. Fearful of what this would do to Unionist sentiment in Maryland and the pending constitutional changes regarding slavery, Lincoln first suspended Hunter's order, then suspended Hunter from command. When the constitutional convention resumed in early September, the new constitution that included the immediate emancipation article was approved, and an October date was set for statewide ratification.[40]

To Lincoln's dismay, he soon received reports that Maryland's proposed new constitution was facing stiff opposition not only for immediate, uncompensated emancipation but also for its required loyalty oath at the polls. It did not help that Lincoln's reelection bid had not been met with full favor in Maryland; Lincoln perhaps prudently declined an invitation to speak at a pro-convention rally scheduled for two days before the ratification vote, although he did send a written message urging passage of the new constitution. The outcome was close, but the new constitution, including the provision for emancipation, prevailed. This would have not been the case had not Union soldiers from Maryland been encouraged to vote, and did so in support of the document.[41] Though several legal challenges were brought against the election's outcome, the new constitution, and with it emancipation, prevailed in Maryland with a final margin of victory of 263 votes out of 59,973 ballots cast.[42] The day before the ratification vote was held, Marylander Roger B. Taney, conservative chief justice of the U.S. Supreme Court and author of the Dred Scott decision, died. In the words of New Yorker George Templeton Strong, an avid diarist of the period, "Two ancient abuses and evils were perishing together."[43]

In Missouri, the only border state to be placed under martial law throughout the war thanks to widespread lawlessness and vicious guerilla tactics, Unionists were anything but unified. Conservative Unionists sought gradual emancipation with compensation along with leniency for rebels, while more radical Unionists demanded immediate abolition and loss of the franchise for secessionists. When Lincoln's 1862 plan for gradual, compensated emancipation was considered, Missouri's State Convention for constitutional revision in Jefferson City met, discussed, and tabled a motion dealing with the president's plan. The following year, public sentiment favoring emancipation had grown in the state, and while the Unionist legislature seemed to favor compensated emancipation, the state's constitution would first need some enabling revisions. Governor Hamilton Gamble called the State Convention back into session on June 15, 1863. A date of 1870 was finally agreed upon by the convention as liberation day for many of Missouri's slaves, with exceptions for slaves forty years and older (who would remain enslaved for life) and those slaves under the age of twelve who would be freed at the age of twenty-three.[44] The radical abolitionists were not pleased with this turn of events, nor were slaves themselves, although President Lincoln continued to see gradual emancipation in Missouri as a desirable option. The *Kansas City Journal of Commerce* reported that many slaves, unwilling to wait for their freedom, had taken matters into their own hands and that these "self-emancipated chattels seem to prefer emancipation without compensation."[45]

A Radical Abolition Convention was called for September 1, 1863, in Jefferson City. One result of this gathering was the selection of a committee to go to Washington to visit with President Lincoln. A large delegation of seventy Missouri abolitionists showed up at the White House on September 30 to demand the ouster of Missouri's military commander, General John Schofield (accused, among other things, of silencing the radical abolitionist press in Missouri), and to complain about Governor Hamilton Gamble. Lincoln had to remind the delegation that his Emancipation Proclamation did not affect Missouri as a loyal state, and explained that while he hoped Missouri would emancipate its slaves, the method they would choose was up to legitimate authorities in the state, and was not his business. Lincoln's junior secretary, John Hay, characterized Lincoln's meeting with the radical Missouri abolitionists as among the most contentious of his presidency. Before the delegation left Washington, Lincoln received an impassioned letter from Governor Gamble warning the president of a "party . . . sprung up in Missouri, which openly and loudly proclaims to purpose to overturn" the state's legitimate government. Referring to the radicals as "corrupt and malignant," Governor Gamble's intemperate approach served further to alienate radical and conservative Unionists, making Missouri in some ways the most problematic of the border states with which Lincoln had to deal. But there was ultimately a happy resolution for the president. In the election of 1864, Lincoln received a substantial majority of Missourians' votes over McClellan—the highest percentage for Lincoln of any of the border states. Thomas Fletcher won the governorship handily, along with voter approval for a new state constitutional convention. The convention acted with speed, and on January 12, 1865, slavery was abolished in Missouri without compensation.[46]

Kentucky's wartime dealings with slavery proved to be a disappointment to Abraham Lincoln. Eager to keep Kentucky loyal, Lincoln had not pressed his native state to enact emancipation legislation, and they did not do so. Kentuckians seemed especially incensed at Lincoln for his Emancipation Proclamation, although it did not directly affect them at the time. On March 10, 1863, at an elaborate and costly public ceremony in Lexington designed to honor Kentucky Colonel Frank Wolford for bravery and valor in his defense of the Union cause, the recipient of the honors used the occasion to launch a ferocious attack against his commander in chief. The president was harshly denounced to the stunned, but somewhat appreciative, audience as a crusher of the Constitution and the rights of the people, a liar regarding the purposes of the war, and a violator of the rules of civilized warfare. General Stephen Burbridge, Union commander in Kentucky, had Wolford arrested, but a forgiving Lincoln intervened and secured his release.[47] While large numbers of Kentucky slaves found their own freedom by escaping to Union lines during the war, slavery did not officially end in the Bluegrass State until the Thirteenth Amendment was ratified in 1865. It was 1976 before Kentucky decided to add its name to the list of states ratifying this amendment.

In Delaware, there was a north-south cultural and political split that was a microcosm of the national experience over slavery. In the tiny state's three counties, New Castle County in the North was largely Republican and antislavery. Southern Sussex County was Democratic and proslavery, while Kent County in the middle of the state was divided. In essence, there were two Delawares.[48] Some Delawareans opted to go south and join the Confederate Army, including the son of former Governor William Ross, and many families found themselves with divided loyalties. Some Delaware clergy found themselves in difficulty with portions of their congregations when they uttered prayers on behalf of President Lincoln and the Union cause. Secessionist talk was not uncommon, but actions were limited to the stealing of a few armaments from the home guard armory and, more injurious to the Union cause, sending supplies, medicine, and information to Maryland and on into Virginia. Partisan politics in Delaware ran rampant, with the town of Smyrna holding separate Fourth of July celebrations for Democrats and Republicans.[49] Despite Southern sympathies in Southern Delaware, there was little organized opposition to Delaware remaining in the Union.[50]

There was also partisan division over Lincoln's offer of compensated emancipation in Delaware. Lincoln's initial offer of three hundred dollars per slave in the state was rejected. Ironically, the largest slaveholder in the state, Benjamin Burton, was a Republican who owned twenty-eight slaves. Delaware Congressman George Fisher arranged for Burton to go to Washington and meet with Lincoln to discuss the situation. Burton told the president that he was certain that, upon a fair offer of compensation, Delaware's slaveholders would gladly give up their Negroes. A delighted Lincoln, who believed that if Delaware went for a compensated emancipation plan other border states would follow, was soon disappointed, as the optimistic Burton returned home to unexpected opposition from all but one other of the state's slave owners.[51] Both of Delaware's U.S. senators also opposed Lincoln's compensated emancipation plan for their state, with Senator Willard Saulsbury attacking it as part of a plot "to elevate the miserable Negro, not only to political rights, but to put him in [the] Army."[52] The Delaware legislature rejected the proposal, and as William C. Harris has noted, due to the tiny number of slaves in the state, "the main issue in its disapproval was not the protection of an economic system or the maintenance of a plantation lifestyle. Slavery was no longer important to the material welfare or white class structure of Delaware. The overriding issue in Delaware's rejection was racial, specifically the state's continued control of blacks. Like Senator Saulsbury, legislators feared that their acceptance of Lincoln's plan would become an entering wedge for antislavery elements in the federal government to impose black equality or rights upon Delaware whites."[53]

The largely negative reaction in Delaware to Lincoln's Preliminary Emancipation Proclamation in the fall of 1862 resulted in a state legislature being elected that fall that, while still Unionist, was highly critical of Mr. Lincoln. When the new legislature met in January 1863, they were critical of both the Emancipation Proclamation and Lincoln's suspension of the writ of habeas corpus, seeing these policies as "a flagrant attempt to exercise absolute power" and "an artful device by persons in authority for the subversion of our form of Government."[54] Anti-Lincoln rhetoric in the U.S. Senate reached new heights thanks to Senator Willard Saulsbury's vitriolic attack in January 1863, in which he denounced Lincoln as "a weak and imbecile man, the weakest that I ever knew in a high place. . . . [N]ever did [I] see or converse with so weak and imbecile a man as Abraham Lincoln, President of the United States." Outraged Senate Republicans thereupon passed a resolution declaring Saulsbury's verbal attack on the president as a violation of the Senate's rules of order, which provoked another attack from Saulsbury on Lincoln and his Republican supporters to the point that Hannibal Hamlin, Lincoln's vice-president and presiding officer of the Senate, ordered the sergeant-at-arms to remove the feisty Delaware senator from the chamber.[55]

The Delaware legislature never did reach a consensus on emancipation during the war, and when elections in the fall of 1864 resulted in Democratic victories in that state, further discussion of emancipation seemed fruitless. Only in December 1865, when the Thirteenth Amendment went into effect nationally, did slavery end in Delaware. The Delaware General Assembly refused to ratify the amendment, rejecting it as an illegal interference over the states by the federal government. By the time the Thirteenth Amendment was implemented, most of Delaware's slaves had already run off, with many of the men having enlisted in black Union regiments in 1863 and 1864. Delaware finally ratified the Thirteenth Amendment on Lincoln's birthday, February 12, 1901.

The northwestern counties of Virginia, containing about one-third of the state's population, provided Lincoln with yet another challenge and opportunity. In November 1861 thirty-four counties sent delegates to Wheeling and voted to secede from Virginia and form the new state of Kanawha. This largely Unionist region of the state claimed to be the "Restored State of Virginia" which the Lincoln administration, as well as Congress, came to view as the legitimate government of the state. The legislature of this region supported the request of the Wheeling convention for separate statehood in 1862. The U.S. Senate passed a resolution allowing statehood for "Kanawha," thenceforward to be known as West Virginia, in June 1862, and the House of Representatives did likewise in December. In taking the issue up with his cabinet, a somewhat hesitant Lincoln received conflicting advice. Attorney General Edward Bates said approval of statehood for the region was clearly unconstitutional. William Seward said it was essential. Gideon Welles raised the delicate issue that, if West Virginia were not admitted to the Union, its 18,500 slaves would be freed when the Emancipation Proclamation would be signed within a couple of days. If admitted as a loyal slave state, those slaves would remain enslaved, at least for the near future. Lincoln decided to sign the legislation admitting West Virginia as a state, and did so on New Year's Eve, 1862, believing that such action, even if constitutionally questionable, was in the best interests of the Union's war effort. He justified his action in part by claiming that "there is still difference enough between secession against the constitution, and secession in favor of the constitution." Lincoln's approval contained a condition; the new state would be required to amend its constitution to provide for compensated emancipation, a promise that was kept a few weeks later in February 1863.[56]

Slavery in the nation's capital had been a galling offense for years to many Northern men in the federal government. The District of Columbia (which included Washington City, Washington County, and Georgetown) had about 75,000 residents when Lincoln began his first presidential term, including approximately 11,000 free blacks and 3,200 slaves. The slave trade had been banned from the capital by the Compromise of 1850, but not slavery itself. The long history of agitation by the African American press must be credited as a significant factor in the achievement of emancipation in the District, along with the work of many whites, including Congressman Abraham Lincoln, who had advocated an emancipation plan for the District, pending local voter approval, during his one term in the House of Representatives.[57]

It should be noted that slavery in the District of Columbia had been an issue years before. In 1846, the community of Alexandria, within the original District limits on the south side of the Potomac River, led a successful fight for Congress to retrocede to Virginia that part of the District of Columbia that is today's Arlington County. Residents of Alexandria were choosing to identify with Virginia rather than with the United States and its capital city. Fear that Congress would at some point end slavery in the District loomed large among the concerns of Alexandrians as they sought, and won, retrocession. Other legitimate concerns about lack of local control and not being represented in Congress deliberately obscured the slavery issue, causing most historians to miss the connection between the 1846 retrocession and the growing sectional divide over slavery.[58]

In March 1862, Alexandrians' fears of sixteen years earlier were realized when an emancipation bill for the nation's capital was introduced in Congress by Senator Henry Wilson of Massachusetts. After heated debate, the measure passed both the House and Senate on April 16, 1862, with every Republican legislator voting in favor, and all but five Democrats voting in opposition. It was the first time that slaves had been freed by an act of Congress, and the voters of the District of Columbia were neither required nor allowed to be participants in the decision. The bill, as passed, included compensation for owners deprived of their "property." A proposed colonization amendment to the bill failed on the first attempt, but was revived and passed a few days later. It was not known if President Lincoln would sign or veto the legislation; since none of the border states had accepted Lincoln's compensated emancipation proposal, it was unclear how this measure in the capital would be received by them. Border-state reaction was always of concern to Lincoln as part of the big picture of the war effort. The Washington *Evening Star* editorialized concerning twenty reasons why an emancipation bill should not be approved, and was likely correct in its assessment that the District's white population did not favor the bill.[59]

A veritable flood of petitions and letters to Washington's newspapers from the District's white citizens bemoaned the inevitable rush of even more poor and unemployed blacks into the nation's capital. But public opinion made little impact on Congress, as no member of that body owed election to the unrepresented voters in the nation's capital. Senator Charles Sumner, sensing the president needed prodding, requested a meeting with Lincoln and in blunt terms told him to his face that he, Abraham Lincoln, was the largest slaveholder in the nation, "for [you] hold all of the 3,000 slaves of the District, which is more than any other person in the country holds."[60] While it is not known what impact Sumner's strategy had on the president, Lincoln signed the bill, and put in writing this very honest explanation: "I have never doubted the Constitutional authority of Congress to abolish slavery in this District. I have ever desired to see the national capital freed from the institution in some satisfactory way. Hence there has never been in my mind any question upon the subject, except the one of expediency, arising in view of all the circumstances."[61]

Frederick Douglass, upon hearing the news of emancipation for the nation's capital, penned a letter to Senator Sumner in which he said, "I trust I am not dreaming, but the events taking place seem like a dream."[62] Washington's black population enjoyed a great day of celebration, particularly in the District's seventeen black churches on the Sunday after the emancipation bill was signed. Black religious leaders in the city issued a joint statement of thanks to God, the president, and Congress and pledged, "by our industry, energy, moral deportment and character, we will prove ourselves worthy of the confidence reposed in us in making us free men. . . . [A]s in the past we have as a people been orderly and law-abiding, so in the future we will strive with might and main to be in every way worthy of the glorious privilege which has now been conferred upon us."[63] Emancipation Day has been celebrated on April 16 by Washington's black community since that time.

To circumvent the emancipation law, a few District slaveholders relocated several hundred of their slaves to various locations in Maryland. Some of these slaves suffered from abusive incarceration conditions until most of them were searched out and liberated in 1863 by Colonel William Birney, in charge of black recruitment for the Union Army in Maryland.[64] The evasive actions of these District of Columbia slave owners were very similar to what occurred in several parts of the Confederacy throughout the war. When Union troops were approaching, planters who could afford to do so often "refugeed" their slaves to safer areas where they would not be liberated, including the vast expanses of remote Texas. In the District of Columbia, after a somewhat difficult process of determining slave values, about $900,000 was paid out to the more cooperative owners of emancipated slaves by the end of January 1863. Fortunately, Congress acted wisely and with foresight in removing Washington's black codes at the same time the emancipation bill passed; otherwise, free blacks would have been banned from certain occupations, would have been required to post bonds for good behavior, and would not have enjoyed freedom of assembly to the same degree as whites. The Senate also removed a ban on colored mail carriers in the District.[65]

One other emancipation bill was passed by Congress in 1862 and signed into law by Lincoln, although it was not referred to as an emancipation act. This legislation fulfilled the agenda of the Republican platforms of 1856 and 1860, that is, the prohibition of slavery in the territories. Long sought after as a means to contain slavery where it already existed,

An Act to Secure Freedom for All Persons Within the Territories of the United States[66] became law on June 19, 1862. In the Senate, one of the twenty-eight "ayes" came from none other than Senator David Wilmot of Pennsylvania, now a Republican, who as a Democratic member of the House had authored the Wilmot Proviso sixteen years earlier. The act provided immediate and uncompensated freedom to a handful of slaves in the Utah and New Mexico territories. The statute did not cover the slaves in the Indian Territory since officially it was an unorganized area governed by treaties.

The situation in Tennessee, the last state to secede and the first of the Confederate states to seek a return to the Union, was a unique case. This was a state that was very divided geographically and ideologically over slavery and secession. Eastern, Appalachian Tennessee consisted mainly of small farms and independent, hardscrabble yeomen with few if any slaves. The middle of the state, with larger farms and plantations, and wider commercial interests, had a significant slave population. West Tennessee, the richest cotton region of the state, was home to the highest concentration of slaves. Consequently, when the secession vote was taken in Tennessee in 1861, most all of the eastern counties were pro-Union, while the middle and western portions of the state favored joining the Confederacy.

The majority of Tennessee's 275,000 slaves managed to obtain freedom before the war ended.[67] As 1862 came to a close, much of Middle and West Tennessee, including Nashville and Memphis, was occupied by the Union Army. By the end of 1863, federal troops also occupied Knoxville and Chattanooga in East Tennessee. An unintended consequence of Union occupation was the significant acceleration of slavery's demise. Early in the war, many Union officers did not permit escaping slaves into Union lines, and some escaped slaves were returned by the army to their Unionist owners. However, thousands of other enslaved men in Tennessee claimed their own freedom by joining the Union Army.

Lincoln had hoped to exempt Tennessee from his Emancipation Proclamation by having elections held in 1862 that would restore Union representation for that state in the U.S. Congress. Lincoln urged the military governor, Democrat Andrew Johnson, to hold such elections in order for the state's loyal white residents to "avoid the unsatisfactory prospect [of forced emancipation through the Emancipation Proclamation] before them," but Johnson was fearful that secessionist candidates might prevail. An alternative plan was promoted by Unionist and former governor William B. Campbell, who drafted a petition asking Lincoln to exempt Tennessee because fair elections among the supposed Unionist majority of voters would not be possible due to the interference of Confederate raiders. Andrew Johnson, and about forty other Tennessee leaders, signed the petition, which was presented to Abraham Lincoln on December 23, 1862.[68] Lincoln agreed, and Tennessee was exempted from the final Emancipation Proclamation of January 1, 1863.

In an unexpected move, Military Governor Andrew Johnson gave a speech on August 29, 1863, in which he called for immediate emancipation in Tennessee. This policy position was much more a function of Johnson's political ambition and his disdain for the state's upper-class slave aristocracy than any concern on Johnson's part for the slaves themselves. Johnson had once owned slaves, and as his later actions as president would demonstrate, he was no friend of the freedmen. Furthermore, "immediate" emancipation would require perhaps a two-year legislative process before it could be implemented. Lincoln sent Johnson a letter urging a rapid revision of the state constitution to move the process along more quickly. Finally, on January 21, 1864, after considerable pressure from free blacks, white Unionists, and Lincoln, Governor Johnson called for a constitutional convention and general reconstruction program for Tennessee that included sworn support for emancipation as a prerequisite for voting rights.[69] The issue of emancipation had still not been resolved in Tennessee by the time Lincoln named Johnson as his vice-presidential running mate on the "Union Party" ticket (a coalition of Republicans and War Democrats) in the 1864 presidential election. Before his departure for Washington to be inaugurated as vice-president, Andrew Johnson had the satisfaction of seeing a statewide referendum on February 22, 1865, approve the state constitutional amendments that brought about immediate emancipation in Tennessee. Tennessee's new civil government began operating under its new constitution on April 5, 1865. That very day, the state legislature unanimously voted to ratify the Thirteenth Amendment to the federal Constitution.

The sense of excitement, joy, and relief experienced by slaves and antislavery advocates during the process of emancipation often masks some dark and disheartening unintended consequences that few historians have addressed. Nobody in the civil government or military forces of the United States, or in antislavery churches and philanthropic organizations, or in the Northern press had foreseen and planned adequately for the massive dislocation, disease, hunger, and general deprivation that large numbers of fugitive and emancipated slaves were forced to endure. Proslavery advocates had predicted that, if slavery ended, the former slaves would go extinct.[70] While this proved to be a gross exaggeration, it did predict some of the severe hardships that freed slaves would face in light of thoroughly inadequate preparation by the government and private agencies to anticipate and meet their needs. As glorious and remarkable an achievement as emancipation was, it must be noted that, as Jim Downs has concluded, "tens of thousands of freed slaves became sick and died due to the unexpected problems caused by the exigencies of war and the massive dislocation triggered by emancipation. The distress and medical crises that freed slaves experienced were a hidden cost of war and an unintended outcome of emancipation."[71]

The massive and devastating outbreak of epidemic diseases among the freed African American population was due not only to their being deprived of basic necessities such as sufficient clothing, food, clean water, and shelter, it was also exacerbated by deficient medical knowledge of germ theory (which also killed hundreds of thousands of soldiers on both sides) and a strange misconception that African Americans differed physiologically from whites and required different medical treatments, some of which were experimental and few of which were effective. Furthermore, medical fiction of the day "blamed the spread of disease on black people's innate vulnerability to illness."[72] It was a massive public health crisis that would continue, especially in the South, for years to come.

Even in states firmly under Confederate control, there was talk of possible limited emancipation if it would further the Confederacy's goal of winning its independence. This was certainly a shift in the position of Confederate President Jefferson Davis, who in his address to the Confederate Congress on November 7, 1864, took the legislators by surprise by recommending limited emancipation for forty thousand slaves who would serve the Confederate military long-term as a workforce of persons, rather than slaves. These slaves, according to Davis's proposal, would be purchased by the Confederate government and ultimately given their freedom "as a reward for faithful service." Davis even went so far as to state that, if the South's white population should ever "prove insufficient for the armies we require and can afford to keep in the field," and "should the alternative ever be presented of subjugation or of the employment of the slave as a soldier, there seems no reason to doubt what should then be our decision."[73]

The idea of using a portion of the slave population as soldiers had surfaced before in the South, such as the proposal advanced by General Patrick Cleburne and other officers of the Army of Tennessee in early 1864 following the Confederate disaster at Chattanooga the previous November. Such pleas had been initially neither well received nor implemented. Perhaps too much was at stake, ideologically, for the South to make such a bold move.

JEFFERSON DAVIS. *Kentucky-born Mississippi slaveholder, U.S. senator, secretary of war, and president of the Confederate States of America. Near the end of the Civil War, Davis advocated the use of slaves in the Confederate army to be followed by their emancipation, but the war ended before such a policy could be implemented. Following his capture by Union forces shortly after the war, he was confined at Fort Monroe for two years and then released.*

However, by early 1865 the Confederate military situation was growing so desperate that the arming of slaves for the Southern cause seemed to be catching on in some quarters. Senator Albert Gallatin Brown introduced a resolution to the Confederate Senate on February 7 permitting President Davis to place up to 200,000 slaves, voluntarily or otherwise, into the armed forces and ultimately to free them. Only two senators joined him in voting for the measure. In what Bruce Levine calls "the most extraordinary and momentous proposal of the war,"[74] Confederate Secretary of State, and former Secretary of War, Judah P. Benjamin asked Robert E. Lee on February 11, 1865, to get a sense of his troops' opinion about the recruitment of slaves for the Confederate forces. Lee readily complied. Because Lee came to see the proposal as a military necessity, he favored it as did many of his men and the officers under him.[75] Recruitment of slaves was approved, but it was too late. The Confederate surrender at Appomattox was just two weeks away.

Perhaps Commander Howell Cobb of Georgia's reserve forces summed it up succinctly in January 1865 in a letter to Confederate Secretary of War James Seddon by stating, "The day you make soldiers of them is the beginning of the end of the revolution. If slaves will make good soldiers our whole theory of slavery is wrong."[76] If the "cornerstone" of the Confederate nation was worth compromising, then perhaps the nation itself was not worth preserving. The end was in sight; Confederate realists saw it coming with Lincoln's reelection in November of 1864. That election was proof that the North would stay the course until the war, whose non-negotiable aims now included Union *and* emancipation, resulted in a Northern victory.

CHAPTER 14

UNION VICTORY AND THE THIRTEENTH AMENDMENT: FREE AT LAST?

Emancipation was progressing in incremental steps, seeming to make more progress than the Union armies. As the war dragged on, Congress had abolished slavery in the District of Columbia and in the territories by legislative enactments in the spring of 1862. That following summer, Congress passed the Second Confiscation Act, which freed the slaves who fled to or became encompassed within Union lines. Lincoln had turned the Confiscation Act on its head with the Emancipation Proclamation by freeing all the slaves in designated areas of the South, whether Union armies had reached them or not. While the Emancipation Proclamation freed the slaves in designated areas in a state of rebellion, the proclamation could not and did not free the slaves in the border states that remained loyal to the Union, or slaves residing in areas already controlled by Union forces or otherwise exempted from the effect of the order. The three fugitive slaves who had first rowed their boat to Fort Monroe were still not free. However, by abolishing slavery in the territories and requiring West Virginia to abolish slavery once it had been granted statehood, Lincoln and the Congress had made an emphatic statement that no slave state would again be admitted to the Union.

The war was destabilizing slavery as an institution throughout the Confederacy, a process that accelerated following Union victories in Atlanta and elsewhere in late 1864 and early 1865. Long before any action took place in Washington to put forth a constitutional ban on slavery, some Southerners had already reconciled themselves to the idea that slavery was going to end, and sooner rather than later. When Lincoln had issued his

"Proclamation of Amnesty and Reconstruction" in late 1863, it was an attempt to get Confederate states to seek readmission to the Union on lenient terms, but the plan did include an end to slavery. The new state governments, under the Amnesty and Reconstruction Plan, would need to acknowledge the "permanent freedom" of the former slaves and provide for their education. However, always the principled pragmatist, Lincoln suggested the possibility that freed slaves could be put into a system of apprenticeships "consistent, as a temporary arrangement, with their present condition as a laboring, landless, and homeless class." This was justified as a means to ameliorate "the confusion and destitution which must, at best, attend all classes by a total revolution of labor" in the former slaveholding states.[1] Although the Lincoln plan was never enacted, many white Southern ears perked up. Even if the Union were restored, perhaps it would be possible to end slavery in a technical sense and yet keep their former slaves as a lowly paid, highly restricted underclass, which is essentially what happened for the next hundred years. As planter D. C. Humphreys of Madison County, Alabama, expressed it in March of 1864, "we prefer the old method" (actual chattel slavery) but, he concluded, "There is really no difference . . . whether we hold them as absolute slaves, or obtain their labor by some other method."[2]

As Lincoln noted in his Second Inaugural Address, slavery was the root cause of the war. If there were to be peace, the future of slavery as an institution in the United States had to be addressed once and for all by constitutional means. On January 11, 1864, Senator John B. Henderson, a Missouri Democrat, broached the subject in the Senate by proposing a constitutional amendment for the abolition of slavery throughout the nation. The amendment was referred to the Senate Judiciary Committee, where a number of other proposals for abolition had been under consideration. Eventually, a joint resolution was voted on in the Senate on April 8, 1864. Before a final vote, however, Senator Willard Saulsbury of Delaware rose to offer a substitute amendment. The amendment contained twenty separate sections for the preservation of slavery, the restoration and extension of the old Missouri Compromise line, making it a crime to "incite a slave to abscond" or to conspire in "any State to interfere with the lawful rights in any other State." In other words, Saulsbury sought to outlaw the abolitionist movement and its Republican allies. Also proposed was the possibility of federal compensation when a state abolished slavery, the permanent prohibition of the African slave trade, and the permanent abolition of slavery after all the states had individually decided to abolish the institution.[3] These proposals harkened back to the proposals of the Crittenden compromise and the Committee of Thirteen in late 1860. The Senate must have sat there aghast, listening to the gentleman from Delaware talk as if there had not been three years of civil war and 400,000 dead over these very issues. The time for compromise on slavery was long past—too much blood had been shed. No official vote on this proposal was taken; the entry in the Congressional Globe merely states, "there being on a division—ayes 2, noes not counted."[4]

The Senate then took a vote on Senator Henderson's main proposal. The outcome was a foregone conclusion. There were fifty members in the Senate, two each for the now twenty-four states including newly admitted West Virginia. Also sitting in the chamber were two senators from the rival Unionist government of Virginia. The Republicans held twenty-eight seats while their Unconditional Unionist allies held an additional four seats for a total of thirty-two, a more than sufficient number for the required two-thirds majority for passage. When the tally was taken, thirty-eight senators voted aye and six no, far above the needed majority. Senator Reverdy Johnson of Maryland was the only Unionist who voted for the amendment. Five senators were absent when the vote was taken, three Democrats and two Unionists.

Among the thirty-eight ayes, three votes cast that day had particular poignancy. James Lane of Kansas, an abolitionist who had barely escaped death at the hands of William Quantrill's Confederate guerillas during their bloody raid on Lawrence in 1863, survived to cast his aye vote. Likewise, the radical abolitionist and victim of the savage attack on the Senate floor by Representative Preston Brooks nearly eight years before, Senator Charles Sumner of Massachusetts, had survived physically as well as politically to relish this moment. Ironically, Brooks, the man who nearly killed Sumner, was now deceased and was spared the pain of witnessing slavery's final demise. Senator John Sherman of Ohio cast an affirmative vote. Unlike his older brother William Tecumseh Sherman, who had lived in the South prior to the war, John Sherman was a staunch abolitionist crusader, serving on and off in the Senate until 1897, where he would fight for the rights of the freed African Americans. Four of the six no votes came from very predictable sources, the senators from Kentucky and Delaware, the two loyal states that were steadfast in their commitment to slavery. Joining these were Thomas A. Hendricks from Indiana and James A. McDougall of California. Prior to the vote, McDougall had indulged in a particularly savage exercise of race baiting, including raising the favorite canard of miscegenation.

When the voting had been completed, Senator Saulsbury declared, "I rise simply to say that I now bid farewell to any hope of reconstruction of the American Union." McDougall then rose to raise an objection to the constitutionality of the vote, stating, "I think our vote now being a final vote should have relation to all the States as recognized by the Constitution." Since the North did not recognize the legitimacy of secession, McDougall was asserting that, even though the Confederate states did not currently have representatives in the Senate, they should have been counted, and therefore the necessary two-thirds vote of the Senate had not been reached. Vice-President Hamlin ruled that a quorum had been present and voting, as required by the Constitution. McDougall then stated for the record that his opinion differed on the matter. With that, the Senate adjourned.[5]

Obtaining the required two-thirds of the House would not be as easy as it was in the Senate. It would take eight months for the House to reach the constitutionally mandated two-thirds vote. While the Republicans were the largest party in the House, they failed to have a clear majority. At the time of the final vote in January 1865, there were eighty-four Republicans, sixty-five Democrats, and an assortment of Unionist, Unconditional Unionist, Independent Republican, and Union Republican parties holding an additional twenty-six seats. Representative William Windom first introduced the emancipation amendment on the House floor on February 15, 1864.[6] On the same day, Representative Isaac Arnold of Minnesota called for a test vote proposing a resolution resolving that the Constitution be amended to abolish slavery without proposing formal language as Windom had done earlier. The resolution was adopted by a vote of seventy-eight to sixty-two, far from the two-thirds majority required to pass an amendment.[7]

The first attempt in the House to approve the Joint Resolution passed by the Senate occurred on June 15, 1864, and it failed badly. There were ninety-three votes in favor, sixty-five against, and twenty-three abstentions. While a majority, it was barely so. But subsequent events would ultimately change the vote. When the House first voted on the proposed Thirteenth Amendment in June of 1864, the war was going badly for the Union. Grant's bloody Overland campaign was giving the Northern public pause on whether continuing the war was worth the sacrifice. Union victory seemed as remote in mid-1864 as it had seemed in the dark days of 1862. It also appeared quite likely that Lincoln and the Republicans would be voted out of office in the November 1864 election. The lower chamber, always more sensitive to the winds of political change, was not in a risk-taking mood. The Republican Party itself, however, had become more radicalized on the issue of emancipation, and at their nominating convention in Baltimore, in June of 1864, some momentous decisions were made by party leaders and delegates, despite what some saw as their gloomy prospects in the fall election. Of course Lincoln was re-nominated, but the party temporarily adopted the name of "National Union Party" to broaden its political base among Northern Democrats, and War Democrat Andrew Johnson of Tennessee was added as Mr. Lincoln's vice-presidential running mate. Equally noteworthy was that the party platform of 1864 called for a constitutional amendment that would prohibit slavery throughout the entire United States:

> 3. Resolved, That as slavery was the cause, and now constitutes the strength of this Rebellion, and as it must be, always and everywhere, hostile to the principles of Republican Government, justice and the national safety demand its utter and complete extirpation from the soil of the Republic; and that, while we uphold and maintain the acts and proclamations by which the Government, in its own defense, has aimed a deathblow at this gigantic evil, we are in favor, furthermore, of such an amendment to the Constitution, to be made by the people in conformity with its provisions, as shall terminate and forever prohibit the existence of Slavery within the limits of the jurisdiction of the United States.[8]

Meanwhile, the Democrats offered a peace platform that was, for the first time in years, silent on the issue of slavery.

Events moved swiftly in the autumn and early winter of 1864, once again changing the political landscape. Lincoln's reelection, thanks in good measure to the fall of Atlanta and other Union advances, strengthened his political muscle; not only was it an endorsement of the president's war policies, but it also could now be viewed as a mandate for emancipation. Important Union victories had indeed begun to signal the death throes of the Confederacy. Atlanta, Cedar Creek, Nashville, Sherman's march to the sea, Savannah, and Fort Fisher were added to the roll call of Union victories between mid-June 1864 and the end of January 1865 when the House again took up the amendment. Lincoln applied political persuasion, and in a spirit of nonpartisanship urged Democrats to rethink their opposition to the amendment. Since it would no doubt be passed by the newly elected Republican majority in the next session of Congress, he asked the lame-duck Congress, "may we not agree that the sooner the better?"[9] Lincoln became more engaged in the legislative process than ever before, using all his charm and the reinvigorated personal authority that his electoral victory had given him to persuade questionable votes in the House to side with the amendment.[10] Lincoln wanted a constitutional amendment prohibiting slavery in process before the war ended, fearful that the Emancipation Proclamation, as a war measure, might be judicially struck down once hostilities ceased.

The final vote was taken in the House on January 31, 1865. Fifteen Democrats, more than three times the previous number voting for the amendment, joined with Republicans and their allies to bring the affirmative vote total to 119. Fifty Democrats were joined by 6 Union Party representatives for a total of 56 nays. The margin of victory in the House that day was provided by 8 Democrats who apparently could not bring themselves to vote for the amendment, but neither did they want to be the cause of its failure. They are recorded as not voting.[11] A future president, James Garfield, was in the chamber as a young representative from Ohio and voted for emancipation.

The final vote also reflected the traditional strongholds of the old Puritan faith and its attendant abolitionist sentiments. Only 2 of New England's representatives failed to cast an affirmative vote, a Democrat from Maine who voted nay and a Democrat from New Hampshire who abstained. The New York delegation split between the abolitionist regions of upstate versus the Copperhead stronghold of New York City and the Hudson Valley. Five downstate Democrats defected to help swing the vote. Reflecting its New England origins, Michigan's delegation of 4 Republicans and 1 Democrat voted in the affirmative, as did the 3 Republicans from Wisconsin. The Upper Midwest was staunchly for the abolitionist cause. Kentucky's delegation voted 4–3 against the amendment while Delaware's only representative, an Unconditional Republican, voted for it. The Democratic regions of Illinois, downstate New York, and Ohio, as well as traditionally Democratic Pennsylvania provided the largest blocks of "no" votes against freedom for the slaves.

The final count was 119 ayes, 56 noes, and 8 present but not voting. The requisite two-thirds requirement was met, and the resolution passed. The document was signed by the President of the Senate and the Speaker of the House, as required. President Lincoln, elated over the successful vote, added his non-required signature, and the amendment was on its way to the states for what was almost certain to be ratification. At the moment the resolution was declared to have passed, the Republican side of the House as well as the galleries erupted in demonstrations of profound joy. According to the *Congressional Globe,* "The announcement was received by the House and by the spectators with an outburst of enthusiasm. The members on the Republican side of the House instantly sprang to their feet and, regardless of the parliamentary rules, applauded with cheers and clapping of hands. The example was followed by male spectators in the galleries, which were crowded to excess, who waved their hats and cheered loud and long, while the ladies, hundreds of whom were present, rose in their seats and waved their handkerchiefs, participating in and adding to the general excitement, and intense interest of the scene. This lasted for several moments."[12] Included in the galleries were several African Americans who had only the previous year been admitted as spectators into sessions of Congress. To add to the celebration, Congress voted to take the rest of the day off, and a hundred-gun salute was fired in Washington. Of course, the war was not yet over, and while it looked promising for the Union, no one knew how soon it would end or how many additional lives would be required.

The following night, President Lincoln gave a rare impromptu, and unrecorded, speech to a crowd that had gathered outside the Executive Mansion. The speech was later summarized in a biography of Lincoln written by his private secretaries John Nicolay and John Hay:

> He [Lincoln] supposed the passage through Congress of the constitutional amendment for the abolishment of slavery throughout the United States was the occasion for which he was indebted for the honor of this call. The occasion was one of congratulation to the country and to the whole world. But there is a task yet before us—to go forward and have consummated by the votes of the States that which Congress had so nobly begun yesterday. He had the honor to inform those present that Illinois had already to-day done the work. Maryland was about half through, but he felt proud that Illinois was a little ahead. He thought this measure was a very fitting if not an indispensable adjunct to the winding up of the great difficulty. He wished the reunion of all the States perfected, and so effected as to remove all causes of disturbance in the future; and to attain this end it was necessary that the original disturbing cause should, if possible, be rooted out. He thought all would bear him witness that he had never shrunk from doing all that he could to eradicate slavery, by issuing the Emancipation Proclamation. But that proclamation falls far short of what the amendment will be when fully consummated. A question might be raised whether the proclamation was legally valid. It might be urged that it only aided those that came into our lines, and that it was inoperative as to those who did not give themselves up; or that it would have no effect upon the children of slaves born hereafter; in fact, it would be urged that it did not meet these evils. But this amendment is the king's cure-all for all the evils. It winds the whole thing up. He would repeat that it was the fitting; if not the indispensable adjunct to the consummation of the great game we are playing. He could not but congratulate all present—himself, the country, and the whole world—upon this great moral victory.[13]

On February 12, 1865, another milestone was reached when the Reverend Henry Highland Garnet, a former slave, became the first African American to address the United States Congress. Garnett was invited to preach a sermon to mark congressional passage of the Thirteenth Amendment. In his moving homily, in which Congress was praised for its actions, Garnet implored the states to complete the ratification process that would finally end slavery throughout the nation:

> With all the moral attributes of God on our side, cheered as we are by the voices of universal human nature—in view of the best interests of the present and future generations—animated with the noble desire to furnish the nations of the earth with a worthy example, let the verdict of death which has been brought in against slavery by the Thirty-eighth Congress be affirmed and executed by the people. Let the gigantic monster perish. Yes, perish now and perish forever![14]

Lincoln did not live to see the final consummation of his great work, but he did see several states make the decision to ratify the Thirteenth Amendment. After Illinois ratified the amendment on February 1, many other states quickly followed. Maryland, which until the previous year had nearly ninety thousand slaves, ratified the amendment on February 3. West Virginia, which had abandoned slavery as the price of statehood, also ratified the amendment on February 3. Kansas, which experienced nearly eleven years of bloodshed over the slavery issue, ratified on February 7. The rump Unionist government of Virginia ratified the amendment on February 9 even though it would be another two months before its rival government in Richmond would be disbanded. Missouri, where slavery had just been abolished, ratified on February 10. On February 17, Louisiana became the first truly reconstructed Confederate state to ratify the Thirteenth Amendment.

Tennessee became the twentieth state to approve the Thirteenth Amendment on April 7, 1865. Two days later, on the afternoon of Palm Sunday, April 9, General Robert E. Lee surrendered his army to General Ulysses S. Grant at Appomattox Court House, Virginia. Lee's surrender effectively marked the end of the South's war to perpetuate slavery. While there were still Confederate armies in the field, they took Lee's lead and surrendered in quick succession. Stand Watie, a Cherokee general fighting on behalf of the Confederacy, surrendered on June 23, bringing the last serious organized resistance to an end.

Lincoln, who had on the morning of April 9 just departed Grant's headquarters after a triumphant tour of the former Confederate capital of Richmond, received the long-awaited news of Lee's surrender from Secretary of War Stanton when the president reached Washington on the steamship *River Queen*. Lincoln's top priority that day was to make a visit to William Seward, recuperating at home from serious injuries suffered in a carriage accident during Lincoln's Virginia tour. Jubilant celebrations had already erupted in the capital among blacks and whites and would be repeated throughout the Union when news of Lee's surrender was telegraphed across the North. On Monday evening, a large crowd gathered outside the White House requesting that the president give a speech, which he had declined to do the night before. Lincoln talked about the future. It was neither a triumphal eulogy over the corpse of the Confederacy nor a vengeful rant demanding what Lincoln had once termed "bloody work" against the former Confederate leaders. Instead, Lincoln called for peace and unity, emphasizing the agenda of "malice toward none, charity for all" for which he had called barely a month before in his Second Inaugural Address. Then, the conservative lawyer who had made a long journey from his racist frontier roots to the new birth of freedom he envisioned in his Gettysburg Address, talked about the franchise for African Americans, especially black veterans. Lincoln was not talking of a future for African Americans with freedom but without equality, which had been the fate of so many blacks in the antebellum North, but a future of freedom *with* equality. Lincoln now dreamed of a new and different future for America. The famed actor John Wilkes Booth was present in the crowd that night. He understood what Lincoln wanted and determined to kill the president before Lincoln and the country had a chance to realize his dream.

The next day, Tuesday April 11, government offices were closed for an official day of celebration, and the celebrations went on throughout the week.[15] On Good Friday, April 14, 1865, the reconstructed government of Arkansas became the twenty-first state to ratify the amendment. That evening, while attending a play at Ford's Theater with Mary and two guests, Abraham Lincoln was fatally shot in the head by Booth. Lincoln died the next morning, and hapless Vice-President Andrew Johnson, a former Tennessee slaveholder upon whom would fall the elusive burden of reuniting the nation with peace and honor, became the unlikely seventeenth president of the United States.

In the midst of national tragedy and transition, the ratification of the Thirteenth Amendment proceeded. Twenty-seven states were needed. Delaware had rejected ratification on February 8, as had Kentucky on February 24. Both states had fought a rear-guard action for slavery within the Union throughout the war. Neither would ratify the amendment until the twentieth century—Delaware in 1901, Kentucky in 1976. New Jersey, a state with an antebellum proslavery bias and still with a handful of its own slaves, also rejected the amendment on March 16, not ratifying it until January 1866, after the amendment was already a part of the Constitution. On December 6, 1865, the reconstructed government of Georgia ratified the amendment, becoming the twenty-seventh state to do so. As a result, Secretary of State William Seward, himself the product of the abolitionist stronghold of upstate New York, had the honor of certifying that the amendment had been duly ratified with an official proclamation dated December 18, 1865. Now part of the U.S. Constitution, the amendment was briefly worded, as had been Lincoln's Gettysburg Address, but it made all the difference in the world to millions of American slaves:

> Section 1.   Neither slavery nor involuntary servitude, except as punishment for crime whereof the party shall have been duly convicted, shall exist within the United States, or any place subject to their jurisdiction.
>
> Section 2.   Congress shall have power to enforce this article by appropriate legislation.

In their biography of Lincoln, Nicolay and Hay concluded their chapter on the Thirteenth Amendment by connecting its ratification with Lincoln's speech at Gettysburg:

> The profound political transformation which the American Republic had undergone can perhaps best be measured by contrasting for an instant the two constitutional amendments which Congress made it the duty of the Lincoln administration to submit officially to the several states. The first was that offered by Thomas Corwin, chairman of the Committee of Thirty-three, in February, 1861, and passed by the House of Representatives, yeas, 133; nays 65; and by the Senate, yeas, 24; nays 12. It was signed by President Buchanan as one of his last official acts, and accepted and endorsed by Lincoln in his inaugural address. The language of the amendment was
>
>> "No amendment shall be made to this Constitution which will authorize or give to Congress the power to abolish or interfere within any State with the domestic institutions thereof, including that of persons held to labor or service by the laws of said State."
>
> Between Lincoln's inauguration and the outbreak of war, the Department of State, under Seward, transmitted this amendment of 1861 to the several States for their action; and had the South shown a willingness to desist from secession and accept it as a peace offering, there is little doubt that the required three-fourths of the States would have made it a part of the Constitution. But the South refused to halt in her

rebellion, and the thunder of Beauregard's guns against Fort Sumter drove away all further thought or possibility of such a ratification; and within four years Congress framed and the same Lincoln administration sent forth the amendment of 1865, sweeping out of existence by one sentence the institution to which it had in its first proposal offered a virtual claim to perpetual recognition and tolerance. The "new birth of freedom" which Lincoln invoked for the nation in his Gettysburg address, was accomplished.[16]

The last vestiges of legalized slavery had been wiped away. America was born again, and now the words of the Declaration of Independence stating, "We hold these truths to be self-evident, that all men are created equal, that they are endowed by their Creator with certain unalienable rights, that among these are life, LIBERTY, and the pursuit of happiness" had a different meaning than before. Now the words applied to ALL men— not as many Americans, North and South, had once believed, to whites only. A new dawn of freedom had arisen, but there was so much more yet to be done.

Epilogue

On March 16, 1995, the Mississippi legislature finally got around to ratifying the Thirteenth Amendment to the U.S. Constitution.[1] The amendment, banning slavery in the United States, had actually gone into effect in December of 1865 after three-fourths of the states approved it. As for implementing the amendment, Mississippi's ratification was meaningless. But in terms of providing insight into the history of emancipation and race relations in America, Mississippi's delayed action speaks loudly. Freedom's delay may have officially ended in December of 1865, but it was a contested freedom that would continue to strain at the very fabric of American society for generations to come. On the steps of the Lincoln Memorial in Washington, D.C., on August 28, 1963, Martin Luther King Jr. began one of America's greatest speeches with the words

> Five score years ago, a great American, in whose symbolic shadow we stand today, signed the Emancipation Proclamation. This momentous decree came as a great beacon light of hope to millions of Negro slaves who had been seared in the flames of withering injustice. It came as a joyous daybreak to end the long night of their captivity.
>
> But one hundred years later, the Negro still is not free. One hundred years later, the life of the Negro is still sadly crippled by the manacles of segregation and the chains of discrimination. One hundred years later, the Negro lives on a lonely island of poverty in the midst of a vast ocean of material prosperity. One hundred years later, the Negro is still languished in the corners of American society and finds himself an exile in his own land.[2]

Resistance to freedom for all Americans before 1865 involved much more than the economic importance of the institution of slavery. Race was at the very heart of that institution, and racial considerations have continued to be at the center of American society into our own day. There was never any legal question that the Thirteenth Amendment gave all Americans freedom from slavery, but the extent of that guaranteed freedom, the extent to which government should be proactive to ensure that freedom, and how responsibility should be divided between state and federal governments on this issue have been open to interpretation over the decades since the amendment went into effect. It became clear after the Civil War that no legislation could instantly change long-held attitudes about race and racial prejudice. As a conflict between preservation of the Union and Southern independence, the Civil War had clear-cut objectives. But when the war, from a Northern perspective, also evolved into a social revolution to end slavery, it became far more complicated to predict or to establish a consensus on what the outcome would, or should, look like.

The years following the Civil War saw an America both radically transformed in many ways and at the same time amazingly impervious to change when it came to freedom and equality for America's former slave population. The turbulent and violent years of Reconstruction, which began with a roar of freedom and ended with a whimper of accommodation to the Old South, resulted in scant permanent improvement in the lives of many of the nation's black population, despite the great price that had been paid for their freedom. In the struggle for true freedom and equality in America, emancipation proved to be, in words used by Winston Churchill pertaining to the Second World War, "not the end, not even the beginning of the end, but perhaps the end of the beginning."[3] It is perhaps as true today as in the post–Civil War era that the nation needs to be reminded of Lincoln's words at Gettysburg: "It is for us the living, rather, to be dedicated here to the unfinished work which they who fought here have thus far so nobly advanced. It is rather for us to be here dedicated to the great task remaining before us." While so much has been achieved, the struggle to complete the unfinished work of realizing liberty and justice for all continues in our own day.

Afterword to the Second Edition

When a second edition of this volume was suggested, it seemed appropriate to add a brief overview of the nation's ongoing engagement with issues related to the American dream of freedom, equality, and justice for African Americans whose slavery ended officially with the thirteenth Amendment to the Constitution. The story told in *Freedom's Delay*, ending as it does in 1865 with the ratification of that constitutional amendment, is foundational, fascinating, but incomplete. This Afterword adds a concise and very selective overview of events and persons involved in the struggle for civil rights for black Americans since 1865. It will conclude that continued vigilance is required to prevent erosion and even erasure of what has been achieved in the quest for liberty and justice for all.

The assassination of President Abraham Lincoln days after the surrender of General Robert E. Lee's Confederate army and the ascension to the Presidency of Vice President Andrew Johnson was very unexpected, tragic, and confusing. At first, Johnson's policies seemed to follow what Lincoln had envisioned for the country after the Civil War. However, it soon became clear that Andrew Johnson would be no friend to the freed slaves. He had been selected for the vice presidency in 1864 for his loyalty to the Union, being the only senator from a seceded state to remain at his post in Washington to represent the loyal people of Tennessee. It was also hoped that a pro-Union Democrat on the ticket with Lincoln would help ensure Lincoln's re-election. However, Johnson soon proved to be a fervent racist who did everything possible to block legislation passed by the Republican Congress to aid the former slaves. Many of Johnson's vetoes were overridden by Congress. A contentious relationship soon developed between the President and Congress over who should control the Reconstruction process. Several issues resulted in the nation's first presidential impeachment. The Senate failed to convict Andrew Johnson on a series of rather dubious charges by a single vote in 1868. Johnson, though retained in office for a few more months, was an unpopular lame duck and not a candidate for election that November. An empowered Congress guided the Reconstruction process without Johnson's interference.

Reconstruction involved a twelve-year period between 1865 and 1877 that attempted to restore the fractured Union and rebuild the devastated South while giving the former slaves and other black residents the rights that were now legally due them. An occupying force of Union soldiers was charged by Congress with helping a new era of race relations to germinate on Southern soil. Reconstruction of the South involved four aspects: political, physical, economic, and perhaps most difficult of all, social reconstruction. Social reconstruction would hopefully persuade white Southerners, as well as white Northerners, to embrace the idea that former slaves should have the freedoms and opportunities now given them by the Constitution's three Reconstruction Amendments. The Thirteenth Amendment legally freed nearly four million slaves, but while it abolished slavery, the legal status of former slaves under state and federal law was not clear. The Fourteenth Amendment, ratified in 1868, clarified the situation by granting citizenship and equal protection of the laws to former slaves, and later to other groups who had been denied these protections. By prohibiting any State from with-holding "the privileges or immunities of citizens of the United States" or depriving "any person of life, liberty, or property, without due process of law" or denying "to any person within its jurisdiction the equal protection of the laws," the Fourteenth Amendment significantly extended the reach of Federal authority into the States. However, no mention of suffrage for former slaves (or women) was included in this Amendment. This issue was addressed by final Reconstruction amendment, Amendment 15. Ratified in 1870, it stated, "The right of citizens of the United States to vote shall not be denied or abridged by the United States or by any State on account of race, color, or previous condition of servitude." Women were still excluded.

Despite occupation of the former Confederacy by Union troops, violence was all too common during Reconstruction. A radical Southern response to the war's loss and Union occupation was the creation of numerous secret societies, the most well-known and enduring being the Ku Klux Klan. The goals of such organizations were to regain control over African Americans and keep them as an oppressed laboring class. Through intimidation, terrorist acts, and restrictive Black Codes, white supremacy could be re-established. Suppression of black voting was also high on the agenda of the Klan and other such secret societies. Even before military occupation of the South ended in 1877, the Klan and similar white secret societies were difficult to control; they wore disguises, met and plotted their activities in secret, and often had support of much of the white population despite the arson, murder, and mayhem they inflicted under a perverse veneer of Christianity. While primarily targeting Negroes, the KKK also went after Catholics, Jews, and immigrants. More than half a century after the Civil War ended, the Ku Klux Klan reached a high point of membership in a not-so-secret attempt to influence national opinion and legislation on racial and immigration policies in the 1920s.

The presidential election of 1876, in the year celebrating the centennial of American independence, was fraught with controversy and unfortunate consequences for the former slave population struggling to find their way into a fair and just American society. During the presidency of Ulysses S. Grant (1869-1877), military occupation of the former Confederate States continued and Federal laws were ostensibly enforced.   Georgia, the last Confederate state to be readmitted to the Union in 1870, joined ten other defeated Confederate States that had all revised their constitutions prohibiting slavery as a condition for rejoining the Union. Grant's second presidential term was ending and in 1876 the Republican candidate for president was Rutherford B. Hayes, the governor of Ohio. His Democratic opponent was Samuel J. Tilden, governor of New York. When it appeared that Hayes had lost both the popular vote and the Electoral College vote, Republican leaders questioned the close election outcome in three Southern states, South Carolina, Florida, and Louisiana. The Republican majority in Congress created a special bipartisan election commission to investigate. The commission consisting of 7 Republicans and 6 Democrats, voted 7-6 along party lines, giving Hayes the presidency by one electoral vote. Tilden agreed to go away quietly if certain Democratic demands were met, including ending military occupation of the former Confederate States. An agreement was finalized only two days before the inaugural ceremony on March 5, 1877. Federal troops were withdrawn from the South, Reconstruction ended, and the enforcement of the rights given to former slaves was left to the States, whose white leadership generally had little enthusiasm for the task. Predictably, this was a severe setback for civil rights gained by former slaves and other African Americans as the South again asserted white supremacy with impunity.

Most of the gains made for black equality after 1865 had been extinguished by the end of the nineteenth century. African Americans experienced discrimination in employment, many facing periods of no work, low wages, and poverty. North and South, they faced segregated housing, shopping, schools, churches, public transportation, lodging, dining, and even cemeteries. Black males who had the Constitutional right to vote were in the post-Reconstruction era increasingly denied voting rights in the South. Not until the civil rights movement of the 1950s and 1960s were African Americans gradually given rights they should have enjoyed many decades earlier.

One bright spot of the Reconstruction period was the work of the Freedmen's Bureau, a Federal Government agency proposed by President Lincoln and begun by Congress in 1865. An attempt by Congress to expand the funding and outreach of the Freedmen's Bureau was vetoed by President

Andrew Johnson in early 1866. Even with inadequate funding, the Bureau was able to provide significant humanitarian and legal aid, as well as educational opportunities for former slaves. Many of the Freedmen's Bureau activities ended by 1870 with its most significant legacy being the establishment of hundreds of schools for blacks in the South. Another bright spot was the rapid growth of Negro churches in the South and the spiritual and material assistance these congregations provided to former slaves.

Among the worst violations of civil rights after Reconstruction was the arrest and imprisonment of African Americans who could then be hired out by local governments to do hard labor. The wording of the Thirteenth Amendment provided an unfortunate legal rationale for a corrupt system of convict slave labor that was fully exploited from the end of Reconstruction well into the twentieth century: "Neither slavery nor involuntary servitude, **except as a punishment for a crime whereof the party shall have been duly convicted**, shall exist within the United States, or any place subject to their jurisdiction" [bold print by author].

The offenses resulting in heavy fines and/or long incarceration were generally minor infractions deliberately enacted to target behavior of freed slaves as well as blacks who had not been slaves. Vagrancy, or inability to demonstrate one had a regular home and employment, was a frequent "crime" as were such horrendous offences as walking on the grass, walking beside a railroad track (a common means of transportation for poor blacks who had no choice but to walk), violating curfews, loitering, breaking a labor contract by quitting a job, holding a job prohibited to black people, and other offences designed to justify arrest. Black people were selectively targeted with such laws rarely if ever applied to white people.

Such discriminatory laws known as "Black Codes" were commonplace in the post-Reconstruction South and were designed to intimidate and control blacks, demonstrate that white supremacy was alive and well, and reduce the economic impact of the end of slavery by enhancing revenues to state and local treasuries. According to historian Douglas Blackmon, whose 2009 Pulitzer Prize winning book provides an excellent investigation into these "Slavery by Another Name" attempts to control black lives, such actions failed to arouse much attention outside the black community then, and even well into the twentieth century. "Sympathy for the victims however brutally they had been abused, was tempered because, after all, they were criminals." According to Blackmon, "Through debt peonage and the worst forms of sharecropping . . . an exponentially larger number of African Americans [were] compelled into servitude through the most informal--and tainted—local courts."[1]

Beginning about 1880, increasing numbers of Southern blacks grew disenchanted with prospects in the South and began leaving for points north and west. White supremacy became re-entrenched in much of Southern society and politics, making black equality and economic prosperity increasingly unlikely. The idea for blacks to depart the rural South and head to northern or western cities or midwestern agricultural opportunities in Kansas and elsewhere grew in popularity. Some Negro leaders including Frederick Douglass were opposed to a mass exodus of blacks from the South, concerned that once relocated, they might not be any better off than before. Southern whites, concerned about losing significant numbers of black laborers, vigorously enforced vagrancy and labor contract laws to try to stem the exodus. The temptation was strong to move to an industrial city in the north or west, Chicago, Los Angeles, and Denver becoming desired destinations where pay was superior to the rural South. Some blacks remained in the South but left rural life and sought employment in southern cities. Many such migrants discovered that the quality of Southern city life had few if any advantages over Southern rural life. One unanticipated problem faced by black urban workers was growing unionization of labor with white attempts to keep blacks out of unions.

In 1900 Booker T. Washington developed a plan to organize, upgrade, and promote black businesses. In Boston he established the National Negro Business League. In less than a decade there were over 300 local branches of the organization. While there had been notable successes among black business enterprises, there were also numerous failures. Several black banks were established in the late nineteenth and early twentieth century, but many of them were short-lived. Booker T. Washington desired to be a non-political non-activist. He had a serious critic in W. E. B. DuBois, the first African American to earn a Ph.D. from Harvard University in 1895. DuBois was concerned that Washington emphasized vocational education and urged blacks to expect and tolerate racism which he felt would eventually end. DuBois was an activist believing in agitation, not accommodation, and helped organize a group of black intellectuals known as the Niagara Movement. This movement promoted goals of full suffrage and equality in American society. In 1909 DuBois and Ida B. Wells, a teacher turned journalist and anti-lynching crusader, joined forces with white activists to form the biracial National Association for the Advancement of Colored People (NAACP).

Approximately 175,000 African American men served overseas in World War I. Many hoped that their patriotism in serving their country would be rewarded when they returned home after the war, but this was not to be. In the summer of 1919, 25 race riots erupted in the United States and 70 lynchings of blacks were reported. Hundreds more black men were violently killed in the United States in the five years after World War I ended than were killed in combat during the war.

In 1915, W. E. B. DuBois died. Marcus Garvey, a Jamaican immigrant and publisher, arrived in Harlem about the time of DuBois's death. Seeing a vacuum in black American leadership following the passing of DuBois, Garvey sought to assert himself as a black leader with goals similar of DuBois, but with a very different twist. Garvey established the Universal Negro Improvement Association (UNIA) that sought to appeal to black soldiers returning from fighting for democracy in Europe during World War I to fight for black freedom and equality in America. Garvey was an activist like DuBois, crusading against lynchings, suppression of black voting rights, and Jim Crow laws. But Garvey, unlike DuBois, abandoned hope that white Americans would ever treat black Americans as equals. Garvey's answer was to argue for segregation of the races. He was critical of mixed-race people and Jews. His movement was global in its outreach and at its peak UNIA claimed six million followers worldwide. Garvey, in his newspaper *Negro World*, called for black pride and self-sufficiency. But his most controversial project was to get African Americans to relocate to Africa. Although he had never been to that continent, Garvey envisioned a unified Africa under his leadership and claimed to be Provisional President of Africa. Marcus Garvey was a divisive figure among African Americans, with most black leaders condemning his back-to-Africa agenda and attacking him for his attempt at rapprochement with the Ku Klux Klan. Garvey was convicted of mail fraud in 1923 and spent two years in a federal prison in Atlanta. He was deported to Jamaica in 1927.

In New York City's Harlem, a cultural scene flourished in the 1920s that came to be known as the Harlem Renaissance. It included an explosion of significant works by black authors, playwrights, actors, musicians, and visual artists. Many of their works brought to America's attention the injustices that continued to be experienced by black Americans. Harlem's high level of black intellectual and artistic success made this community the black cultural and intellectual capital of America. Jazz, originating in New Orleans, soon found an artistic home in Harlem where many upper-class whites came to hear black musicians perform jazz at the Cotton Club. Ironically, only whites were allowed to attend the Cotton Club and black performers were forbidden to mingle with the audience.

At the time of Harlem's renaissance, race riots were all too common in other American cities. The most egregious race riot occurred in the spring of 1921 resulting in the virtual destruction by whites of 35 blocks of the black Greenwood section of Tulsa, Oklahoma. This was the richest black community in the nation, called by many the "Negro Wall Street," an enclave of prosperous black shops, homes, and professional services. Most of the community was torched and 68 black residents were killed.[2] Harlem, on the other hand, was a relatively peaceful intellectual center for what was claimed to be the "New Negro." The New Negro movement emphasized black self-confidence, pride, intellectual, artistic, and economic success, and the ability to take charge of one's own situation while rejecting the old "Sambo" image and other derogatory stereotypes.

The Great Depression hit black Americans especially hard. Noted historian John Hope Franklin determined that in 1934, 17 percent of whites and 38 percent of blacks were categorized as "incapable of self-support in any occupation." "In Atlanta, in 1935, 65 percent of the Negro employables were in need of public assistance, while in Norfolk no less than 80 percent of the group were on relief." Franklin concluded, 'Small wonder that there was utter distress and pessimism among Negroes generally. Added to the denials of freedom and democracy was the specter of starvation."[3]

America's entry into World War II saw nearly one million African Americans serving in the military. However, while in the service of a nation that was fighting for democracy and freedom overseas, segregated black troops were limited to lower ranks and given the most undesirable and often most dangerous jobs. In 1944, the worst stateside war disaster occurred at California's Port Chicago Naval Weapons Station where two ships were being loaded with ammunition for use in the Pacific theater of the war. Hundreds of African American servicemen, not trained for the work they were required to do, were killed and injured when a massive explosion occurred, measuring on the Richter scale and shattering windows in San Francisco several miles away. The explosion killed over 300 men instantly while nearly 400 others were injured. African American servicemen, serving under white officers, made up the vast majority of the dead and injured. After the blast, white officers were given convalescent leaves while black sailors who survived were ordered to resume work. Fifty of them demanded safer conditions before returning to work and were charged with mutiny and court-martialed. In 2024, on the eightieth anniversary of the blast, these servicemen were posthumously officially exonerated.

A disturbing situation involving German military prisoners-of-war housed in Georgia and Utah developed during the Second World War.

African American servicemen were often denied access to restaurants and other public places due to Jim Crow laws while German POWs under guard were often admitted. This was disheartening to black American troops who were amazed that Nazi military prisoners had more privileges in the United States than they did. President Truman ended segregation in the US military with Executive Order 9981 on July 26, 1948. Both praised and criticized at the time, the order set a new path toward racial justice.

The 1950s and 1960s saw dramatic events that galvanized African Americans and other minorities to push harder for a long overdue equal share in the promise of America. The 1954 US Supreme Court case *Brown vs. Board of Education of Topeka Kansas* has often been characterized as the most important Supreme Court ruling in our history. This case, which declared racially segregated schools as inherently unequal and thus unconstitutional, was a stinging rebuke to the 1896 *Plessy vs Ferguson* Supreme Court decision that racially segregated schools were not in violation of the US Constitution, provided the schools were "separate but equal." This impressive victory for civil rights achieved through this unanimous Supreme Court decision encouraged the increased successful use of legal challenges to civil rights inequities. In the *Brown vs. Board of Education* case the Supreme Court insisted on implementation of their ruling "with all deliberate speed" which did not happen. By 1957 President Eisenhower felt it necessary to send U.S. troops to enforce racial integration at Central High School in Little Rock, Arkansas over the protests of many residents.

A 1955 bus boycott by black residents of Montgomery, Alabama lit a fire of protest and catapulted Rev. Martin Luther King Jr. to a key leadership role in the struggle for racial justice. On December 1, 1955, black seamstress Rosa Parks was arrested for refusing to give up her seat on a public bus to a white passenger. This action triggered a boycott of Montgomery busses by the African American community. Black ministers set a date of December 5 for a one-day boycott of Montgomery busses by black riders that was highly successful. Later that day the city's black ministers and other leaders met and decided to establish the Montgomery Improvement Association and selected a young pastor, Rev. Martin Luther King Jr., to be its president and voice. Despite city protests and attempts to intimidate Dr. King by bombing his home, the boycott by African American bus riders persisted throughout all of 1956. Despite Montgomery obtaining injunctions against the boycott and punishing black cab drivers for aiding the boycotters, the busses remained empty of black riders. Black Montgomery residents walked or car-pooled as needed and followed the examples King urged them to follow of Jesus and Ghandi by responding to opposition and hate without violence. In June of 1956 a federal district court ruled segregation of busses was unconstitutional, and in November of 1956 the US Supreme Court upheld the federal court ruling banning segregation on public busses. On December 20, 1956, Dr. King called for an end to the bus boycott. King became a nationally and internationally known figure for his non-violent leadership role in this protest of injustice. While his pastoral role would continue, he would spend increasing time and energy as a respected civil rights leader.

Dr. Martin Luther King Jr.'s leadership predominated the civil rights movement during his life but was not without dissenting opinions and opposition in both black and white communities. King's unwavering insistence on non-violence and Christ's example of love, even towards those who hate and do unjustly both appealed to many African Americans while being rejected by others, such as Malcolm X and Stokely Carmichael. King's defense of non-violence while calling for active resistance and protest toward injustice is contained in his *Letter from Birmingham Jail* that is regarded as a classic example of protest literature.

The 1960s saw increased national interest in civil rights issues and the growth of important organizations challenging racial discrimination and segregation. The Southern Christian Leadership Conference, the Student Nonviolent Coordinating Committee, and the Congress of Racial Equality were major players in advocating racial equality while using non-violent tactics. The Black Panther Party, founded in Oakland, California had a more aggressive and militant agenda including urging blacks to arm themselves for self-protection. The Black Panthers, like Malcolm X, shunned King's insistence on non-violence as ineffective, and focused on confronting police brutality with armed resistance. The Black Panther Party provided food and social services in areas beyond the American South.

The US Supreme Court declared that facilities used in interstate bus travel, such as bus terminals and restrooms, could not be racially segregated. However, most Southern states ignored the court order and maintained unconstitutional segregation in bus terminals. In May 1961 a group of 13 black and white "Freedom Riders," including future member of Congress John Lewis, boarded two public busses in Washington, DC heading toward New Orleans. At stops along the route the Freedom Riders ignored segregation signs and moved at will through the bus terminals. One of the busses was firebombed and Freedom Riders were beaten in South Carolina. Unable to continue, they were replaced by another group of Freedom Riders in a pattern that was repeated as more violence was experienced and white mobs beat Freedom Riders at various stops. On May 29,

Attorney General Robert F. Kennedy ordered the Interstate Commerce Commission to enforce bans on segregation involving busses engaged in interstate transportation.

The most widely publicized and carefully planned civil rights event of the 1960s was the nation's largest protest event to that time as an estimated crowd of 250,000 persons arrived in Washington DC for a march on August 28, 1963, and a gathering at the Lincoln Memorial. The Kennedy Administration, worried about possible violence, was originally opposed to the event but acquiesced as the protest leaders met and assured President Kennedy that the marchers would be non-violent and order would be maintained. Speaking from the steps of the Lincoln Memorial, Martin Luther King Jr. delivered his now famous "I have a Dream" speech which is considered one of America's greatest speeches. The event went as planned, attracted national and international attention, enhanced the reputation of Dr. King, and gave black Americans a sense of pride for the movement. President Kennedy attempted to push significant civil rights legislation through Congress but was assassinated in November 1963 before such legislation was enacted.

The assassination of President John F. Kennedy shocked the nation and world. It was a disheartening blow to civil rights leaders and activists who now realized that Vice President Lyndon Johnson, a Texas Democrat whose earlier actions were not seen as friendly to African Americans was now President of the United States. Johnson's full embrace of Kennedy's hopes for civil rights legislation came as a pleasant surprise to African Americans as well as whites in sympathy with the civil rights struggle. Johnson pushed Congress hard to pass the Civil Rights Act of 1964, a stronger version of the bill Kennedy had proposed the previous summer. Johnson's bill targeted racial discrimination in voting, segregation of public facilities, and employment. Johnson demonstrated solidarity with Martin Luther King Jr., maintaining close contact with him during a series of civil rights proposals that the President sent to Congress. The Voting Rights Act of 1965 was the next legislative victory won by Johnson, following a march of civil rights supporters bloodied by Alabama State Police at Selma's Edmund Pettus Bridge. The nation was stunned by days of racial rioting in the Watts section of Los Angeles just days after the Voting Rights Act was approved. Some blamed Johnson for giving African Americans too much too quickly. Johnson's support for ending racial and ethnic discrimination saw him sign the Immigration and Nationality Act (the Hart-Celler Act) in October 1965, ending the discriminatory immigration quota system in place for decades. It was now possible for skilled workers and those with family in

America to immigrate to the U.S. without regard for race or national origin. In 1968 Lyndon Johnson's prowess in navigating civil rights legislation through Congress was again on display as one week following Dr. Martin Luther King's assassination Johnscn was able to sign the Civil Rights Act of 1968 (the Fair Housing Act) outlawing discrimination in the sale, rental, and financing of property based on national origin, race, or religion. Lyndon Johnson's impressive support for civil rights was overshadowed by his continued support for the Vietnam War despite growing public opposition to it. The positive relationship between the President and Martin Luther King Jr. nearly collapsed as King became a frequent critic of the war.

Since 1968 there has been a surge of black Americans elected to public office at local, state, and national levels, many of them being women. Organizations created to support black politicians include the Congressional Black Caucus established in 1971 and the National Conference of Black Mayors begun in 1974. Shirley Chisholm became the first black woman elected to the House of Representatives in 1968. In 1992 Carol Moseley Brown was the first black woman U.S. Senator, and the second black woman US Senator, Kamala Harris, was elected Vice President of the United States in 2020. In 2008 and 2012 Barack Obama was elected and re-elected as the first black president of the United States.

DESPITE PROGRESS, SOME WARNING SIGNS

The progress made by black Americans since the end of legal slavery in the United States in 1865 is impressive. The constant struggle for equal rights and opportunities, and the resilience and engagement of black Americans inspires admiration and hope. The fight for the cause of civil rights equality by other Americans is meritorious. However, there is yet work to be done.

In the current political climate of the United States, a dangerous trend has surfaced designed to scale back and even remove safeguards that have allowed civil rights and racial equity to be more accessible to more Americans than ever before. Presidential executive orders have ended the government's DEI (diversity, equity, and inclusion) programs and dismissed employees who worked for these programs. Educational institutions and private corporations have been threatened with consequences if they do not dismantle such programs that were designed to promote fairness and equity. The ranks of top black leadership in the American military have been reduced. Recent voter suppression laws and practices create barriers to participation in elections by making voter registration more difficult, reducing voting periods, restricting mail-in voting, and discouraging voter participation by undermining trust and confidence in election integrity and the legitimate outcomes of elections. The United States Supreme Court has made recent rulings that have weakened the Voting Rights Act so ardently fought for by President Lyndon Johnson in 1965.

African Americans continue to be disproportionally subjected to use of police force. Blacks are also arrested, convicted, and incarcerated at much higher levels than the Anglo population. Attempts to remedy these disparities such as the George Floyd Justice in Policing Act have been denied approval by the US Senate.

Peaceful protest and free expression of dissent have long been fundamental rights and practices of the American people. Recent laws and law enforcement tactics have discouraged certain demonstrations and protests including those focused on human rights issues. Use of national guard troops by the Executive Branch of the Federal Government to patrol supposedly "high crime" American cities with large minority populations has not strengthened American democracy or improved race relations.

While censorship is nothing new, there appears to be at this time in our nation's history a renewed, more aggressive attempt by some politicians, organizations, and self-proclaimed cultural watchdogs to redirect the way certain aspects of our national past are taught. In some cases, certain unpleasant topics are viewed as best minimized or even eliminated from our classrooms, museums, and historical sites. This should be of serious concern to teachers and professors of history who may be subject to guidelines in the practice of their craft that will whitewash, distort, or eliminate historical realities from educational curricula at levels from elementary school through university programs. School Boards and state legislatures, as well as leaders of our federal government, should be challenged about why the teaching and presentation of American history should not be entrusted to the expert historians which abound in our nation. Neither government edicts nor public opinion, but truth and facts, should be the final arbiter about what is appropriate in the telling of our national past.

Attempts to minimize or ignore unpleasant aspects of the American past, including racism, slavery, treatment of Native Americans, discriminatory immigration policies, and the restricted roles of women in many aspects of national life (among many possible topics) will not create better informed and knowledgeable citizens. Those who want to remake the telling of the past into a story that will make students feel more positive and patriotic about America are not acting in the best interests of truth, democracy, good government, and good citizenship as we move into the future. Truth matters. We must be on guard against attempts to diminish the importance of slavery and the struggle for civil rights in our national past, or to remove and rearrange facts to align with partisan ideologies of the American story. Attempts to fabricate a more positive but less realistic view of the American past by being less than honest about the struggle against slavery and for equal rights denies an important aspect at the very heart of the American experience. It is a story that must be told well and remembered well.

Notes

PREFACE

1. Texas Secession Convention, "A Declaration of the Causes Which Impel the State of Texas to Secede from the Federal Union," Feb. 2, 1861, in James W. Loewen and Edward H. Sebasta, eds., *The Confederate and Neo-Confederate Reader: The Great Truth about the Lost Cause* (Jackson: University Press of Mississippi, 2010), 143.
2. See Pauline Maier's thorough and enlightening analysis of the Declaration of Independence and the ways its meaning has changed over time in her *American Scripture: The Making of the Declaration of Independence* (New York: Random House, 1998).
3. Abraham Lincoln, *Gettysburg Address,* Nov. 19, 1863.
4. William Henry Seward, "Irrepressible Conflict" speech (1858), in William Jennings Bryan, ed., *The World's Famous Orations* (New York: Funk and Wagnalls, [1906]), vol. 10; www.bartleby.com/268/.
5. See Edward Bartlett Rugemer's *The Problem of Emancipation: The Caribbean Roots of the American Civil War* (Baton Rouge: Louisiana State University Press, 2008), as a good starting place for strong advocacy of a transatlantic perspective in understanding the background to the American Civil War.
6. John 8:32.

1. SLAVERY AND REVOLUTION

1. John Adams to Abigail Adams, July 3, 1776, in Frank Shuffelton, ed., *The Letters of John and Abigail Adams* (New York: Penguin Books, 2004), 192.
2. Thomas Jefferson, *Notes on the State of Virginia,* Query 18, 168–69.
3. Qtd. in Peter A. Dorsey, *Common Bondage: Slavery as Metaphor in Revolutionary America* (Knoxville: University of Tennessee Press, 2009), 141.
4. Donald Jackson, *Thomas Jefferson and the Rocky Mountains: Exploring the West from Monticello* (Norman: University of Oklahoma Press, 1993), 25–26.
5. Matthew Mason, *Slavery and Politics in the Early American Republic* (Chapel Hill: University of North Carolina Press, 2006), 35.
6. Acts 17:26.
7. Thomas S. Kidd, *God of Liberty: A Religious History of the American Revolution* (New York: Basic Books, 2010), 142.
8. Allen Carden, *Puritan Christianity in America: Religion and Life in Seventeenth-Century Massachusetts* (Grand Rapids, Mich.: Baker Book House, 1990), 137–38.
9. See Carden, *Puritan Christianity in America,* 137 n 15.
10. Kenneth A. Lockridge, *A New England Town: The First Hundred Years: Dedham, Massachusetts, 1636–1736* (New York: Norton, 1970), 10–11, 16.

11. Qtd. in Stephen Foster, *Their Solitary Way: The Puritan Social Ethic in the First Century of Settlement in New England* (New Haven, Conn.: Yale University Press, 1971), 12, 41.
12. Margaret Ellen Newell, "The Changing Nature of Indian Slavery in New England, 1670–1720," in Colin G. Calloway and Neal Salisbury, eds., *Reinterpreting New England Indians and the Colonial Experience* (Boston: Colonial Society of Massachusetts, 2003), 110.
13. Ibid., 107–8, 127.
14. See Carden, *Puritan Christianity in America,* 138 n 19.
15. Bernard Bailyn, *The Ideological Origins of the American Revolution* (Cambridge, Mass.: Harvard University Press, 1992), 232.
16. John Dickinson, *Letters from a Farmer in Pennsylvania* (Philadelphia, 1768), John Harvard Library, Pamphlet 23, 38.
17. *Declaration of the Causes and Necessity of Taking Up Arms,* July 5, 1775, in Julian P. Boyd, ed., *The Papers of Thomas Jefferson* (Princeton, N.J.: Princeton University Press, 1950), vol. 1: 213.
18. Mercy Otis Warren, *History of the Rise, Progress, and Termination of the American Revolution,* ed. Lester H. Cohen (Indianapolis: Liberty Fund, 1990), vol. 1: 24–25.
19. David Ramsay, *The History of the American Revolution,* ed. Lester H. Cohen (Indianapolis: Liberty Classics, 1990), vol. 1: 24.
20. Edmund S. Morgan, *American Slavery, American Freedom: The Ordeal of Colonial Virginia* (New York: Norton, 1975), 386.
21. David Brion Davis, *Inhuman Bondage: The Rise and Fall of Slavery in the New World* (Oxford, U.K.: Oxford University Press, 2006), 145.
22. Ramsay, *History of the American Revolution* 1: 29–30.
23. Bailyn, *Ideological Origins,* 234.
24. Jay Fliegelman, *Declaring Independence: Jefferson, Natural Language, and the Culture of Performance* (Palo Alto, Calif.: Stanford University Press, 1993), 141.
25. Qtd. in Bailyn, *Ideological Origins,* 158–59.
26. James Brewer Stewart, *Holy Warriors: The Abolitionists and American Slavery,* rev. ed. (New York: Hill and Wang, 1996), 14–17.
27. Mason, *Slavery and Politics,* 11–12, 14.
28. John Locke, *The Second Treatise of Government,* ed. Thomas P. Peardon (1689; New York: Liberal Arts Press, [c. 1952]), vol. 4: 16.
29. Qtd. in Bailyn, *Ideological Origins,* 236.
30. Thomas Jefferson, *A Summary View of the Rights of British America,* in Merrill Jensen, ed., *Tracts of the American Revolution, 1763–1776* (Indianapolis: Bobbs-Merrill, 1967), 269, 264.
31. Qtd. in Don E. Fehrenbacher, *The Slaveholding Republic: An Account of the United States Government's Relations to Slavery* (Oxford, U.K.: Oxford University Press, 2001), 16.
32. Qtd. in Bailyn, *Ideological Origins,* 237.
33. Qtd. in Roger Bruns, ed., *Am I Not a Man and a Brother? The Antislavery Crusade of Revolutionary America* (New York: Chelsea House Publishers, 1977), 101.

34. Qtd. in Bailyn, *Ideological Origins,* 238.
35. Stephen Hopkins, "An Essay on the Trade of the Northern Colonies," in Jensen, ed. *Tracts of the American Revolution,* 10–11.
36. Qtd. in Fliegelman, *Declaring Independence,* 193.
37. Dorsey, *Common Bondage,* xii.
38. U.S. Continental Congress, *Journals of the Continental Congress, 1774–1789* (Washington, D.C.: Government Printing Office, 1906), vol. 6: 1096.
39. Maier, *American Scripture,* 146.
40. *Journals of the Continental Congress* 4: 258.
41. Fehrnebacher, *The Slaveholding Republic,* 17.
42. Maier, *American Scripture,* 26.
43. Benjamin Quarles, *The Negro in the American Revolution* (Chapel Hill: University of North Carolina Press, 1996), 42–43.
44. Dorsey, *Common Bondage,* xii.
45. Jefferson, *Papers* 2: 672–73. An excellent analysis of slavery in the revolutionary and early national periods is Eva Sheppard Wolf's *Race and Liberty in the New Nation: Emancipation in Virginia from the Revolution to Nat Turner's Rebellion* (Baton Rouge: Louisiana State University Press), 2006.
46. Gary B. Nash, *Race and Revolution* (Madison, Wis.: Madison House Publishers, 1990), 11–12.
47. Qtd. in Nash, *Race and Revolution,* 12.
48. Qtd. in Fehrenbacher, *Slaveholding Republic,* 18.
49. Fehrenbacher, *Slaveholding Republic,* 15.
50. Maier, *American Scripture,* 35–36.
51. Samuel Johnson, *The Works of Samuel Johnson,* vol. 10, *Political Writings,* ed. Donald J. Greene (New Haven, Conn.: Yale University Press, 1977), 454.
52. Mason, *Slavery and Politics,* 32.
53. Bruns, ed., *Am I Not a Man and a Brother?* 385–86.
54. Winthrop D. Jordan, *White Over Black: American Attitudes Toward the Negro, 1550–1812* (New York: Pelican Books, 1969), 297–99.
55. Quarles, *Negro in the American Revolution,* 44.
56. Fehrenbacher, *Slaveholding Republic,* 18.
57. Quarles, *Negro in the American Revolution,* 13.
58. Fehrenbacher, *Slaveholding Republic,* 19.
59. Quarles, *Negro in the American Revolution,* 54, 52, 56, 57.
60. Fehrenbacher, *Slaveholding Republic,* 20; Quarles, *Negro in the American Revolution,* 62–63.
61. Quarles, *Negro in the American Revolution,* 71.
62. John Ferling, *Almost a Miracle: The American Victory in the War of Independence* (Oxford, U.K.: Oxford University Press, 2007), 342.
63. Quarles, *Negro in the American Revolution,* 113, 115, 119, 125, 127–28, 152.
64. Qtd. in Sidney Kaplan and Emma N. Kaplan, *The Black Presence in the American Revolution* (Amherst University of Massachusetts Press, 1989), 3.
65. Quarles, *Negro in the American Revolution,* 158–59, 166.
66. Fehrenbacher, *Slaveholding Republic,* 15.
67. Washington to Benjamin Harrison, May 6, 1783, in *The Writings of George Washington from the Original Manuscript Sources, 1745–1799,* ed. John C.

Fitzpatrick (Washington, D.C.: U.S. Government Printing Office), vol. 26: 401.

68. Quarles, *Negro in the American Revolution,* 173–75.

69. Bruns, ed. *Am I Not a Man and a Brother?* 476–77, 485.

70. See Nash, *Race and Revolution,* chap. 1.

71. Nash, *Race and Revolution,* xiv.

2. Slavery and the Constitution

1. Richard Beeman, *Plain, Honest Men: The Making of the American Constitution* (New York: Random House, 2009), 216.

2. Qtd. in Joseph J. Ellis, *American Creation: Triumphs and Tragedies at the Founding of the Republic* (New York: Vintage Books, 2007), 93.

3. Qtd. in David Waldstreicher, *Slavery's Constitution* (New York: Hill and Wang, 2009), 110.

4. David O. Stewart, *The Summer of 1787: The Men Who Invented the Constitution* (New York: Simon & Schuster, 2007), 105.

5. Lawrence Goldstone, *Dark Bargain: Slavery, Profits, and the Struggle for the Constitution* (New York: Walker & Co., 2005), 193.

6. James Madison, *The Constitutional Convention: A Narrative History from the Notes of James Madison,* ed. Edward J. Larson and Michael P. Winship (New York: Modern Library, 2005), 69.

7. Mason, *Slavery and Politics,* 33.

8. Goldstone, *Dark Bargain,* 13.

9. Fehrenbacher, *Slaveholding Republic* 47, 36, 39–40.

10. Goldstone, *Dark Bargain,* 94.

11. Waldstreicher, *Slavery's Constitution,* 104.

12. Ibid., 73.

13. Goldstone, *Dark Bargain,* 104.

14. Beeman, *Plain, Honest Men,* 161.

15. Fehrenbacher, *Slaveholding Republic,* 41.

16. Max Farrand, ed. *The Records of the Federal Convention of 1787,* rev. ed. (New Haven, Conn.: Yale University Press, 1966), vol. 1: 201, 208.

17. Beeman, *Plain, Honest Men,* 213–14.

18. James H. Hutson, *Supplement to Max Ferrand's The Records of the Federal Convention of 1787* (New Haven, Conn.: Yale University Press, 1987), 158.

19. Goldstone, *Dark Bargain,* 144.

20. Farrand, *Records of the Federal convention of 1787* 2: 221–23.

21. Beemer, *Plain, Honest* Men, 317.

22. See Beeman, *Plain, Honest Men,* 474, note 41. Also see Waldstreicher, *Slavery's Constitution,* 176, note 30.

23. See Richard B. Morris, *The Forging of the Union* (New York: Harper and Row, 1987), 232–44.

24. George W. Van Cleve, *A Slaveholders' Union: Slavery, Politics, and the Constitution in the Early American Republic* (Chicago: University of Chicago Press, 2010), 153.

25. Ibid., 156.
26. Beeman, *Plain, Honest Men,* 217–18.
27. Van Cleve, *Slaveholders' Union,* 154.
28. Qtd. in Waldstreicher, *Slavery's Constitution,* 87–88.
29. Van Cleve, *Slaveholders' Union,* 154.
30. Stewart, *Summer of 1787,* 135–36.
31. Beeman, *Plain, Honest Men,* xxi.
32. Waldstreicher, *Slavery's Constitution ,* 93–94.
33. Qtd. in Beeman, *Plain, Honest Men,* 319.
34. Qtd. in Waldstreicher, *Slavery's Constitution,* 94–95.
35. Christopher Collier and James Lincoln Collier, *Decision in Philadelphia: The Constitutional Convention of 1787* (New York: Ballantine Books, 2007), 228.
36. Qtd. in Collier and Collier, *Decision in Philadelphia,* 232.
37. Farrand, *Records of the Federal Convention of 1787* 2: 370.
38. Qtd. in Goldstone, *Dark Bargain,* 171.
39. Collier and Collier, *Decision in Philadelphia,* 234.
40. Beeman, *Plain, Honest Men,* 334.
41. Mason, *Slavery and Politics,* 15,18.
42. Qtd. in Collier and Collier, *Decision in Philadelphia,* 235.
43. Van Cleve, *Slaveholders' Union,* 146.
44. Goldstone, *Dark Bargain,* 172.
45. Ibid., 173.
46. Fehrenbacher, *Slaveholding Republic,* 36.
47. Qtd. in Stewart, *Summer of 1787,* 239.
48. Pauline Maier, *Ratification: The People Debate the Constitution, 1787–1788* (New York: Simon & Schuster, 2010), 36.
49. Ibid., 70–71.
50. The rhetorical use of slavery by the Anti-Federalists is laid out well in Dorsey, *Common Bondage,* chap. 8.
51. *The Debate on the Constitution: Federalist and Antifederalist Speeches, Articles, and Letters during the Struggle over Ratification* (New York: Viking Press, 1993), vol. 1: 915–16.
52. Qtd. in Maier, *Ratification,* 248, 249.
53. Ibid., 274.
54. *Debate on the Constitution* 2: 706–7.
55. John Hope Franklin, *From Slavery to Freedom: A History of Negro Americans,* 5th ed. (New York: Alfred A. Knopf, 1980), 96.

3. Stumbling Forward

1. See U.S. Census for 1790.
2. Anne Farrow, Joel Lang, and Jennifer Frank, *Complicity: How the North Promoted, Prolonged, and Profited from Slavery* (New York: Random House, 2005), xxvi.
3. See Mason, *Slavery and Politics,* chap. 1, 10–41.
4. Qtd. in Gene Dattel, *Cotton and Race in the Making of America: The Human Costs of Economic Power* (Chicago: Ivan R. Dee, 2009), 16.

5. Arthur Zilversmit, *The First Emancipation: The Abolition of Slavery in the North* (Chicago: University of Chicago Press, 1967), 19.
6. Farrow, et al., *Complicity*, xii.
7. See Robert C. Twombley and Robert H. Moore, "Black Puritan: The Negro in Seventeenth-Century Massachusetts," *William and Mary Quarterly* 24 (Apr. 1967): 224–42; Carden, *Puritan Christianity in America*, 138–39.
8. Zilversmit, *First Emancipation*, 61.
9. Qtd. in Zilversmit, *First Emancipation*, 58, 59.
10. Ibid., 99.
11. See U.S. Census for 1790.
12. Joanne Pope Melish, *Disowning Slavery: Gradual Emancipation and "Race" in New England, 1780–1860* (Ithaca, N.Y.: Cornell University Press, 1998), 64n31.
13. Gordon S. Wood, *Empire of Liberty: A History of the Early Republic, 1789–1815* (Oxford, U.K.: Oxford University Press, 2009), 517.
14. Melish, *Disowning Slavery*, 65.
15. The details of this case and related cases can be found in Emily Blanck, "Seventeen Eighty-three: The Turning Point in the Law of Slavery and Freedom in Massachusetts," *New England Quarterly*, 75, no. 1 (Mar. 2002): 24–51.
16. Charles Deane, "Letters and Documents Relating to Slavery in Massachusetts," *Collections of the Massachusetts Historical Society* (Boston: The Society, 1877), ser. 5, vol. 3: 401–2.
17. Blanck, "Seventeen Eighty-three," 28, 29. The Massachusetts Superior Court of Judicature was renamed the Supreme Judicial Court in 1780.
18. Ibid., 29.
19. Zilversmit, *First Emancipation*, 115.
20. Blanck, "Seventeen Eighty-three," 30, 31.
21. Ibid., 43–45.
22. Qtd. in Zilversmit, *First Emancipation*, 116.
23. Ibid., 122–23.
24. See Census of 1790 and 1810.
25. Melish, *Disowning Slavery*, 76n53.
26. See U.S. Census for 1790 and 1840.
27. Qtd. in Zilversmit, *First Emancipation*, 116–17.
28. Ibid., 117.
29. "New Hampshire," in *The Complete Poetical Works of John Greenleaf Whittier* (Cambridge, Mass.: Riverside Press, 1895), 293. John Langdon was a leading politician of New Hampshire during the revolutionary era and early republic. He helped frame New Hampshire's constitution and was a delegate to the U.S. Constitutional Convention who voted against the proslavery clauses. John Stark was a military man, but it is not clear why Whittier mentions him.
30. See U.S. Census for 1840; Zilversmit, *First Emancipation*, 117.
31. Melish, *Disowning Slavery*, 12–13; Wood, *Empire of Liberty*, 516.
32. Zilversmit, *First Emancipation*, 119.
33. Ibid., 120, 121.

34. Census of 1840.
35. Benjamin Quarles, *The Negro in the Making of America* (New York: Simon & Schuster, 1987), 54.
36. Jean R. Soderlund, *Quakers and Slavery: A Divided Spirit* (Princeton, N.J.: Princeton University Press, 1985), 184–85.
37. Qtd. in Leon F. Litwack, *North of Slavery: The Negro in the Free States, 1790–1860* (Chicago: University of Chicago Press, 1961), 7.
38. Zilversmit, *First Emancipation*, 125–27.
39. Ibid., 127–31.
40. Ibid., 132; Nash and Soderlund, *Freedom by Degrees*, 202.
41. U.S. Census of 1790–1840.
42. Qtd. in David Herbert Donald, *Lincoln* (New York: Simon & Schuster, 1996), 202, 221.
43. James Oliver Horton and Lois E. Horton, *Hard Road to Freedom* (New Brunswick, N.J.: Rutgers University Press, 2001), 81–82.
44. Franklin, *From Slavery to Freedom*, 109.
45. Horton and Horton, *Hard Road to Freedom*, 101.
46. Qtd. in Franklin, *From Slavery to Freedom*, 178–79.

4. Forward to the Past

1. David Hackett Fischer, *Albion's Seed: Four British Folkways in America* (New York: Oxford University Press, 1989), 210.
2. Ibid., 212–14.
3. See William R. Taylor, *Cavalier and Yankee: The Old South and American National Character* (New York: George Braziller, 1961), 15–22.
4. Elizabeth Fox-Genovese and Eugene Genovese, *The Mind of the Master Class: History and Faith in the Southern Slaveholders' Worldview* (Cambridge, U.K.: Cambridge University Press, 2005), 92.
5. Ibid., 94.
6. Bruce Levine, *Half Slave and Half Free: The Roots of Civil War* (New York: Hill and Wang, 2005), 100.
7. Alan T. Nolan, *Lee Considered: General Robert E. Lee and Civil War History* (Chapel Hill: University of North Carolina Press, 1991), 168.
8. James C. Cobb, *Away Down South: A History of Southern Identity* (Oxford, U.K.: Oxford University Press, 2005), 22.
9. Qtd. in Taylor, *Cavalier and Yankee*, 7.
10. Qtd. in Fox-Genovese and Genovese, *Mind of the Master Class*, 662.
11. Qtd. in Bertram Wyatt-Brown, *The Shaping of Southern Culture: Honor, Grace, and War, 1760s–1880s* (Chapel Hill: University of North Carolina Press, 2001), 180.
12. Qtd. in Wyatt-Brown, *Shaping of Southern Culture*, 180.
13. Levine, *Half Slave and Half Free*, 95.
14. Many of these developments and their relationship to slavery, particularly in the Mississippi Valley, are explored in detail in Walter Johnson, *River of Dark Dreams: Slavery and Empire in the Cotton Kingdom* (Cambridge, Mass.: Harvard University Press, 2013).

15. Donald G. Nieman, *Promises to Keep: African-Americans and the Constitutional Order, 1776 to the Present* (New York: Oxford University Press, 1991), 17.
16. Qtd. in Paul Finkelman, *Slavery and the Founders: Race and Liberty in the Age of Jefferson*, 2nd ed. (Armonk, N.Y.: M. E. Sharpe, Inc., 2001), 100.
17. Dattel, *Cotton and Race,* 29–30, 37.
18. Qtd. in W. E. B. Du Bois, *The Suppression of the African Slave-Trade to the United States of America, 1638–1870* (1896; rpt. Mineola, N.Y.: Dover Publications, 1999), 95.
19. Wood, *Empire of Liberty,* 526.
20. Finkelman, *Slavery and the Founders,* 151.
21. Wood, *Empire of Liberty,* 524.
22. United States of America, by Authority of Congress, 2 Statutes at Large, 426; The Act of 1807, Section I (Record of the Ninth Congress, Sess. 2, Ch. 22, 1807), pub. 1845 by Charles C. Little and James Brown, Boston.
23. Du Bois, *Suppression of the African Slave-Trade,* 96.
24. John Craig Hammond, "Uncontrollable Necessity: The Local Politics, Geopolitics, and Sectional Politics of Slavery Expansion," in Hammond and Mason, eds., *Contesting Slavery,* 144.
25. U.S. Census data for 1810, 1820, 1840, 1860.
26. Patrick Henry to Robert Pleasants, Jan. 18, 1773 in Bruns, ed., *Am I Not a Man and a Brother?* 222.
27. Peter Kolchin, *American Slavery: 1619–1877,* rev. ed. (New York: Hill and Wang, 2003), 94.
28. Fox-Genovese and Genovese, *Mind of the Master Class,* 35.
29. Ibid., 35–36.
30. Wood, *Empire of Liberty,* 530.
31. Dattel, *Cotton and Race,* 55.
32. Stewart, *Holy Warriors,* 25–26.

5. THE ARITHMETIC OF EMANCIPATION

1. See Mason, *Slavery and Politics,* 40–41.
2. Wood, *Empire of Liberty,* 529.
3. Qtd. in Wood, *Empire of Liberty,* 369.
4. Jon Kukla, *A Wilderness So Immense: The Louisiana Purchase and the Destiny of America* (New York: Random House, 2004), 292–93.
5. Mason, *Slavery and Politics,* 39.
6. Ibid., 55–57.
7. Ibid., 25- 26.
8. Horton and Horton, *Hard Road to Freedom,* 88–89.
9. Andrew Burstein and Nancy Isenberg, *Madison and Jefferson* (New York: Random House, 2010), 394–95.
10. Wood, *Empire of Liberty,* 372, 373.
11. Qtd. in Kukla, *Wilderness So Immense,* 293–94.
12. Qtd. in Burstein and Isenberg, *Madison and Jefferson,* 397, 398.

13. Thomas Jefferson to John Holmes, Apr. 22, 1820, www.loc.gov/exhibits, transcript of letter.
14. Mason, *Slavery and Politics,* 42.
15. A. J. Langguth, *Union 1812: The Americans Who Fought the Second War of Independence* (New York: Simon & Schuster, 2006), 134–35.
16. Qtd. in Langguth, *Union 1812,* 135.
17. Ibid., 338.
18. Qtd. in Mason, *Slavery and Politics,* 43.
19. Julius W. Pratt, *Expansionists of 1812* (New York: Peter Smith, 1949), 131; Mason, *Slavery and Politics,* 44.
20. Annals of Congress, 12th Congress, 2nd sess., 569–570.
21. Mason, *Slavery and Politics,* 50.
22. Kevin Phillips, *The Cousins' Wars: Religion, Politics, and the Triumph of Anglo-America* (New York: Basic Books, 1999), 336–37.
23. Mason, *Slavery and Politics,* 52.
24. Sean Wilentz, *The Rise of American Democracy: Jefferson to Lincoln* (New York: W.W. Norton & Co., 2005), 165–66; see also Theodore Dwight, *History of the Hartford Convention* (New York: Da Capo Press, 1970).
25. Qtd. in Alan Taylor, *The Civil War of 1812: American Citizens, British Subjects, Irish Rebels, and Indian Allies* (New York: Random House, 2011), 135.
26. Ibid., 136.
27. Qtd. in Taylor, *Civil War of 1812,* 328.
28. Burstein and Isenberg, *Madison and Jefferson,* 525.
29. Sam W. Haynes, *Unfinished Revolution: The Early American Republic in a British World* (Charlottesville: University of Virginia Press, 2010), 6. The six new states added between 1816 and 1821 were Indiana, Mississippi, Illinois, Alabama, Maine, and Missouri.
30. Qtd. in Mason, *Slavery and Politics,* 180.
31. See Albert E. Castel, *The Yeas and the Nays: Key Congressional Decisions, 1774–1945* (Kalamazoo, Mich.: New Issues Press, Western Michigan University, 1975), 33–34.
32. Qtd. in Daniel Walker Howe, *What Hath God Wrought: The Transformation of America, 1815–1848* (Oxford, U.K.: Oxford University Press, 2007), 148.
33. Qtd. in Mason, *Slavery and Politics,* 177; David S. Heidler and Jeanne T. Heidler, *Henry Clay: The Essential American* (New York: Random House, 2010), 146.
34. Mason, *Politics and Slavery,* 179.
35. Wilentz, *Rise of American Democracy,* 232.
36. William W. Freehling, *The Road to Disunion* (Oxford, U.K.: Oxford University Press, 1990), vol. 1: 153.
37. See Castel, *The Yeas and the Nays,* 35–36.
38. Howe, *What Hath God Wrought,* 155–56.
39. Qtd. in Wood, *Empire of Liberty,* 737.
40. Qtd. in Freehling, *Road to Disunion* 1: 155.

6. The Sunset of Northern Slavery

1. Ira Berlin and Leslie M. Harris, eds., *Slavery in New York* (New York: New Press, 2005), 286.
2. David N. Gellman, *Emancipating New York: The Politics of Slavery and Freedom 1777–1827* (Baton Rouge: Louisiana State University Press, 2006), 3.
3. Edgar J. McManus, *A History of Negro Slavery in New York* (Syracuse, N.Y.: Syracuse University Press, 1966), 161.
4. Zilversmit, *First Emancipation,* 148–49.
5. Qtd. in Litwack, *North of Slavery,* 8.
6. Zilversmit, *First Emancipation,* 151–52.
7. Gellman, *Emancipating New York,* 153.
8. McManus, *History of Negro Slavery in New York,* 174–75.
9. Graham Russell Hodges, *Root and Branch: African Americans in New York and East Jersey, 1613–1863* (Chapel Hill: University of North Carolina Press, 1999), 170.
10. Gellman, *Emancipating New York,* 175.
11. Hodges, *Root and Branch,* 170.
12. Patrick Rael, "The Long Death of Slavery," in Berlin and Harris, eds., *Slavery in New York,* 129.
13. Shane White, *Somewhat More Independent: The End of Slavery in New York City, 1770–1810* (Athens: University of Georgia Press, 1991), 49.
14. Rael, "The Long Death of Slavery," 130.
15. Hodges, *Root and Branch,* 193.
16. Qtd. in Zilversmit, *First Emancipation,* 211.
17. Gellman, *Emancipating New York,* 207.
18. Ibid., 208–12.
19. Litwack, *North of Slavery,* 88–89.
20. Qtd. in Henry Scofield Cooley, *A Study of Slavery in New Jersey* (Baltimore: Johns Hopkins University Press, 1896), 23.
21. Qtd. in Edgar J. McManus, *Black Bondage in the North* (Syracuse, N.Y.: Syracuse University Press, 1973), 161.
22. Qtd. in Dorsey, *Common Bondage,* 15.
23. Qtd. in Zilversmit, *First Emancipation,* 102.
24. Cooley, *Study of Slavery in New Jersey,* 26–27.
25. Zilversmit, *First Emancipation,* 193.
26. Hodges, *Root and Branch,* 192.
27. Ibid., 194–98.
28. Qtd. in Cooley, *Study of Slavery in New Jersey,* 27.
29. Ibid., 28–29.
30. U.S. Census data, 1810, 1820, 1830, 1850, 1860.
31. Zilversmit, *First Emancipation,* 200.
32. U.S. Census data, 1820, 1840.
33. *Journals of the Continental Congress* 33 (Friday, Oct. 5, 1787): 610; Christopher P. Lehman, *Slavery in the Upper Mississippi Valley, 1787–1865* (Jefferson, N.C.: McFarland & Co., 2011), 12.

34. Lehman, *Slavery in the Upper Mississippi Valley,* 28–29.

35. Ibid., 30–31.

36. Francis Thorpe, *The Federal and State Constitutions, Colonial Charters, and Other Organic Laws of the States, Territories, and Colonies Now or Heretofore Forming the United States of America. Compiled and Edited under the Act of Congress of June 30, 1906* (Washington, D.C.: Government Printing Office, 1909), vol. 2, 1010.

37. Lehman, *Slavery in the Upper Mississippi Valley,* 47.

38. Lerone Bennett Jr., *Forced Into Glory: Abraham Lincoln's White Dream* (Chicago: Johnson Publishing, 2007), 278.

39. Donald, *Lincoln,* 103–4.

40. Ronald C. White Jr., *A. Lincoln: A Biography* (New York: Random House, 2009), 75.

41. Norman Dwight Harris, *History of Negro Slavery in Illinois and of the Slavery Agitation in That State* (Chicago: A. C. McClurg & Co., 1904), 48; for a detailed account of the attempt to hold a pro-slavery constitutional convention in Illinois, see Harris's chapter 4, "The Contest for a Convention," 27–48.

42. Gary W. Gallagher, *The Union War* (Cambridge, Mass.: Harvard University Press, 2011), 4.

43. Alexis de Tocqueville, *Democracy in America,* ed. Phillips Bradley (New York: Alfred A. Knopf), vol. 1: 359–60, 373.

44. Qtd. in Litwack, *North of Slavery,* 67.

45. Ibid., 106.

7. THE WOLF BY THE EAR

1. Thomas Jefferson to John Holmes, Monticello, Apr. 22, 1820. Library of Congress manuscript at memory loc.gov/master/mss/mtj1/051/1200/1238.jpg.

2. Jefferson Davis, "Message to the Confederate Congress," Jan. 12, 1863, in Loewen and Sebesta, eds., *Confederate and Neo-Confederate Reader,* 198.

3. Eugene D. Genovese, *From Rebellion to Revolution: Afro-American Slave Revolts in the Making of the Modern World* (Baton Rouge: Louisiana State University Press, 1979), xxiii.

4. Postmaster Gideon Granger to Senator James Jackson, qtd. in Levine, *Half Slave and Half Free,* 12–13.

5. Levine, *Half Slave and Half Free,* 10, 11, 146; Charles Johnson and Patricia Smith, *Africans in America: America's Journey through Slavery* (New York: Harcourt, 1998), 255–57; Quarles, *Negro in the Making of America,* 98; John Hope Franklin, *From Slavery to Freedom,* 153.

6. John Hope Franklin and Loren Schweninger, *Runaway Slaves: Rebels on the Plantation* (Oxford, U.K.: Oxford University Press, 1999), 12.

7. The best and most thorough account to date of the German Coast revolt is to be found in Daniel Rasmussen, *American Uprising: The Untold Story of America's Largest Slave Revolt* (New York: HarperCollins, 2011).

8. Rasmussen, *American Uprising,* 209.

9. Michael P. Johnson, "Denmark Vesey and His Co-Conspirators," *William and Mary Quarterly*, 3rd ser., vol. 58, no. 4 (Oct. 2001): 976.

10. Horton and Horton, *Slavery and the Making of America*, 93–95.

11. Davis, *Inhuman Bondage*, 208–9; Horton and Horton, *Slavery and the Making of America*, 112–13.

12. James Oakes, *Slavery and Freedom: An Interpretation of the Old South* (New York: W. W. Norton & Co., 1998), 154–55.

13. Qtd. in Freehling, *Road to Disunion* 1: 182.

14. Qtd. in Christopher M. Curtis, "Can These Be the Sons of Their Fathers? The Defense of Slavery in Virginia, 1831–1832," master's thesis, Virginia Polytechnic Institute, 1997, unnumbered page immediately following table of contents.

15. Wolf, *Race and Liberty in the New Nation*, xi.

16. A strong argument is built for this interpretation in Curtis, "Can These Be the Sons of Their Fathers?"

17. Wolf, *Race and Liberty in the New Nation*, xiii.

18. Franklin and Schweninger, *Runaway Slaves*, 274–75.

19. Ibid., 297.

20. Franklin, *From Slavery to Freedom*, 191–92.

21. Ibid., xiv—xv, 200–203.

22. Brian Schoen, "Positive Goods and Necessary Evils: Commerce, Security, and Slavery in the Lower South, 1787–1837," in Hammond and Mason, eds., *Contesting Slavery*, 176.

23. *David Walker's Appeal*, 3rd ed., ed. Charles M. Wiltse (1830; New York: Hill and Wang, 1965), 76.

24. Johnson and Smith, *Africans in America*, 341–43.

25. Robert Walker Johannsen, *Stephen A. Douglas* (New York: Oxford University Press, 1973), 817.

26. Qtd. in Ira Berlin, *Many Thousands Gone: The First Two Centuries of Slavery in North America* (Cambridge, Mass.: Harvard University Press, 1998), 282.

27. Horton and Horton, *Slavery and the Making of America*, 105.

28. Ibid., 107.

29. Franklin and Schweninger, *Runaway Slaves*, 134–35.

30. Oakes, *Slavery and Freedom*, 170.

31. Ibid., 181.

32. John Craig Hammond, *Slavery, Freedom, and Expansion in the Early American West* (Charlottesville: University of Virginia Press, 2007), 143–45.

33. David F. Ericson, "Slave Smugglers, Slave Catchers, and Slave Rebels," in Hammond and Mason, eds., *Contesting Slavery*, 192–93.

34. There is a scholarly debate over the birthplace of Olaudah Equiano, who claimed to have been born in West Africa near the Niger River. Other evidence points to his birthplace as being in South Carolina. In either case, there is no disputing his powerful account of the middle passage, but whether it was from firsthand experience (as Equiano claimed) or based on the stories of those who actually made the crossing, the impact of his book was significant for the abolitionist movement.

35. Henry Mayer, *All on Fire: William Lloyd Garrison and the Abolition of Slavery* (New York: W. W. Norton & Co., 1998), 51–57.
36. Christopher Leslie Brown, *Moral Capital: Foundations of British Abolitionism* (Chapel Hill: University of North Caroline Press, 2006), 27.
37. Ibid., 27–28.
38. Ibid., 5.
39. Qtd. in Simon Schama, *The American Future: A History* (New York: HarperCollins, 2010), 178, 180.
40. Ibid., 182.
41. Henry B. Stanton, ed., *Debate at the Lane Seminary, Cincinnati* (Boston: Garrison & Knapp, 1834), 3. Available at www.oberlin.edu/external/EOG/LaneDebates/Resources.html.
42. Ibid., 4.
43. Ibid., 16.
44. Stewart, *Holy Warriors,* 59, 60.
45. Mayer, *All on Fire,* xiii.
46. William Lloyd Garrison, July 4, 1329, qtd. in Kai Wright, ed., *The African-American Experience: Black History and Culture through Speeches, Letters, Editorials, Poems, Songs, and Stories* (New York: Black Dog & Leventhal Publishers, 2009), 158–59.
47. Philip F. Gura, *American Transcendentalism: A History* (New York: Hill and Wang, 2007), 245.
48. Qtd. in Richard S. Newman, *The Transformation of American Abolitionism: Fighting Slavery in the Early Republic* (Chapel Hill: University of North Carolina Press, 2002), 13.
49. Howard Holman Bell, *A Survey of the Negro Convention Movement 1830–1861* (New York: Arno Press and New York Times, 1969), 6–7.
50. Ibid., 16, 32, 26.
51. Ibid., 56.
52. Henry Highland Garnet, "Let Your Motto Be Resistance" (1843), in Manning Marable and Leith Mullings, eds., *Let Nobody Turn Us Around: An African American Anthology* (Lanham, Md.: Rowman and Littlefield, 2000), 60.
53. Bell, *Survey of the Negro Convention Movement,* 76.
54. David S. Cecelski, *The Fire of Freedom: Abraham Galloway and the Slaves' Civil War* (Chapel Hill: University of North Caroline Press, 2012), 139–40.
55. See Frederick Douglass, *My Bondage and My Freedom* (1855; rpt. New York: Dover Publications, 1969); John Stauffer, *Giants: The Parallel Lives of Frederick Douglass and Abraham Lincoln* (New York: Hachette Book Group, 2008).
56. Maurice O. Wallace and Shawn Michelle Smith, eds., *Pictures and Progress: Early Photography and the Making of African American Identity* (Durham, N.C.: Duke University Press, 2012), 5.
57. See Laura Wexler, "A More Perfect Likeness: Frederick Douglass and the Image of the Nation," in Wallace and Smith, eds., *Pictures and Progress,* 18–40; quote on 37.
58. *United States v. The Libellants and Claimants of the Schooner Amistad,* 40 US 518.

59. See Davis, *Inhuman Bondage,* 12–26; Horton and Horton, *Slavery and the Making of America,* 116–17; Earl M. Maltz, *Slavery and the Supreme Court, 1825–1861* (Lawrence: University Press of Kansas, 2009), 66.

60. For a thorough and well-researched treatment of the Amistad episode, see Marcus Rediker, *The Amistad Rebellion: An Atlantic Odyssey of Slavery and Freedom* (New York: Viking Penguin, 2012).

61. James Oakes, *Freedom National: The Destruction of Slavery in the United States, 1861–1865* (New York: W. W. Norton & Co., 2013), 22–25.

62. Charles W. Hanna, *African American Recipients of the Medal of Honor: A Biographical Dictionary, Civil War through Vietnam War* (Jefferson, N.C.: McFarland & Co. 2002), 11; Gary Gilmore, "African Americans Continue Tradition of Distinguished Service," *U.S. Department of Defense News,* www.defense.gov/news/newsarticle.aspx?ID=2897

63. Nelson D. Lankford, *Richmond Burning: The Last Days of the Confederate Capital* (New York: Viking, 2002), 130–31.

8. FREEDOM'S FAITH

1. George Pack, ed., "Religion in America," *Methodist Quarterly Review,* 3rd ser., vol. 5 (Oct. 1845): 496.

2. Robert Baird, *Religion in the United States of America* (1844; New York: Arno Press and New York Times, 1969), 424.

3. Ibid, 55.

4. Timothy Lawrence Smith, *Revivalism and Social Reform in Mid-Nineteenth Century America* (New York: Abingdon Press, 1957), 24, 36.

5. Adam L. Tate, "Confronting Abolitionism: Bishop John England, American Catholicism, and Slavery," *Journal of the Historical Society* 9, no. 3 (Sept. 2009): 375, 398–99.

6. Qtd. in Nash, *Race and Revolution,* 15.

7. Lucius C. Matlack, *The History of American Slavery and Methodism, from 1780 to 1849; and History of the Wesleyan Methodist Connection of America* (New York, 1849), 323. Matlack not only attended the February 1843 convention, he served as secretary pro tem.

8. *Journals of the General Conference of the Methodist Episcopal Church,* vol. 2 (New York: Carlton and Lanaham, 1844), 23.

9. Lucius C. Matlack, *The Anti-Slavery Struggle and Triumph in the Methodist Episcopal Church* (New York: Negro University Press, 1969), 152.

10. "Methodist General Conference," *Liberator,* June 14, 1844, 94.

11. J. M. Buckley, *A History of Methodists in the United States* (New York: Charles Scribner's Sons, 1900), 409.

12. Donald G. Mathews, *Slavery and Methodism: A Chapter in American Morality, 1780–1845* (Princeton, N.J.: Princeton University Press, 1965), 252; *Journal of the General Conference of 1844,* 33.

13. *Journal of the General Conference of 1844,* 64.

14. J. T. Peck, "General Conference of 1844," *Methodist Quarterly Review* (Apr. 1870): 170.

15. *Journal of the General Conference of 1844,* 100–101.

16. Mathews, *Slavery and Methodism,* 257.
17. *Journal of the General Conference of 1844,* 95.
18. Matlack, *Anti-Slavery Struggle,* 160–61.
19. James Porter, "General Conference of 1844," *Methodist Quarterly Review* (Apr. 1871): 242. Nothing is known about Porter other than that he was an abolitionist delegate present in 1844.
20. *Journal of the General Conference of 1844,* 203–11.
21. Ibid., 135–37.
22. William Warren Sweet, *Methodism in American History* (New York: Methodist Book Concern, 1933), 255.
23. See *The True Wesleyan,* qtd. in William Goodell, *Slavery and Anti-Slavery: A History of the Great Struggle in Both Hemispheres; With a View of the Slavery Question in the United States* (Negro Universities Press, New York, 1968), 149–50.
24. Mathews, *Slavery and Methodism,* 277.
25. Matlack, *History of American Slavery,* app. 9.
26. Sweet, *Methodism in American History,* 260, 272.
27. For a detailed account of the arguments used in such a case in New York City, see a pamphlet printed by the Southern church entitled *Decision of the United States Circuit Court in the Case of the Methodist Episcopal Church, South vs the Methodist Episcopal Church, North, Pronounced by His Honor, Judge Nelson in the City of New York* (San Francisco: Christian Observer, 1852).
28. William Gammell, *History of American Baptist Missions in Asia, Africa, Europe, and North America* (Boston: Gould, Kendall and Lincoln, 1849), 17–20.
29. Albert H. Newman, *A History of the Baptist Churches in the United States* (New York: Christian Literature Co., 1894), 305.
30. Orland Kay Armstrong and Marjorie M. Armstrong, *The Indomitable Baptists* (Garden City, N.Y.: Doubleday and Co., 1967), 164.
31. Newman, *History of the Baptist Churches,* 443.
32. Gammell, *History of American Baptist Missions,* 174.
33. Roger G. Torbet, *A History of the Baptists* (Valley Forge, Pa.; Judson Press, 1963), 288.
34. William Wright Barnes, *The Southern Baptist Convention, 1845–1953* (Nashville: Broadman Press, 1954), 23.
35. Edmund F. Merriam, *A History of American Baptist Missions* (Philadelphia: American Baptist Publication Society, 1900), 53.
36. Robert A. Baker, *A Baptist Source Book* (Nashville: Broadman Press, 1966), 98.
37. Torbet, *History of the Baptists,* 289.
38. Jess L. Boyd, *A History of Baptists in America, Prior to 1845* (New York: American Press, 1957), 162–63.
39. Qtd. in Baker, *Baptist Source Book,* 94.
40. "The Baptists in Trouble," *Liberator,* Sept. 29, 1843, 153.
41. Roger B. Torbet, *Venture of Faith: The Story of the American Baptist Foreign Mission Society and the Woman's American Baptist Foreign Mission Society, 1814–1954* (Philadelphia: Judson Press, 1955), 111.

42. "Triennial Convention," *Baptist Memorial and Monthly Chronicle* 3 (June 1844): 185.

43. "The Baptist Brotherhood of Thieves," *Liberator,* May 17, 1844, 79.

44. American Baptist Home Mission Society, *Twelfth Annual Report of the American Baptist Home Mission Society* (New York: American Baptist Home Mission Rooms, 1844), 5–6.

45. *Minutes of the Meetings of the American Baptist Home Mission Society and of Its Executive Committee,* Book 2 (New York: Entry for Oct. 7, 1844), 303, rpt. in Baker, *Baptist Source Book,* 106.

46. "Reply of the Acting Board, Boston, Dec. 18, 1844," *Baptist Missionary Magazine* 25 (Aug. 1845): 222.

47. "Intelligence: America: Secession from the Amer. Bapt. Bd. of Foreign Missions," *Baptist Magazine* (London), vol. 37 (May 1845): 247.

48. John B. Lawrence, *History of the Home Mission Board* (Nashville: Broadman Press, 1958), 17.

49. "The Southern Baptist Convention," *Baptist Memorial and Monthly Record* 4 (July 1845): 219–21.

50. Newman, *History of the Baptist Churches,* 455.

51. William Hosmer, *The Higher Law, in Its Relation to Civil Government with Particular Reference to Slavery and the Fugitive Slave Law* (New York: Negro Universities Press, 1969), 99.

52. Luther Lee, *Slavery Examined in the Light of the Bible* (Syracuse, N.Y.: Wesleyan Methodist Book Room, 1855), 48.

53. Hosmer, *Higher Law,* 106.

54. Francis Wayland qtd. in Richard Fuller, *Domestic Slavery Considered as a Scriptural Institution: In a Correspondence between the Rev. Richard Fuller, of Beaufort, S.C., and the Rev. Francis Wayland, of Providence, R.I.* (New York: Lewis Colby, 1845), 74, 100.

55. Psalm 12:5, Isaiah 58:6, qtd. in Charles Elliott, *Sinfulness of American Slavery: Proved from Its Evil Sources; Its Injustice; Its Wrongs; Its Contrariety to Many Scriptural Commands, Prohibitions, and Principles, and to the Christian Spirit; and from Its Evil Effects; together with Observations on Emancipation, and the Duties of American Citizens in Regard to Slavery* (New York: Negro Universities Press, 1968), vol. 1: 260–61.

56. Elliott, *Sinfulness of American Slavery* 1: 20, 305.

57. General Conference of the Mennonite Churches, *Worship Together* (pub. for the Mennonite Brethren Churches, Fresno, Calif., by The Christian Press, 1995), hymn 308.

58. Joshua R. Balme, *American States, Churches, and Slavery* (New York: Negro Universities Press, 19690, 257.

59. Elliott, *Sinfulness of American Slavery* 1: 106–8.

60. Wayland, qtd. in Fuller, *Domestic Slavery Considered,* 26.

61. Qtd. in Matlack, *Anti-Slavery Struggle,* 248.

62. Wayland qtd. in Fuller, *Domestic Slavery Considered,* 81.

63. Elliott, *Sinfulness of American Slavery* 1: 302.

64. Lee, *Slavery Examined,* 13.

65. Ibid., 23.
66. Elliott, *Sinfulness of American Slavery* 1: 127.
67. Ibid., 279–80.
68. J. S. May, "The Liberty Bell Is Not of the Liberty Party," *The Liberty Bell* (Boston, Massachusetts Anti-Slavery Fair, 1845), 159.
69. "Observations on Men, Books, and Things: Massachusetts Anti-Slavery Society," *Christian Observatory* 4 (Mar. 1850): 143.
70. Eugene Genovese, *The Political Economy of Slavery: Studies in the Economy and Society of the Slave South* (New York: Pantheon, 1965), 8.
71. Qtd. in Ralph E. Morrow, "The Pro-Slavery Argument Revisited," *Mississippi Valley Historical Review* 48 (June 1961): 87.
72. Qtd. in Charles G. Sellers Jr., "The Travail of Slavery," in Joel H. Silbey, ed., *National Development and Sectional Crisis, 1815–1860* (New York: Random House, 1970), 127.
73. Qtd. in William Sumner Jenkins, *Pro-slavery Thought in the Old South* (Chapel Hill: University of North Carolina, 1935), 206–7.
74. Qtd. in Elliott, *Sinfulness of American Slavery* 1: 29.
75. Fred Augustus Ross, *Slavery Ordained of God* (New York: Negro Universities Press, 1969), 97.
76. John Fletcher, *Studies on Slavery, in Easy Lessons: Compiled into Eight Studies, and Subdivided into Short Lessons for the Convenience of Readers* (1852; Miami: Mnemosyne Pub. Co., 1969), 18.
77. Fuller, *Domestic Slavery Considered,* 7.
78. Thomas C. Thornton, *An Inquiry into the History of Slavery; Its Introduction into the United States, Causes of Its Continuance, and Remarks upon the Abolition Tracts of William E. Channing* (1841; rpt. Detroit: Negro History Press, 1969), 70.
79. Fletcher, *Studies on Slavery,* 90.
80. Thornton, *An Inquiry into the History of Slavery,* 108.
81. See George S. Sawyer, *Southern Institutes or, An inquiry into the Origin and Early Prevalence of Slavery and the Slave-Trade . . . with Notes and Comments in Defence of the Southern Institutions* (New York: Negro Universities Press, 1969), 160–65.
82. Jenkins, *Pro-slavery Thought in the Old South,* 204.
83. Henry Clay to Dr. W. A. Booth, Apr. 7, 1845 in *The Private Correspondence of Henry Clay,* ed. Calvin Colton (New York: A. S. Barnes & Co., 1856), 525.
84. John Calhoun, *The Papers of John C. Calhoun,* ed. Robert L. Meriwether (Columbia: University of South Carolina Press, 2003), vol. 27 (*1848–1850*): 199.
85. Abraham Lincoln, *The Lincoln-Douglas Debates of 1858,* ed. Robert W. Johannsen (New York: Oxford University Press, 1965), 313–14, 317.
86. For an excellent analysis of this theme in Lincoln's speech, see Ronald C. White Jr., *Lincoln's Greatest Speech: The Second Inaugural.* New York: Simon & Schuster, 2002), 101–20.

9. SLAVERY AND MANIFEST DIVISION

1. *Richmond Times,* qtd. in Richard Kluger, *Seizing Destiny: The Relentless Expansion of American Territory* (New York: Random House, 2008), 460.
2. Ibid., 415.
3. Robert W. Merry, *A Country of Vast Designs: James K. Polk, the Mexican War, and the Conquest of the American Continent* (New York: Simon & Schuster, 2009), 183.
4. Steven E. Woodworth, *Manifest Destinies: America's Westward Expansion and the Road to the Civil War* (New York: Alfred E. Knopf, 2010), 127.
5. Merry, *Country of Vast Designs,* 186–87.
6. Qtd. in Merry, *Country of Vast Designs,* 68.
7. For a good analysis of British interests in Texas, and American concerns about this, see Haynes, *Unfinished Revolution,* 230–20.
8. See Leonard L. Richards, *The Slave Power: The Free North and Southern Domination 1780–1860* (Baton Rouge: Louisiana State University Press, 2000), for a thorough and insightful analysis of the "Slave Power" conspiracy and reality.
9. Merry, *Country of Vast Designs,* 287.
10. Woodworth, *Manifest Destinies,* 297.
11. Ibid., 298.
12. Ibid.
13. Eric Foner, *Free Soil, Free Labor, Free Men: The Ideology of the Republican Party Before the Civil War* (1970; Oxford, U.K.: Oxford University Press, 1995), 73.
14. Wilentz, *Rise of American Democracy,* 506.
15. Foner, *Free Soil,* 78–80.
16. Bangor *Platform,* May 6, 1849, qtd. in Foner, *Free Soil,* 80.
17. Ann Arbor, Mich., *Signal of Liberty,* Sept. 15 and Oct. 13, 1841, qtd. in Wilentz, *Rise of American Democracy,* 549.
18. Qtd. in Wilentz, *Rise of American Democracy,* 617.
19. Ibid., 618.
20. Ray Allen Billington, *Westward Expansion: A History of the American Frontier* (New York, MacMillan Publishing Co., 1974), 452; Frank McLynn, *Wagons West: The Epic Story of America's Overland Trails* (New York: Grove Press, 2002), 42.
21. A phrase used by Clay to emphasize the urgency of resolving the issue. For an insightful analysis of the Compromise of 1850 and Henry Clay's role in it, see Robert V. Remini, *At the Edge of the Precipice: Henry Clay and the Compromise That Saved the Union* (New York: Basic Books, 2010).
22. Qtd. in Leonard L. Richards, *The California Gold Rush and the Coming of the Civil War* (New York: Alfred A. Knopf, 2007), 94.
23. Qtd. in Remini, *At the Edge of the Precipice,* 63–64.
24. Ibid, 55.
25. Richards, *California Gold Rush,* 100; Remini, *At the Edge of the Precipice,* 54–56.
26. Qtd. in Richards, *California Gold Rush,* 95.

27. Remini, *At the Edge of the Precipice,* 54.
28. See S. C. Gwynne, *Empire of the Summer Moon* (New York: Scribner, 2010), 78–82.
29. Kluger, *Seizing Destiny,* 481.
30. Qtd. in Steven Lubet, *Fugitive Justice: Runaways, Rescuers, and Slavery on Trial* (Cambridge, Mass.: Harvard University Press, 2009), 41.
31. Ibid., 42–43.
32. Wilentz, *Rise of American Democracy,* 471–73.
33. Remini, *At the Edge of the Precipice,* 67.
34. Qtd. in Remini, *At the Edge of the Precipice,* 73.
35. Ibid., 81.
36. Qtd. in Richards, *California Gold Rush,* 104.
37. Heidler and Heidler, *Henry Clay,* 462, 464.
38. Qtd. in Remini, *At the Edge of the Precipice,* 79.
39. *Congressional Globe,* 31st Congress, vol. 21, 1st sess., 451–55.
40. Wilentz, *Rise of American Democracy,* 639–40.
41. *Congressional Globe,* 31st Congress, vol. 21, 1st sess., 656–57.
42. Qtd. in Remini, *At the Edge of the Precipice,* 88.
43. Ibid.
44. Wilentz, *Rise of American Democracy,* 640; Remini, *At the Edge of the Precipice,* 100–105.
45. Heidler and Heidler, *Henry Clay,* 469–70.
46. Remini, *At the Edge of the Precipice,* 132.
47. See Heidler and Heidler, *Henry Clay,* 474–75.
48. Ibid., 476.
49. Qtd. in Remini, *At the Edge of the Precipice,* 148–49; 150–51.
50. Wilentz, *Rise of American Democracy,* 637.
51. David M. Potter, *The Impending Crisis, 1848–1861* (New York: Harper & Row, 1976), 91–120.

10. Rushing toward Disunion

1. Lubet, *Fugitive Justice,* 48–49.
2. Qtd. in Michael F. Holt, *The Political Crisis of the 1850s* (New York: John Wiley & Sons, 1978), 90.
3. Seward, "Irrepressible Conflict," 268.
4. Abraham Lincoln, *Collected Works,* ed. Roy P. Basler, Marion Delores Pratt, and Lloyd A. Dunlap (New Brunswick, N.J.: Rutgers University Press), vol. 2: 461–62.
5. Qtd. in Stanley Harrold, *Border War: Fighting Over Slavery before the Civil War* (Chapel Hill: University of North Carolina Press, 2010), 145.
6. Freehling, *Road to Disunion* 1: 503.
7. Harrold, *Border War,* 137.
8. Lubet, *Fugitive Justice,* 49.
9. U.S. National Park Service, *Underground Railroad* (official National Park Handbook; Washington, D.C.: U.S. Dept. of the Interior, 1998), 45.
10. Ibid., 53–54.

11. David S. Reynolds, *Mightier than the Sword: Uncle Tom's Cabin and the Battle for America* (New York: W. W. Norton & Co., 2011), xiv.
12. Ibid., 28, 41.
13. www.harrietbeecherstowecenter.org/hbs
14. Potter, *Impending Crisis,* 140.
15. Reynolds, *Mightier than the Sword,* 158–60.
16. Qtd. in Fox-Genovese and Genovese, *Mind of the Master Class,* 387.
17. Reynolds, *Mightier than the Sword,* 166.
18. Qtd. in Michael Burlingame, *Abraham Lincoln: A Life* (Baltimore: Johns Hopkins University Press, 2008), vol. 2: 728.
19. Harriet Ann Jacobs, *Incidents in the Life of a Slave Girl Written by Herself* (1861; Lexington, Ky.: Simon & Brown, 2012), 6.
20. Solomon Northup, *Twelve Years a Slave. Narrative of Solomon Northup, a Citizen of New-York, Kidnapped in Washington City in 1841 and Rescued in 1853, From a Cotton Plantation Near the Red River in Louisiana* (Auburn, NY: Derby and Miller, 1853), 109.
21. *Journal of the Executive Proceedings of the Senate of the United States of America* (Washington, D.C.: 1828–87), vol. 9: 238–40, 260–315.
22. Potter, *Impending Crisis,* 183.
23. Qtd. in Potter, *Impending Crisis,* 192.
24. Ibid.
25. 10 Statutes at Large 277.
26. Qtd. in Donald, *Lincoln,* 168.
27. Ibid., 168.
28. New York *Tribune,* Mar. 17, May 24, June 17, 1854.
29. Eric Foner, *Free Soil,* 127–28.
30. Ibid., 287.
31. Ibid., 158.
32. Potter, *Impending Crisis,* 239.
33. Nicole Etcheson, *Bleeding Kansas: Contested Liberty in the Civil War Era* (Lawrence: University Press of Kansas, 2004). See the excellent "Introduction," 1–8.
34. Robert E. McGlone, *John Brown's War against Slavery* (Cambridge, U.K.: Cambridge University Press, 2009), 10; Beecher qtd. in Debby Applegate, *The Most Famous Man in America: The Biography of Henry Ward Beecher* (New York: Doubleday, 2006), 282.
35. Harrold, *Border War,* 171–72.
36. Holt, *Political Crisis of the 1850s,* 205.
37. The full text of Sumner's speech can be found in the *Congressional Globe,* 34th Congress 1st sess., app., 529–44.
38. Ibid, 530.
39. Ibid, 543.
40. Qtd. in David Herbert Donald, *Charles Sumner and the Coming of the Civil War,* (1960; Naperville, Ill.: Sourcebooks, 2009), 239.
41. Qtd. in Donald, *Charles Sumner and the Coming of the Civil War,* 240.
42. Ibid., 241.

43. For a thorough and engaging recent volume detailing the Sumner caning episode, the reader is referred to Stephen Puleo's *The Caning: The Assault that Drove America to Civil War* (Yardley, Pa.: Westholme Publishing, 2012).

44. *Congressional Globe,* 34th Congress, 1st sess., app., 629.

45. Qtd. in Puleo, *Caning,* 118.

46. Hinton Rowan Helper, *The Impending Crisis of the South: How to Meet It* (1857; Memphis: General Books, 2010), 2.

47. Ibid., 2.

48. Ibid., 6.

49. Ibid.,10.

50. Ibid., 18, 19.

51. Ibid., 31.

52. Ibid., 46.

53. Ibid., 54, 133.

54. Maltz, *Slavery and the Supreme Court,* 210–11.

55. Ibid., 212.

56. The details of the multiple trials and appeals of the Dred Scott case prior to its finalization in the U.S. Supreme Court are well presented in Maltz, *Slavery and the Supreme Court,* 213–23.

57. Ibid., 224.

58. Elizabeth R. Varon, *Disunion! The Coming of the American Civil War, 1789–1859* (Chapel Hill: University of North Carolina Press, 2008), 296–97.

59. *Dred Scott v Sandford,* 60 US 393 (1856 Term).

60. Varon, *Disunion!* 298.

61. Ralph Waldo Emerson, *The Complete Works of Ralph Waldo Emerson, with a Biographical Introduction and Notes by Edward Waldo Emerson, and a General Index* (Boston: Houghton, Mifflin and Co., 1903–4), vol. 11: 268–70.

62. For a discussion of Brown's literary support, see William Keeney, "Hero, Martyr, Madman: Representations of John Brown in the Poetry of John Brown Year 1859–1860," in *Terrible Swift Sword: The Legacy of John Brown,* ed. Peggy A. Russo and Paul Finkelman (Athens: Ohio University Press, 2005), 141–75.

63. Louis Ruchames, *A John Brown Reader; The Story of John Brown in His Own Words, in the Words of Those Who Knew Him, and in the Poetry and Prose of the Literary Heritage* (New York: Abelard-Schuman, 1959), 125–26.

64. Ibid., 159.

65. Revelation 7:14.

66. Mayer, *All on Fire,* 495.

67. Loewen and Sebasta, eds., *The Confederate and Neo-Confederate Reader,* 128.

11. PRESIDENTIAL POLITICS AND THE WAR FOR SLAVERY

1. Svend Petersen, *A Statistical History of the American Presidential Elections* (New York: Ungar, 1963), 3–4, table 1: "Electoral votes to which each state is entitled." Subtract two votes per state (senators), and the result is the representation for each state in the House.

2. Petersen, *Statistical History,* 37–38, table 21: "Election of 1860: Electoral and Popular Vote," and subsequent unnumbered table, "Percentage of Popular Vote."

3. Petersen, *Statistical History.* Calculations based on information from the tables.

4. Table based on information from Petersen, *Statistical History.*

5. Ibid.

6. John Quincy Adams is difficult to categorize. Often he is listed as a "National Republican" as the party system had broken down at that point. He was certainly no friend of Jackson, a true Democrat.

7. Qtd. in Freehling, *Road to Disunion* 2: 310.

8. Margaret E. Wagner et al., eds., *The Library of Congress Civil War Desk Reference* (New York: Simon & Schuster, 2009), 124.

9. White, *A. Lincoln,* 324.

10. See Doris Kearns Goodwin, *Team of Rivals: The Political Genius of Abraham Lincoln* (New York: Simon & Schuster, 2005).

11. Petersen, *Statistical History,* table 21, 37–38.

12. Ibid., 37–38.

13. Benjamin Palmer, "Thanksgiving Sermon," in Loewen and Sebasta, eds., *The Confederate and Neo-Confederate Reader,* 107–8.

14. Ibid., 108.

15. Qtd. in William W. Freehling and Craig M. Simpson, eds., *Secession Debated: Georgia's Showdown in 1860* (New York: Oxford University Press, 1992), 46–47.

16. Freehling, *Road to Disunion* 2: 348.

17. Charles B. Dew, *Apostles of Disunion: Southern Secession Commissioners and the Causes of the Civil War* (Charlottesville: University of Virginia Press, 2001), 16–17.

18. "Declaration of the Immediate Causes Which Induce and Justify the Secession of South Carolina from the Federal Union," Dec. 24, 1860, in Loewen and Sebasta, eds., *Confederate and Neo-Confederate Reader,* 116–17.

19. Qtd. in Dew, *Apostles of Disunion,* 12–13.

20. Georgia Committee of Seventeen, "Report on Causes for Secession," Jan. 29, 1861, in Loewen and Sebasta, eds., *Confederate and Neo-Confederate Reader,* 139.

21. Texas Secession Convention, "Declaration of the Causes Which Impel the State of Texas to Secede," 143.

22. Qtd. in Freehling and Simpson, eds., *Secession Debated,* 55.

23. Michael P. Johnson, *Toward a Patriarchal Republic: The Secession of Georgia* (Baton Rouge: Louisiana State University Press, 1977), xx-xxi.

24. Farewell Address of Senator Robert Toombs, in Thomas Ricaud Martin, ed., *The Great Parliamentary Battle and Farewell Addresses of the Southern Senators on the Eve of the Civil War* (New York: Neale Publishing Co., 1905), 157, 164, 165, 167, 169, 171.

25. Farewell Address of Senator Jefferson Davis, in Martin, ed., *Great Parliamentary Battle and Farewell Addresses,* 184–85.

26. Farewell Address of Senator Clement Claiborne Clay, in Martin, ed., *Great Parliamentary Battle and Farewell Addresses,* 202–4.
27. Dew, *Apostles of Disunion,* 18–19.
28. Qtd. in Dew, *Apostles of Disunion,* 23.
29. Ibid., 54.
30. Ibid., 56.
31. Ibid., 77–79.
32. Alexander H. Stephens, "African Slavery: The Corner-Stone of the Southern Confederacy," Mar. 22, 1861, in Loewen and Sebasta, eds., *Confederate and Neo-Confederate Reader,* 188.
33. White, *Lincoln's Greatest Speech,* 87, 90.
34. Qtd. in Henry Steele Commager, ed., *The Defeat of the Confederacy: A Documentary Survey* (Princeton, N.J.: Van Nostrand, 1964), 19.

12. Thenceforward, and Forever Free

1. White, *A. Lincoln,* 39.
2. Ibid., 75.
3. Eric Foner, *The Fiery Trial: Abraham Lincoln and American Slavery* (New York: W. W. Norton and Co., 2010), 22.
4. Stauffer, *Giants,* 119.
5. Qtd. in Donald, *Lincoln,* 64.
6. Henry Clay, *The Papers of Henry Clay,* ed. James F. Hopkins (Lexington: University of Kentucky Press, 1959–92), vol. 9: 81, 278–82.
7. Herndon's later biography of Lincoln and his painstaking work of interviewing persons directly associated with Lincoln has provided historians with much valuable information, much of it long ignored and only recently finding acceptance within the community of Lincoln scholars.
8. Qtd. in Mark E. Neely Jr., *The Last Best Hope of Earth: Abraham Lincoln and the Promise of America* (Cambridge, Mass.: Harvard University Press, 1993), 43.
9. Qtd. in Lewis E. Lehrman, *Lincoln at Peoria: The Turning Point* (Mechanicsburg, Pa.: Stackpole Books, 2003), 10.
10. Lincoln, *Collected Works* 2: 222–23.
11. Ibid., 271.
12. Qtd. in Lehrman, *Lincoln at Peoria,* 310.
13. Foner, *Fiery Trial,* 64.
14. Lincoln, *Collected Works* 2: 247–81.
15. Ibid., 262–65.
16. Roy Morris Jr., *The Long Pursuit: Abraham Lincoln's Thirty-Year Struggle with Stephen Douglas for the Heart and Soul of America* (New York: HarperCollins Publishers, 2008), 77.
17. See Morris, *The Long Pursuit,* 87; Donald, *Lincoln,* 191–92.
18. Qtd. in James F. Simon, *Lincoln and Chief Justice Taney: Slavery, Secession, and the President's War Powers* (New York: Simon & Schuster, 2006), 137–39.
19. Qtd. in Donald, *Lincoln,* 206.

20. Lincoln and Douglas, *Lincoln-Douglas Debates,* 159.
21. Bennett, *Forced Into Glory,* 66, 635, 349.
22. Foner, *Fiery Trial,* 127.
23. White, *A. Lincoln,* 278.
24. Lincoln, *Collected Works* 3: 204–5.
25. William Lee Miller, *Lincoln's Virtues: An Ethical Biography* (New York: Alfred A. Knopf, 2007), 364.
26. Allen C. Guelzo, *Lincoln and Douglas: The Debates that Defined America* (New York: Simon & Schuster, 2008), 303, 306.
27. Harold Holzer, *Lincoln at Cooper Union: The Speech That Made Abraham Lincoln President* (New York: Simon & Schuster, 2004), 1, 5.
28. Ibid., 129.
29. Text of Cooper Union speech in Holzer, *Lincoln at Cooper Union,* 270, 275, 276, 280, 283, 284.
30. Qtd. in Holzer, *Lincoln at Cooper Union,* 284.
31. Foner, *Fiery Trial,* 141; Donald, *Lincoln,* 239.
32. Lincoln, *Collected Works* 4: 141.
33. See Donald, *Lincoln,* 261.
34. See Harold Holzer, *Lincoln President-Elect: Abraham Lincoln and the Great Secession Winter, 1860–1861* (New York: Simon & Schuster, 2008).
35. Qtd. in Burlingame, *Abraham Lincoln* 2: 30–31.
36. Stauffer, *Giants,* 256–57.
37. Abraham Lincoln, *Abraham Lincoln, Slavery, and the Civil War: Selected Writings and Speeches,* ed. Michael P. Johnson (Boston: St. Martin's, 2001), 114.
38. Donald, *Lincoln,* 283–84.
39. Stauffer, *Giants,* xii.
40. Lincoln, *Abraham Lincoln, Slavery, and Civil War,* 205.
41. Salmon P. Chase, *Inside Lincoln's Cabinet: The Civil War Diaries of Salmon P. Chase,* ed. David Herbert Donald (New York: Longmans, Green and Co., 1954), 149–50.
42. Preliminary Emancipation Proclamation, in Lincoln, *Abraham Lincoln, Slavery, and Civil War,* 206.
43. Neely, *Last Best Hope,* 113–14.
44. Donald Stoker, *The Grand Design: Strategy and the U.S. Civil War* (Oxford, U.K.: Oxford University Press, 2010), 29–30.
45. Emancipation Proclamation, in Lincoln, *Abraham Lincoln, Slavery, and Civil War,* 219.
46. Bruce Levine, *The Fall of the House of Dixie: The Civil War and the Social Revolution That Transformed the South* (New York: Random House, 2013), 125.
47. Allen C. Guelzo, *Lincoln's Emancipation Proclamation: The End of Slavery in America* (New York: Simon & Schuster, 2004), 211, 213.
48. Qtd. in Levine, *Fall of the House of Dixie,* 140.
49. Qtd. in Stauffer, *Giants,* 16.
50. Lincoln, *Collected Works* 6: 374–75.
51. Stauffer, *Giants,* 16.

13. Slavery's Death Throes

1. Gallagher, *Union War,* 2.
2. Varon, *Disunion!* 337.
3. Abraham Lincoln, Second Inaugural Address, reprinted in Ronald C. White Jr., *Lincoln's Greatest Speech: The Second Inaugural* (New York: Simon & Schuster, 2002), 17–19.
4. Foner, *Fiery Trial,* 170; Adam Goodheart, *1861: The Civil War Awakening* (New York: Alfred A. Knopf, 2011), 301.
5. Stauffer, *Giants,* 222–23.
6. Benjamin Butler, *Autobiography and Personal Reminiscences of Major-Genera Benj. F. Butler; Butler's Book* (Boston: A. M. Thayer, 1892), 256–59.
7. Query by Union General Benjamin Butler to Secretary of War Simon Cameron, July 30, 1861, in Bob Blaisdell, ed., *Famous Documents and Speeches of the Civil War* (Mineola, N.Y.: Dover Books, 2006), 39.
8. It should be noted that as of January 1, 1863, such slaves were not *technically* free according to the Emancipation Proclamation; had they remained in Rebel territory they would have been *technically,* though often not *practically,* free.
9. Mary Beth Corrigan, "Whether They Be Ours or No, They May Be Heirs of the Kingdom," in Paul Finkelman and Donald R. Kennon, eds., *In the Shadow of Freedom: The Politics of Slavery in the National Capital* (Athens: Ohio University Press, 2011), 169.
10. Horton and Horton, *Slavery and the Making of America,* 182–83.
11. See the official Robert Smalls Foundation website at www.robertsmalls.org.
12. 12 Statutes at Large, 319.
13. *Congressional Globe,* 37th Congress 1st Sess., 319.
14. Stauffer, *Giants,* 225.
15. William C. Harris, *Lincoln and the Border States: Preserving the Union* (Lawrence: University Press of Kansas, 2011), 208.
16. Foner, *Fiery Trial,* 175–76.
17. Donald, *Lincoln,* 314.
18. Qtd. in Burlingame, *Abraham Lincoln* 2: 202–3.
19. Lincoln, *Collected Works* 4: 506.
20. Qtd. in White, *A. Lincoln,* 454.
21. Qtd. in Burlingame, *Abraham Lincoln* 2: 203.
22. Stauffer, *Giants,* 226.
23. Qtd. in Stauffer, *Giants,* 455.
24. Lincoln, *Abraham Lincoln, Slavery, and Civil War,* 184–85.
25. Qtd. in James McPherson, *Battle Cry of Freedom: The Civil War Era* (Oxford, U.K.: Oxford University Press, 1988), 357.
26. Abraham Lincoln, "By the President of the United States of America. A Proclamation," in *Lincoln on War: Our Greatest Commander-in-Chief Speaks to America,* ed. Harold Holzer (Chapel Hill, N.C.: Algonquin Books, 2011), 133–34.
27. Qtd. in Levine, *Fall of the House of Dixie,* 126–27.
28. *Congressional Globe,* 37th Congress, 1st sess., 222–23, 258–62.

29. Qtd. in McPherson, *Battle Cry of Freedom,* 358.
30. *Congressional Globe,* 37th Congress, 2nd sess., 15.
31. Qtd. in McPherson, *Battle Cry of Freedom,* 495.
32. Harris, *Lincoln and the Border States,* 3.
33. Lincoln, *Collected Works* 5: 144–46.
34. Lincoln was not being very generous, or even realistic, with his estimated compensation, as prime field slaves were selling in the New Orleans market in 1860 for fifteen hundred dollars. See Neely, *Last Best Hope,* 106.
35. Foner, *Fiery Trial,* 198; Charles Lewis Wagandt, *The Mighty Revolution: Negro Emancipation in Maryland, 1862–1864* (Baltimore: Maryland Historical Society, 2004), 56–60.
36. Qtd. in Wagandt, *Mighty Revolution,* 62.
37. Ibid., 66.
38. Ibid., 67.
39. Harris, *Lincoln and the Border States,* 293–95.
40. Ibid., 296–97.
41. Ibid., 299–300; McPherson, *Battle Cry of Freedom,* 805.
42. Wagandt, *Mighty Revolution,* 263.
43. Qtd. in Foner, *Fiery Trial,* 277.
44. Harrison Anthony Trexler, *Slavery in Missouri, 1804–1865* (Baltimore: Johns Hopkins Press, 1914), 233–38.
45. Qtd. in Foner, *Fiery Trial,* 323, 278.
46. Harris, *Lincoln and the Border States,* 326–29, 332, 344–45.
47. William H. Townsend, *Lincoln and the Bluegrass: Slavery and Civil War in Kentucky* (Lexington: University of Kentucky Press, 1955), 322–23.
48. Patience Essah, *A House Divided: Slavery and Emancipation in Delaware, 1638–1865* (Charlottesville: University Press of Virginia, 1996), 153.
49. Harold Bell Hancock, *Delaware During the Civil War: A Political History* (Wilmington: Historical Society of Delaware, 1961), 83–94.
50. Essah, *House Divided,* 161.
51. Ibid., 106–7.
52. Qtd. in Harris, *Lincoln and the Border States,* 161.
53. Ibid., 162.
54. Qtd. in Harris, *Lincoln and the Border States,* 208.
55. *Congressional Globe,* 37th Congress, 3rd sess., 1862–63, vol. 1: 545–50, 558, 584; Harris, *Lincoln and the Border States,* 208–9.
56. Foner, *Fiery Trial,* 239; Burlingame, *Abraham Lincoln* 2: 459–61.
57. Richlyn F. Goddard, "Henceforth and Forever Free: The African American Press and Emancipation in the District of Columbia," in Elizabeth Clark-Lewis, ed., *First Freed: Washington, D.C., in the Emancipation Era* (Washington, D.C.: Howard University Press, 2002), 38–68; Foner, *Fiery Trial,* 198.
58. See A. Glenn Crothers, "The 1846 Retrocession of Alexandria," in Finkelman and Kennon, eds., *In the Shadow of Freedom,* 141–68.
59. David Taft Terry, "A Brief Moment in the Sun: The Aftermath of Emancipation in Washington, D.C., 1862–1869," in Clark-Lewis, ed., *First Freed,* 75.
60. Qtd. in Ernest B. Furgurson, *Freedom Rising: Washington in the Civil War* (New York: Random House, 2005), 170.

61. Qtd. in Furgurson, *Freedom Rising,* 171.

62. Qtd. in Horton and Horton, *Slavery and the Making of America,* 179.

63. Qtd. in Furgurson, *Freedom Rising,* 171.

64. Foner, *Fiery Trial,* 200–201; Clark-Lewis, ed., *First Freed,* 77.

65. 12 Statutes at Large 432, chap. 111

66. Ira Berlin et al., eds., *The Destruction of Slavery* (New York: Cambridge University Press, 1985), 268.

67. John Cimprich, *Slavery's End in Tennessee, 1861–1865* (University: University of Alabama Press, 1985), 100–101.

68. Ibid., 102–5.

69. David Williams, *Bitterly Divided: The South's Inner Civil War* (New York: New Press, 2008), 200; Benjamin Quarles, *The Negro in the Civil War* (1953; Boston: Da Capo Press, 1988), 180.

70. Jim Downs, *Sick from Freedom: African-American Illness and Suffering during the Civil War and Reconstruction* (Oxford, U.K.: Oxford University Press, 2012), 165.

71. Ibid., 7.

72. Ibid., 35, 163.

73. Qtd. in Emory M. Thomas, *The Confederate Nation 1861–1865* (New York: Harper Perennial, 1979), 291.

74. Bruce Levine, *Confederate Emancipation: Southern Plans to Free and Arm Slaves During the Civil War* (Oxford, U.K.: Oxford University Press, 2006), 116, 114.

75. Ibid., 113–17.

76. Qtd. in Thomas, *Confederate Nation,* 292.

14. Union Victory and the Thirteenth Amendment

1. Qtd. in Burlingame, *Abraham Lincoln* 2: 595.

2. Qtd. in Levine, *Fall of the House of Dixie,* 205–6; See also Douglas A. Blackmon, *Slavery by Another Name: The Re-Enslavement of Black Americans from the Civil War to World War II* (New York: Random House, 2009).

3. *Congressional Globe* 38th Congress 1st Session, 1489–90.

4. Ibid.,1490.

5. Ibid., 1490.

6. Ibid., 659.

7. Ibid., 660.

8. Donald Bruce Johnson, *National Party Platforms* (Urbana: University of Illinois Press, 1978), vol. 1: 35.

9. Qtd. in Donald, *Lincoln,* 554.

10. Steven Spielberg's masterful 2012 film, *Lincoln,* while taking some artistic liberties, brings to life this aspect of Lincoln's political genius and determination.

11. *Congressional Globe,* 38th Congress, 1st sess., 531.

12. Ibid.

13. John G. Nicolay and John Hay, *Abraham Lincoln: A History* (New York: Century Co., 1914), vol. 10: 87–88.

14. Henry Highland Garnet, "Let the Monster Perish," in *A Just and Lasting Peace: A Documentary History of Reconstruction,* ed. John David Smith (New York: Signet Classics, 2013), 42.
15. White, *A. Lincoln,* 670–71.
16. Nicolay and Hay, *Abraham Lincoln,* vol. 10: 89–90.

EPILOGUE

1. This gets even more intriguing (and embarrassing). After watching the Steven Spielberg film, *Lincoln,* a Mississippi professor did some historical research and discovered that the ratification process was not officially completed because the U.S. Archivist had never been notified of the Mississippi state legislature's ratification action in 1995. This paperwork omission was corrected, and the State of Mississippi officially went on record as having ratified the Thirteenth Amendment banning slavery as of February 7, 2013. (The Associated Press story was carried on February 18, 2013, by many newspapers as well as television news outlets.)
2. In Wright, ed. *African-American Experience,* 531–32.
3. Winston Churchill, "The End of the Beginning Speech," Nov. 10, 1942, qtd. in *Winston Churchill War Speeches,* comp. Charles Eade, 2nd ed. (London: Cassell, 1963–65), vol. 2: 343.

AFTERWORD TO THE SECOND EDITION

1. Douglas Blackmon, *Slavery by another Name: The Re-Enslavement of Black Americans from the Civil War to World War II.* (New York: Vintage Books, 2009), 3.
2. Henry Louis Gates and Donald Yacovone, *The African Americans: Many Rivers to Cross.* (Wolfesboro, NH: SmileyBooks, 2013), 189–90.
3. John Hope Franklin, *From Slavery to Freedom: A History of Negro Americans,* 5th edition. (New York: Alfred A. Knopf, 1980), 360.

Bibliography

Abbott, Richard H. *The Republican Party and the South, 1855–1877.* Chapel Hill: University of North Carolina, 1986.

Achenbach, Joel. *The Grand Idea: George Washington's Potomac and the Race to the West.* New York: Simon & Schuster, 2005.

Adams, John. *The Letters of John and Abigail Adams.* Ed. Frank Shuffelton. New York: Penguin Books, 2004.

Ahlstrom, Sydney E. *A Religious History of the American People.* New Haven, Conn.: Yale University Press, 1972.

American Baptist Home Mission Society. *Twelfth Annual Report of the American Baptist Home Mission Society.* New York: American Baptist Home Mission Rooms, 1844.

Applegate, Debby. *The Most Famous Man in America: The Biography of Henry Ward Beecher.* New York: Doubleday, 2006.

Armstrong, Orland Kay, and Marjorie M. Armstrong. *The Indomitable Baptists: A Narrative of Their Role in Shaping American History.* Garden City, N.Y.: Doubleday and Co., 1967.

Ayers, Edward L. and Martin, Carolyn R., eds. *America on the Eve of the Civil War.* Charlottesville: University of Virginia Press, 2010.

Bailyn, Bernard. *The Ideological Origins of the American Revolution.* Cambridge, Mass.: Harvard University Press, 1992.

———, ed. *Pamphlets of the American Revolution,* Cambridge, Mass.: Harvard University Press, 1965.

Baird, Robert. *Religion in the United States of America.* 1844. New York: Arno Press and New York Times, 1969.

Baker, Robert Andrew. *A Baptist Source Book.* Nashville: Broadman Press, 1966.

Balme, Joshua R. *American States, Churches, and Slavery.* New York: Negro Universities Press, 1969.

Baptist Magazine 37 (May 1845).

Baptist Memorial and Monthly Chronicle 3 (June 1844).

Baptist Memorial and Monthly Record 4 (May–July 1844).

Baptist Missionary Magazine 25 (Aug. 1845, Nov. 1845) and 26 (Jan. 1846).

Barnes, William Wright. *The Southern Baptist Convention, 1845–1953.* Nashville: Broadman Press, 1954.

Beeman, Richard. *Plain, Honest Men: The Making of the American Constitution.* New York: Random House, 2009.

Bell, Howard Holman. *A Survey of the Negro Convention Movement 1830–1861.* New York: Arno Press and New York Times, 1969.

Bennett, Lerone, Jr. *Forced Into Glory: Abraham Lincoln's White Dream.* Chicago: Johnson Publishing Co., 2007.

Berlin, Ira. *Many Thousands Gone: The First Two Centuries of Slavery in North America.* Cambridge, Mass.: Harvard University Press, 1998.

———. *Slaves without Masters: The Free Negro in the Antebellum South.* Oxford, U.K.: Oxford University Press, 1974.

———, et al., eds. *The Destruction of Slavery*. New York: Cambridge University Press, 1985.

———, Marc Favreau, and Steven F. Miller, eds. *Remembering Slavery: African Americans Talk About their Personal Experiences of Slavery and Emancipation*. New York: New Press, 1996.

———, and Leslie M. Harris, eds. *Slavery in New York*. New York: New Press, 2005.

Billington, Ray Allen. *Westward Expansion: A History of the American Frontier*. New York: MacMillan Publishing Co., 1974.

Blackmon, Douglas A. *Slavery by Another Name: The Re-Enslavement of Black Americans from the Civil War to World War II*. New York: Random House, 2009.

Blaisdell, Bob, ed. *Famous Documents and Speeches of the Civil War*. Mineola, N.Y.: Dover Publications, 2006.

Blanck, Emily. "Seventeen Eighty-three: The Turning Point in the Law of Slavery and Freedom in Massachusetts." *New England Quarterly* 75, no. 1 (Mar. 2002): 24–51.

Blight, David W. *Race and Reunion: The Civil War in American Memory*. Cambridge, Mass.: Harvard University Press, 2001.

Boyd, Jesse L. *A History of Baptists in America, Prior to 1845*. New York: American Press, 1957.

Braeman, John. *The Road to Independence: A Documentary History of the Causes of the American Revolution: 1763–1776*. New York: G. P. Putnam's Sons, 1963.

Brands, H. W. *The Age of Gold: The California Gold Rush and the New American Dream*. New York: Random House, 2002.

———. *The Man Who Saved the Union: Ulysses Grant in War and Peace*. New York: Random House, 2012.

Bridges, Kenneth. *Freedom In America*. Upper Saddle River, N.J.: Pearson Prentice Hall, 2008.

Broadie, Alexander, ed. *The Scottish Enlightenment: An Anthology*. Edinburgh, U.K.: Canongate Classics, 1997.

Broussard, James H. *The Southern Federalists, 1800–1816*. Baton Rouge: Louisiana State University Press, 1978.

Brown, Christopher Leslie. *Moral Capital: Foundations of British Abolitionism*. Chapel Hill: University of North Carolina Press, 2006.

Bruns, Roger, ed. *Am I Not a Man and a Brother? The Antislavery Crusade of Revolutionary America 1688–1788*. New York: Chelsea House Publishers, 1977.

Bryan, William Jennings, ed. *The World's Famous Orations*. 10 vols. New York: Funk and Wagnalls Co., [1906].

Buckley, J. M. *A History of Methodists in the United States*. New York: Charles Scribner's Sons, 1900.

Burlingame, Michael. *Abraham Lincoln: A Life*. 2 vols. Baltimore: Johns Hopkins University Press, 2008.

Burstein, Andrew, and Nancy Isenberg. *Madison and Jefferson*. New York: Random House, 2010.

Burton, Orville Vernon. *The Age of Lincoln*. New York: Hill and Wang, 2007.

Butler, Benjamin F. *Autobiography and Personal Reminiscences of Major-General Benj. F. Butler; Butler's Book.* Boston: A. M. Thayer, 1892.

Calhoun, John C. *The Papers of John C. Calhoun.* Ed. Robert L. Meriwether. 28 vols. Columbia: University of South Carolina Press, 1959–2003.

Calloway, Colin G., and Neal Salisbury, eds. *Reinterpreting New England Indians and the Colonial Experience.* Boston: Colonial Society of Massachusetts, 2003.

Carden, Allen. *Puritan Christianity in America: Religion and Life in Seventeenth-Century Massachusetts.* Grand Rapids, Mich.: Baker Book House, 1990.

Carlisle, Rodney P., general ed., *Life In America: The Colonial and Revolutionary Era.* New York: Infobase Publishing, 2010.

Castel, Albert E. *The Yeas and the Nays: Key Congressional Decisions, 1774–1945.* Kalamazoo, Mich.: New Issues Press, Western Michigan University, 1975.

Cecelski, David S. *The Fire of Freedom: Abraham Galloway and the Slaves' Civil War.* Chapel Hill: University of North Carolina Press, 2012.

Chadwick, Bruce. *Lincoln for President: An Unlikely Candidate, an Audacious Strategy, and the Victory No One Saw Coming.* Naperville, Ill.: Sourcebooks, 2009.

Chase, Salmon P. *Inside Lincoln's Cabinet; the Civil War diaries of Salmon P. Chase.* Ed. David Herbert Donald. New York: Longmans, Green and Co., 1954.

Christian Observatory 4 (Mar. 1850).

Cimprich, John. *Slavery's End in Tennessee, 1861–1865.* University: University of Alabama Press, 1985.

Clark-Lewis, Elizabeth, ed. *First Freed: Washington, D.C., in the Emancipation Era.* Washington, D.C.: Howard University Press, 2002.

Clay, Henry. *The Papers of Henry Clay.* Ed. James F. Hopkins. 11 vols. Lexington: University of Kentucky Press, 1959–92.

———. *The Private Correspondence of Henry Clay.* Ed. Calvin Colton, New York: A. S. Barnes & Co., 1856.

Cobb, James C. *Away Down South: A History of Southern Identity.* Oxford, U.K.: Oxford University Press, 2005.

Collier, Christopher, and James Lincoln Collier. *Decision in Philadelphia: the Constitutional Convention of 1787.* New York: Ballantine Books, 2007.

Commager, Henry Steele, ed. *The Defeat of the Confederacy: A Documentary Survey.* Princeton, N.J.: Van Nostrand, 1964.

Cooley, Henry Scofield. *A Study of Slavery in New Jersey.* Baltimore: Johns Hopkins University Press, 1896.

Cooper, William J. *We Have the War Upon Us: The Onset of the Civil War.* New York: Alfred A. Knopf, 2012.

———. *The South and the Politics of Slavery, 1828–1856.* Baton Rouge: University of Louisiana Press, 1973.

Craven, Avery O. *The Growth of Southern Nationalism 1848–1861.* Baton Rouge: University of Louisiana Press, 1953.

Curtis, Christopher M. "Can These Be the Sons of Their Fathers? The Defense of Slavery in Virginia, 1831–1832." Master's thesis, Virginia Polytechnic Institute, 1997.

Dattel, Gene. *Cotton and Race in the Making of America: The Human Costs of Economic Power.* Chicago: Ivan R. Dee, 2009.

Davis, David Brion. *Inhuman Bondage: The Rise and Fall of Slavery in the New World.* Oxford, U.K.: Oxford University Press, 2006.

Davis, Kenneth C. *A Nation Rising.* New York: HarperCollins, 2010.

Davis, William C. *Look Away! A History of the Confederate States of America.* New York: Free Press, 2002.

Deane, Charles. "Letters and Documents Relating to Slavery in Massachusetts." *Collections of the Massachusetts Historical Society.* Boston: The Society, 1877. Ser. 5, vol. 3: 373–442.

The Debate on the Constitution: Federalist and Antifederalist Speeches, Articles, and Letters during the Struggle over Ratification. 2 vols. New York: Viking Press, 1993.

Decision of the United States Circuit Court in the Case of the Methodist Episcopal Church, South vs the Methodist Episcopal Church, North, Pronounced by His Honor, Judge Nelson in the City of New York. San Francisco: Christian Observer, 1852.

Dershowitz, Alan. *America Declares Independence.* Hoboken, N.J.: John Wiley & Sons, 2003.

Dew, Charles B. *Apostles of Disunion: Southern Secession Commissioners and the Causes of the Civil War.* Charlottesville: University of Virginia Press, 2001.

Dickinson, John. *Letters from a Farmer in Pennsylvania.* Philadelphia, 1768. John Harvard Library, Pamphlet 23.

Donald, David Herbert. *Charles Sumner and the Coming of the Civil War.* 1960. Naperville, Ill.: Sourcebooks, 2009.

———. *Lincoln.* New York: Simon & Schuster, 1996.

Dorsey, Peter A. *Common Bondage: Slavery as Metaphor in Revolutionary America.* Knoxville: University of Tennessee Press, 2009.

Douglass, Frederick. *My Bondage and My Freedom.* 1855. Rpt. New York: Dover Publications, 1969.

———. *On Slavery and the Civil War: Selections from His Writings.* Ed. Philip S. Foner. 1945. Rpt. Mineola, N.Y.: Dover Publications, 2003.

Downs, Jim. *Sick from Freedom: African-American Illness and Suffering during the Civil War and Reconstruction.* Oxford, U.K.: Oxford University Press, 2012.

Du Bois, W. E. B. *The Suppression of the African Slave-Trade to the United States of America, 1638–1870.* 1896. Rpt. Mineola, N.Y.: Dover Publications, 1999.

Dwight, Theodore. *History of the Hartford Convention.* 1833. Rpt. New York: Da Capo Press, 1970.

Egerton, Douglas R. *Year of Meteors: Stephen Douglas, Abraham Lincoln, and the Election that Brought On the Civil War.* New York: Bloomsbury Press, 2010.

Elkins, Stanley M. *Slavery: A Problem in American Institutional and Intellectual Life.* 3rd ed. Chicago: University of Chicago Press, 1976.

Elliott, Charles. *Sinfulness of American Slavery: Proved from Its Evil Sources; Its Injustice; Its Wrongs; Its Contrariety to Many Scriptural Commands,*

Prohibitions, and Principles, and to the Christian Spirit; and from Its Evil
Effects; together with Observations on Emancipation, and the Duties of
American Citizens in Regard to Slavery. Ed. B. F. Tefft. 2 vols. New York:
Negro Universities Press, 1968.

Ellis, Joseph J. *American Creation: Triumphs and Tragedies at the Founding of
the Republic.* New York: Vintage Books, 2007.

———. *Founding Brothers: The Revolutionary Generation.* New York: Alfred A.
Knopf, 2001.

Emerson, Ralph Waldo. *The Complete Works of Ralph Waldo Emerson, with
a Biographical Introduction and Notes by Edward Waldo Emerson, and a
General Index.* 12 vols. Boston: Houghton, Mifflin and Co., 1903–4.

Engs, Robert F. and Randall M. Miller, eds. *The Birth of the Grand Old Party:
The Republicans' First Generation.* Philadelphia: University of Pennsylvania
Press, 2002.

Equiano, Olaudah. *The Interesting Narrative of the Life of Olaudah Equiano.*
Ed. Robert J. Allison. 1794. Boston: St. Martin's, 2007.

Essah, Patience. *A House Divided: Slavery and Emancipation in Delaware, 1638–
1865.* Charlottesville: University Press of Virginia, 1996.

Etcheson, Nicole. *Bleeding Kansas: Contested Liberty in the Civil War Era.*
Lawrence: University Press of Kansas, 2004.

Farrand, Max, ed. *The Records of the Federal Convention of 1787.* 4 vols. 1937.
Rev. ed. New Haven, Conn.: Yale University Press, 1966.

Farrow, Anne, Joel Lang, and Jennifer Frank. *Complicity: How the North
Promoted, Prolonged, and Profited from Slavery.* New York: Random House,
2005.

Fehrenbacher, Don E. *The Slaveholding Republic: An Account of the United
States Government's Relations to Slavery.* Ed. and completed by Ward M.
McAfee. Oxford, U.K.: Oxford University Press, 2001.

Ferling, John. *Almost a Miracle: The American Victory in the War of
Independence.* Oxford, U.K.: Oxford University Press, 2007.

Finkelman, Paul. *Defending Slavery: Proslavery Thought in the Old South: A
Brief History with Documents.* Boston: Bedford/St. Martin's, 2003.

———. *Slavery and the Founders: Race and Liberty in the Age of Jefferson.*
Armonk, N.Y.: M. E. Sharpe, Inc., 2001.

———, and Donald R. Kennon, eds.. *In the Shadow of Freedom: The Politics of
Freedom in the National Capital.* Athens: Ohio University Press, 2011.

Fischer, David Hackett. *Albion's Seed: Four British Folkways in America.* New
York: Oxford University Press, 1989.

Fleming, Thomas. *The Perils of Peace: America's Struggle for Survival After
Yorktown.* New York: HarperCollins, 2007.

Fletcher, John. *Studies on Slavery, in Easy Lessons: Compiled into Eight Studies,
and Subdivided into Short Lessons for the Convenience of Readers.* 1852.
Miami: Mnemosyne Pub. Co., 1969.

Fliegelman, Jay. *Declaring Independence: Jefferson, Natural language, and the
Culture of Performance.* Palo Alto, Calif.: Stanford University Press, 1993.

Flood, Charles Bracelen. *1864—Lincoln at the Gates of History.* New York:
Simon & Schuster, 2009.

Fogel, Robert William. *Without Consent or Contract: The Rise and Fall of American Slavery*. 1991. New York: W. W. Norton & Co., 1994.

———, and Stanley L. Engerman. *Time on the Cross: The Economics of American Negro Slavery*. 1989. New York: W. W. Norton & Co., 1995.

Foner, Eric. *The Fiery Trial: Abraham Lincoln and American Slavery*. New York: W. W. Norton, 2010.

———. *Forever Free: the Story of Emancipation and Reconstruction*. New York: Alfred A. Knopf, 2005.

———. *Free Soil, Free Labor, Free Men: The Ideology of the Republican Party Before the Civil War*. 1970. Oxford, U.K.: Oxford University Press, 1995.

———. *Reconstruction: America's Unfinished Revolution, 1863–1877*. New York: HarperCollins, 1989.

———, ed. *Our Lincoln: New Perspectives on Lincoln and His World*. New York: W. W. Norton & Company, 2008.

Foote, Shelby. *The Civil War: A Narrative: Red River to Appomattox*. New York: Vintage Books: Random House, 1974.

Foreman, Amanda. *A World on Fire: Britain's Crucial Role in the American Civil War*. New York: Random House, 2010.

Foster, Stephen. *Their Solitary Way: The Puritan Social Ethic in the First Century of Settlement in New England*. New Haven, Conn.: Yale University Press, 1971.

Fox-Genovese, Elizabeth, and Eugene D. Genovese. *The Mind of the Master Class: History and Faith in the Southern Slaveholder's Worldview*. Cambridge, U.K.: Cambridge University Press, 2005.

Franklin, John Hope. *From Slavery to Freedom: A History of Negro Americans*. 5th ed. New York: Alfred A. Knopf, 1980.

———, and Loren Schweninger. *Runaway Slaves: Rebels on the Plantation*. Oxford, U.K.: Oxford University Press, 1999.

Freehling, William W., *The Road to Disunion*. 2 vols. New York: Oxford University Press, 1990.

———, and Craig M. Simpson, eds. *Secession Debated: Georgia's Showdown in 1860*. New York: Oxford University Press, 1992.

Fuller, Richard, *Domestic Slavery Considered as a Scriptural Institution: In a Correspondence between the Rev. Richard Fuller, of Beaufort, S.C., and the Rev. Francis Wayland, of Providence, R.I.* New York: Lewis Colby, 1845.

Furgurson, Ernest B. *Freedom Rising: Washington in the Civil War*. New York: Random House, 2005.

Gallagher, Gary W. *The Union War*. Cambridge, Mass.: Harvard University Press, 2011.

Gammell, William, *A History of American Baptist Missions in Asia, Africa, Europe, and North America*. Boston: Gould, Kendall and Lincoln, 1849.

Gellman, David N. *Emancipating New York: The Politics of Slavery and Freedom 1777–1827*. Baton Rouge: University of Louisiana Press, 2006.

General Conference of the Mennonite Brethren Churches. *Worship Together*. Published for the Mennonite Brethren Churches, Fresno, Calif., by the Christian Press, 1995.

Genovese, Eugene D. *The Political Economy of Slavery: Studies in the Economy and Society of the Slave South*. New York: Pantheon, 1965.

————. *Roll, Jordan, Roll: the World the Slaves Made.* New York: Random House, 1976.

Gienapp, William E. *Abraham Lincoln and Civil War America: A Biography.* Oxford, U.K.: Oxford University Press, 2002.

————. *The Origins of the Republican Party 1852–1856.* New York: Oxford University Press, 1987.

Goldfield, David. *America Aflame: How the Civil War Created a Nation.* New York: Bloomsbury Press, 2011.

Goldstone, Lawrence. *Dark Bargain: Slavery, Profits, and the Struggle for the Constitution.* New York: Walker & Co., 2005.

Goodell, William. *Slavery and Anti-Slavery: A History of the Great Struggle in Both Hemispheres; With a View of the Slavery Question in the United States.* New York: Negro Universities Press, 1968.

Goodheart, Adam. *1861: The Civil War Awakening.* New York: Alfred A. Knopf, 2011.

Goodwin, Doris Kearns. *Team of Rivals: The Political Genius of Abraham Lincoln.* New York: Simon & Schuster, 2005.

Greene, Lorenzo Johnston, *The Negro in Colonial New England, 1620–1776.* New York: Columbia University Press, 1942.

Guelzo, Allen C. *Lincoln and Douglas: The Debates that Defined America.* New York: Simon & Schuster, 2008.

Gura, Philip F. *American Transcendentalism: A History.* New York: Hill and Wang, 2007.

Gwynne, S. C. *Empire of the Summer Moon.* New York: Scribner, 2010.

Hamburger, Joseph. *John Stuart Mill on Liberty and Control.* Princeton, N.J.: Princeton University Press, 1999.

Hammond, James Henry. *Secret and Sacred: The Diaries of James Henry Hammond, a Southern Slaveholder.* Ed. Carol Bleser. Columbia: University of South Carolina Press, 1997.

Hammond, John Craig. *Slavery, Freedom, and Expansion in the Early American West.* Charlottesville: University of Virginia Press, 2007.

————, and Matthew Mason, eds. *Contesting Slavery: The Politics of Bondage and Freedom in the New American Nation.* Charlottesville: University of Virginia Press, 2011.

Hancock, Harold Bell. *Delaware During the Civil War: A Political History.* Wilmington: Historical Society of Delaware, 1961.

Hanna, Charles W. *African American Recipients of the Medal of Honor: A Biographical Dictionary, Civil War through Vietnam War.* Jefferson, N.C.: McFarland & Co., 2002.

Hardin, David. *After the War: The Lives and Images of Major Civil War Figures After the Shooting Stopped.* Chicago: Ivan R. Dee, 2010.

Harris, Norman Dwight. *The History of Negro Servitude in Illinois, and of the Slavery Agitation in That State, 1719–1864.* Chicago: A. C. McClurg & Co., 1904.

Harris, William C. *Lincoln and the Border States: Preserving the Union.* Lawrence: University Press of Kansas, 2011.

Harrold, Stanley. *Border War: Fighting Over Slavery before the Civil War.* Chapel Hill: University of North Caroline Press, 2010.

Havers, Grant N. *Lincoln and the Politics of Christian Love.* Columbia: University of Missouri Press, 2009.

Haynes, Sam W. *Unfinished Revolution: The Early American Republic in a British World.* Charlottesville: University of Virginia Press, 2010.

Haynes, Stephen R. *Noah's Curse: The Biblical Justification of American Slavery.* Oxford, U.K.: Oxford University Press, 2002.

Heidler, David S., and Jeanne T. Heidler. *Henry Clay: The Essential American.* New York: Random House, 2010.

Helper, Hinton Rowan. *The Impending Crisis of the South: How to Meet It.* 1857. Memphis: General Books, 2010.

Herndon, William Henry. *Herndon's Lincoln: The True Story of a Great Life . . . The History and Personal Recollections of Abraham Lincoln.* 3 vols. Chicago: Belford Clarke & Co., 1889.

Hodges, Graham Russell, *Root and Branch: African Americans in New York and East Jersey, 1613–1863.* Chapel Hill: University of North Carolina Press, 1999.

Holt, Michael F. *The Political Crisis of the 1850s.* New York: John Wiley & Sons, 1978.

Holt, Thomas C. *Children of Fire: A History of African Americans.* New York: Hill and Wang, 2010.

Holzer, Harold. *Lincoln at Cooper Union: The Speech That Made Abraham Lincoln President.* New York: Simon & Schuster, 2004.

———. *Lincoln President-Elect: Abraham Lincoln and the Great Secession Winter 1860–1861.* New York: Simon & Schuster, 2008.

Horton, James Oliver, and Lois E. Horton. *Hard Road to Freedom: The Story of African America.* New Brunswick, N.J.: Rutgers University Press, 2001.

———. *Slavery and the Making of America.* Oxford, U.K.: Oxford University Press, 2005.

Hosmer, William. *The Higher Law, in Its Relation to Civil Government with Particular Reference to Slavery and the Fugitive Slave Law.* New York: Negro Universities Press, 1969.

Howe, Daniel Walker. *What Hath God Wrought: The Transformation of America, 1815–1848.* Oxford, U.K.: Oxford University Press, 2007.

Hudson, Winthrop S. *Religion in America.* 3rd ed. New York: Charles Scribner's Sons, 1981.

Hutson, James H. *Supplement to Max Farrand's The Records of the Federal Convention of 1787.* New Haven, Conn.: Yale University Press, 1987.

Jackson, Donald. *Thomas Jefferson and the Rocky Mountains: Exploring the West from Monticello.* Norman: University of Oklahoma Press, 1993.

Jackson, Maurice. *Let This Voice Be Heard: Anthony Benezet, Father of Atlantic Abolitionism.* Philadelphia: University of Pennsylvania Press, 2009.

Jacobs, Harriet Ann. *Incidents in the Life of a Slave Girl Written by Herself.* 1861. Lexington, KY: Simon & Brown, 2012.

Jefferson, Thomas. *Notes on the State of Virginia.* Ed. Frank Shuffelton, New York: Penguin Books, 1999.

———. *The Papers of Thomas Jefferson.* Ed. Julian P. Boyd. 37 vols. Princeton, N.J.: Princeton University Press, 1950–2009.

Jenkins, Sally, and John Stauffer. *The State of Jones: The Small Southern County that Seceded from the Confederacy*. New York: Random House, 2010.

Jenkins, William Sumner. *Pro-slavery Thought in the Old South*. Chapel Hill: University of North Carolina Press, 1935.

Jensen, Merrill, ed. *Tracts of the American Revolution 1763–1776*. Indianapolis: Bobbs-Merrill, 1967.

Johnson, Charles, and Patricia Smith. *Africans in America: America's Journey through Slavery*. New York: Harcourt, 1998.

Johnson, Donald Bruce, comp. *National Party Platforms*. 2 vols. Rev. ed. Urbana: University of Illinois Press, 1978.

Johnson, Michael P. "Denmark Versey and His Co-Conspirators." *William and Mary Quarterly*, 3rd ser., vol. 58, no. 4 (Oct. 2001): 915–76.

———. *Toward a Patriarchal Republic: The Secession of Georgia*. Baton Rouge: Louisiana State University Press, 1977.

Johnson, Samuel. *The Works of Samuel Johnson*. Vol. 10. *Political Writings*. Edited by Donald J. Greene. New Haven, Conn.: Yale University Press, 1977.

Johnson, Walter. *River of Dark Dreams: Slavery and Empire in the Cotton Kingdom*. Cambridge, Mass.: Harvard University Press, 2013.

Jordan, Don, and Michael Walsh. *White Cargo: the Forgotten History of Britain's White Slaves in America*. New York: New York University Press, 2007.

Jordan, Winthrop D. *White Over Black: American Attitudes Toward the Negro, 1550–1812*. New York: Pelican Books, 1969.

Kammen, Michael, ed. *The Origins of the American Constitution: A Documentary History*. New York: Penguin Books, 1986.

Kaplan, Sidney, and Emma N. Kaplan *The Black Presence in the Era of the American Revolution*. Amherst: University of Massachusetts Press, 1989.

Keegan, John. *The American Civil War*. New York: Random House, 2009.

Kidd, Thomas S. *God of Liberty: A Religious History of the American Revolution*. New York: Basic Books, 2010.

Kline, Michael J. *The Baltimore Plot: The First Conspiracy to Assassinate Abraham Lincoln*. Yardley, Pa.: Westholme Publishing, 2008.

Kluger, Richard. *Seizing Destiny: The Relentless Expansion of American Territory*. New York: Random House, 2008.

Kolchin, Peter. *American Slavery: 1619–1877*. Rev. ed. New York: Hill and Wang, 2003.

Krannawitter, Thomas L. *Vindicating Lincoln: Defending the Politics of our Greatest President*. Lanham, Md.: Rowman & Littlefield, 2008.

Kukla, Jon. *A Wilderness So Immense: The Louisiana Purchase and the Destiny of America*. New York: Random House, 2003.

Lane, Ann J., ed. *The Debate Over Slavery: Stanley Elkins and His Critics*. Urbana: University of Illinois Press, 1971.

Langguth, A. J. *Driven West: Andrew Jackson and the Trail of Tears to the Civil War*. New York: Simon & Schuster, 2010.

———. *Union 1812: The Americans who Fought the Second War of Independence*. New York: Simon & Schuster, 2006.

Lankford, Nelson D. *Richmond Burning: The Last Days of the Confederate Capital*. New York: Viking, 2002.

Larsen, Edward J. and Winship, Michael P. *The Constitutional Convention: A Narrative History from the Notes of James Madison.* New York: Random House, 2005.

Larson, John Lauritz. *The Market Revolution in America: Liberty, Ambition, and the Eclipse of the Common Good.* Cambridge, U.K.: Cambridge University Press, 2010.

Lawrence, John B. *History of the Home Mission Board.* Nashville: Broadman Press, 1958.

Lee, Luther. *Slavery Examined in the Light of the Bible.* Syracuse, N.Y.: Wesleyan Methodist Book Room, 1855.

Lehman, Christopher P. *Slavery in the Upper Mississippi Valley, 1787–1865.* Jefferson, N.C.: McFarland & Co., 2011.

Lehrman, Lewis E. *Lincoln at Peoria: The Turning Point.* Mechanicsburg, Pa.: Stackpole Books, 2008.

Levine, Bruce. *Confederate Emancipation: Southern Plans to Free and Arm Slaves During the Civil War.* Oxford, U.K.: Oxford University Press, 2006.

———. *The Fall of the House of Dixie: The Civil War and the Social Revolution That Transformed the South.* New York: Random House, 2013.

———. *Half Slave and Half Free: The Roots of Civil War.* Rev. ed. New York: Hill and Wang, 2005.

Liberator (Boston, Mass.). Sept. 24, 1843; May 17, 1844; June 14, 1844.

Lillback, Peter A. *George Washington's Sacred Fire.* Bryn Mawr, Pa.: Providence Forum Press, 2006.

Lincoln, Abraham. *Abraham Lincoln, Slavery, and the Civil War: Selected Writings and Speeches.* Ed. Michael P. Johnson. Boston: St. Martin's, 2001.

———. *Collected Works.* Ed. Roy P. Basler, Marion Delores Pratt, and Lloyd A. Dunlap. 9 vols. New Brunswick, N.J.: Rutgers University Press, 1953–55.

———. *The Lincoln-Douglas Debates: Abraham Lincoln and Stephen A. Douglas.* Ed. Robert W. Johannsen. Mineola, N.Y.: Dover Publications, 2004.

———, and Stephen A. Douglas. *The Lincoln-Douglas Debates of 1858.* Ed. Robert W. Johannsen. New York: Oxford University Press, 1965.

Litwack, Leon F. *North of Slavery: The Negro in the Free States, 1790–1860.* Chicago: University of Chicago Press, 1961.

Locke, John. *The Second Treatise of Government.* Vol. 4. Edited by Thomas P. Peardon. 1689. New York: Liberal Arts Press, [c. 1952].

Lockridge, Kenneth A. *A New England Town: The First Hundred Years: Dedham, Massachusetts, 1636–1736.* New York: Norton, 1970.

Loewen, James W., and Edward H. Sebesta, eds. *The Confederate and Neo-Confederate Reader: The "Great Truth" about the "Lost Cause."* Jackson: University Press of Mississippi, 2010.

Lubet, Steven. *Fugitive Justice: Runaways, Rescuers, and Slavery on Trial.* Cambridge, Mass.: Harvard University Press, 2010.

Luthin, Reinhard H. *The First Lincoln Campaign.* Cambridge, Mass.: Harvard University Press, 1944.

Madison, James. *The Constitutional Convention: A Narrative History from the Notes of James Madison.* Ed. Edward J. Larson and Michael P. Winship. New York: Modern Library, 2005.

Maier, Pauline. *American Scripture: The Making of the Declaration of Independence.* New York: Vintage Books, 1998.

———. *Ratification: The People Debate the Constitution, 1787–1788.* New York: Simon & Schuster, 2010.

Maltz, Earl M. *Slavery and the Supreme Court, 1825–1861.* Lawrence: University Press of Kansas, 2009.

Marable, Manning, and Leith Mullings, eds. *Let Nobody Turn Us Around: Voices of Resistance, Reform, and Renewal: An African American Anthology.* Lanham, Md.: Rowman and Littlefield, 2000.

Martin, Thomas Ricaud, ed. *The Great Parliamentary Battle and Farewell Addresses of the Southern Senators on the Eve of the Civil War.* New York: Neale Publishing Co., 1905.

Marty, Martin E. *Righteous Empire: The Protestant Experience in America.* New York: Harper and Row, 1970.

Mason, Matthew. *Slavery and Politics in the Early American Republic.* Chapel Hill: University of North Carolina Press, 2006.

Masur, Louis P. *The Civil War: A Concise History.* Oxford, U.K.: Oxford University Press, 2011.

Mathews, Donald G. *Slavery and Methodism: A Chapter in American Morality, 1780–1845.* Princeton, N.J.: Princeton University Press, 1965.

Matlack, Lucius C. *The Antislavery Struggle and Triumph in the Methodist Episcopal Church.* New York: Negro Universities Press, 1969.

———. *The History of American Slavery and Methodism, from 1780 to 1849; and History of the Wesleyan Methodist Connection of America.* New York: 1849.

May, Gary. *John Tyler.* New York: Henry Holt and Co., 2008.

May, S. J. "The Liberty Bell Is Not of the Liberty Party." *The Liberty Bell.* Boston: Massachusetts Anti-Slavery Fair, 1845. 159–63.

Mayer, Henry. *All on Fire: William Lloyd Garrison and the Abolition of Slavery.* New York: W. W. Norton & Co., 1998.

McClintock, Russell. *Lincoln and the Decision for War: The Northern Response to Secession.* Chapel Hill: University of North Carolina Press, 2008.

McCurry, Stephanie. *Confederate Reckoning: Power and Politics in the Civil War South.* Cambridge, Mass.: Harvard University Press, 2010.

McGlone, Robert E. *John Brown's War against Slavery.* Cambridge, U.K.: Cambridge University Press, 2009.

McLynn, Frank. *Wagons West: The Epic Story of America's Overland Trails.* New York: Grove Press, 2002.

McManus, Edgar J. *Black Bondage in the North.* Syracuse, N.Y.: Syracuse University Press, 1973.

———. *A History of Negro Slavery in New York.* Syracuse, N.Y.: Syracuse University Press, 1966.

McPherson, James M. *Battle Cry of Freedom: The Civil War Era.* Oxford, U.K.: Oxford University Press, 1988.

———. *This Mighty Scourge: Perspectives on the Civil War.* Oxford, U.K.: Oxford University Press, 2009.

———. *Tried by War: Abraham Lincoln as Commander in Chief.* New York: Penguin Books, 2008.

———. *What They Fought For, 1861–1865.* New York: Random House, 1995.

———, et al. *Blacks in America: Bibliographical Essays.* New York: Doubleday & Co., 1971.

Meacham, Jon. *American Gospel: God, the Founding Fathers, and the Making of a Nation.* New York: Random House, 2006.

———. *American Lion: Andrew Jackson in the White House.* New York: Random House, 2008.

Melish, Joanne Pope. *Disowning Slavery: Gradual Emancipation and "Race" in New England, 1780–1860.* Ithaca, N.Y.: Cornell University Press, 1998.

Merriam, Edmund Franklin. *A History of American Baptist Missions.* Philadelphia: American Baptist Publication Society, 1900.

Merry, Robert W. *A Country of Vast Designs: James K. Polk, the Mexican War, and the Conquest of the American Continent.* New York: Simon & Schuster, 2009.

Methodist Episcopal Church. *Journals of the General Conference of the Methodist Episcopal Church.* Vol. 2: *1840–44.* Vol. 3: *1848–1856.* New York: Carlton & Lanahan, 1844, 1856.

Miller, William Lee. *Arguing About Slavery: John Quincy Adams and the Great Battle in the United States Congress.* New York: Random House, 1996.

———. *Lincoln's Virtues: An Ethical Biography.* New York: Alfred A. Knopf, 2007.

Morgan, Edmund S. *American Slavery, American Freedom: The Ordeal of Colonial Virginia.* New York: Norton, 1975.

———. *The Birth of the Republic, 1763–89.* 3rd ed. Chicago: University of Chicago Press, 1992.

Morris, Richard B. *The Forging of the Union.* New York: Harper and Row, 1987.

Morris, Roy, Jr. *The Long Pursuit: Abraham Lincoln's Thirty-Year Struggle with Stephen Douglas for the Heart and Soul of America.* New York: HarperCollins, 2008.

Morrow, Ralph E. "The Pro-Slavery Argument Revisited." *Mississippi Valley Historical Review* 48 (June 1961): 79–94.

Napolitano, Andrew P. *Dred Scott's Revenge: A Legal History of Race and Freedom in America.* Nashville: Thomas Nelson, 2009.

Nash, Gary B. *Freedom By Degrees: Emancipation in Pennsylvania and Its Aftermath.* New York: Oxford University Press, 1991.

———. *Race and Revolution.* Madison, Wis.: Madison House Publishers, 1990.

Neely, Mark E. *The Last Best Hope of Earth: Abraham Lincoln and the Promise of America.* Cambridge, Mass.: Harvard University Press, 1993.

Nelson, Scott, and Carol Sheriff. *A People at War: Civilians and Soldiers in America's Civil War, 1854–1877.* New York: Oxford University Press, 2008.

Newman, Albert Henry. *A History of the Baptist Churches in the United States.* New York: Christian Literature Co., 1894.

Newman, Richard S. *The Transformation of American Abolitionism: Fighting Slavery in the Early Republic.* Chapel Hill: University of North Carolina Press, 2002.

Nicolay, John G., and John Hay. *Abraham Lincoln: A History.* 10 vols. 1890. New York: Century Co., 1914.

Nieman, Donald G. *Promises to Keep: African Americans and the Constitutional Order, 1776 to the Present.* New York: Oxford University Press, 1991.

Nolan, Alan T. *Lee Considered: General Robert E. Lee and Civil War History.* Chapel Hill: University of North Carolina Press, 1991.

Northup, Solomon. *Twelve Years a Slave. Narrative of Solomon Northup, a Citizen of New-York, Kidnapped in Washington City in 1841 and Rescued in 1853 From a Cotton Plantation near the Red River in Louisiana.* Auburn, NY: Derby and Miller, 1853.

Oakes, James. *Freedom National: The Destruction of Slavery in the United States, 1861–1865.* New York: W. W. Norton & Co., 2013.

———. *The Radical and the Republican: Frederick Douglass, Abraham Lincoln, and the Triumph of Antislavery Politics.* New York: W. W. Norton, 2007.

———. *Slavery and Freedom: An Interpretation of the Old South.* New York: W. W. Norton & Co., 1990.

Peck, George, ed. "Religion in America." *Methodist Quarterly Review* (Oct. 1845): 485–503.

Peck, J. T. "General Conference of 1844." *Methodist Quarterly Review* (Apr. 1870): 165–88.

Perman, Michael. *Emancipation and Reconstruction, 1862–1879.* Arlington Heights, Ill.: Harlan Davidson, 1987.

Petersen, Svend, *A Statistical History of the American Presidential Elections.* New York: Ungar, 1963.

Phillips, Kevin. *The Cousins' War: Religion, Politics, and the Triumph of Anglo-America.* New York: Basic Books, 1999.

Porter, James, "General Conference of 1844." *Methodist Quarterly Review* (Apr. 1871): 234–50.

Potter, David M. *The Impending Crisis, 1848–1861.* New York: Harper & Row, 1976.

Pratt, Julius William. *Expansionists of 1812.* New York: P. Smith, 1949.

Puleo, Stephen. *The Caning: The Assault that Drove America to Civil War.* Yardley, Pa.: Westholme Publishing, 2012.

Quarles, Benjamin. *Black Abolitionists.* New York: Oxford University Press, 1969.

———. *The Negro in the American Revolution.* Chapel Hill: University of North Carolina Press, 1996.

———. *The Negro in the Civil War.* 1953. Boston: Da Capo Press, 1988.

———. *The Negro in the Making of America.* 3rd ed. New York: Simon and Schuster, 1987.

Ramsay, David. *The History of the American Revolution.* Ed. Lester H. Cohen. 2 vols. Indianapolis: Liberty Classics, 1990.

Rasmussen, Daniel. *American Uprising: The Untold Story of America's Largest Slave Revolt.* New York: HarperCollins, 2011.

Rediker, Marcus. *The Amistad Rebellion: An Atlantic Odyssey of Slavery and Freedom.* New York: Viking Penguin, 2012.

Remini, Robert V. *At the Edge of the Precipice: Henry Clay and the Compromise That Saved the Union.* New York: Basic Books, 2010.

Reynolds, David S. *Mightier than the Sword: Uncle Tom's Cabin and the Battle for America.* New York: W. W. Norton & Co., 2011.

Rice, David. *Slavery Inconsistent with Justice and Good Policy*. 1792. Rpt. New York: Arno Press, 1969.

Richards, Leonard L. *The California Gold Rush and the Coming of the Civil War*. New York: Alfred A. Knopf, 2007.

———. *The Slave Power: The Free North and Southern Domination 1780–1860*. Baton Rouge: Louisiana State University Press, 2000.

Roediger, David, and Martin H. Blatt. *The Meaning of Slavery in the North*. New York: Garland Publishing, 1998.

Ross, Frederick Augustus. *Slavery Ordained of God*. New York: Negro Universities Press, 1969.

Ruchames, Louis, *A John Brown Reader; The Story of John Brown in His Own Words, in the Words of Those Who Knew Him, and in the Poetry and Prose of the Literary Heritage*. New York: Abelard-Schuman, 1959.

Rugemer, Edward Bartlett. *The Problem of Emancipation: The Caribbean Roots of the American Civil War*. Baton Rouge: Louisiana State University Press, 2008.

Russo, Peggy A., and Paul Finkelman, eds. *Terrible Swift Sword: The Legacy of John Brown*. Athens: Ohio University Press, 2005.

Sandburg, Carl. *Abraham Lincoln: The Prairie Years and the War Years*. 1954. New York: Sterlin Publishing, 2011.

Sawyer, George S. *Southern Institutes or, An inquiry into the Origin and Early Prevalence of Slavery and the Slave-Trade . . . with Notes and Comments in Defence of the Southern Institutions*. New York: Negro Universities Press, 1969.

Schama, Simon. *The American Future: A History*. New York: HarperCollins, 2009.

———. *Rough Crossings: Britain, the Slaves, and the American Revolution*. New York: HarperCollins, 2006.

Sellers, Charles, Jr. *The Market Revolution: Jacksonian America, 1815–1846*. New York: Oxford University Press, 1991.

———. "The Travail of Slavery." In *National Development and Sectional Crisis*, comp. Silbey. 119–145.

Silbey, Joel H., comp. *National Development and Sectional Crisis, 1815–1860*. New York, Random House, 1970.

Simon, James F. *Lincoln and Chief Justice Taney: Slavery, Secession, and the President's War Powers*. New York: Simon & Schuster, 2006.

Sinha, Manisha, and Penny Von Eschen, eds. *Contested Democracy: Freedom, Race and Power in American Democracy*. New York: Columbia University Press, 2007.

Smith, John David, ed. *A Just and Lasting Peace: A Documentary History of Reconstruction*. New York: Signet Classics, 2013.

Smith, Timothy Lawrence. *Revivalism and Social Reform in Mid-Nineteenth-Century America*. New York: Abingdon Press, 1957.

Snyder, Christina. *Slavery in Indian Country: The Changing Face of Captivity in Early America*. Cambridge, Mass.: Harvard University Press, 2010.

Soderlund, Jean R. *Quakers and Slavery: A Divided Spirit*. Princeton, N.J.: Princeton University Press, 1985.

Stampp, Kenneth M. *The Peculiar Institution: Slavery in the Ante-Bellum South*. New York: Random House, 1956.

———, ed. *The Causes of the Civil War*. 3rd ed. New York: Simon & Schuster, 1991.

Stanton, Henry B., ed. *Debate at the Lane Seminary, Cincinnati. Speech of James A. Thome, of Kentucky, Delivered at the Annual Meeting of the American Anti-slavery Society, May 6, 1834. Letter of the Rev. Dr. Samuel H. Cox, against the American Colonization Society*. Boston: Garrison & Knapp, 1834.

Stanton, Lucia. *"Those Who Labor for My Happiness": Slavery at Thomas Jefferson's Monticello*. Charlottesville: University of Virginia Press, 2012.

Stauffer, John. *Giants: The Parallel Lives of Frederick Douglass and Abraham Lincoln*. New York: Hachette Book Group, 2008.

Stewart, David O. *The Summer of 1787: The Men who Invented the Constitution*. New York: Simon & Schuster, 2007.

Stewart, James Brewer. *Abolitionist Politics and the Coming of the Civil War*. Amherst: University of Massachusetts Press, 2008.

———. *Holy Warriors: The Abolitionists and American Slavery*. Rev. ed. New York: Hill and Wang, 1996.

Stoker, Donald. *The Grand Design: Strategy and the U.S. Civil War*. Oxford, U.K.: Oxford University Press, 2010.

Sweet, William Warren. *Methodism in American History*. New York: Methodist Book Concern, 1933.

Takaki, Ronald. *A Different Mirror: A History of Multicultural America*. New York: Back Bay Books, 2008.

———. *A Larger Memory: A History of Our Diversity, with Voices*. Boston: Little, Brown, and Co., 1998.

Tate, Adam L. "Confronting Abolitionism: Bishop John England, American Catholicism, and Slavery." *Journal of the Historical Society* 9, no. 3 (Sept. 2009): 373–404.

Taylor, Alan. *The Civil War of 1812: American Citizens, British Subjects, Irish Rebels, and Indian Allies*. New York: Random House, 2011.

Taylor, William R. *Cavalier and Yankee: The Old South and American National Character*. New York: George Braziller, 1961.

Thomas, Emory M. *The Confederate Nation: 1861–1865*. 1979. New York: HarperCollins, 2011.

Thornton, Thomas C. *An Inquiry into the History of Slavery; Its Introduction into the United States, Causes of Its Continuance, and Remarks upon the Abolition Tracts of William E. Channing*. 1841. Rpt. Detroit: Negro History Press, 1969.

Tocqueville, Alexis de. *Democracy in America*. Ed. Phillips Bradley. 2 vols. New York: A. A. Knopf, 1989.

Torbet, Robert G. *A History of the Baptists*. Rev. ed. Valley Forge, Pa.: Judson Press 1963.

———. *Venture of Faith: The Story of the American Baptist Foreign Mission Society and the Woman's American Baptist Foreign Mission Society, 1814–1954*. Philadelphia: Judson Press, 1955.

Townsend, William H. *Lincoln and the Bluegrass: Slavery and Civil War in Kentucky*. Lexington: University of Kentucky Press, 1955.

Trexler, Harrison Anthony. *Slavery in Missouri, 1804–1865*. Baltimore: Johns Hopkins Press, 1914.

Turner, Frederick Jackson. *The Frontier in American History*. New York: Barnes & Noble, 2009.

Twombley, Robert C., and Robert H. Moore. "Black Puritan: The Negro in Seventeenth-Century Massachusetts." *William and Mary Quarterly* 24 (Apr. 1967): 224–42.

Unger, Harlow Giles. *Lion of Liberty: Patrick Henry and the Call to a New Nation*. Cambridge, Mass.: Da Capo Press, 2010.

U.S. Continental Congress. *Journals of the Continental Congress, 1774–1789*. Ed. Worthington Chauncey Ford. 34 vols. New York: Johnson Reprint Corp., 1968.

U.S. National Park Service, Division of Publications. *Underground Railroad*. Washington, D.C.: Dept. of the Interior, 1998.

Van Cleve, George William. *A Slaveholders' Union: Slavery, Politics, and the Constitution in the Early American Republic*. Chicago: University of Chicago Press, 2010.

Varon, Elizabeth R. *Disunion! The Coming of the American Civil War, 1789–1859*. Chapel Hill: University of North Carolina Press, 2008.

Wagandt, Charles. *The Mighty Revolution: Negro Emancipation in Maryland, 1862–1864*. Baltimore: Maryland Historical Society, 2004.

Wagner, Margaret E., Gary W. Gallagher, and Paul Finkelman, eds. *The Library of Congress Civil War Desk Reference*. New York: Simon & Schuster, 2002.

Waldstreicher, David. *Slavery's Constitution*. New York: Hill and Wang, 2009.

Walker, David. *David Walker's Appeal, in Four Articles, together with a Preamble, to the Coloured Citizens of the World, but in Particular, and Very Expressly, to Those of the United States of America*. Ed. Charles M. Wiltse. New York: Hill and Wang, 1965.

Wallace, Maurice O., and Shawn Michelle Smith, eds. *Pictures and Progress: Early Photography and the Making of African American Identity*. Durham, N.C.: Duke University Press, 2012.

Ward, Andrew. *The Slaves' War: The Civil War in the Words of Former Slaves*. Boston: Mariner Books, 2008.

Warren, Mercy Otis. *History of the Rise, Progress and Termination of the American Revolution*. Ed. Lester H. Cohen. 2 vols. Indianapolis: Liberty Fund, 1990.

Washington, George. *The Writings of George Washington from the Original Manuscript Sources, 1745–1799*. Ed. John C. Fitzpatrick. 39 vols. Washington, D.C.: U.S. Government Printing Office, 1931–44.

Waugh, John C. *Lincoln and McClellan: The Troubled Partnership Between a President and his General*. New York: Palgrave-MacMillan, 2010.

Weber, Karl, ed., *Lincoln: A President for the Ages*. New York: Public Affairs, 2012.

Weinstein, Allen, and Frank Otto Gatell, eds. *American Negro Slavery: A Modern Reader*. New York: Oxford University Press, 1973.

White, Ronald C., Jr. *A. Lincoln: A Biography*. New York: Random House, 2010.

————. *Lincoln's Greatest Speech: The Second Inaugural*. New York: Simon & Schuster, 2002.

White, Shane. *Somewhat More Independent: The End of Slavery in New York City, 1770–1810* Athens: University of Georgia Press, 1991.

Wilentz, Sean. *The Rise of American Democracy: Jefferson to Lincoln*. New York: W. W. Norton & Co., 2006.

Willey, Austin. *The History of the Antislavery Cause in State and Nation*. New York: Negro Universities Press, 1969.

Williams, David. *Bitterly Divided: The South's Inner Civil War*. New York: New Press, 2008.

Wolf, Eva Sheppard. *Race and Liberty in the New Nation: Emancipation in Virginia from the Revolution to Nat Turner's Rebellion*. Baton Rouge: Louisiana State University, 2006.

Wood, Gordon S. *Empire of Liberty: A History of the Early Republic, 1789–1815*. Oxford, U.K.: Oxford University Press, 2009.

Woodworth, Steven E. *Manifest Destinies: America's Westward Expansion and the Road to the Civil War*. New York: Alfred A. Knopf, 2010.

Wright, Kai, ed. *The African-American Experience: Black History and Culture through Speeches, Letters, Editorials, Poems, Songs, and Stories*. New York: Black Dog & Leventhal Publishers, 2009.

Wyatt-Brown, Bertram. *The Shaping of Southern Culture: Honor, Grace, and War, 1760s–1880s*. Chapel Hill: University of North Carolina Press, 2001.

Zilversmit, Arthur. *The First Emancipation: The Abolition of Slavery in the North*. Chicago: University of Chicago Press, 1967.

Index

abolition/abolitionism/abolitionists, 65, 71, 101, 110, 119–26, 128–30, 132–47, 151–55, 164–65, 176, 185, 188, 201–2, 209, 225, 231, 241, 244, 250, 266, 271, 290, Baptists and, 142–43; Benezet, Anthony, 55; in Boston, 6, 183; Catholic hostility toward, 136; Cazenovia (NY) meeting, 185; in churches, 138–42, 146–47; in Connecticut, 51; constitutional amendment proposal, 286; Douglass, Frederick, 128–30; election of Lincoln, 222; Emancipation Proclamation and, 255, 257; finance John Brown's raid, 110, 207; Franklin, Benjamin, 47; free blacks and, 126; Fremont, John C., 265; La Amistad case, 132; Lane, James, 287; Lincoln at odds with, 250–51, 268; Lincoln's views on, 237, 243; in Missouri, 273–74; myths about, xiv; in New Jersey, 96–97; in New York, 90, 97; Oberlin College founded by, 124; Phillips, Wendell, 126, 269; Seward, William H., 218, 247, 249; Sumner, Charles, 198; in Syracuse (NY), 128; Transcendentalists and, 126; Tubman, Harriet, 186; Weld, Theodore Dwight, 122; West Virginia, 285; Wilmot, David, 163

Act prohibiting the African slave trade (1807), 66–67
Adams, Abigail, 1
Adams, Charles Francis, 166
Adams, John, 1, 12, 14, 15
Adams, John Quincy, 86, 131, 166, 174, 215, 320n6
Adams-Onis Treaty (1819), 160, 171
African Methodist Episcopal Church, 127
Alabama, 68, 143, 215, 223, 227, 229
Alexandria (DC/VA), 277–78
Allen, Richard, 127
Alton (IL), 156, 237
American Anti-Slavery Society, 124, 128
American Colonization Society, 58, 122, 127, 238
American Party, 194, 213, 221
Ames, Fisher, 75–77
Amistad Case, 130–32
Anderson, Robert A., 266
Andrew, James O., 138
Annapolis (MD), 261
Antietam, Battle of, 253–54
Anti-Federalists, 40

Appeal to the Coloured Citizens of the World, 115
Appomattox Court House (VA), 284, 292
Arkansas, 71, 78, 215, 217, 223, 228, 293
Armstrong, John, 83
Arnold, Isaac, 288
Articles of Confederation, 23, 25, 28, 30, 34, 42, 43, 173, 246
Asbury, Francis, 136
Ashmore, John, 217
Atchison, David, 167, 192, 196
Atlanta (GA), 285, 289
Atlantic slave trade, 74
Augusta (GA), 145

Bailey, Gamaliel, 194
Baird, Robert, 135
Baja California, 172
Baldwin, Henry, 132
Baltimore (MD), 119, 138, 143, 166, 217, 272, 289
Baptists: 135–36, 141–43; Alabama Baptist convention, 143; American Baptist Home Mission Society, 142; American Baptist Anti-Slavery Convention, 143; American Baptist Free Mission Society, 144; Baltimore Compromise, 143; clergymen as abolitionists, 142; General Convention, 142; General Missionary Convention, 142; Georgia Baptist Convention, 145; in New England, 142; Southern Baptist Convention, 145
Barnburners (anti-slavery Democrats), 164–65
Barnwell, Robert, 167
Bates, Edward, 218, 277
Baumfree, Isabella. See Truth, Sojourner
Beauregard, Pierre, 232, 295
Bedford (MA), 128
Beecher, Catharine, 187
Beecher, Henry Ward, 187
Beecher, Lyman, 122, 186
Beecher's Bibles, 196
Beeman, Richard, 31, 34
Belknap, Jeremy, 53
Bell, Howard Holman, 127
Bell, John, 220, 223–24
Benezet, Anthony, 11, 55
Benjamin, Judah P., 284
Bennett, Jr. Lerone, 243–44
Benton, Thomas Hart, 167, 175
Berkeley, William, 61